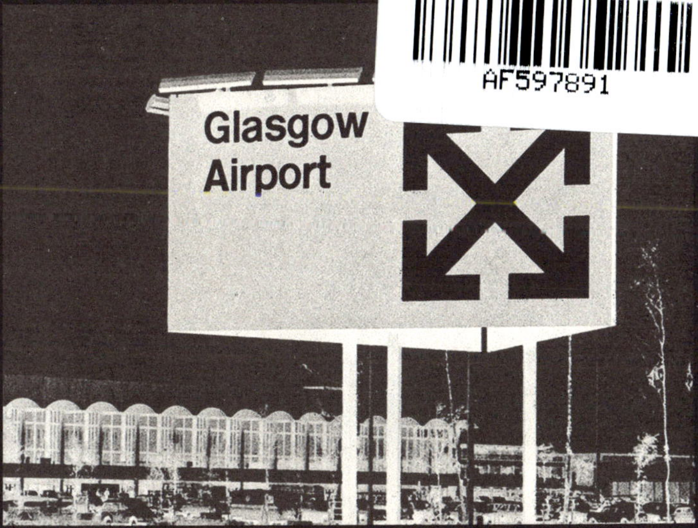

Glasgow airport logo by British designer Margaret Calvert (1964)

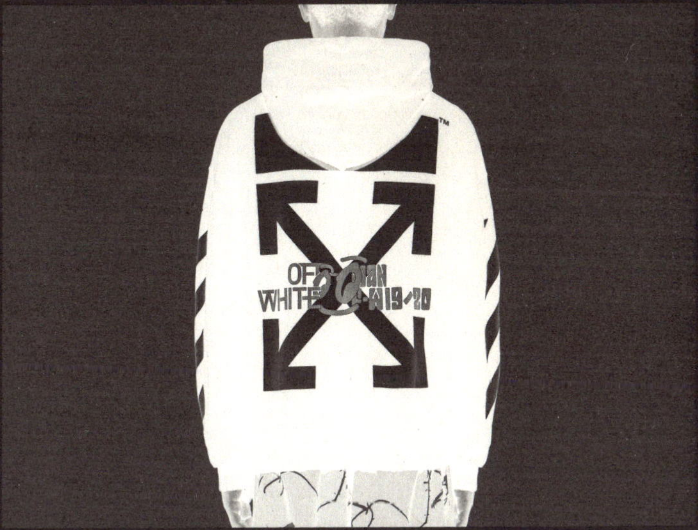

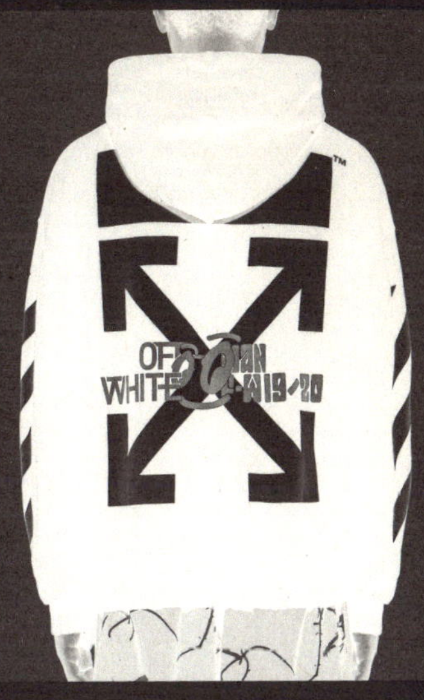

Off-White logo by Virgil Abloh (2018)

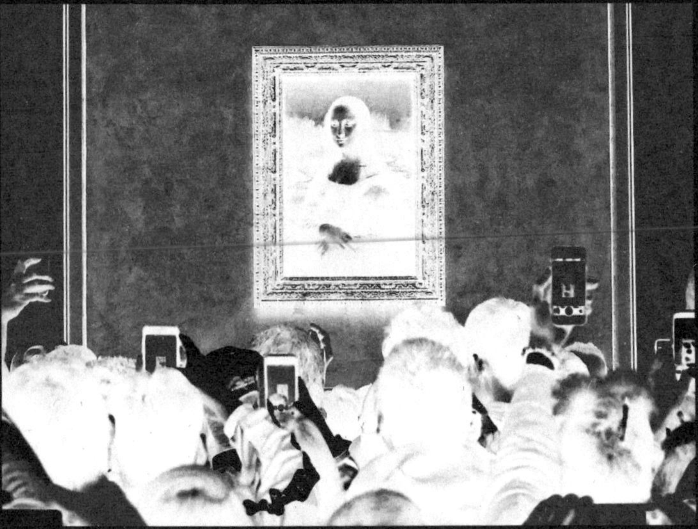

Leonardo da Vinci, *Mona Lisa* (1503)

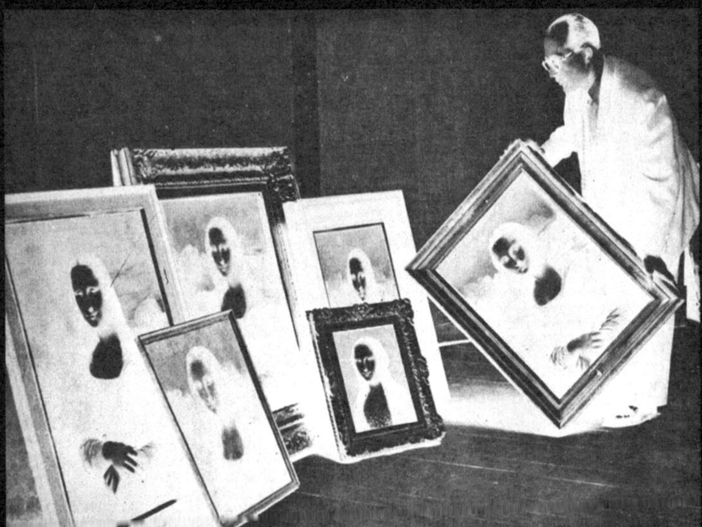

Exhibition of Mona Lisa fakes curated by police detective Guy Isnard (1955)

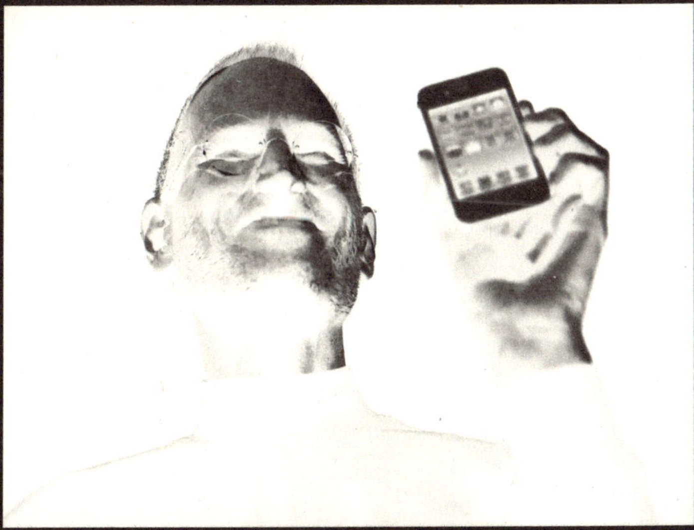

Steve Jobs demonstrating the first iPhone (2007)

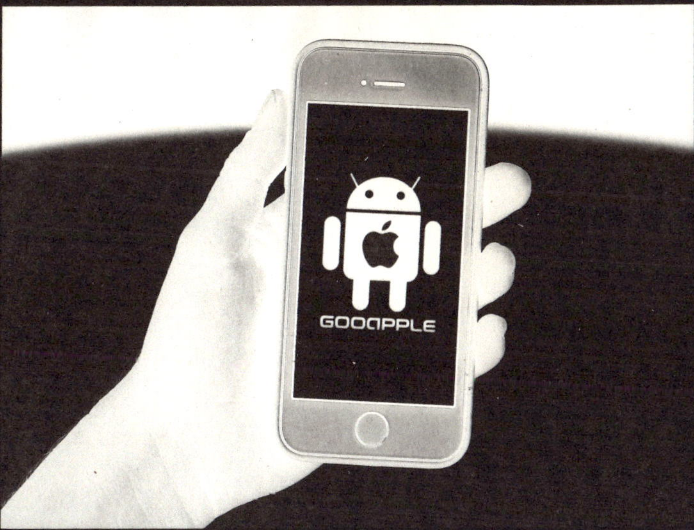

The GooApple shanzhai phone combining the iPhone's shape with Google Android's OS (c. 2011)

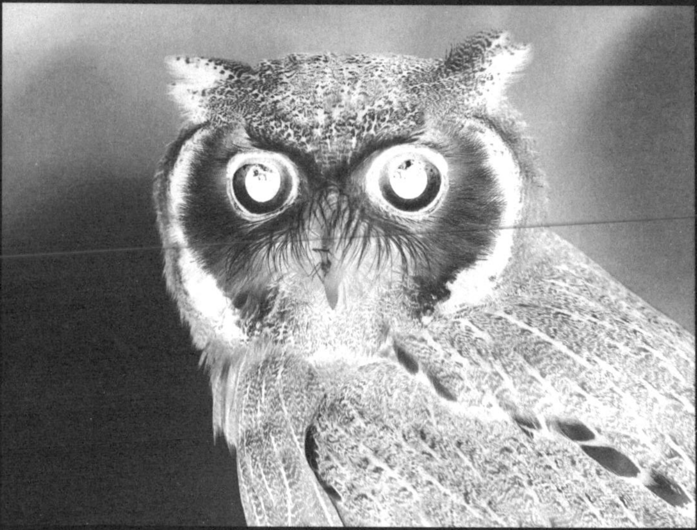

Southern White-Faced Owl

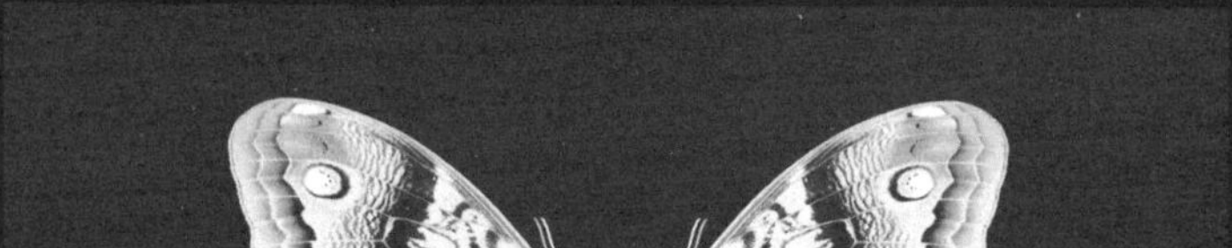

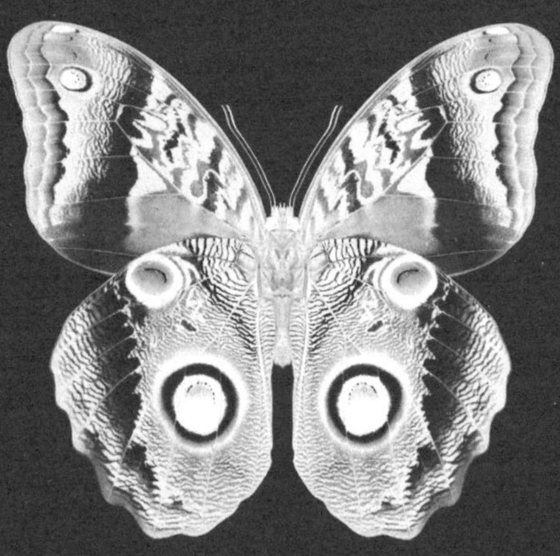

Caligo Owl Butterfly with spots that mimic an owl's eyes to fool potential predators

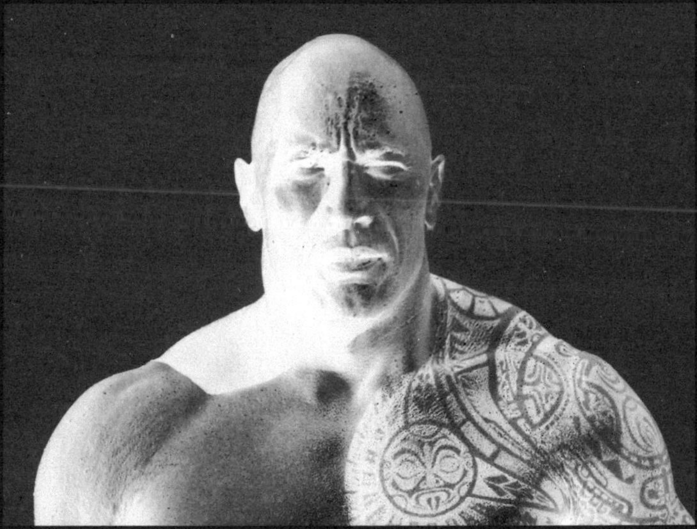

Actor, and professional wrestler, Dwayne Johnson aka The Rock

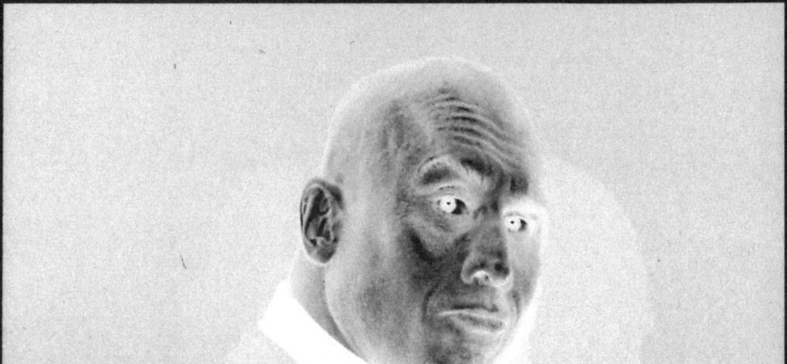

Tanoai Reed, best known as a stunt double for his cousin, The Rock

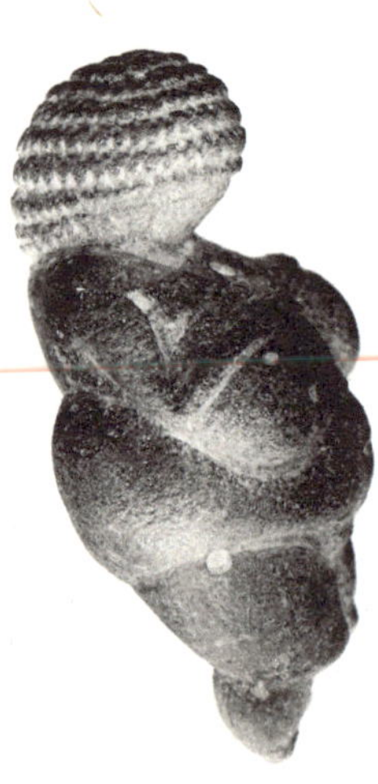

Venus of Willendorf sculpture (c. 25,000 BP)

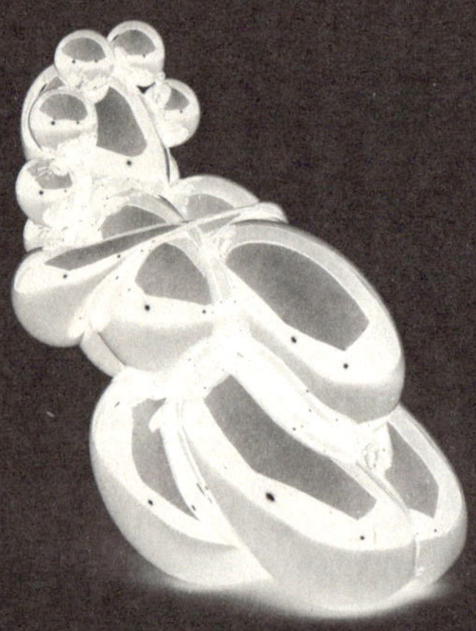

Jeff Koons, *Balloon Venus* (2008–12)

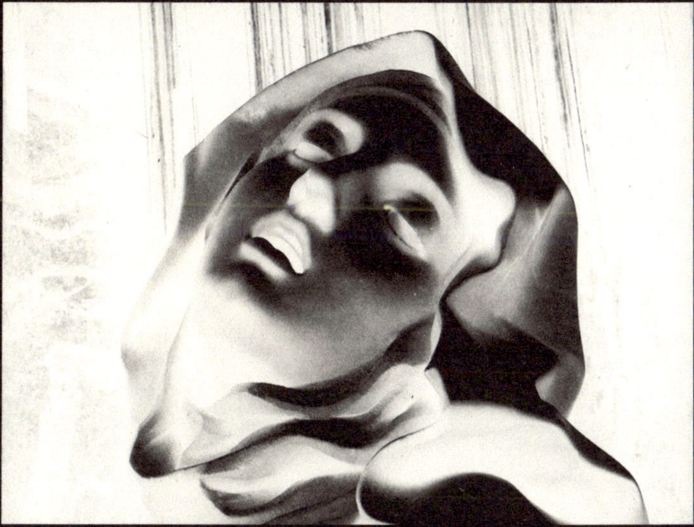

Gian Lorenzo Bernini, *The Ecstasy of Saint Teresa*, detail (1647)

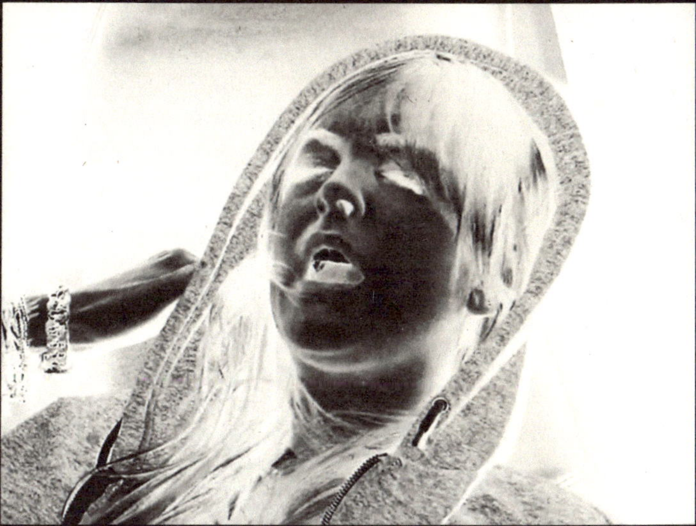

Tabloid photograph of Lindsay Lohan asleep in her car (2007)

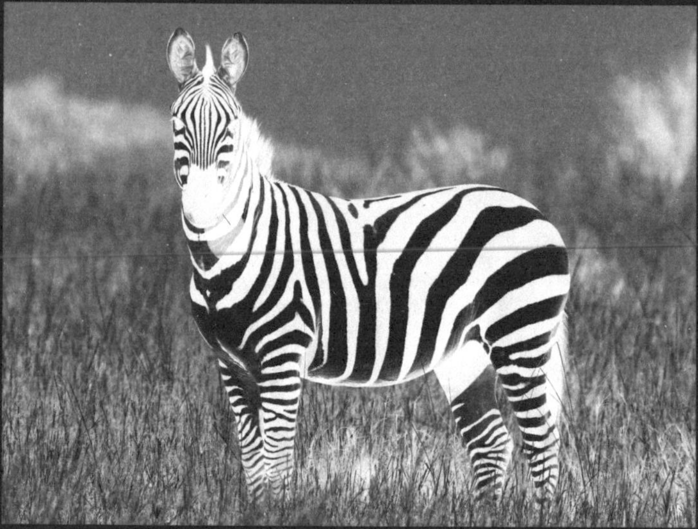

Zebra in the grasslands of the Serengeti

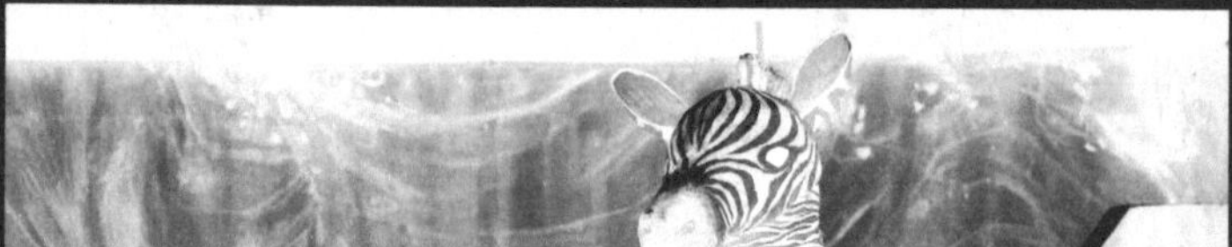

Zookeeper wearing a Zebra costume during an animal escape drill in a Tokyo zoo

UNLICENSED:
Bootlegging as Creative Practice

UNLICENSED:
Bootlegging as Creative Practice

Ben Schwartz

Published by Valiz
with Source Type

Contents

UNLICENSED Interviews

References

Introduction: Under the Cover of Darkness

Ben Schwartz

This might all be futile. By its very nature, a bootleg defies definition. It travels in black markets and hides in unmarked record sleeves; it communicates in the errors of cheap production and escapes into the loopholes of property law. It cares little for the stability a definition might offer. To define a bootleg would be to contain it. It creates order where mess is much more welcome. Definitions, language, and names clarify, but they also tend to pin things down. A bootleg's survival is dependent on its ambiguity. Maybe we can talk about a bootleg while resisting the urge to define it. Maybe we can open it up, explore its edges, extend them outward, or destroy them altogether.

I began my bootleg research at the Walker Art Center in 2018, at a moment when the act seemed precariously balanced on a brink of either evolution or implosion. (As an aside I've come to appreciate the term "bootleg research," as not only a description of what I was studying, but also how: in the time and space outside of "legitimate" work, embracing an element of non-professionalism, and finding pleasure in the scrappy nature of my efforts.) My interest in the subject began with my background in music and grew further with a collision of creative observations. On one end, I became aware of a particular visual trend in graphic design, and on the other, I was witnessing an increasing number of unexpected fashion collaborations: Vetements/DHL, Telfar/White Castle, Balenciaga/Bernie Sanders. Where they overlapped was an awkward juxtaposition of high and low culture, corporate branding and lo-fi aesthetics, critical irony and authentic fandom. There were moments when I felt genuinely excited to see bootlegging embraced on such a public scale. Like how conversations around homage, appropriation, and theft—which feel normal in the world of contemporary art—were now being reimagined in the spaces of popular culture, social media, and the creative industry as a whole. At other times I felt the gesture growing stale and superficial, reduced to a set of Photoshop effects implemented to tap into a viral cultural zeitgeist.

I began an interview series published by The Gradient[1] called Unlicensed in an attempt to learn from artists and designers who seemed to deploy bootlegging in unexpected or abstract ways. I questioned what the act meant at a time when copying is embedded in nearly every aspect of our culture. Could the gesture remain potent, liberating, subversive, transgressive? Could bootlegging transcend objects? Is it possible to bootleg yourself? And how might the act become a tool of resistance? In China, for example, where strict censorship policies prevent the dissemination of globalized media, bootlegging is an essential tool for freedom of expression and dissent. And while my research focuses on bootlegging as an artistic gesture, it's important to acknowledge that the act outside of this context is often one of economic or political necessity. Hopefully, these conversations will bring further awareness to the communities who depend on its effects in their day to day lives.

What follows is an attempt to begin to unpack the possibilities of bootlegging today… ways that the bootleg itself might be bootlegged, smuggled from its place in tradition and history into new contexts, concepts, and ideas.

I. Cover Version

For one day in 2016, the art practice OOIEE draped the works on display at the Aspen Art Museum with a textile printed with an image of the sky. Wrapped in pieces of the sky, works by Ryan Gander, Anna Sew Hoy, and Diana Thater became air... but they also became covers, like a punk version of a Robert Breer. In the act of covering the pieces, OOIEE also managed to *cover* the pieces. You know what I mean? A cover can envelop the work but it can also open it up. The best covers tend to create space; between the original and the reproduction, between "the artist" and OOIEE, between the thing and well... everything else, even the sky? A cover asks what is possible within what is given. These artworks, these amorphous sheets of blue, demonstrate what a cover is capable of when put to task... which is really a lot more than we've come to expect. Like on Cat Power's *The Covers Record* where she performs *Satisfaction* without even singing the chorus. Is it even the same song? Maybe we're asking the wrong questions.

Lately I've been thinking of a cover as a type of translation. A good translation is more than just semantic. A translator must find what is "unfathomable, mysterious, and poetic"[2] in the original and interpret this essence in a new language. Translation becomes "a form of displacement, a way to enrich life."[3] Coleman Barks, a renowned Rumi translator, describes his process as a trance. His translations prioritize feeling over fidelity. "It feels like a different kind of something outside the mind. I call it the heart of the soul, but it's somewhere different than my ordinary mentality."[4] A translation doesn't come *from*, it moves *through*. Like a translation or a cover, a bootleg might aspire to something greater than a reproduction. It should open up space for the possibility to transform and, when pushed, maybe even transcend. But of course not all covers are created with such grand aspirations. Let's look at a cover in its simplest form, one that measures its success through the fidelity of its reproduction. Let's call it a mimetic cover.

In the global subculture of Elvis impersonation (which includes an intense competitive circuit), greatness is defined by how closely one can get to becoming the King. There is no intent to adjust or update, rather the self disappears and in its place is a white leather jumpsuit, thick sideburns, and gold rimmed glasses. But an Elvis impersonator must do more than look the part… it involves research, practice, and nuance. "My respect for Elvis should shine through. I know I'm not Elvis, but I hope that when I perform, people might forget that for a moment."[5] Elvis impersonators perform mimetic covers, an act perhaps closest to our traditional understanding of a bootleg. A counterfeit Louis Vuitton bag is successful only when it performs as the real thing. At the core of a mimetic cover is homage. But a cover's ability to celebrate its source can go further, and in doing so can become something else. Let's call this an interpretive cover.

Anthony Huberman describes homage as falling somewhere between admiration and research. "A tribute is neither an analysis nor just a party. Giving a toast is about making people care, not about making them understand." A cover, then, opens up the possibility to express admiration in a way that emphasizes *affect* over *effect*, "I love it" over "I get it."[6] Let me give you an example… The song *All Along the Watchtower* was written and recorded by Bob Dylan in 1967 and appeared on the album *John Wesley Harding*. The sparse and wandering track sparked curiosity for its enchanting lyrical mysticism. One year later, Jimi Hendrix, after hearing an early tape of the track, recorded a cover. Using the same foundational elements as Dylan's original, Hendrix transformed the folk saga into a psychedelic anthem. "It overwhelmed me, really" said Dylan, "He found things that other people wouldn't think of finding in there. I took license with the song from *his* version, actually, and continue to do it to this day." Hendrix's cover is an interpretive one, an evolution through the stylistic sensibilities of a new performer. An interpretive cover begins to demonstrate how something new might come from within the constraints of the original. It's a powerful gesture of transformation, but still, maybe a cover can do more...

The song *Respect* was first recorded by Otis Redding and was released on the 1965 album *Otis Blue*. On top of the track's soulful groove, Redding chauvinistically demands respect from "his woman" after a long day at work. But the *Respect* most of us are familiar with isn't Redding's. Two years after the original, Aretha Franklin recorded her own rendition of the song. The track surpasses a stylistic interpretation with added lyrics that have become its signatures: the R-E-S-P-E-C-T breakdown and the repetition of "Sock it to me." The most powerful change, however, is the context of "respect" considering the realities of Franklin as a Black woman in the late 1960s, early 1970s. The song was able to tap into a much broader social consciousness. It aligned with the civil rights and women's rights movements, and propelled the track from a misogynist jingle into an anthem of liberation. "The song was a demand for something that could no longer be denied. She had taken a man's call for respect from a woman... and flipped it. The country had never heard anything like it."[7]

The track demonstrates that even in repetition there is always a "quality of difference"— a cover is never *just* "the same thing but rather a progression or regression" providing "philosophical insight about the shape of time and history."[8] "Respect" is a transcendent cover. If a mimetic cover repeats and a transformational cover shifts, then a transcendent cover "stutters."

Just as Gilles Deleuze used the idea of making language stutter through exposing and subverting its constraints, so too can a cover infiltrate an original and reveal its borders. And despite this necessity of a cover to work within the limitations of its original, there remains a possibility (as demonstrated by Franklin) for these structures to be manipulated. Constraints can become expansive when turned against themselves. To consider a bootleg as a cover allows the gesture to unfold beyond celebration and homage. As we cover or bootleg we also update, evolve, shift, deconstruct; at times we even destroy.

II. Anti-Illusion

In physics the term "dark matter" is used to describe that which makes up as much as 83% of the universe, yet is virtually undetectable. Dark matter can only be perceived by its effects on other things. "Dark matter neither emits nor scatters light. It is believed to be fundamentally important in the cosmos and yet there is essentially no direct evidence of its existence and little understanding of its nature."[9] Taken outside of the realm of science, we can think of dark matter as a form of invisible social scaffolding… organizations, structures, attitudes, and ideals that are vague and indefinite yet produce very real effects. Take, for example, a pair of Nikes. These shoes are the result of the company's corporate policies and culture, the legal frameworks it works within, wider societal fashions, creative trend forecasting, and various economic and environmental considerations… all of this is the dark matter.

Our current form of globalized capitalism is another form of dark matter. It is a considerable force in nearly every decision we make, yet manages to remain almost entirely undetectable. The products of such a society are complicit in keeping this dark matter (the violence and inequality upon which the system relies) dark. Its effects only become tangible in the detritus that falls outside of its oversight. A bootleg is an example of this debris. It's an anachronism, an inconsistency, a glitch in the capitalist matrix. A bootleg stares into the audience from its place on stage and breaks the fourth wall. It becomes a disruption to a much greater collective illusion… we might even call it an anti-illusion.[10]

Anti-illusionist theatre was developed by the playwright Bertolt Brecht, who considered traditional theater a "branch of the narcotics business." He believed that at any given performance the audience would "hang up their brains with their hats in the cloakroom."[11] Brecht had witnessed the power of political propaganda during both World Wars and understood how entertainment can easily distract from more pressing political and social issues. To break this spell, he devised the concept of "epic theater," a set of techniques to transform the grandiose into the grotesque. "Anti-illusions" (also translated as "alienation effects") were an essential element to this newly conceived theory. Brecht began formulating alienation effects following a performance by Mei Lanfang's theater company in Moscow. Throughout the play he was struck by the actors' expressed awareness of being watched. "Their purpose, it seemed, was to appear strange and even surprising to the audience."[12] Brecht was interested in the way this level of absurdity created distance between the drama and the audience. The spectator becomes more inclined to engage with the play on a cerebral (rather than emotional) level and is less likely to be consumed by the illusion. Let me give you some examples…

> Narration: A reminder that the play is a presentation of a story. This might involve revealing events before they happen so as to prevent the audience from getting invested in the storyline.
>
> Breaking the scene: The character removes themself from the current situation so as to comment, as the actor, on how that character might be feeling.
>
> Performing the mechanics: The actor calls out stage directions such as "cue the violins" to bring attention to the methods that influence emotion.

Brecht saw these devices not just as creative techniques, but as social strategies of resistance. From the absurdity, we are brought back to reality. The bootleg works in a similar way. In its often absurd use of language, materials, and graphics, it becomes an anti-illusion calling attention to the oppressive and inequitable systems from which it was created. As it travels, it causes ripples and holes in the "grey curtain of capitalism."[13] The bootleg, even in the innocuous form of a T-shirt or mobile phone, yields power.

The GooApple is a bootleg smartphone from China that looks identical to the iPhone but uses an Android operating system that's customized to resemble Apple's iOS.[14] It's an example of shanzhai, a term used to describe a fake, copy, or counterfeit in Chinese culture. The neologism gained popularity around 2008 in the field of consumer electronics and has since evolved to encompass read/write culture, copy/paste creativity, and anti-authoritarian grassroots efforts. Shanzhai has infiltrated nearly every industry in China. There are shanzhai garments, shanzhai TV shows, shanzhai galas, and even a Shanzhai Nobel Prize. These products, once universally ridiculed, have become celebrated by creative think tanks for embracing a DIY attitude unbothered by copyright and IP. Their disregard for notions of "originality," "authenticity," and "ownership" is flaunted in their logo flips and brand name bricolage. The GooApple phone is a 21st century Dadaist collage, a rejection of the rationale of modern capitalist society. The device chooses to embrace the absurdity often hidden beneath the gleam of the surface.

The anti-illusionist language of Shanzhai culture might best be captured in the counterfeit graphic T-shirts archived by the collective Shanzhai Lyric. With their research, artists Ming Lin and Alex Tatarsky frame TikTok truisms from bootleg shirts into an ongoing poem sourced from the detritus of consumerism. With phrases like "ART IS WAY OF CHIC," shiny "broken" English becomes both decoration and description, indicating rupture on a wider level."[15] The smooth language of capitalism breaks down and the dark matter is exposed. The graphic design studio Metahaven understood the capacity of a joke to "resist and overturn the frame of reference imposed by any political status quo."[16] Shanzhai T-shirts, often humorous in their level of absurdity, might do the same. To consider the bootleg as an anti-illusion is to understand it as a disruptor, an agitator, an instigator. As it moves, it flaunts the scars left by dark matter to remind us of its dislocation, marginalization, and violence. Its refusal (or failure?) to conform serves as a reminder of the fragility of the capitalist illusion. It is a demonstration that one of the most powerful effects of the fake is to remind us of what is real.

III. Alternative Archive

By 2025, MoMA will have 1.2 petabytes (1.2 million gigabytes) of artworks stored digitally on magnetic tape...Warhol's film archive alone takes up half a petabyte. The magnetic tape, necessary to account for file corruption or obsolete formats, is stored in small cases, which are collectively held in a black box in the basement of the museum. It's an example of various archiving systems working in tandem… physical works, occupying digital space, converted back to a tangible container, all hidden away in a dusty (albeit enormous) basement.[17] Traditional archives take on many forms: from specialized facilities with meticulously regulated rooms like those of MoMA, to a shoebox of photos kept underneath the bed. Archives can be libraries, or museums, or most recently digital spaces... the internet itself is even archived. But traditional archives double in their function of preservation, in that they also act as storage. And sometimes things in storage are easy to forget. Let me give you an example…

From 2016 to 2018 I worked as the graphic design fellow for the Walker Art Center in Minneapolis.

The museum is made up of seven galleries, spread out over five floors. The building, designed by Herzog & de Meuron, is intentionally disorienting, providing an opportunity for visitors to spend a day getting lost… after all, isn't that the purpose of contemporary art? Below the galleries, mostly unbeknownst to visitors, lies an equally complex and vast cultural labyrinth… the library. Although only a fraction of the size of the exhibition spaces above it, this "universe (which others call the Library) is composed of an indefinite, perhaps infinite number of...galleries."[18] Designers often sought the library as respite. Cell service was poor underground and a trip to the library meant an excuse to leave an email unanswered or dodge a co-worker looking for last-minute changes. On one particular occasion I decided to revisit the entire set of the Walker's in-house magazine, *Design Quarterly* and was struck by issue 89, 'Mindscapes.' The red cover was punctuated by silver display type: "SOTSASS" in layered lettering mimicking his Ultrafragola mirror, and "SUPER-STUDIO" in typography recalling the dimensional grids of the collectives' photomontages. We decided to bootleg the cover graphic onto a T-shirt. We produced a limited run and gave them to anyone interested. This small gesture transferred the *Design Quarterly* issue from one archive to another… from a library to a "cotton archive"[19] able to be accessed and disseminated by the simple act of wearing. 'Mindscapes,' once safely stored (and all but forgotten) in the stacks, was reactivated on an intimate level… quite literally enveloping any *body* interested in the radical Italian designers. The publication and the ideas within had been resurrected in a new and different form, liberated from the traditional archive and brought back to life to walk among us.

Walter Benjamin was also curious about the idea of resurrecting books. Benjamin all but names the act of bootlegging when listing the methods that a collector might apply to revive a forgotten treasure… "collecting is only one process of renewal; other processes are the painting of objects, the cutting out of figures, the application of decals…"[20] But what a bootleg makes up for in access, it forgoes in accuracy. A traditional archive is meticulous in its record keeping, a bootleg admittedly less so. Maybe there's something to be learnt in this slippage...

Shakespeare's First Folio, published seven years after his death, was thought to be the legitimate compendium of the playwright's works. The texts were compiled by friends of Shakespeare who made it their goal to be as faithful as possible to the playwright's original intent. The full title *Mr. William Shakespeare's comedies, histories, & tragedies. Published according to the true original copies* is a mouthful, but the last section, *Published according to the true original copies* is worth noting….Throughout his career William Shakespeare chose not to authorize written versions of his plays, instead wanting them to be exclusively for the stage. But the absence of tangible copies only forced fans of the playwright to become more entrepreneurial. In the likeness of latter-day Deadheads, audience members at the Globe Theatre would transcribe versions of the plays for reproduction and dissemination. These copies, full of errors and editorial liberties, became known as the Bad Quarto. In these versions, Hamlet's famous soliloquy goes as follows: "To be, or not to be; ay, there's the point. To die, to sleep–is that all? Ay, all." Despite the errors, the Bad Quarto (a Shakespeare bootleg) played a key role "in saving England's finest body of drama from oblivion."[21] Some historians have even questioned if its discrepancies are the result of other contextual factors like an actor stumbling over his lines, or an early draft of a work in progress. Thought of this way, is the Bad Quarto any different from a live bootleg of The Beatles or The Stones? In such instances, it's the slippage that makes them iconic. It has a way of bringing us closer, breaking down the divide of the stage or the studio...maybe even time?

As an alternative archive, a bootleg becomes a "parallel canon," a version of history running alongside, supporting, or at times undermining authorized accounts of the past. "Bootlegs open up and mine an imaginative space" they can "fill in the gaps," or leave room for "imagined artifacts."[22] Looking at both the authorized and unauthorized versions of a history allows the actual image "to emerge out of the cloud of virtual similars and dissimilars."[23] And the dissimilarities are significant, no matter how insignificant they might seem. Let me explain…

Leon Trotsky, in his text "The ABC of Materialist Dialectics," makes the argument that "a letter A is never equal to another letter A—it is not even equal to itself." In other words, to change is at the core of what it means to exist. Then perhaps the variations over generations of bootlegs are not the effects of shoddy production or the errors of an amateur archivist… they're signs of life. They're the bruises that occur when an idea or object is "compressed, reproduced, ripped, remixed, as well as copied and pasted into other channels of distribution."[24] All of which are the risks of forgoing an archive for a continued, unpredictable existence.

Another thing about traditional archives is that they seem to appreciate a certain amount of distance... In a traditional archive, you're often asked to wear a pair of white gloves to handle the work, so that even when you're touching an object you're not really *grasping* it. The philosopher Roland Barthes thought about this distance when differentiating between the ideas of "Text" and "Work." As he describes it, a "Work" is something static and complete, analyzed and classified. A "Text," on the other hand, invites us in. It's malleable and prone to shift and stray and evolve and expand with each interaction. A "Text" "decants the work from its consumption and recuperates it as play, task, production, practice." Barthes calls on us to "play the text, release it, make it go."[25] A bootleg does that too, it invites us in. It requires no gloves or permissions. It asks us to engage so that it might remain in motion. But as we interact with bootlegs, how can we bring others into the process?

One last thing about a traditional archive, it's generally a solitary experience. But bootlegs are reliant on community ... a shared "visual bond."[26] In 2012 artist/curator/publisher Shannon Michael Cane launched the first iteration of Printed Matter's Bootleg T-shirt Show.[27] The show featured bootleg shirts designed by a selection of artists and designers, with graphics from music, queer history, and capitalist critique. Its proximity to Printed Matter is no coincidence. Bootlegs, especially when thought of as tools for preservation, can be easily embedded into the world of independent publishing: "Similar to how zines work, these shirts are about finding people already within our small community that share a very 'deep' interest in something very specific."[28] The bootleg also becomes an archival mechanism for underrepresented communities. "It naturally becomes something that we perceive as aligned with diversity, minorities, activist political voices, queer culture—because no one is censoring it, which is so often what is happening in mainstream publishing, fashion, music, media, et cetera. It's a platform for raw expression."[29]

It's within these subcultures that we can understand the bootleg as a means of preservation in its most vital sense. As an alternative archive, a bootleg allows ideas and information to move through time, not as something fixed, but as something malleable. Walter Benjamin said, "to live means to leave traces,"[30] and that's what a bootleg does. Its existence is dependent on those around it to maintain it; it leaves traces and picks up new ones as it passes from hand to hand.

IV. Method Actor

A friend recently sent an article to me of an animal escape exercise at a zoo in Japan. In one photo, two people dressed up in a ridiculous zebra costume perform as the fugitive animal. The two actors not only look the part, they act the way you might expect a zebra to in this situation… skittish, confused, and weary of any passing human. In another image, the costumed creature stands outside the actual zebra's habitat, where the animal stares at the abomination with a look of sheer existential dread. I suppose you have to admire the zookeeper's dedication. The whole situation reminded me of another story…

In 1943 Marlon Brando began studying under Stella Adler, one of the teachers responsible for developing the method acting technique. In one exercise, she told her students to pretend to be chickens preparing for the attack of an atomic bomb. The students frantically waddled around the room. They made their arms into wings and they clucked and screamed at their impending doom. Brando, however, sat still, stoic, a bit confused. When Adler asked Brando to give reason for his odd behavior, he replied, "I'm a chicken, what the hell do I know about bombs?" While Brando is often credited as the pioneering force for the method technique, it was in fact an actor by the name of Dilip Kumar who was the first to develop and employ the approach. In Indian cinema, he's regarded as "the ultimate method actor."[31] Kumar specialized in tragedy, and his work earned him respect for bringing a sense of realism to Bollywood. In fact, his connection with characters was so strong that he suffered a serious depression after performing a string of melancholy roles. A psychiatrist eventually gave him the advice to pursue comedy. Kumar developed his own technique out of a need to reconcile reality with the fantasy of cinema. "If the director comes up to me for a scene and says 'This is your mother. And she is now dead.' And every faculty of yours is against the idea that this woman is your mother...in a situation like that, your imagination needs to function. And that is when the brain starts to bring in memories of your own mother, and sometimes directly, sometimes indirectly, puts you in touch with your emotions.'[32]

Method acting involves foregrounding the "art of experience," Kumar said. It requires a sense of embodiment greater than hitting marks and memorization. Method acting requires the actor to live in feelings analogous to those of the character in order to communicate authentically. To method act is to follow in the path of Jorge Luis Borges's Pierre Menard in his attempt to rewrite *Don Quixote* not by copying it, but by *becoming* Cervantes... by creating the conditions necessary so that the words arrive no differently to Menard than they did to their original creator. Or in the case of the artist Robert Gober who, upon first seeing an Ellsworth Kelly painting, was utterly confused, "I couldn't figure out whether it was a joke or it was really smart, but it was way beyond me, like a language I didn't know how to read. I remember I went home and in the basement of our house I remade the painting to try to understand it."[33] The bootleg as a method actor is a form of research, a way to better understand an original. It embraces copying as a process and acknowledges that creation "demands long intense engagement with what has been in order to move forward."[34]

In China, ancient practice considered it a high honor for a painter to infiltrate the collection of a connoisseur with a forgery of an Old Master. If one succeeds, the forger becomes equal to the master.[35] Today the area of Dafen Village, located in Shenzhen, China, has become renowned for its community of artists specializing in oil painted replicas of past masters like Van Gogh, Dalí, da Vinci, and Rembrandt. In 1989, an oil painting dealer from Hong Kong came to the small village to commission copies of iconic paintings. Today Dafen has over 8,000 workers in the oil painting industry and its output makes up nearly 70% of the commercial paintings in Europe and American markets. But as the artists were copying, they were also studying and learning. They grew a discerning eye for light, color, composition, and gesture which lead to a "synthesis of a new personal style expressive of the individual and the copied past; a seeing double."[36] It reminds me of a group of works by the artist Allen Ruppersberg…

In 1973, the artist copied the entirety of Henry David Thoreau's *Walden*[37] by hand. For Ruppersberg, the process was a way of entering into a personal discussion with the author. It was a way to reactivate the text.[38] A year later, he copied the entirety of Oscar Wilde's *The Picture of Dorian Gray* onto twenty wall-sized canvases, working six days a week over the course of several months. The time-intensive method was "the only way of getting to the heart of the work. ... The second line of the poem which prefaces *Dorian Gray* reads: 'To reveal art and conceal the artist is art's aim.' Anonymity can be a strategy in an ego-centric culture."[39] In one last piece of epic transcription titled *The Singing Posters*, Ruppersberg copied the entirety of Allen Ginsberg's *HOWL* phonetically onto a series of fluorescent signs. "Generation" becomes "je-nuh-RAY-shin"... the phonetics are a way to inhabit the work, to decipher and resuscitate each word as if learning to speak for the first time. To read *The Singing Posters* is to perform it, and in the process we become Ginsberg... we become *HOWL*, we become the protest, we become the oral tradition, we become the words and we become their meanings.

The artist Matt Olson once told me a story about bootlegging Guy de Cointet. Olson and his studio at the time, RO/LU, were creating furniture pieces lifted from shapes and objects found in the scenography of the artist. Posters from de Cointet performances were reimagined in the studio's signature plywood. At a certain point in the process, as Olson tells it, one begins to think about time and money and efficiency and output... the sort of things that try and make art rational, which is never really how it should be. Fed up, he cried out "Why in the fuck are we even doing this?" to which someone in the studio replied, "We're learning from these things in ways that no one could teach us." It's about process... not so much the thing, but what the thing does to us. How it changes us, how we "become the things, people, and ideas we love."[40] It's about method acting. The bootleg as a method actor is about transformation, it's an act of *becoming*... but maybe not as we'd expect. As we learn through reenactment, through copying, through bootlegging, it is less about a relationship to a character from a script, and more about the process of becoming ourselves.

V: Knock Up

A knock up is not a knock off, it's an important distinction to make. A knock off is a counterfeit produced to deceive and pass as "authentic." A knock up is different. In China, there's a rating system for how accurate knock off products are in their deception. AAA-rated knock offs are near perfect, at times even better than the original—like a pair of Adidas with an added Nike swoosh. On the other end, Z-rated counterfeits are so far off from the original that they operate better as jokes than actual products. In China, knock-off products are often manufactured in the same factories as their "official" counterparts. In these day-night factories "you make shoes for Nike during the day, then you make Nike shoes for you during the night."[41] It's a mode of production that only further blurs the line between the original and the fake, disrupting the hierarchy that each implies. But as I mentioned, a knock up is not a knock off. The term knock up was created by the designer Daniel Day, better known as Dapper Dan.

Dan was a hustler-turned-designer in Harlem during the 1970s and 1980s. His interest in clothing stemmed from the realization that on the street in his neighborhood, fashion was power. Dan eventually opened up his own boutique selling fur coats and leather jackets, and soon evolved to making custom versions of each for select clients. It wasn't until Dan witnessed the excitement surrounding a customers' Louis Vuitton bag that he understood the cachet of aspirational brands. At the time, "luxury goods were becoming status symbols, and European heritage brands that nobody had ever heard of, like Louis, Fendi, and Gucci, were entering the mainstream."[42] But the power of a luxury brand is predicated on limited access and exclusivity. These brands cater to a wealthy white audience despite growing interest and demand from other communities. Dan's goal was, in his own words, to "blackenize"[43] these brands. To create a design and production strategy to reclaim their signs and symbols for his community.

His first custom piece was a jacket with patterned sleeves made from a deconstructed Gucci garment bag. The jacket created a considerable amount of hype in the neighborhood, and with each new customer Dan was challenged to continuously one-up the last. As the designs deviated further from the brand's standard offerings, it became increasingly more apparent to audiences that Dan's items were not "authentic." "I knew none of [my customers] would be caught dead in a knock off, so I had to convince them that, while it had the high-end materials and craftsmanship of a luxury item, it was something new and different. They had to see that I had taken these brands and pushed them into new territory. I knocked them up, I didn't knock them off."

A knock up is a copy that chooses difference as a sign of resistance. Unlike a knock off, which aspires to pass as legitimate, a knock up displays its illegitimacy as a refusal to participate in the oppressive structures it was created to challenge. I am reminded here of the artist David Hammons, or rather how the artist, writer, and curator Coco Fusco frames the work of Hammons. In a 1995 essay for *Frieze* magazine, Fusco addresses Hammons's work in parallel to the idea of "signifyin," a concept first proposed by the literary critic Henry Louis Gates Jr. According to Gates, signifyin "involves taking, twisting and transforming English to make it otherwise. It implicitly revindicates 'imitation' as a creative gesture, over and against a legacy of negative, Eurocentric appraisal of black literature and culture as unoriginal." Thought of in the context of Hammons's work "signifyin allows the artist to be influenced (by Dada and Klein, for instance) yet to twist the influence, blacken it, pastiche it, own it."[44] For Dapper Dan, a knock up does the same. It becomes a tool for the marginalized to "benefit from a capitalist model intended to exclude."[45] A knock up embraces illegitimacy," and in doing so "refuses to rely on the violence that organizes the social space of annunciations."[46] In the 1980s, the popularity of Dan's "knock ups" led to intense copyright litigation. Unable to keep up with exorbitant court fees, Dan was forced to close his business.

Illegitimacy is tricky. Although it often leaves a visual trace, aesthetics alone can be deceiving. The recent trend of "official" bootlegs shows how quickly illegitimacy can be used as strategy. It's an easy way to claim something as "authentic"... which just makes the whole thing feel inauthentic. Let me give you an example...

In the 2018 Gucci Cruise Show, creative director Alessandro Michele premiered a jacket that was basically an exact replica of a piece by Dapper Dan from 1989 (the original was designed with Louis Vuitton monograms, which Gucci converted to Gucci Gs). Although the brand backtracked by justifying the jacket as an homage, the stunt felt ill conceived given Dan was never consulted. Also, Gucci was one of the corporations that had prosecuted Dan in the past for copyright infringement. (Let's consider the Gucci jacket as a "knock down.") In the same show, the brand premiered a dress prominently displaying the text "GUCCY," a clear allusion to the misspellings often found on the brand's bootlegs. The entire show might have been considered progressive—a brand recognizing its imitators as essential to its popularity—but since then, the Gucci legal team has become no more relaxed. Clearly, if anyone's going to knock off Gucci, it's going to be Gucci.

Because illegitimacy can be so easily manipulated, it's worth considering how the idea might move past something tangible. Is it possible to knock up an idea or institution? In 2019, Czar Kristoff, an artist in the Philippines, began a project called Temporary UnRelearning Academy (Temporary URL) in response to the country's monolithic art education. What began as a book-pirating workshop led to classes, research sessions, and lectures while squatting at cyber cafes: "The idea of doing a workshop or organizing a school is based on the conditioning of what a school is supposed to be. You could look at what we were doing as a bootleg of an institution."[47]

Thinking about a bootleg institution, I am reminded of Stefano Harney and Fred Moten's work *The Undercommons*. "It cannot be denied that the university is a place of refuge, and it cannot be accepted that the university is a place of enlightenment.

In the face of these conditions one can only sneak into the university and steal what one can. To abuse its hospitality, to spite its mission, to join its refugee colony ... to be in but not of—this is the path of the subversive intellectual in the modern university."[48] Moten embraces the idea of unprofessionalism, bootlegging its definition as not beneath but beyond professionalization, an escape. A knock up, in its quest for illegitimacy, offers the same.

***

Recently, I read an article on Hyperpop, a Gen-Z music genre that seems, even to its fans, both clear and confusing. It's one of those "you know it when you hear it" situations... more about a feeling than a definition. A.G. Cook is Hyperpop, but so is Kate Bush and J Dilla. Its very appeal is its resistance to classification. It reminded me of bootlegging. When I interviewed people for *Unlicensed*, I always began by asking them how they define a bootleg. The answers varied and at times contradicted themselves. Shirts were bootlegs but so were schools, sculptures, processes. Most people I spoke with never considered bootlegging a part of their practice; some failed to see the connection even after we spoke. That's what makes it so great, it's impossible to pin down. And really, these conversations and investigations might have only made things messier. Like I said… this might all be futile. Anthony Huberman says, "confusion is at the heart of wisdom" and as we remain open to the possibility of what bootleg is, or was, or might be in the future, it leaves us with far more questions than answers. But maybe that's OK. Maybe all that really means is that today the bootleg is alive and well... and just when we think we've created any sort of definition, it slips away from us under the cover of darkness.

Notes

1. The Gradient is the Walker Art Center's online graphic design publishing vertical.

2. Walter Benjamin, "The Task of the Translator," in *Illuminations* (London: The Bodley Head Ltd, 2015), pp. 78–91.

3. Camilo Jiménez Santofimio, "'To Me, Art Is a Place of Transit,'" *C& AMÉRICA LATINA*, amlatina.contemporaryand.com/ editorial/ a-arte -para-mim-e-um-espaco-edgar-calel-de-transito-edgar-calel/.

4. Tami Simon and Coleman Barks, "Coleman Barks: Rumi, Grace, and Human Friendship," *Sounds True*, August 20, 2020, resources.soundstrue.com/podcast/ coleman-barks-rumi-grace-human-friendship/.

5. Andreas Beck, "'People Think All It Takes Is Sideburns': Life as an Elvis Impersonator," *The Guardian*, August 18, 2017, www.theguardian.com/music/2017/ aug/18/all-takes-sideburns-elvis-impersonator-forty-years.

6. Anthony Huberman, "Take Care," *Circular Facts*, ed. Binna Choi, Mai Abu ElDahab, and Emily Pethick (Berlin and New York: Sternberg Press, 2011), pp. 9–17.

7. DeNeen L. Brown "How Aretha Franklin's 'Respect' Became an Anthem for Civil Rights and Feminism," *The Washington Post*, August 14, 2020, www.washington post. com/news/retropolis/wp/ 2018/ 08/14/how-aretha-franklins-respect-became-an-anthem-for-civil-rights-and-feminism/.

8. James Snead, "Repetition as a Figure of Black Culture," *Black Literature and Literary Theory*, ed. Henry Louis Gates Jr. (New York: Routledge, 2016), pp. 59–60.

9. Dan Hill, *Dark Matter and Trojan Horses: A Strategic Design Vocabulary* (Moscow: Strelka Press, 2015).

10. A great debt is owed to Canal Street Research Association (@canal_street_research) for bringing to light this connection between Brecht and bootlegs in an Instagram post on December 12, 2020.

11. "Epic Theatre and Brecht: Why Is Brecht so Important?," GCSE Drama

Revision, BBC Bitesize, *BBC News*, www.bbc.co.uk/bitesize/guides/zwmvd2p/revision/2.

12. Bertolt Brecht, *Brecht On Theatre*, ed. Marc Silberman, Steve Giles, and Tom Kuhn (London: Bloomsbury Academic, 2019).

13. Mark Fisher, *Capitalist Realism: Is There No Alternative?* (London: Zero Books, 2010).

14. Xiao Yuefan, "Maoism and Disruptive Creativity: Shanzhai—an Alternative Perspective," *Boredom, Shanzhai, and Digitisation in the Time of Creative China*, ed. Jeroen de Kloet et al. (Amsterdam: Amsterdam University Press, 2019), pp. 186–210; JSTOR www.jstor.org/stable/j.ctvqr1bnw.15. Accessed April 26, 2021.

15. See Shanzhai Lyric in this book, pp. 118–147.

16. Metahaven, *Can Jokes Bring Down Governments? Memes, Design and Politics* (Moscow: Strelka Press, 2014).

17. Kyle Chayka, "How Do You Back Up the Museum of Modern Art?," *Vice*, July 20, 2015, www.vice.com/en/article/gvy7q3/how-do-you-back-up-the-museum- of-modern-art

18. Jorge Luis Borges, *The Library of Babel* (Boston: David R. Godine, 2000).

19. See Experimental Jetset in this book, pp. 68–87.

20. Walter Benjamin, "Unpacking My Library," in *Illuminations* (London: The Bodley Head Ltd, 2015), pp. 78–91.

21. Clinton Heylin, *Bootleg: The Secret History of the Other Recording Industry* (New York: St. Martin's Griffin, 1996).

22. See Mark Owens in this book, pp. 384–395.

23. Marcus Boon, *In Praise of Copying* (Cambridge, MA: Harvard University Press, 2013)

24. Hito Steyerl, "In Defense of the Poor Image," *e-flux Journal #10* (November 2009), www.e-flux.com/journal/ 10/61362/in-defense-of-the-poor-image/.

25. Roland Barthes, "From Work to Text," *The Rustle of Language*, trans. Richard Howard (Berkeley and Los Angeles: University of California Press, 2010).

26. Steyerl 2009 (note 24).

27. The show has als been staged in 2015 and 2017.

28. See Experimental Jetset in this book, pp. 68–87

29. Ibid.

30. Walter Benjamin, “Paris: Capital of the Nineteenth Century,” in *Reflections: Essays, Aphorisms, Autobiographical Writings*, ed. Peter Demetz (New York: Schocken Books, 2007).

31. “Dilip Kumar: Lesser Known Facts,” *The Times of India*, December 10, 2014, timesofindia.indiatimes.com/entertainment/hindi/bollywood/photo-features/dilip-kumar-lesser-known-facts/photostory/

32. Shriram Iyengar, “The Secret of Dilip Kumar’s ‘Method’, Revealed by the Actor Himself,” *Cinestaan*, www.cinestaan.com/articles/2018/oct/12/15537.

33. Hilton Als, exh. cat. *Robert Gober: The Heart Is Not A Metaphor* (New York: Museum of Modern Art, 2014), p. 105.

34. Byung-Chul Han, *Shanzhai: Deconstruction in Chinese*, trans. Philippa Hurd (Cambridge: MIT Press, 2017).

35. Ibid.

36. “Princeton—News—Copying and Imitation in the Arts of China on View at the Princeton University Art Museum,” *Princeton University*, The Trustees of Princeton University, pr.princeton.edu/news/01

37. As an aside, a fellow Jan van Eyck participant Gamal Fouad built a hut in the garden of the institution where he lived and wrote for six weeks. It was a way for him to enter into a dialogue with Thoreau and Walden, a form of method acting.

38. “Allen Ruppersberg with Constance Lewallen,” *The Brooklyn Rail*, April 24, 2018, brooklynrail.org/2018 / ALLEN-RUPPERSBERG.

39. “Allen Ruppersberg,” De Appel, deappel.nl/en/exhibit/allen-ruppersberg.

40. See Matt Olson in this book, pp. 160–179.

41. Christopher Kirkley et al., “Bandits Brought Technology to This World: Shanzhai Culture in China,” in *The*

Pirate Book, ed. Marie Lechner (Ljubljana: Aksioma, 2015).

42. Daniel R. Day and Mikael Awake, *Dapper Dan: Made in Harlem: A Memoir* (New York: Random House, 2019).

43. Ibid.

44. Coco Fusco, "Wreaking Havoc on the Signified: David Hammons," *Frieze* 7 (May 1995), www.frieze.com/article/wreaking-havoc-signified.

45. Anna Harsanyi, "Canal Street Research Association: Shanzhai Lyric," *The Brooklyn Rail*, February 9, 2021, brooklynrail.org/2021/02/artseen/Canal-Street- Research-Association-Shanzhai-Lyric.

46. See Babak Radboy in this book, pp. 148–159.

47. See Clara Balaguer and Czar Kristoff in this book, pp. 240–263.

48. Stefano Harney and Fred Moten, *The Undercommons: Fugitive Planning & Black Study* (London/New York: Minor Compositions/Autonomedia, 2013).

An Incomplete History of Bootlegs (1440–2023)

Ben Schwartz

Because of bootleggings existence underground and resistance to any clear definition, it remains impossible to compile anything close to a comprehensive chronology of it. What follows then, are notable milestones I have encountered in my research and in conversations with the people in this publication. Included as well are key moments from related gestures such as "appropriation," "copying," "pirating," "sampling," and "remixing," further embracing the blurry borders that may (or may not) separate these ideas. Additionally, legislation related to U.S. and European copyright law are woven into the text to create a framework of the oppositional structures a majority of contributors in this book are up against. In giving a history of bootlegging, it is my hope that readers will gain a foundational understanding of the act, which is challenged and expanded upon by the interviews in the latter part of this book.

Fig. 1

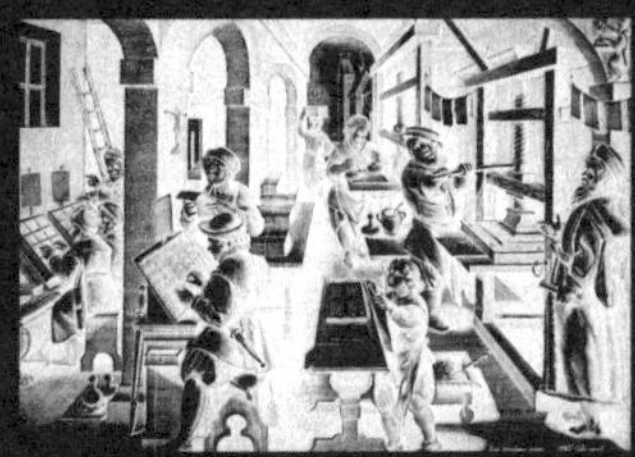

c.1440: The German goldsmith Johannes Gutenberg invents the printing press, allowing for the production of books and the spread of information on a mass scale. With printing out of the hands of the clergy comes the possibility for dissidents to produce politically subversive content as well as "bootlegs"—copies of existing works re-typeset, printed, and distributed illegally. (Fig. 1)

1603: William Shakespeare's first quarto of Hamlet is published. This play, along with other early transcribed Shakespeare performances, would later be collected into one edition known together as the Bad Quarto. These unauthorized and error-ridden "bootlegs" were compiled from audience transcriptions of the playwright's live performances. Despite the inaccuracies, these played a crucial role in preserving Shakespeare's legacy.

1710: The British Parliament creates the first copyright law known as The Statute of Anne. The regulation gave publishers 14 years of legal protection for works made after 1709, and 21 years of protection for pre-existing works.

1790: The first United States Congress creates The Copyright Act of 1790, which offers authors and proprietors exclusive rights to print and publish works for a 14 year period.

1886: The Berne Convention creates standard copyright rules across all major European countries. Additionally, the Convention declares a work as having copyright status from the moment of its creation, rather than needing it to be published or registered to ensure protection.

1901: Lionel Mapleson, the librarian at New York Metropolitan Opera House, creates unauthorized live tapings of performances while working at the venue. Despite their poor quality, these tapes, known as the Mapleson Cylinders, are praised for preserving an era of works that would have otherwise been lost to history. (Fig. 2)

Fig. 2

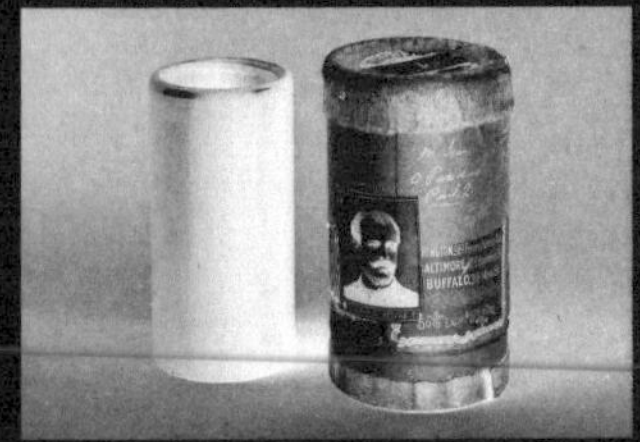

1909: The U.S. passes the Copyright Act of 1909, which extends the period of copyright protection from 14 years to 28 years, with a possible 28 year renewal. In addition, it approves the use of a symbol consisting of a "c" in a circle (©) plus a year, to mark copyright protection.

Fig. 3

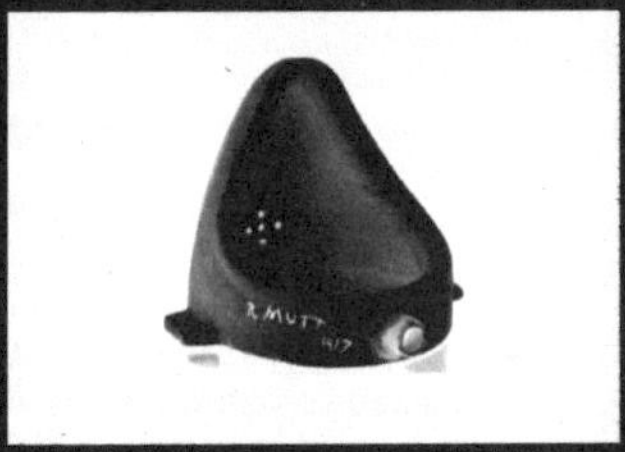

1917: French artist Marcel Duchamp enters a mass-produced urinal titled *Fountain* into a landmark exhibition at the Society of Independent Artists in New York. The piece sparked outrage at the society and, after a vote, was never shown. The artwork, which Duchamp referred to as a "readymade," is considered one of the first pieces in the genre of appropriation art. (Fig. 3)

1920: Prohibition in the United States becomes a nationwide law restricting the sale of alcohol. It was at this time that the word "bootleg" was coined to refer to the smuggling of illegal bottles of alcohol in the leg of one's boot. Those who took part in creating and distributing this moonshine were deemed "bootleggers." (Fig 4)

Fig. 4

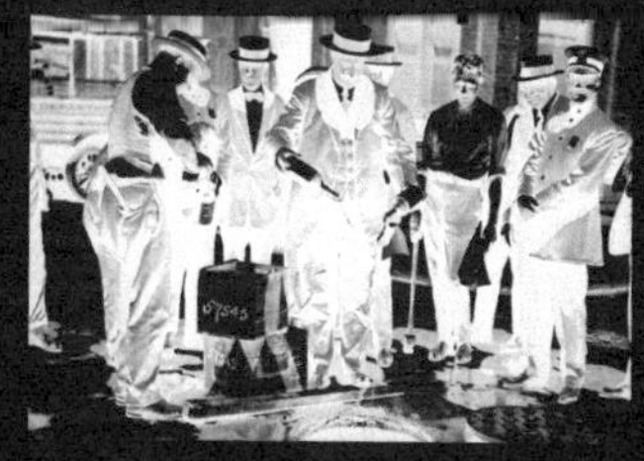

c. 1930: In the 1930s Agloe, NY appears on General Drafting Co. maps as a copyright trap (also known as a fictitious entry). Agloe is an example of a phantom settlement, or paper town—made-up locations on maps that are used to catch plagiarism. If a new map contained the invented location, then it was clear it had been copied. Twenty years later the Agloe General Store opened, taking its name from the fictional town, creating a strange twist where the imaginary location now existed in reality. Today the general store has closed and Agloe has all but disappeared from maps.

1933: Prohibition is repealed in the U.S. with the passage of the Twenty First Amendment.

1948: The French composer Pierre Schaeffer composites bits and pieces of preexisting recorded material, creating the genre known as musique concrète. These avant-garde recordings are widely considered to be one of the first instances of what we would today consider sampling. (Fig. 5)

Fig. 5

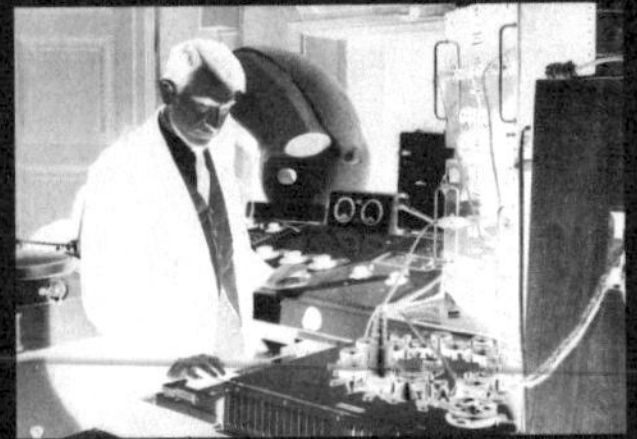

1952: The Recording Industry Association of America (RIAA) is formed to combat the burgeoning music pirating industry whose culprits include major mafia members.

Fig. 6

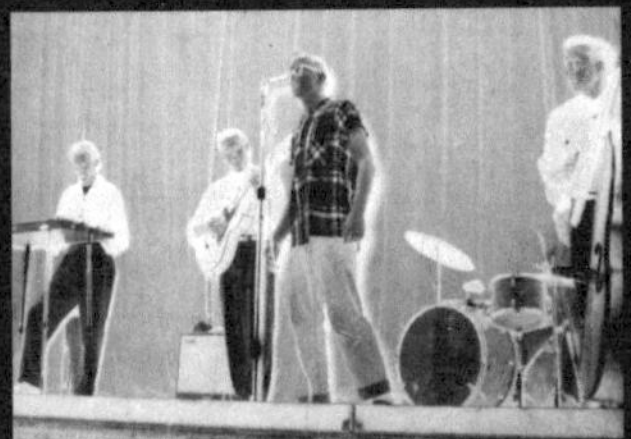

1954: American performer Carl "Cheesie" Nelson, known as the first Elvis impersonator, gains a local following from singing "That's All Right, Mama" and "Blue Moon of Kentucky" on WLAC radio. The covers attract the attention of Elvis himself, and the two perform together later that year. (Fig. 6)

Fig. 7

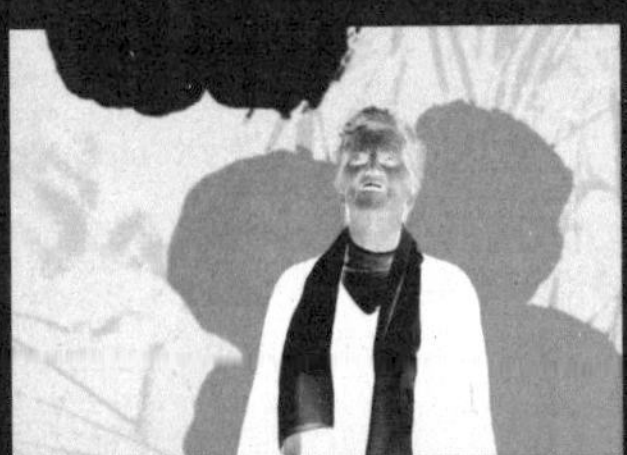

1968: American artist Elaine Sturtevant, known for replicating existing works of art, produces a version of Andy Warhol's silkscreen flower paintings. The works were created using screens provided by Warhol himself. In an interview with Warhol, when asked how he creates his works, he responded, "I don't know. Ask Elaine." (Fig. 7)

1969: Bob Dylan's *Great White Wonder*, widely considered to be the first rock bootleg, is released by the newly formed underground record label Trademark of Quality. (Fig. 8)

Fig. 8

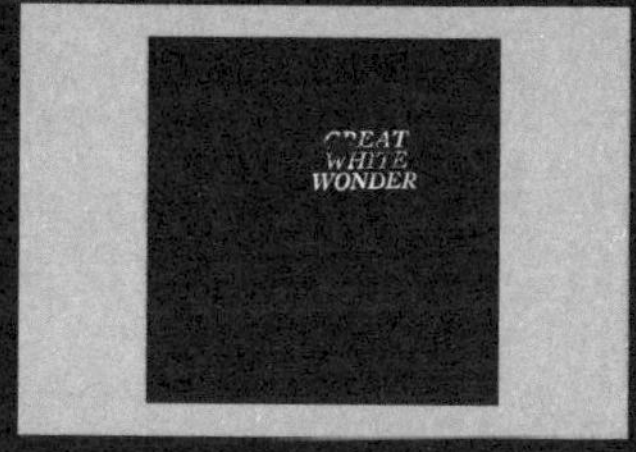

1971: The South African composer John Kongos releases the track "He's Gonna Step on You Again," which is cited in the Guinness Book of World Records as the first commercially available song to contain a sample—in this case, a tape loop of African drumming. This claim is often disputed, citing the track "Burundi Black" by Mike Steiphensen (also released in 1971) as the first use of a sample.

1973: DJ Kool Herc performs "Merry-Go-Round" at a Bronx house party, where he extends a drum break by playing the same record back-to-back on two turntables. This performance is widely considered to be the first remix.

1974: Post-It Notes are invented by 3M employee Art Fry, using a "low-tack" adhesive created by co-worker Dr. Spencer Silver. The product was created in accordance with the company's "permitted bootlegging" policy which allows staff to use 15% of their time to work on their own projects. This idea would later be implemented at Google, where Gmail was conceived on "bootlegged" time.

1976: The U.S. Copyright Act of 1976 declares a work as copyrighted from the moment it is created. Previously, authors would need to publish or register works to acquire protected status. This adjustment brought U.S. copyright law closer in line to the Berne Convention of 1886. Additionally the law created the doctrine of "fair use" which establishes a set of conditions where permission is not needed from the copyright holder.

1976: American computer engineer Li-Chen Wang, responsible for the Palo Alto Tiny BASIC programming language, creates the idea of "copyleft." In the programming language's distribution papers, Wang writes "COPYLEFT ALL WRONGS RESERVED." The idea becomes a foundational principle of future open-source programming, ensuring that material under copyleft status can be edited and redistributed freely as long as new versions of material circulate as copyleft content.

1980s: The American artist Richard Prince begins to exhibit his *Cowboy* series where he rephotographs ads from Marlboro cigarettes featuring cowboys riding through the desert. When asked about his intention, Prince stated, "I wanted to re-present the closest thing to the real thing." (Fig. 9)

Fig. 9

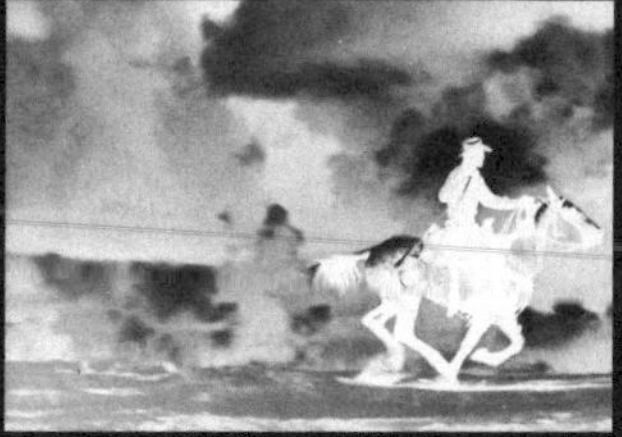

1981: American photographer Sherrie Levine stages her landmark show 'After Walker Evans' at the gallery Metro Pictures, New York. The works are photographs of depression-era photographs taken by Walker Evans. By simply rephotographing the images, Levine makes a powerful statement about "'authenticity,' 'the genius,' 'the masterpiece,' and 'the hand.'" (Fig. 10)

Fig. 10

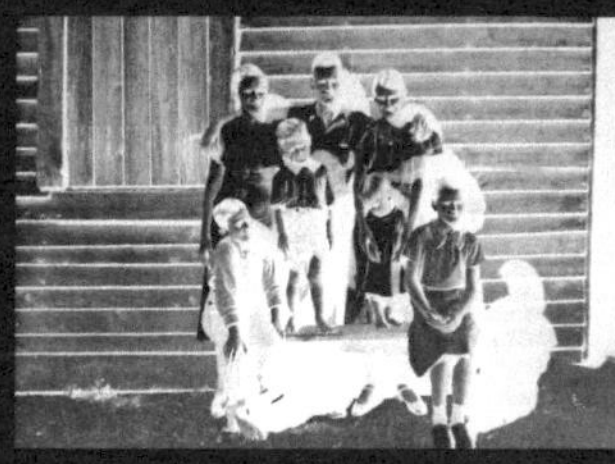

Fig. 11

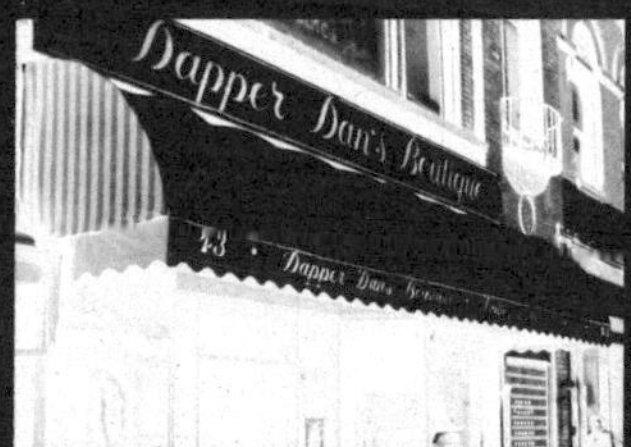

1982: Dapper Dan, considered by many to be the father of bootleg fashion, opens his Harlem boutique.

The store becomes popular for its signature “knock-up” items that use high-end logos on garments designed for the Black community. (Fig. 11)

Fig. 12

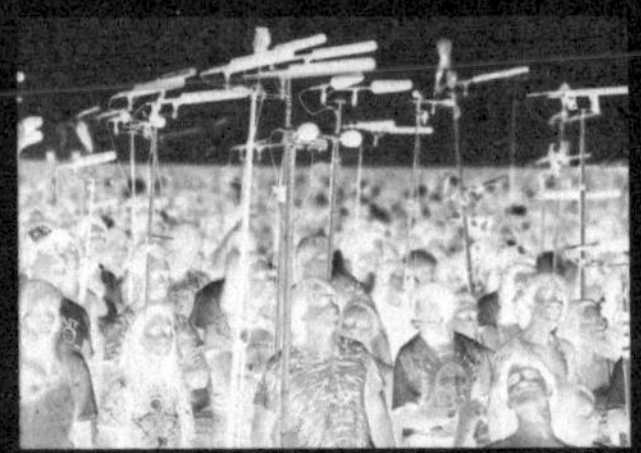

1984: The Grateful Dead play their first show with a designated “tapers’ section” inviting bootleggers to record their Berkeley Community Theater set from directly behind the sound booth. The iconic “tapers’ section,” and resulting recordings, helped to create and connect the band’s devoted fanbase. The tapes, along with other bootleg merchandise, were often sold outside of Grateful Dead concerts in makeshift marketplaces known as “Shakedown Street.” (Fig 12)

Fig. 13

1987: Prince cancels the release of his new album and demands Warner Bros. Records to destroy all copies. By the time of cancellation, advanced radio promos have already been distributed, and are used as source files for widely circulated bootleg versions. The record, dubbed *The Black Album* (due to its plain black cover), is often considered the best selling bootleg of all time. (Fig. 13)

Fig. 14

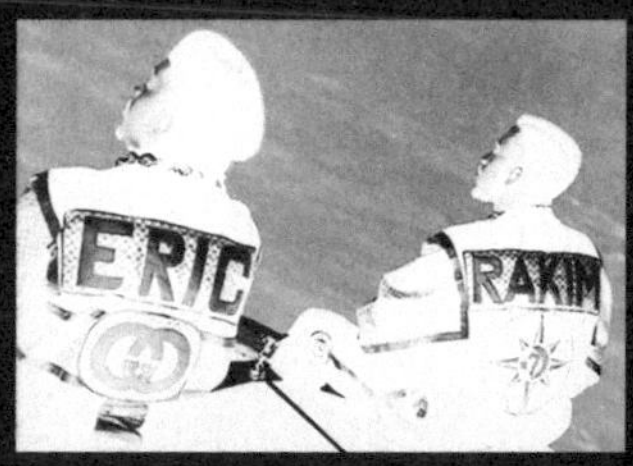

1988: Dapper Dan appears on the hit television show *Yo! MTV Raps* alongside Fab 5 Freddy and Eric B. Later that year, rappers Eric B & Rakim release their hit album *Follow The Leader*. On the cover, the duo wear custom outfits designed by Dapper Dan, bringing further attention to his work. (Fig. 14)

1988: The United States establishes the Berne Convention Implementation Act which more closely aligns U.S. Copyright Law with the tenants of the Berne Convention.

Fig. 15

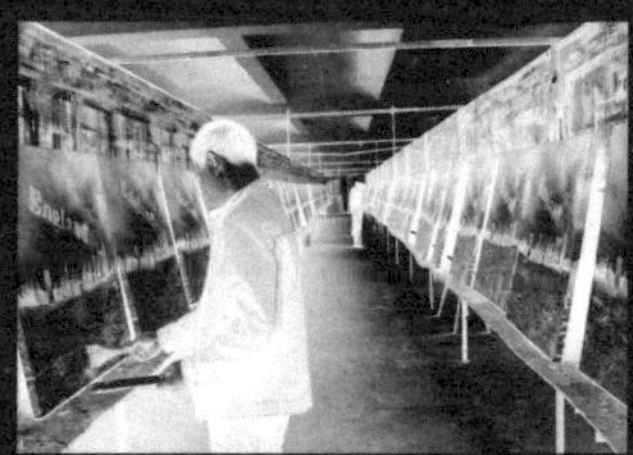

1989: The Chinese painter Huang Jiang, known for his copies of masterworks, creates the renowned art replica industry of Dafen Village. Jiang, along with a group of 20 trained artists, moved to the Shenzhen neighborhood and produced nearly a dozen paintings a day. After sending a painting to Walmart to gauge sales interest, the megastore placed an order for 50,000 copies, which needed to be fulfilled in a month and a half. (Fig. 15)

1989: The animated television show *The Simpsons* premieres on FOX. The wild success of the series is coupled with an inundation of merchandise, both official and unauthorized. Bootleggers focused their attention on one character, the charmingly abrasive adolescent Bart. Fan knockoffs transformed Bart in a variety of ways, from a gym rat to a war hero. One specific niche that gained traction was "Black Bart." Ernest White, a call-in radio show host that often spoke about the character, said, "The presence of the Black Bart T-shirt says there is an association with the underdog, a need to fight the establishment." (Fig. 16)

Fig. 16

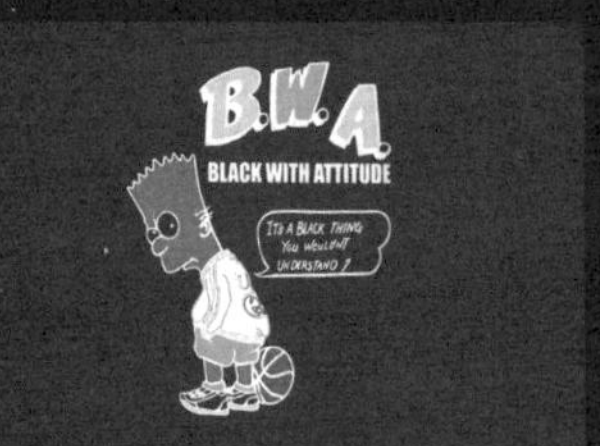

1992: Dapper Dan is forced to shut down his boutique after losing a trademark infringement case to the luxury brand Fendi.

1996: The *Seinfeld* episode "The Little Kicks" premieres, featuring a plot line with Jerry and Kramer befriending a video bootlegger. Jerry eventually realizes his talent for creating pirate films, and orchestrates a scheme to create the best bootleg of all time. (Fig. 17)

Fig. 17

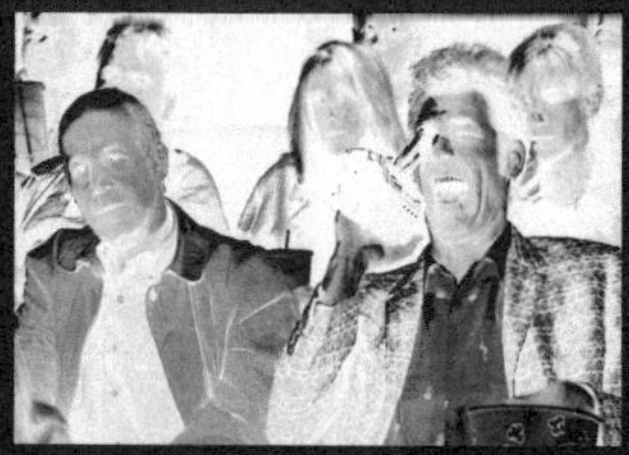

1998: The U.S. Congress passes The Digital Millennium Copyright Act (DMCA) which brings copyright law up to speed with the development of the internet. The law seeks to navigate the relationship between service providers and users in copyright infringement cases, allows for greater protections online for copyrighted works, and makes it unlawful to remove pertinent copyright information from online sources.

1999: Napster, a peer-to-peer file sharing application, is launched, allowing people to illegally download music for free from their home computers.

2001: The Dutch design studio Experimental Jetset creates the iconic John & Paul & Ringo & George T-shirt for the fashion label 2K/Gingham. The "&&&" format becomes bootlegged, remade, and parodied countless times. (p. 68)

2003: The Pirate Bay, an online peer-to-peer file sharing site, is launched. On The Pirate Bay, users had access to a wide variety of media that could be downloaded and uploaded for free, sparking controversy around the legality of file sharing and becoming a major voice in the anti-copyright movement. In 2009, the founders of the site were found guilty of copyright infringement and were sentenced to jail time and a fine. In many countries, Internet Service Providers have been ordered to block access to the site including China, France, Germany, and the UK.

2005: Art dealer Mike Weiss calls the police to remove New York-based artist Eric Doeringer from W. 24th Street in Manhattan, where he had been selling bootleg artworks since 2001. Weiss stated that Doeringer's stand is "bad for his business." (p. 356)

2010: Bootleg phones made in China, known as "Shanzhai phones," account for nearly twenty percent of the global market (most are found in China or other developing countries). The spread of these phones is demonstrative of a larger integration and acceptance of Shanzhai products into daily life.

2011: Designer Mark Owens and curator Alex Klein collaborate on a bootleg Ulm Stool for an exhibition at the Los Angeles gallery LAXART. The piece uses a Memphis Bacterio pattern laminate designed by Ettore Sottsass to cover Max Bill's iconic modernist piece of furniture. (p. 384)

2012: Artist/designer/publisher Shannon Michael Cane hosts the first 'Bootleg T-Shirt Show' at Printed Matter. The show exhibited and sold bootleg shirts from artists such as Peter Sutherland, Matt Connors, Benjamin Critton, Mungo Thomson, Chris Castillo, Shannon Michael Cane, Eliza Koch, and Marc Hundley. Subsequent versions of the show would be held in 2015 and in 2017. (p. 102)

2012: Paris-based designer Olivier Lebrun publishes *A Pocket Companion to Books from The Simpsons* with Rollo Press. The book contains 174 unauthorized stills of books featured in *The Simpsons*. The book immediately sells out and is reprinted four times. (p. 318)

2013: Clara Balaguer, Czar Kristoff, Kristian Henson, and Dante Carlos form Hardworking Goodlooking, a publishing "houz" often making work in and about the Philippines. The studio develops a unique research interest and visual language on the complexities of cultural mimicry. (p. 240)

2013: Virgil Abloh creates the brand Off-White (originally called PYREX VISION in 2012) which garnered popularity for pieces reliant on appropriation, reference, and readymades. The logo for the company is taken from the Glasgow Airport logo created by the British designer Margaret Calvert (Fig. 18).

Fig. 18

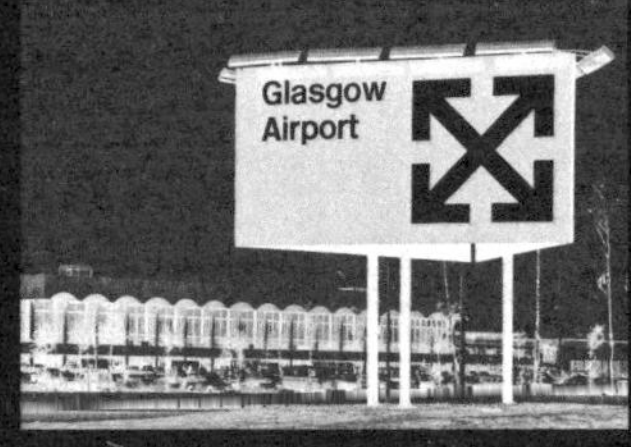

2013: The Canadian rapper Drake releases *Nothing Was The Same*. The record becomes the most illegally downloaded album in history, having been pirated over 10 million times. (Fig. 19)

Fig. 19

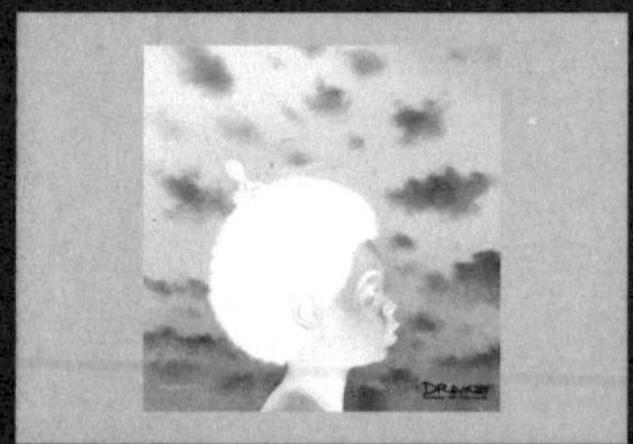

2014: Georgian designers Demna and Durum Gvasalia begin the brand VETEMENTS. In 2016 the brand gains attention for their bootleg of a DHL uniform T-shirt. The brothers continue to build a reputation for their unorthodox approach to fashion, including the memorable "Official Fake" garage sale in which VETEMENTS sold official versions of their own knockoffs. In 2019, Demna left VETEMENTS and the line is now solely run by Durum. (Fig. 20)

Fig. 20

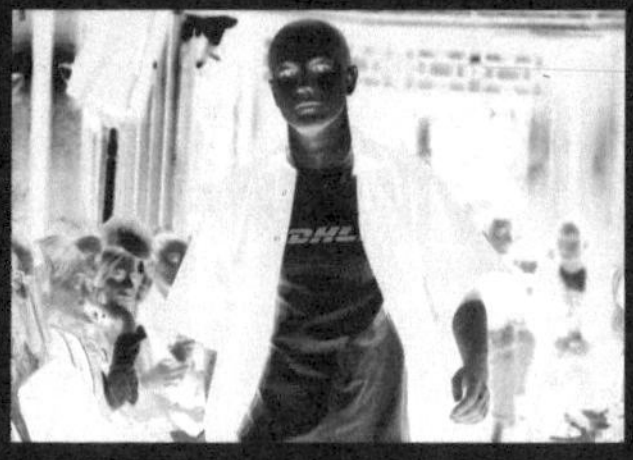

2015: New York-based designer Kevin McCaughey launches Boot Boyz Biz, a project producing bootleg merchandise from a variety of subcultures. The brand's mission statement on their website reads that bootlegging serves "as a model for association, for reflecting on histories and ideas, for capturing essence to organize a collective memory that guides our future." (p. 198)

2015: Demna Gvasalia becomes the creative director of Balenciaga. Under his leadership, the brand becomes a pioneering force in the industry, embracing the idea of "fashion as a mirror for what is going on around us." One particularly notable "bootleg" moment for the brand is a 2017 collection featuring a logo resembling the Bernie Sanders campaign wordmark. (Fig. 21)

Fig. 21

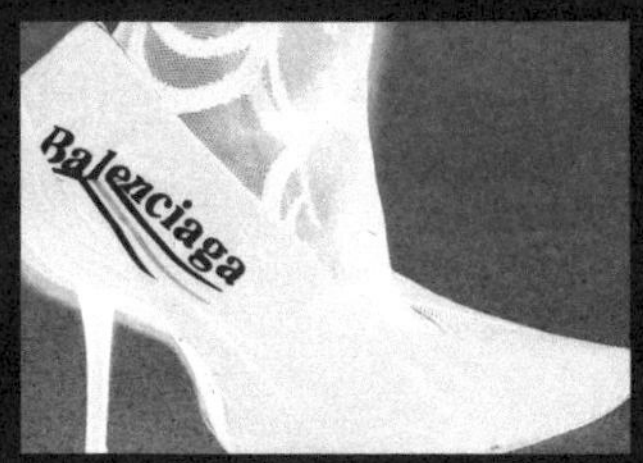

2015: Berlin-based artist Jonathan Monk, who often works in the realm of appropriation, posts on Instagram a restaurant receipt featuring an illustration of the artist Alighiero Boetti. Monk sells the receipt for the price of the dinner, creating the first work in his *Restaurant Drawing* Series. (p. 226)

2015: New York-based artists Ming Lin and Alexandra Tatarsky begin Shanzhai Lyric, an archive that collects and reframes awkward slogans from bootleg T-shirts into an ongoing poem. (p. 118)

2016: Minneapolis-based design studio OOIEE lead by Matt Olson launches their exhibition 'No Separation' at the Aspen Art Museum. In the show pieces on display in the galleries are covered by a textile printed with a picture of the sky from above the institution. (p. 160)

2016: Elisa van Joolen creates her One-to-One collection by inking garments from one brand and printing them onto items from another brand. (p. 88)

2016: LA-based brand Online Ceramics is launched by Alix Ross and Elijah Funk. (p. 370)

2017: Gucci creative director Alessandro Michele premieres a jacket in the brand's 2017 Cruise Collection fashion show, with a striking similarity to a 1989 piece from Dapper Dan. The brand claimed the piece was an homage, while much of the public was upset that luxury labels that had previously sued Dan were now stealing from him. In 2018, the brand and designer partnered for Gucci-Dapper Dan: The Collection. (Fig. 22)

Fig. 22

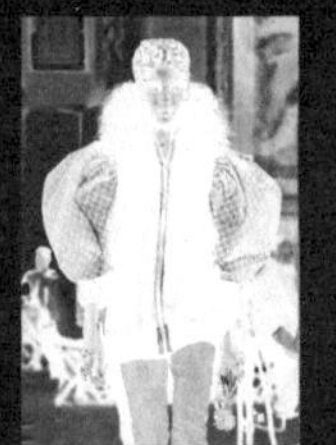

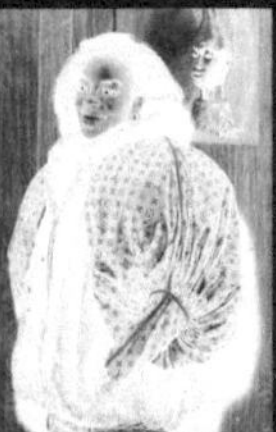

2017: The New York-based fashion designer Telfar Clemens creates new uniforms for the fast food chain White Castle under the creative direction of Babak Radboy. (p. 148)

2018: Virgil Abloh becomes the creative director of Louis Vuitton menswear collection.

2018: The London-based artist Akinola Davies Jr. debuts his film *Boot/Leg* at Art Basel (p. 306)

2018: Upon graduating from Amsterdam's Rietveld Academie, graphic designer Line Arngaard and fashion researcher Sonia Oet produce *A March Issue*, a page-by-page remake of the March issue of *Vogue* magazine. (p. 180)

2018: New York-based artist Nat Pyper creates the font Robert Ford using type treatments from Ford's 1989 magazine *THING*. The font would become the first in their series A Queer Year of Love Letters, in which Pyper redraws and distributes seminal letterforms from queer history. (p. 396)

2018: New York-based designer Hassan Rahim creates the iconic Sun Ra Arkestra bootleg shirt with the brand Total Luxury Spa. The shirt commemorates a fictional 1980 concert from the band at the Great Western Forum in Los Angeles. (p. 408)

2018: New York-based artist SHIRT restages David Hammons's iconic *Bliz-aard Ball Sale* (1983) selling snowballs on the street in New York. (p. 286)

2018: Sony announces plans to develop a film based on the life of Dapper Dan.

2019: Czar Kristoff creates Temporary UnReLearning Academy (Temporary URL) in Calabarzon. According to the program's mission statement, Temporary URL is a "migratory school interested in queering artistic and cultural formation/production in the Philippines through interventions of public spaces and exploring vernacular technology and tools." The program uses bootleg techniques (photocopying, lo-fi publishing, squatting in internet cafes) and is itself a sort of bootleg, demonstrating the potential of the act beyond objects and into structures and ideas.

2019: Uzbekistan-based photographer Hassan Kurbanbaev begins the photo series *Logomania: Owning the World at Half Price*. The series documents and investigates the bootleg obsession of the Uzbekistan people. (p. 276)

2019: Paris-based fashion label BLESS produce the Multicollection T-Shirt from the BLESS N°67 collection. The shirt is an official bootleg, copied from an unofficial fan bootleg, spotted at the Ooga Booga bookstore in Los Angeles. (p. 264)

2020: During the COVID lockdowns in New York Shanzhai Lyric open up a temporary storefront on Canal Street under the name Canal Street Research Association. The project celebrates the history of the surrounding neighborhood (known for its bootleg markets) through performances, communal archives, exhibitions, and storytelling. (p. 118)

2021: Virgil Abloh passes away from cancer.

2021: The artist SHIRT produces the work *You Can Copy Someone To A T (It Will Never Be The Same)* (2021) which bootlegs a 2018 shirt from Virgil Abloh. The shirt is permanently in-stock and is sold with the design file, so the buyer is able to reprint the graphic as they desire. (p. 286)

2021: New York-based architect Oana Stănescu, along with German architecture office Something Fantastic, organize a lecture for the School of Architecture at Syracuse University on cover versions, celebrating the gesture throughout history across a wide range of media. (p. 344)

2023: DeviantArt, Midjourney, and Stability AI are sued by a group of artists over copyright infringement in the generation of AI images. The three companies use Stable Diffusion, an artificial intelligence software created from a dataset using unauthorized artworks. The artists claim that the use of these artworks in the dataset, and thus the use of the dataset, violates copyright law. The case prompts urgent questions around authorship asAI becomes more readily available.

2023: The publication *UNLICENSED: Bootlegging as Creative Practice* is co-published by Valiz and Source Type. The book contains a collection of interviews from various art and design practices reflecting on the act of bootlegging in the 21st Century.

UNLICENSED
Interviews

PROVO

Experimental Jetset (EJ)

Experimental Jetset is a Dutch graphic design studio consisting of Marieke Stolk, Erwin Brinkers, and Danny van den Dungen. The members of the studio are, at their core, fans. As a result, their work often feels like an homage to their obsessions, from punk to Provo, Beatles to Bauhaus, all filtered through their iconic typographic voice. In 2016 the studio made their John & Paul & Ringo & George T-shirt, sparking a wildfire of remakes, covers, parodies, and bootlegs, and creating what is perhaps the first graphic design meme. In another series of works, the studio reinterpreted a piece by Ellsworth Kelly using album covers in one instance, and in another A4 sheets of paper that eventually were bound into a book. The projects demonstrate how different "versions" of an idea can travel through culture, changing but also staying the same. Interview by Ben Schwartz (BS).

BS: As a design studio that seems very invested in punk, anarchist, and activist movements, I'm curious how you define bootlegging. In what ways do you see bootlegging connected to these interests?

EJ: What makes the term "bootlegging" interesting in the first place is perhaps the very fact that its definition is so open and ambiguous. If the origin of the word indeed comes from the practice and culture of smuggling (carrying contraband in the leg of your boot—hence, "bootleg"), then it's not far-fetched to say that the word "bootleg" itself is a bootleg—a term that can carry multiple definitions, a device that can be used to smuggle opposite meanings from one place to another. It's a word with porous borders—ideal for trespassers like us.

So it's a fascinating term. However, it's not a word we use very often in our own practice. In cases in which we explicitly referred to existing work (as facsimile, as re-enactment, or as citation), we sometimes used the word "cover version," which is a term we like very much as well, referring to the idea of rock bands covering songs by other bands, as tribute or homage. For example, the subtitle of our work *Kelly 1:1* from 2002 (in which we recreated a painting by Ellsworth Kelly) was indeed *A Cover Version*.

What we like about the notion of the "cover version" is that whole tension between the "standard" and the "variation"—the idea that a standardized format can still serve as a platform for subversive accents and critical dialects. We talked a bit about cover versions (and the standard/variation dialectic) in a conversation we had with Metahaven a while ago, in the October 2011 issue of *Print Magazine*.[1]

Returning to the word "bootlegging," and contemplating some of the given definitions, it's interesting that the notion of bootlegging as the "counterfeit reproduction of luxury goods" almost seems to touch on the very root of graphic design: the printing of the bible by Johannes Gutenberg, circa 1450.

Of course, before Gutenberg, bibles used to be "luxury goods"—unique pieces, calligraphed by monks, owned by the church, and kept away (at safe distance) from the peasants. Gutenberg broke that spell by basically bootlegging the bible, making it (more or less) available to the common people—thereby destabilizing the Catholic empire, fueling both reformation and renaissance, causing major revolutions and upheavals throughout Europe. Speaking of Gutenberg, we have always been admirers of Régis Debray's 2007 essay "Socialism and Print"[2] (originally published by *New Left Review*, currently to be found online under the title "Socialism: A Life-Cycle"), in which Debray refers to the invention of the printing press as the start of the "graphosphere," that dizzying amalgamation of modernism and socialism, in which graphic workers (from printers to typographers) played such an important role.

Of course, the invention of the printing press can also be seen as the dawn of modern capitalism—after all, the printed book was the first-ever mass-produced product.In that sense, the birth of the printing industry (and thus of graphic design) already carries in itself that beautiful paradox that also can be found in the current practice of bootlegging—that electrifying tension between emancipation and exploitation.

Taking it back to the historical origin of the word, and the culture of smuggling, contrabandism, illegal trespassing, et cetera, it's interesting to see that the current practice of bootlegging often involves smuggling as well: carrying information from one sphere to another, crossing borders between "high culture" and "low culture," between the subcultural and the

pp. 72–73: Experimental Jetset, *Kelly 1:1* (2002)

mainstream, between academic culture and working-class culture, et cetera. Because of its roots in smuggling, bootlegging will always be regarded as slightly illegal, immoral, vulgar.

And this metaphor of smuggling goes for graphic design as well. After all, what is graphic design but the practice of pushing materialized information from one sphere to another, forever crossing the porous borders between art and industry, between poetry and pornography, between pop and politics?- Graphic design is a practice that was born in the vague borderlands between disparate disciplines, so trespassing feels natural to us. Graphic designers are bootleggers, forgers, smugglers—and because of that, graphic design will always be regarded as a slightly clandestine discipline, as a lumpen-activity, as a practice without any real morals (other than the proverbial "honor among thieves"). And that's exactly what makes graphic design such a relevant force in culture, we think.

On a completely different note, one other aspect that is quite striking about the practice of bootlegging is its archiving function. To bootleg is to archive. This was already true in the era of bootleg records—albums that often contained illegally-taped concerts of rock bands, thus creating alternative archives (and parallel canons) of those bands.

But this archivist dimension can also be found in more current examples of bootlegging. In that regard, we should mention Kevin McCaughey's ongoing Boot Boyz Biz project and the way in which McCaughey uses the medium of T-shirts to document crucial moments in (sub)cultural history. It really is an archive made of cotton.In fact, in an old interview from 2008, we (briefly) mentioned exactly this idea:

the potential of a T-shirt to function as a social-democratic archive, as a manifestation of living memory.

BS: In your vast body of work, I'm curious what projects might come to mind when speaking about bootlegging?

EJ: We already mentioned *Kelly 1:1*, an installation (and publication) we made in 2002, in which we recreated an iconic painting by Ellsworth Kelly, using 150 A4-sized sheets of colored paper. By copying (in a low-fi, low-tech, low-res way) an archetypical painting by Kelly, we tried to transform the function of a particular space; a site-specific intervention, in short. Also, by turning those 150 sheets into a publication as well, we hoped to reflect on the relationship between "the original" and "the copy"—and the role of graphic design therein. Most of all, it was a tribute to Ellsworth Kelly (in that sense, it truly was a "cover version"), so we were very flattered to learn that, in 2003, Kelly bought five copies of the publication, through Printed Matter in New York. (First we were slightly nervous that those five copies would be sent straight to his lawyers, for legal matters, but luckily we never heard from them). We later revisited *Kelly 1:1* a couple of times. For example, in 2007, we translated the same Ellsworth Kelly painting into 100 monochrome 12-inch record sleeves (for 'Ultramoderne,' a group exhibition on the relationship between modernism and pop-culture).

Another project in which we explicitly referred to existing work was *Zang Tumb Tumb (If You Want It)*, a print we created in 2003. In that piece, we tried

pp. 76–77: Experimental Jetset, *Kelly 1:1* (2007)

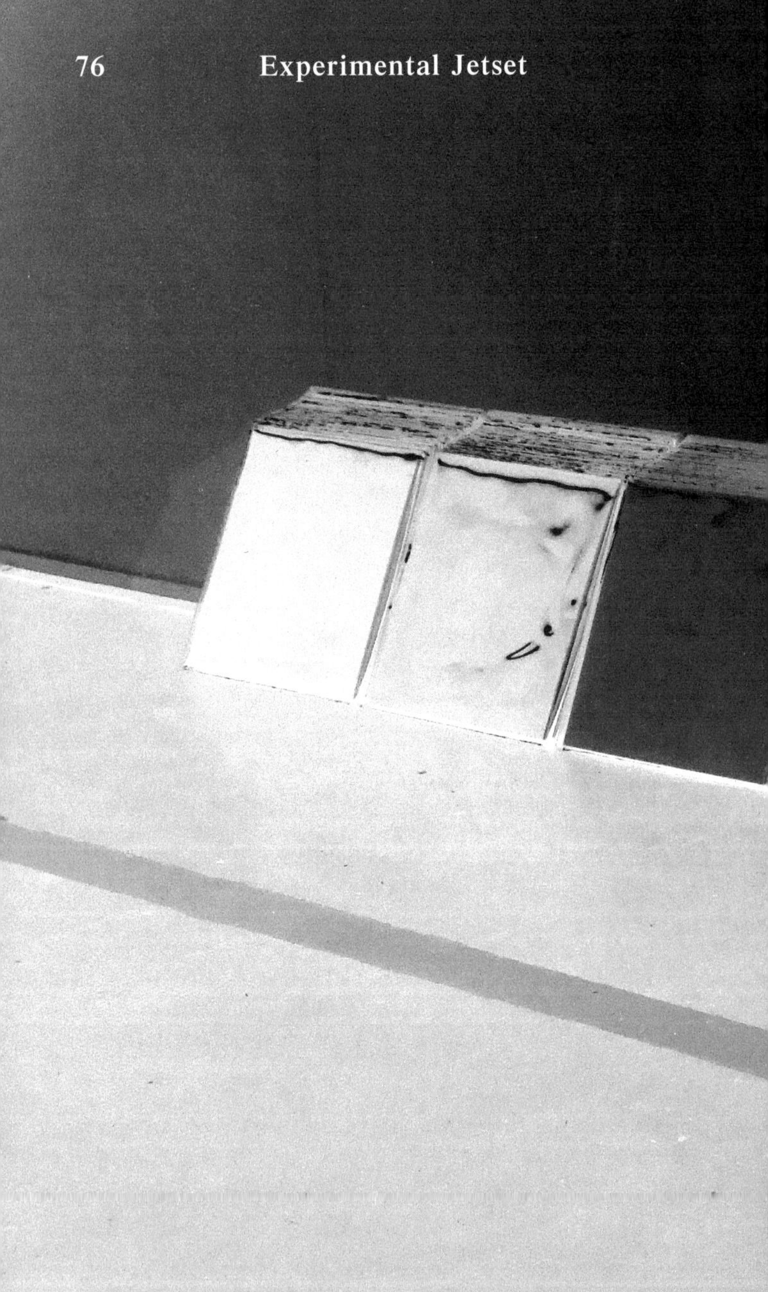

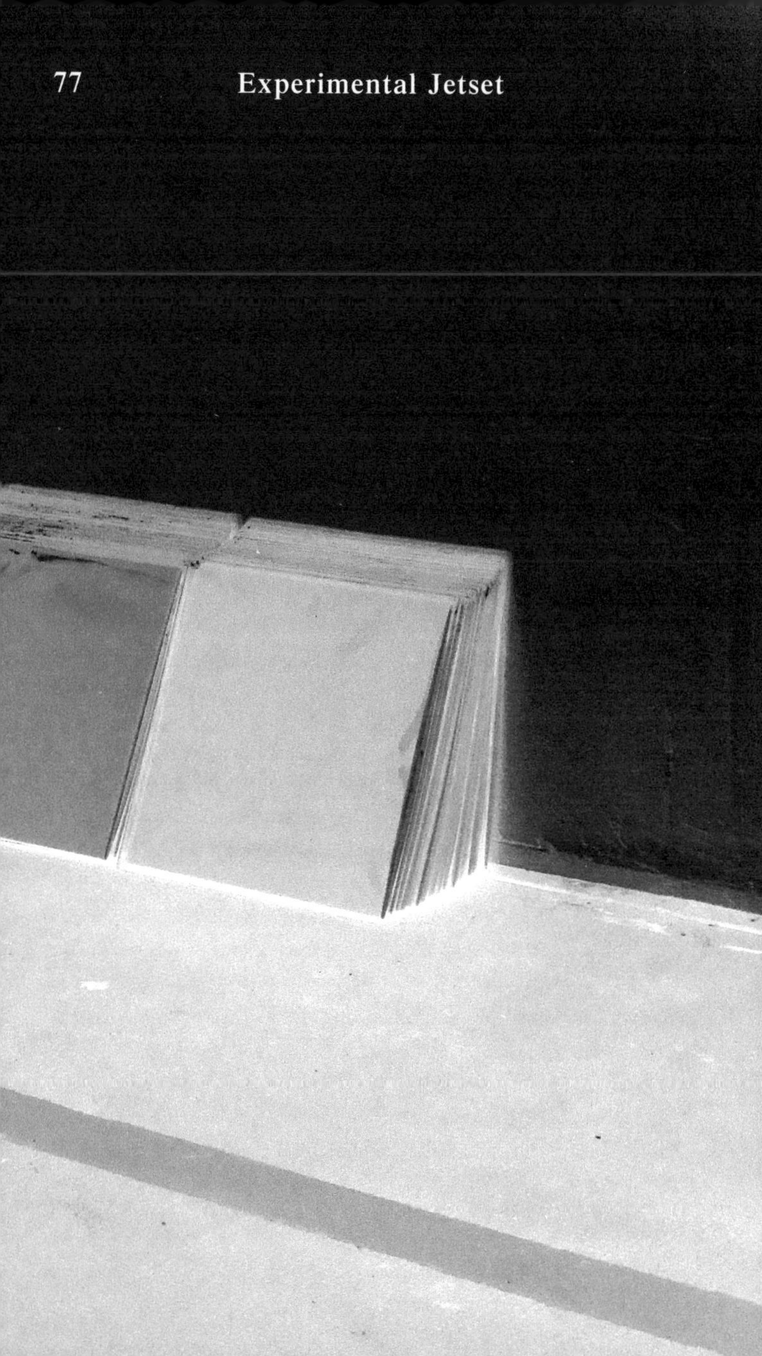

to synthesize two seemingly contrasting forces within modernism: Futurism and Fluxus. In fact, a lot of our work revolves around this theme, trying to reflect on the plurality within modernism, treating it not as a static monolithic movement but, rather, as a maelstrom of conflicting accents and dialects. (Actually, in the poster, we also referred to yet another strand of modernism: post-punk. After all, Zang Tumb Tumb was also the record label of Frankie Goes to Hollywood—but that's another story, for another time). A couple of years later, we were invited to transform this poster into a mural, during the group exhibition 'Ecstatic Alphabets / Heaps of Language' (MoMA, 2012).

A very similar project (attempting to synthesize two seemingly opposite strands of modernism) can be found in *Dark Side of the Bauhaus* (2003), a series of three record sleeves in which we referred to both the famous Pink Floyd album cover (originally designed by Hipgnosis in 1973), and the historical "square/triangle/circle" emblem of the Bauhaus school. Again, a way to pay tribute to two of our main influences, early modernism and psychedelic pop culture.What's interesting about *Dark Side of the Bauhaus* is the fact that a couple of years later, our friend Mark Owens (of Life of the Mind) bootlegged this bootleg—by giving the Germs' iconic *G.I.* sleeve the Bauhaus treatment as well (for his 2006 essay "Graphics Incognito"), thus creating a sort of "meta-bootleg."

One last example we would like to mention is the facsimile we created in 2011, reproducing the first issue of *Provo* (originally published in 1965), a facsimile that was part of 'Two or Three Things I

p. 79: Experimental Jetset, *Zang Tumb Tumb (If You Want It)* (2003)

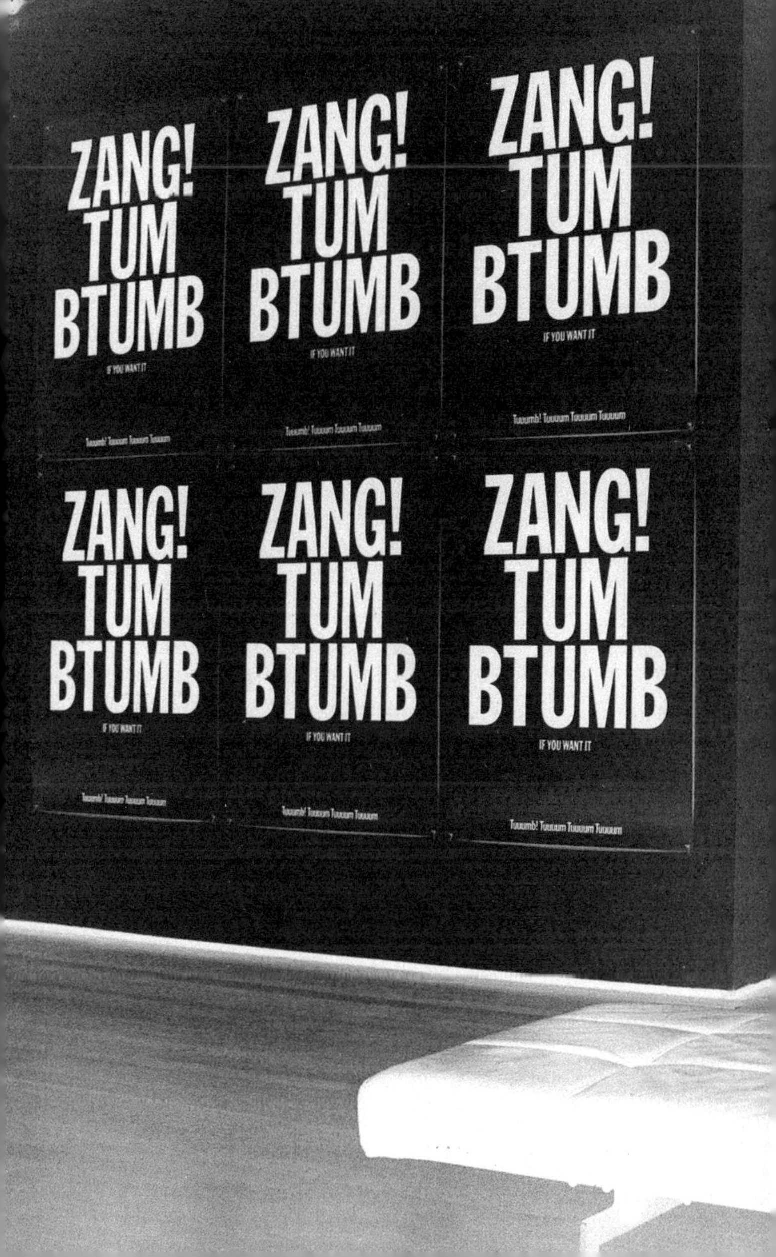

Experimental Jetset

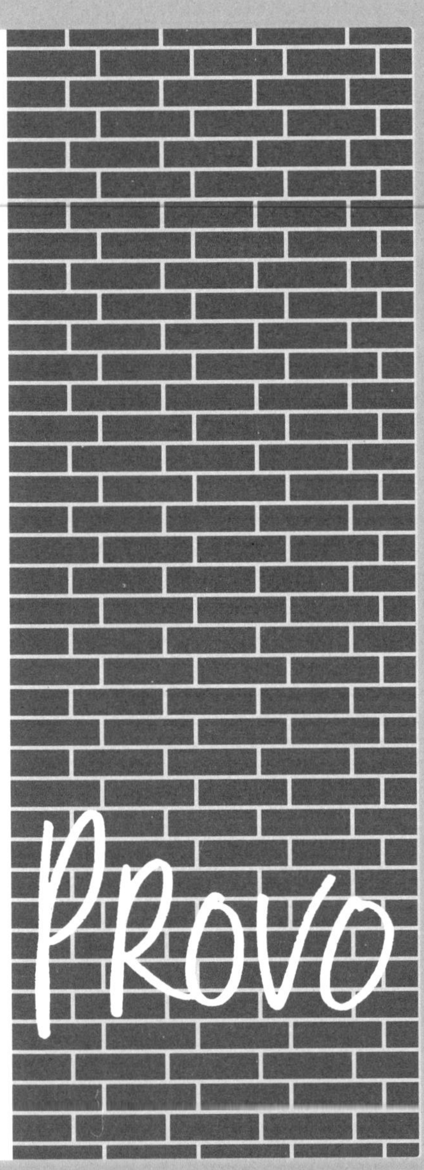
PROVO

Know About Provo,' an exhibition we curated in the beginning of 2011 for W139, an art space in Amsterdam. In short, *Provo* was a monthly magazine published by the Provo movement, an anarchist group active in Amsterdam from 1965 to 1967. Of the 500 copies printed of the first issue, 400 were immediately confiscated by the police (this all took place in July 1965), so only 100 copies of the original first issue remained. In order to fill up this historical gap, we decided to reprint the missing 400 copies. It really was a labor of love to carefully recreate this publication—and we're still very proud of this facsimile.In fact, because the facsimile is so faithfully reproduced (and because the original is almost impossible to obtain), some institutions and archives have actually acquired our facsimile for their collections. For example, when the Walker Art Center showed a full series of *Provo* (during the 'Hippie Modernism' exhibition of 2015–2016), the first issue was actually our facsimile. Also, when the Van Abbe Museum showed the full Provo Series (in 2013), the first issue was our facsimile as well. Again, it shows the archivist potential of bootlegging.

BS: I often think of your &&& shirt as the first graphic design meme. It's spawned a seemingly infinite amount of bootlegs taken into worlds as diverse as LA gangster rap ('Dre & Eazy & Cube & Ren.') to hit TV sitcoms ('Jerry & George & Cosmo & Elaine.'). How did it feel to be on the other side of the bootleg, from the "bootlegger," to the "bootlegged?"

p. 80: Experimental Jetset, *Provo Magazine*, facsimile (2011)

EJ: Of course, when we created the &&& shirt (in itself quite a hermetic, esoteric piece, revolving around themes such as self-referentiality, iconoclasm, abstraction, et cetera.), we had no idea it would be copied on such a massive scale. We had no idea it would be copied at all. But we are actually quite humbled by it.

Fact is, we are very much the products of fanzine culture: all three of us come from a post-punk/ DIY background. So to see all these people using the &&& format as a platform for fandom—as a low-fi way to announce their love for bands, teams, groups, collectives, political causes—most of the time (with only a few exceptions) that's quite a thrill to behold. It reminds us of that famous punk-rock diagram: "this is a chord / this is another / this is a third… now form a band." In a way, that's exactly how the &&& format works: "this is an ampersand / this is another / this is a third… now make a shirt."

BS: You mentioned your *Provo* facsimile. I'm know you're connected to this movement both as researchers and personally (with Marieke's parents a part of the movement). Given your appreciation for these sorts of activist movements, I wonder in what way you see bootlegging as a political gesture?

EJ: We're of the school of thought that regards copying as an intrinsically political act. Multiplying, printing, publishing—it always signifies a movement from the individual to the collective, from solitude to multitude, from one to many. In that sense, we still believe (foolishly, perhaps) that graphic design is an inherently social-democratic practice. Even when subjected to the most neoliberal circumstances, even when used for the most capitalist causes, we still maintain that, at its very core, graphic design has a social-democratic dimension.

The same goes for bootlegging. We believe that the contrabandist nature of bootlegging (smuggling information from one sphere to another) is ultimately a progressive impulse — even when the intentions of the bootlegger are far from progressive. After all, we see culture as a maelstrom of conflicting ideas, a model we borrowed from the late, great philosopher Marshall Berman:

> *To be modern is to experience personal and social life as a maelstrom, to find one's world and oneself in perpetual disintegration and renewal, trouble and anguish, ambiguity and contradiction: to be part of a universe in which all that is solid melts into air. To be a modernist is to make oneself somehow at home in the maelstrom, to make its rhythms one's own, to move within its currents in search of the forms of reality, of beauty, of freedom, of justice, that its fervid and perilous flow allows.*

So we do feel that culture (at large) benefits from being constantly contaminated with other ideas, coming from all kinds of different spheres — turning society into an ever-accelerating maelstrom of clashing ideas. And then we hope (we know, we are being quite hopeful here) that, somehow, out of this dialectical "cold fusion"—like collision, new ideas will

pp. 84–85: Various fan bootlegs of the &&& T-shirt originally designed by Experimental Jetset (2001)

John&
Paul&
Ringo&
George.

Bacon&
Lettuce&
Tomato&
Bacon

flour&
water&
yeast&
salt

Kanye&
Akon&
T-Pain&
Fab&
Weezy.

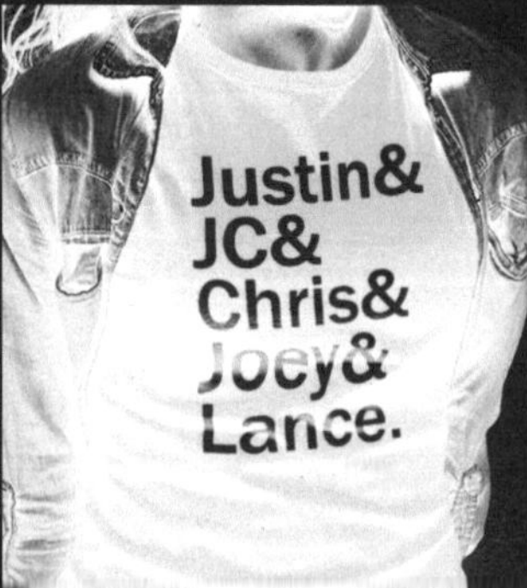

First&
Second&
Third&
Fourth.

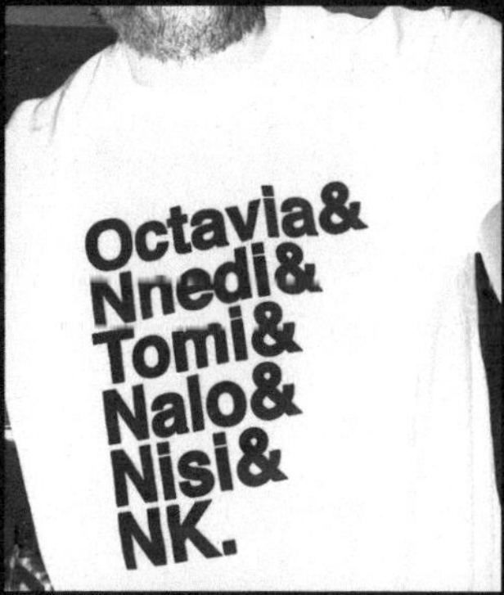

Octavia&
Nnedi&
Tomi&
Nalo&
Nisi&
NK.

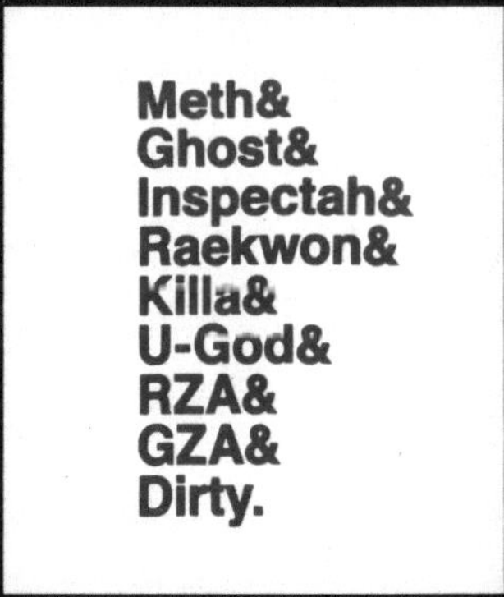

Meth&
Ghost&
Inspectah&
Raekwon&
Killa&
U-God&
RZA&
GZA&
Dirty.

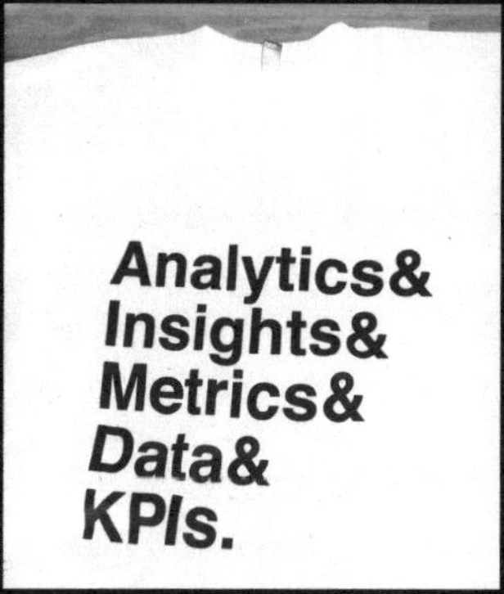

Analytics&
Insights&
Metrics&
Data&
KPIs.

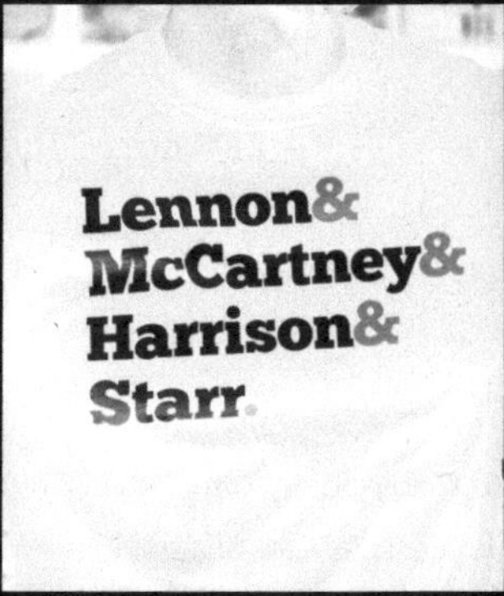

Lennon&
McCartney&
Harrison&
Starr.

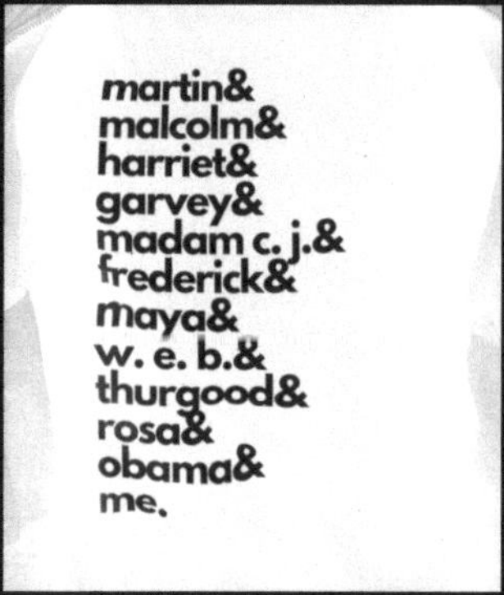

martin&
malcolm&
harriet&
garvey&
madam c. j.&
frederick&
maya&
w. e. b.&
thurgood&
rosa&
obama&
me.

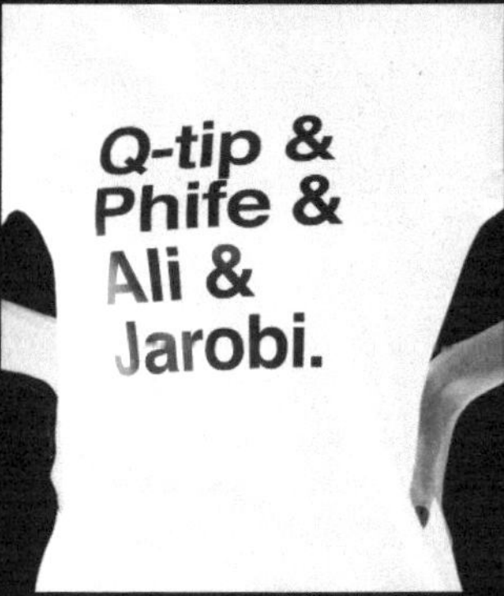

Q-tip &
Phife &
Ali &
Jarobi.

appear, better ideas, more progressive ideas, socialist ideas. Speaking of contamination, the following words by Boris Groys (from his book *In the Flow*) seem quite relevant as well:

> *Modernism is a history of infections; by political movements, by pop-culture and consumerism … Openness is an essential characteristic of the modernist inheritance, and that inheritance is the will to reveal the Other within oneself, to become Other, to become infected by Otherness.*

Ultimately, we think that's the progressive, modernist potential of both bootlegging and graphic design: to keep the boundaries porous; to keep contaminating culture; and to keep trespassing, crossing the borders between "high culture"' and "low," between the subcultural and the mainstream, between academic culture and working-class culture, et cetera.

To give a very personal example: as working-class teens, growing up in non-academic surroundings, it was through subcultures such as punk and new wave that we first learned about movements such as Surrealism, Futurism, and Dada. In that sense, post-punk was a form of education for us. If it wasn't for people such as Malcolm McLaren and Jamie Reid (who basically "bootlegged" avant-garde principles, liberated these ideas from the academic sphere, and pushed them into the mainstream through punk and new wave), we would have probably never heard about the Lettrists and the Situationists. We talk a bit about these dynamics in a 2016 interview for *It's Nice That*.

Maybe McLaren's motives were indeed exploitative, opportunistic, and irresponsible. But in the end, the role he fulfilled was totally progressive. He took information from the academic sphere, and spread these ideas around (through record sleeves, through T-shirts, through commercial products), thereby educating tens of thousands of working-class teenage kids (like us), inspiring them to go to art school, to become artists, designers, poets (which goes to show a bootlegs educational dimension).

Bootleggers (and thus graphic designers) are gate-crashers rather than gatekeepers. The bootleg (in fact, the printed object in general) is a total social mobility machine, puncturing straight through all social layers and economic classes, distributing information and aesthetics in a collectivist, egalitarian, almost jacobine way. Smuggling is the great equalizer. Of course, the intentions of smugglers won't always be so noble. Sometimes their motives might be crassly commercial, grossly opportunistic, downright exploitative (to speak with Malcolm McLaren: "cash from chaos").

But despite all this, we do believe in the progressive potential of the act of smuggling itself. And that's also how we regard bootlegging, and graphic design—as practices that might be driven by opportunistic motives, but that are ultimately progressive.

Title page (p. 68): Writing taken from Experimental Jetset's *Provo Magazine* facsimile (2011)

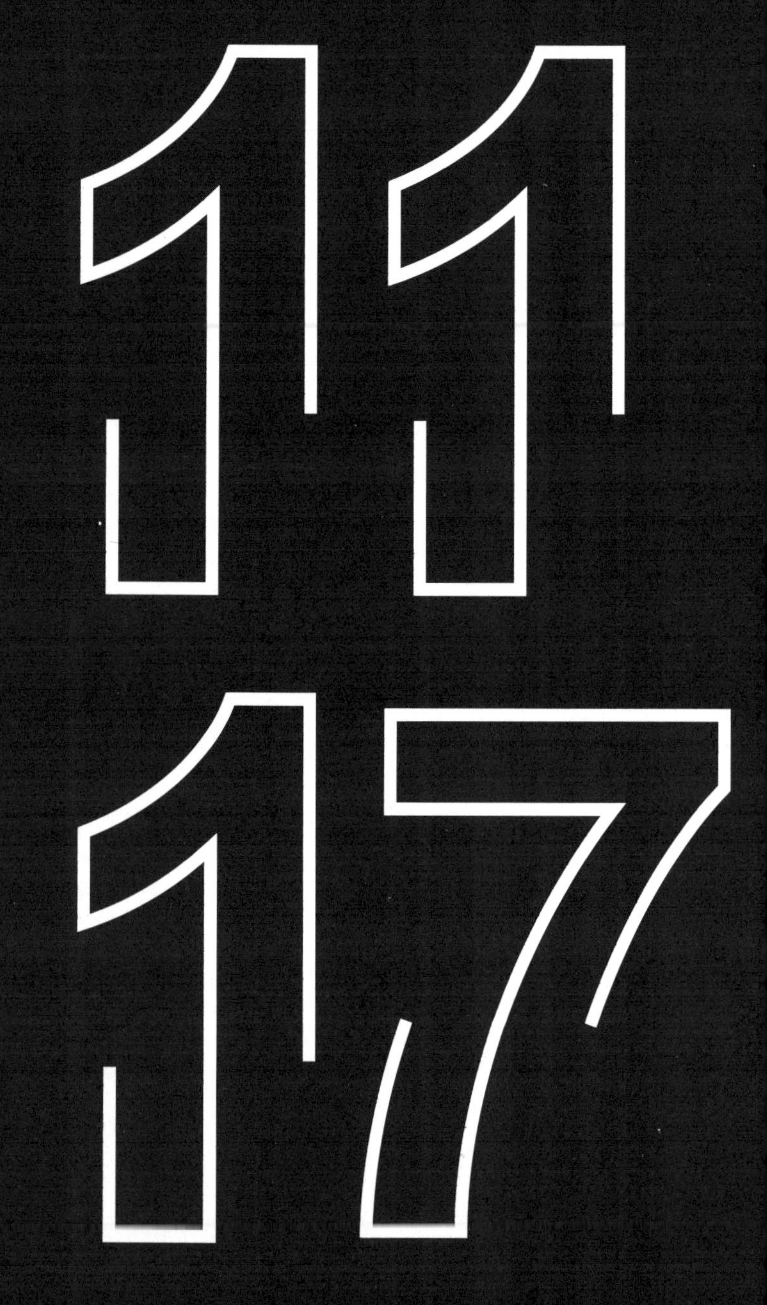
11
17

Elisa van Joolen (EVJ)

Elisa van Joolen is an Amsterdam-based artist whose work involves appropriating, combining, and printing on existing pieces of clothing to turn them into unique one-off garments. In her series One-to-One, for example, van Joolen inks up garments from one brand and uses them to print on another. The new Frankensteined garment becomes a sort of trademark mashup, calling into question any idea of authorship. In her process, the artist advocates for a new form of "open bootlegging" that is inclusive rather than clandestine, a means of collaboration rather than subversion. For van Joolen, bootlegging is an act of generosity, a process in which participants are invited into a dialogue to exchange ideas on value, ownership, and labor. Interview by Ben Schwartz (BS).

> BS: How do you define bootlegging, and in what ways do you see the gesture as related to your practice?

EVJ: A bootleg is an alternate version, a take on the original, a spinoff. In my eyes, it is something that is often done without consent. To be honest, I have never used the word bootleg in relation to my practice, because I feel it has a somewhat negative connotation. However, my work is very much concerned with the political gesture of bootlegging through appropriation and subversion. I would like to add to the definition of "bootlegging:" openness, kindness, politeness. Bootlegging to open up, to start a conversation. So nothing is done behind someone's back, or in secret.

In my practice, I involve people working for different clothing brands. We have a conversation and sometimes they donate samples, dead stock, or archive pieces, which I use as raw material. The conversation is very much part of the "bootleg." It's important for me to emphasize that I like to work with, rather than against, brands. We have seen a lot of *anti-fashion* design or art in the past years, but it doesn't lead us anywhere. I believe that the way forward is to find new ways to work together.

> BS: I really like this idea of a friendly form of bootlegging. So often we think of a bootleg as working against authority or brands—can you talk more about this idea of bootlegging *with* brands?

EVJ: One example of "bootlegging" in my practice would be the 11" × 17" sweaters: a series of garments that consist of multiple brands. When I started this project in 2012, it was already very popular to collaborate in the fashion industry. For example, Comme des Garçons was collaborating with H&M, Opening Ceremony with Levi's. Yet it was always a one-on-one

p. 91: Elisa van Joolen, 11"× 17" (2013). Russell Athletic × Rockwell by Parra × G-StarRAW, donated by Suzanne and Alexander. Photo: Blommers/Schumm

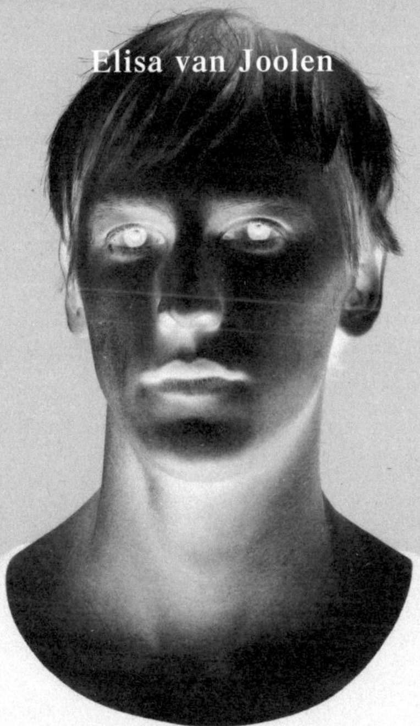

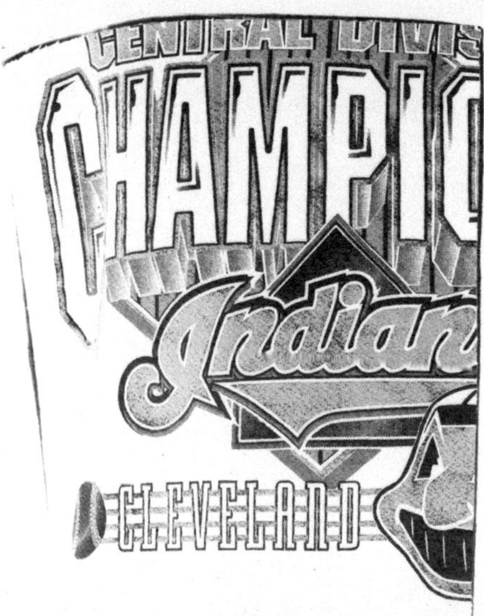
CLEVELAND

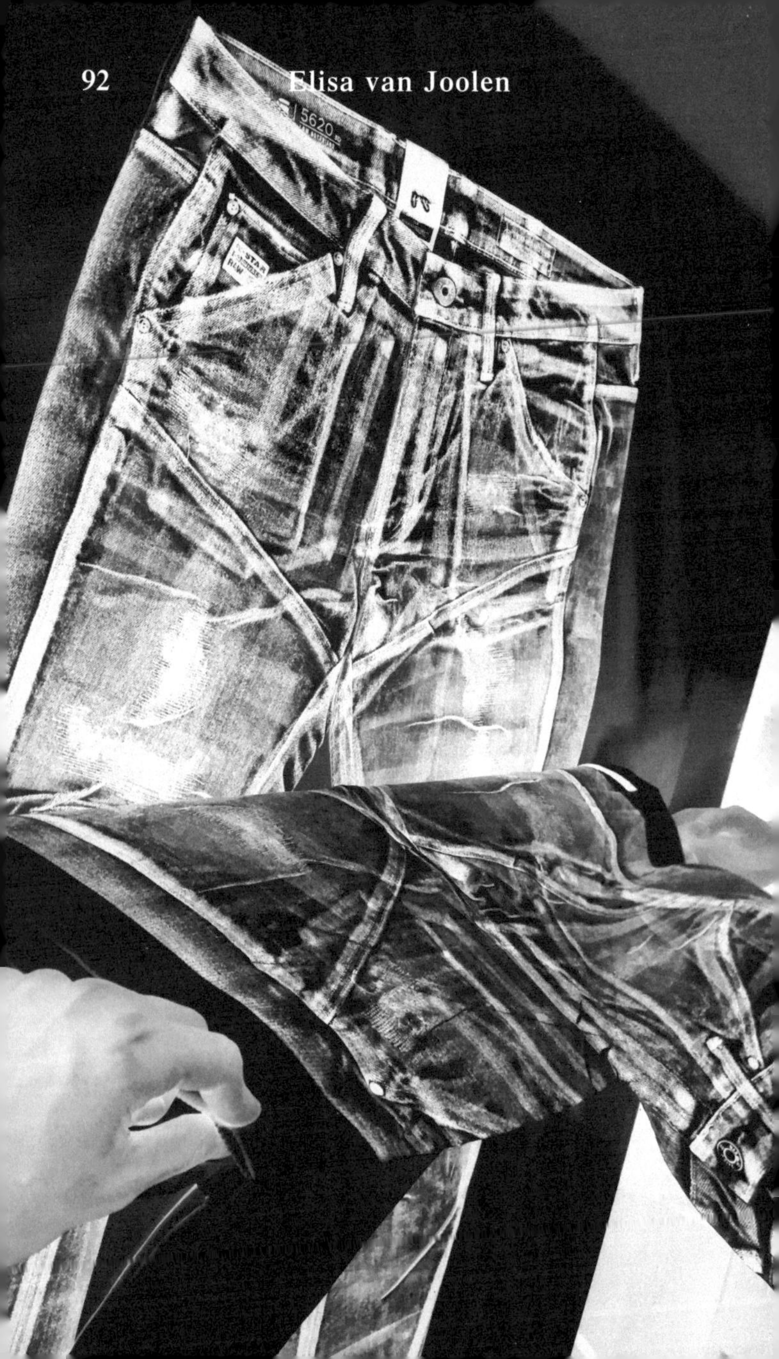
5620

collaboration: a designer or label worked with a multinational company to make a series of new products, often a cheaper version of the original, marketed towards the masses. It would never be a collaboration involving multiple partners. That was what I was looking for in 11" × 17" — to combine the whole scope of fashion in one item of clothing. Just like how we dress in everyday life, and what our wardrobe looks like: designer items next to mass-produced items. The reality of fashion, if you like.

I started contacting employees working at different brands and explained to them briefly that I intended to reuse a selection of donated pieces and make them into one collection. I explained that the purpose of the project was to bring together different layers of production and value from the fashion industry. With the donated items, I created the following procedure: I cut an 11" × 17" inch piece out of different kinds of sweaters, and swapped these cut out pieces between the different items of clothing. I treated all garments equally (didn't matter what brand it was, each received the same 11" × 17" cuts). The resulting sweaters were an assemblage, composed through a cut-out method from a variety of existing clothing items. Whenever I show the sweaters, I always credit all the brand names that are a part of it.

The main difference between bootlegging in my work and bootlegging in music or video is that the cutting and pasting is more definite. "Cutting" in these latter cases is really a matter of "copying;" when we "appropriate" a certain beat, there is no less of that beat in the world, only more. However, the crew neck

p. 92: Process documentation of the production of Elisa van Joolen's One-to-One series (2018)

sweaters cut up in 11" × 17" are forever gone (or new, depending on how you want to view it). Another key component of my "bootlegging" practice is the importance of materiality. In fashion collaborations such as those mentioned above, the label states only the collaboration, so it remains on an immaterial level; it's about added brand value for the parties involved. It never mentions the actual materials that are combined. I do mention this in 11" × 17".

> BS: I'm curious how your work addresses ideas of originality and authorship and how these ideas might reflect the nuanced differences between copying, appropriation, and bootlegging.

EVJ: I like to blur the lines between these different concepts in my practice. For example, in the One-to-One series, the garments I made are both copies and originals. I inked donated items of clothing and used these as a tool for printing on other pieces. Each item is therefore both carrier and receiver; they serve as a stamp and are stamped on at the same time. So I literally printed one garment on top of the other. By doing this, certain aspects of the clothing are lost. The color, for example, is not transferred in this process, but other aspects are really brought to the forefront, such as the stitching and seams; the fabric structure as well as the size of the garment are all transferred very accurately (which is where the title comes from). The prints are like X-rays: a meticulous registration. This enables a view beyond the mostly one-dimensional image created by the fashion industry. It's a way to observe the garment's actual material qualities in a very detailed manner. It is almost like a process of "unbranding." Usually a brand's logo is printed on a garment, but now the structure of another garment, from another brand, is also pressed onto the garment.

In the end, I think nowadays there is little difference between bootlegging, copying, and appropriation. The main difference for all three is not *what* you do, but *how* you do this. And the how for me relates to how you involve others (the originals); how open you are about the process of bootlegging, copying, and/or appropriating; and how you communicate this.

This is one of the reasons I made the *One to One Reader* to go with the garments. To me, it is as important as the garments themselves. The reader documents the process and outcomes of the *One-to-One* project and explores the implications and possibilities of this working method in the broader context of the fashion system through contributions by different authors.

This conversation we are having reminds me of artist and educator Corita Kent. She gave her students a beautiful assignment once: "Look at two dandelions for five minutes. List how they are different from each other. Take two leaves from the same tree and do the same. Nothing is the same. No thing is the same. Everything is itself and one of a kind." Through her eyes everything is unique. More radically: there is no such a thing as a copy; everything is one of a kind.

> BS: What are your thoughts on luxury brands such as Gucci or Off-White who have begun to take ownership of bootlegs and create "official" versions while still pursuing and prosecuting knockoffs?

EVJ: In the spring of 2017, I was contacted by an Off-White HR manager asking if I would be interested in collaborating; they wanted me to be a shoe designer consultant for their new collection. I wrote back that I was interested and sent my CV. We emailed back and forth for a while, but at a certain point I didn't receive any emails from them anymore. I moved on and forgot about it until the fall of 2017, when I saw their new sneaker release. The Ten sneaker looked very similar to Invert Footwear (a series of sneakers I "unmade" in 2013). Off-White used the word "SAMPLE" on the exact same spot, and the sneaker had similar "unmade" aesthetics.

In the fall of 2017, I posted on Instagram that I understood why Off-White asked me if I would be interested in working for them. The post took on a life of its own, and people started to comment that my work was a copy of Nike SB's, which I think is hilarious. I used actual SB sneakers. I obtained these sneakers from Sheilah, a Nike SB designer in Portland, Oregon. She sent me a box full of samples that were not fit for production.

So if you talk about the relationship between bootlegging and irony, and in a larger sense bootlegging and capitalism, the sneakers I used for Invert Footwear were real, actual samples, not the ironic take on "samples" Virgil Abloh and his team used. Mind the quotation marks, which are a key design element for the Off-White label. In an interview with the Berlin-based magazine *032c*, Thom Bettridge writes about this tactic: "Quotation marks are one of the many tools that Abloh uses to operate in a mode of ironic detachment. He describes Marcel Duchamp as his 'lawyer,' the art-historical grounds onto which he can absorb preexisting intellectual property into his reference system. Abloh rejects the who-did-it-first mentality of previous generations in favor of the copy-paste logic of the Internet and its inhabitants. His new order is protected by a fortress of irony."

Despite the similarity in looks, the core of my work is very different. For Invert Footwear I turned the sneakers literally inside out and made new soles out of flip-flops, while using the soles of the sneakers to create new sandals. With this treatment I invited people to look at these shoes with fresh eyes, to see them independently from their original brands and accompanying marketing campaigns. The inversion process allowed the stitch lines that are normally hidden within the shoes to emerge. These are the marks of factory workers—working in Vietnam, in Taiwan—and their presence in the production process is made explicitly visible.

I find it interesting that on online platforms like Instagram, Pinterest, and Tumblr, images are available, easy to copy paste, yet the context, the framework of why and how something is made, is not visible. The image is copied but the realness, content, materiality is not. My work is not meant as an ironic take on fashion, but the contrary; I am looking for inclusive, transparent ways to work in fashion. I am more interested in challenging existing value systems in fashion and proposing new ways of working.

BS: I've been thinking about the bootleg as a lens through which one can understand an object or subject better than an original. But I'm also curious how this might apply

p. 98: Elisa van Joolen, Invert Footwear, SP13-MNASKT -732/ 325548 PC (2013). Donated by Jesi and Sheilah Photo: Blommers/Schumm
p. 99: Off-White Court leather high-top sneakers (2017)

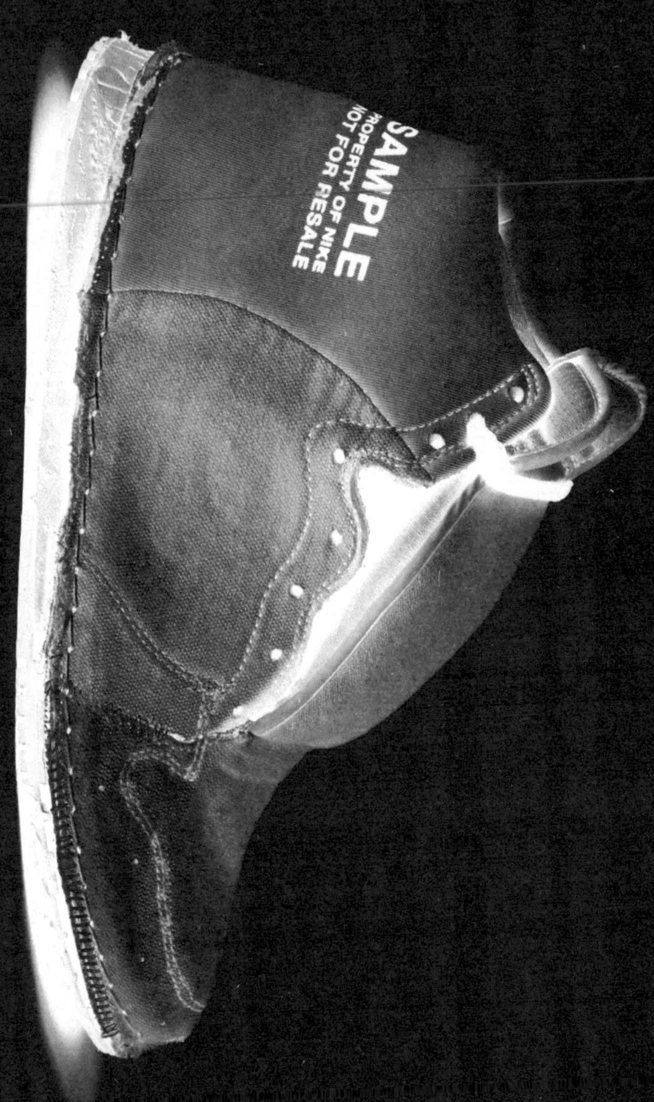
SAMPLE
PROPERTY OF NIKE
NOT FOR RESALE

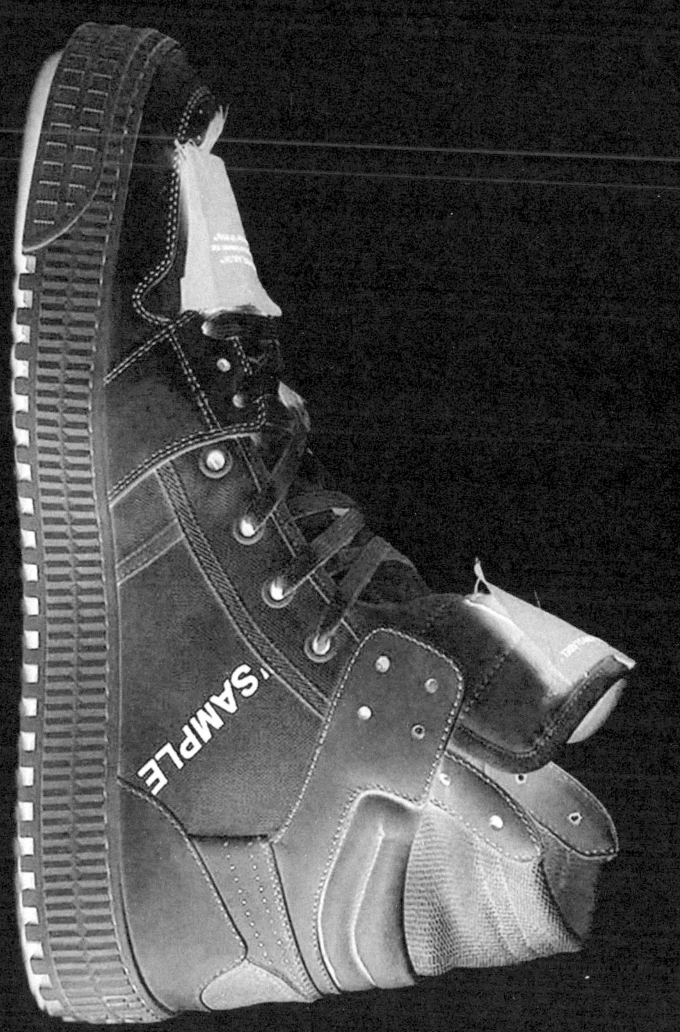
SAMPLE

to value. When does a bootleg become more valuable than an original?

EVJ: Value is constantly shifting; it is very much dependent on context. Everyone has a different idea of what makes something valuable. $500 is only the monetary value, but what about the emotional value of a garment? I think it is interesting when a bootleg s selling for a lot of money, especially with the knowledge that some garments from different brands are made in the same factory, bootleg or non-bootleg.

In 2017 I (un)made a series garments for the project One-to-One (R. Mariz) that were all produced in the same factory. The specific idea for One-to-One (R. Mariz) was born during a conversation I had with the founders of Bonne Suits. They told me that their suits are produced in the same factory as the collections of other brands like Patta, by Parra, and Ontour.

So the garments are, so to speak, "brought to life" in the same factory, with the same producer: R. Mariz. What I thought was really interesting and beautiful is that these garments are a family in the material sense. So I approached the brands that were producing their clothes in this factory: Patta, by Parra, and Ontour. I explained what I wanted to do, and they were up for it. I wanted to investigate the similarities between these garments through the printing process. As I explained before, through printing items of clothing on other items, details such as the stitching, the seams, and fabric structure are brought to the surface. I wanted to see if there were differences or similarities in the ways the garments were stitched. I find it peculiar that the factory itself is never mentioned, or hardly mentioned, in fashion, while it is such an essential part of the production of clothing.

BS: In today's remix culture, your garments feel particularly relevant to conversations about the complexity of ownership. They seem to float in this nebulous area, unable to be claimed by any of the involved brands. What are your thoughts around ideas of property and ownership?

EVJ: Who owns an idea, product or brand is a very intriguing topic nowadays. For the 11" × 17" project, many brands did not want to donate clothing, and I think that in itself is really interesting. Are there different rules when it comes to working with donated items, as opposed to going to a shop and buying the pieces I want to work with there? Do I only own something when I exchange money for it? I had really interesting conversations with brand representatives about these kinds of things. Some reacted with, "No, you are destroying our whole legacy." Well, how does that work? When is it yours? When is it mine? Who decides?

Title page (p. 88): Excerpt from the 11"×17" identity designed by Our Polite Society

Tom Of
England

Printed Matter, Jordan Nassar (JN) & Christopher Schulz (CS)

For Shannon Michael Cane, bootlegging was a prompt that allowed him to celebrate the things he loved, and bring together people to share them with. As curator of Printed Matter's book fairs and editions, Shannon oversaw the inimitable NY and LA Art Book Fairs, events that summon a diverse and energetic array of artists, publishers, and fans to share their love of all things printed: books, posters, records, zines, and quite frequently, T-shirts. In his personal practice, Shannon regularly created his own shirts, bootlegging obscure publications, art practices, and logos as a way of illustrating their relevance today. In 2012, he took this practice a step further by launching the first iteration of 'The Bootleg T-Shirt Show', in which he invited artists and designers to create their own bootleg T-shirts to be exhibited and sold at Printed Matter. This exhibition was followed three years later with 'The Bootleg T-Shirt Show II', and then again in late 2017 with the most recent installment.

Shannon sadly passed away before the third show was completed, and his friends New York-based artist/designer/publisher Christopher Schulz and New York based-artist Jordan Nassar completed the exhibition in his stead. Interview by Emmet Byrne (EB).

EB: Why are T-shirts such a big part of the art-book world?

CS: Printed Matter's primary focus is on publications made by artists. Many of those artists self-publish to make their work accessible outside of mainstream systems, and printing on T-shirts is a part of that practice. Although T-shirts are not artist books, they're made in the same spirit, produced in a similar way, and accomplish much of the same thing in terms of distribution and disruption. Especially now, in a digital age, printed shirts are more akin to artist books because they're literally printed matter. At the book fairs, there are T-shirts being sold at practically every other booth, so the printed T-shirt is an instinctive form to this community of artists. The main difference is dissemination—a T-shirt spreads its message more quickly than a zine.

JN: In the self-publishing realm, there's zines, there's posters, and there's T-shirts as the primary vehicles for creativity. Of course, people make all sorts of objects, but T-shirts seem to just always be a part of it. I think the act of making bootleg T-shirts is also about availability. We all gotta wear clothes. I'm constantly having this fight with my husband, as my closet overflows with T-shirts that he perceives as things I rarely wear—that this is like collecting any other piece of art or ephemera, it's about valuing them as a type of artwork. And of course, yes, there is the element of conveying a message. Whether it's just sporting something you like that you think is cool and makes you feel good (T-shirts as fashion);

p. 105: Jordan Nassar, Israeli Black Panther T-Shirt (2015)

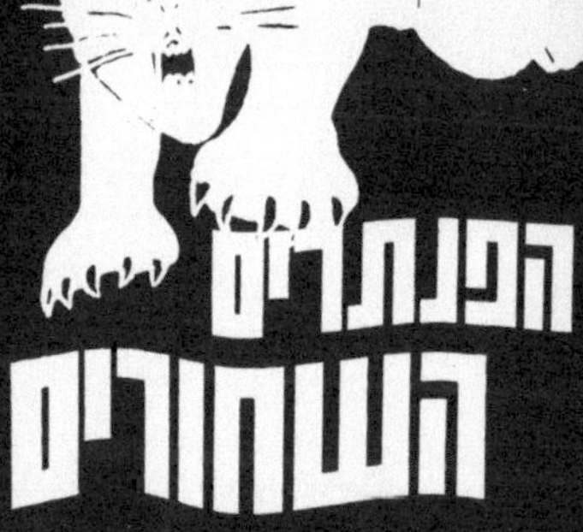
הפנתרים
השחורים

to those "special" shirts that are rare or super precious to you (T-shirts as artwork); to more serious political or socially active statements (T-shirts as message); conveying something is always a part of it. I think these bootlegs are always doing at least one of those things, and sometimes even doing all three at once.

> EB: Would you consider these T-shirts publications? How do you read a T-shirt? Is there a front and a back cover? Is there a subtext? Can you read between the lines?

CS: A lot of artists play with the front and back. The best example is a shirt called Life & Death by Ed Davis. The front is printed with the *LIFE* magazine logo, and the back is printed with the logo of the metal band, Death. The scale of quick reads versus in-depth examination is inherent to all the shows. I personally gravitate toward the in-depth stuff. I get excited when I have an aha moment with something I see. I like to have a connection to the images I wear.

JN: I also think, similar to how zines work, these shirts are about finding people already within our small community that share a very "deep" interest in something very specific. If you make a shirt that is referencing something obscure, and a couple people freak out and love it, then you've found someone that shares a very niche interest of yours—that's a really fun part of it. On the other hand, you can also use the platform to teach people about something they might not be aware of; for example, in 2015 my

p. 107: Ed Davis, Life & Death T-Shirt, front (2015)

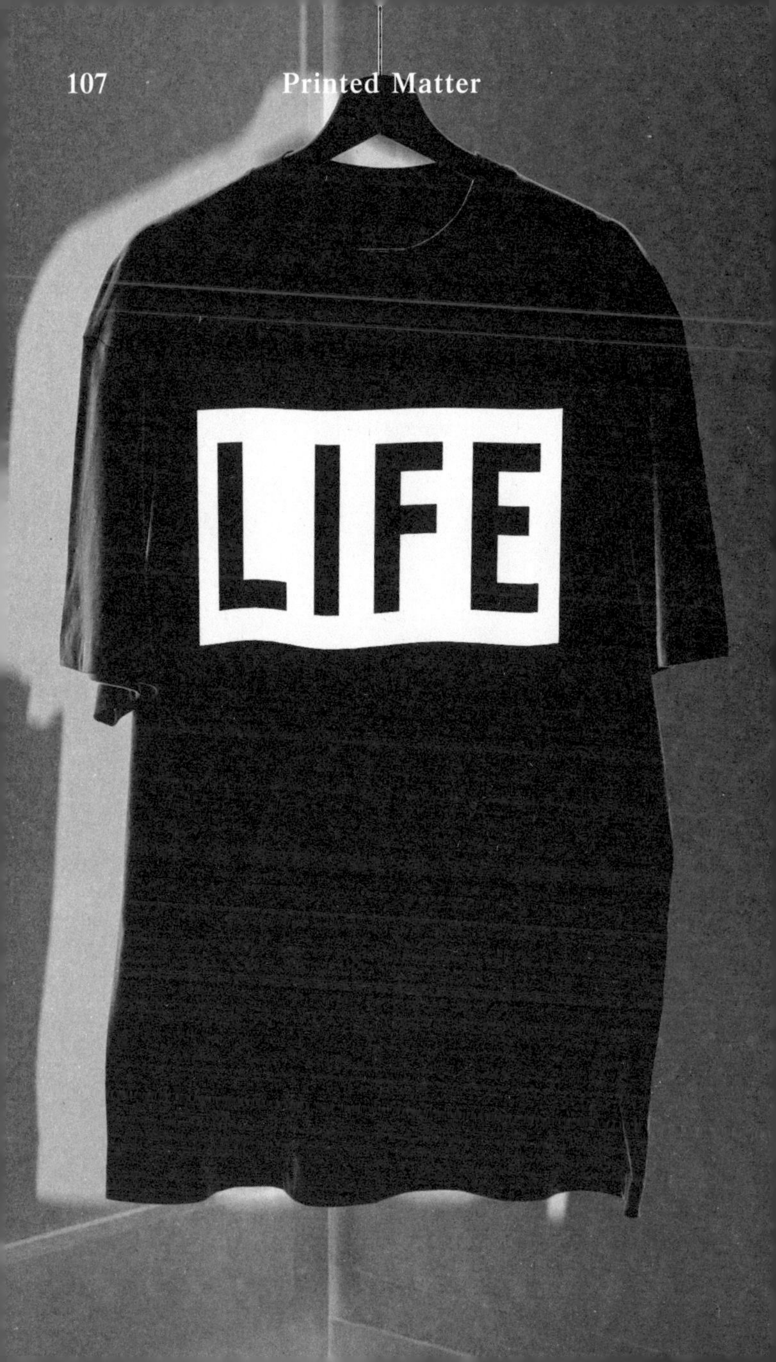

LIFE

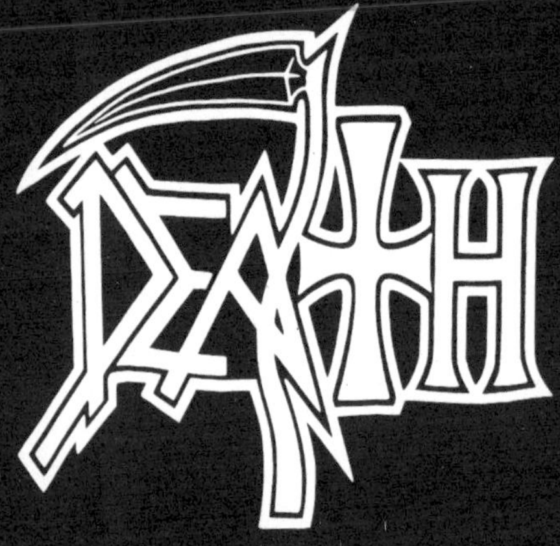
DEATH

bootleg was a rip on the logo of the Israeli Black Panthers, with the classic Black Panther image but juxtaposed with the logo in Hebrew. This was a movement that happened in the 1970s in Israel, a civil rights movement on behalf of "brown" Jews in Israel, largely from Arab countries, and which is something that many don't know about.

EB: How were artists chosen to participate?

CS: This part was 100% Shannon. He always wanted to include artists whose work he admired, and often tapped those in the artist book world, like James Unsworth, an artist best known for his insane and highly explicit drawings of Teenage Mutant Ninja Turtles fucking each other. Obviously there's some sticky legal stuff there. Marc Hundley and Dean Sameshima are both known for their screen-printed shirts. Hundley usually prints lyrics from pop songs, and Sameshima revives book covers from queer literature, like John Rechy's *Numbers*. Kevin McCaughey (Boot Boyz Biz), based in Chicago, is a regular maker of bootleg tees that often reference underground music, like a Chris and Cosey *Heartbeat* tee that sold out and I'm extremely bitter that I didn't get one! Artists Matt Connors, Andrew Kuo, and Matt Chambers have been featured in all three bootleg shows. The motivation behind the show is rooted in a tradition among a community of artists in Printed Matter's circle who are engaged in counterculture and independent publication.

EB: What does "bootleg" mean to you?

p. 108: Ed Davis, Life & Death T-Shirt, back (2015)

CS: When I think about the word "bootleg" the first thing that comes to mind is "knock-off." But when it comes to the bootleg T-shirts that Shannon crafted and curated—those are presented as print editions. I'm not personally interested in illegal operations or the cache of fashion labels, so for me what's compelling about the bootleg T-shirt is that it's a mode of publication that gets disseminated by the wearer. The first show addressed the question "what is a bootleg?" head-on and resolved that there's no one answer. Shannon welcomed all interpretations. He simply invited artists that he liked, and gave no parameters. This loose approach was key—it left "bootleg" open and allowed each show to exemplify a wide range of approaches: facsimiles, logo mashups, appropriated artworks, fanzine tour shirts, merchandise that never was but should have been, etc.

A few examples of these different bootlegging strategies: the famous Sonic Youth album cover *Goo* by Raymond Pettibon was reinterpreted in Taravat Talepasand's T-shirt as "Islamic Youth;" Andrew Kuo mashed up the Black Flag and Windows 95 logos; JD Samson turned L.L. Bean into "LesBian;" Cali Thornhill DeWitt turned "Purdue," the pharmaceutical company, into a party supply company; Matt Connors printed the graphic from the cover of the 1983 *Gay Areas Telephone Directory*; Frank Rodriguez reprinted the image of a Nob Hill Cinema ad by New Man that appeared in the 1975 issue of San Francisco gay lifestyle magazine, *Vector*, et cetera. The idea of a bootleg T-shirt is simply a prompt to mine culture for ideas that can then be augmented in some way.

One of my favorites is the Death Factory T-shirt, a Throbbing Gristle remake by Scott Treleaven. This bootleg is one hell of a deep cut. Death Factory was the name of the Throbbing Gristle recording studio, and in the early days the band made DIY T-shirts that simply said "Death Factory" to look like worker shirts. They were not merchandised, so the reference lives on in old photos.

EB: What do you think about the state of copyright laws today in terms of creative activities like visual arts, music, performance, fashion, etc.?

CS: It's all very confusing. With music, you can copyright and license a recording. With dance you can't copyright movement but you can copyright choreography on paper. Richard Prince has proven that copyright laws around fine art can be very gray. Social media has blurred the lines when it comes to distribution. Think about a blog service like Tumblr, with a social feed: someone might find an image on the Web and will post it to their blog without citing the source, and it gets reblogged by others, distributed over and over without its original context. The author disappears and the image takes on a life of its own. So we're all engaging in a kind of lawless area when it comes to the digital distribution of images and recordings. That said, it makes sense that the notion of bootlegging has infiltrated all creative platforms.

As far as I know the only copyright dispute we faced with the T-shirt shows was regarding a Tom of Finland bootleg. The artist posted the design to Instagram and the Tom of Finland Foundation saw it and sent a cease-and-desist letter. So that one didn't get produced after all. There was also an Adidas logo that had been appropriated and the artist was very

ING SOON

nervous to submit it. It was off the table for a while, but it went to print at the very last minute.

EB: It feels like this is a project that connects a variety of different perspectives and subcultures. I know Shannon was responsible in part for bringing this passion for inclusion to the book fairs. Did this spirit live in the T-shirt shows as well? Why do hybrid projects like this—Printed Matter, the book fairs, independent publishing in general—align so closely with diversity, minorities, politics, queer culture, free thinking, transgressive thinking, love, etcetera.?

JN: I think that's the nature of DIY and self-publishing—the whole point of it is availability to everyone. Anyone can make some copies on a copy machine. So it naturally becomes something that we perceive as aligned with diversity, minorities, activist political voices, queer culture—because no one is censoring it, which is so often what is happening in mainstream publishing, fashion, music, media, etc. It's a platform for raw expression.

CS: The bootleg shows represent Shannon's spirit. Shannon was a transgressive-thinking queer (he preferred "homo"). He was the axis of the book fairs, fundraising editions, various Printed Matter exhibitions, and the bootleg shows. Shannon tied them all together. He folded me into the community that he nurtured, and kept me connected to Printed Matter over many years. I'm sure the same can be said for

p. 115: Scott Treleaven, Death Factory T-Shirt (2015)

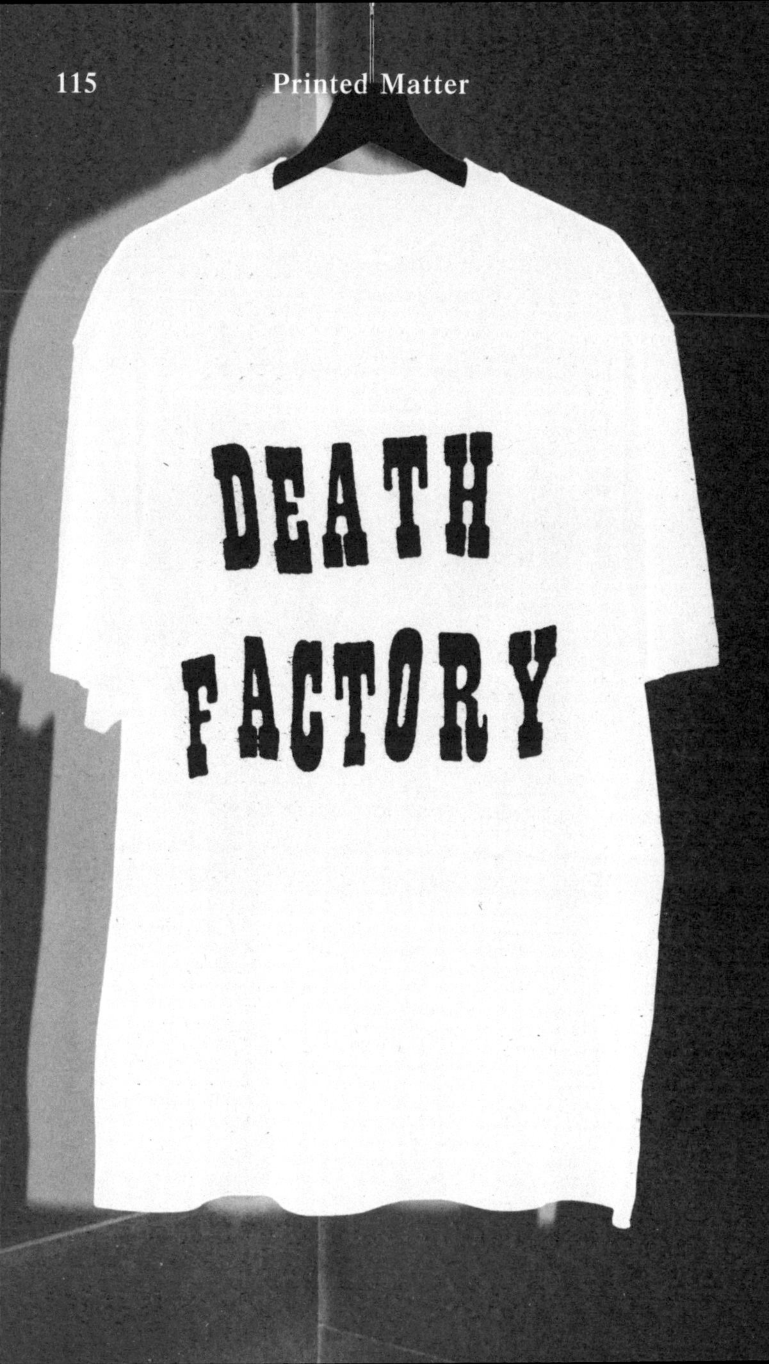

DEATH
FACTORY

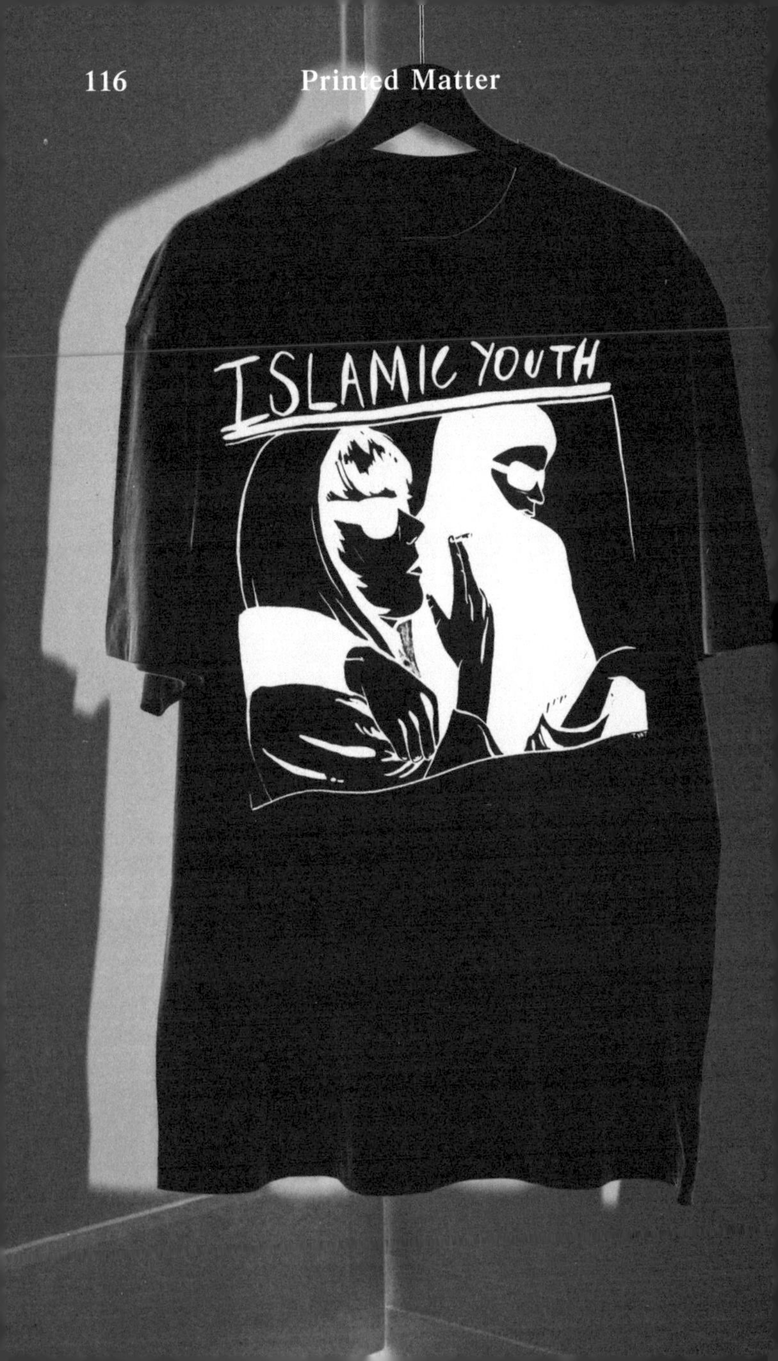

ISLAMIC YOUTH

many, if not all, of the artists in these shows. The third bootleg show had gotten pretty far under way before he passed. It was important for Jordan and me to see the show to fruition because it was Shannon's final project—a final celebration of the things he loved.

p. 116: Taravat Talepasand, Islamic Youth T-Shirt (2015)
Title page (p. 102): Tom of England bootleg T-shirt designed by Shannon Michael Cane on the occasion of the New York Art Book Fair (2017)

SCHOOL RUINED MY UFF

Shanzhai Lyric (SL)

Shanzhai Lyric is a "poetic research and archival unit" that documents and transforms awkwardly translated slogans from Chinese bootleg T-shirts into an ongoing poem. The term "shanzhai" originated during the Song Dynasty (960–1279) and translates to "mountain fortress," referring to camps of bandits located on the outskirts of cities beyond government control. Today, however, the word describes an array of Chinese counterfeit products, from cellphones to designer shoes to bootleg shirts. In their practice, Shanzhai Lyric presents their growing archive of garments online through Instagram as well as in physical form through various interventions including publications, performance-lectures, and installations.

In 2020, as a result of COVID shutdowns in New York, Shanzhai Lyric took over a temporary storefront on Canal Street and opened Canal Street Research Association (CSRA). During their time in the storefront, the artists interacted with fellow merchants; opened their doors to the community; collected memories, souvenirs, and artworks; and restaged iconic Canal Street performances. Under the guise of CSRA, Ming Lin and Alexandra Tatarsky of Shanzhai Lyric have closed the gap from bootleg archivists to bootleggers themselves, deploying the process as a form of research and understanding. Interview by Ben Schwartz (BS).

> BS: I was first introduced to Shanzhai Lyric through its Instagram account (I assume this might be the case for many familiar with your work). I'd love to hear some background on the project. What led you to archiving and posting this particular genre of graphic T-shirt?

SL: "Shanzhai Lyric" is the name of both the project and the phenomenon we are trying to identify—an anonymously and collectively authored ongoing poem emerging out of the detritus of consumerism. The name Shanzhai Lyric itself can be read as a kind of bootleg, eliding distinction as an attempt at expressing solidarity with the aesthetic philosophy and politics of this hybrid English, while not claiming ownership over the found phrases that we are gathering as our subject.

We are less interested in producing our own bootlegs as we are in identifying shanzhai strategies and sharing them across various platforms through experiments in publication, performance, curation, archive, installation, and conversation. Our aim is to place shanzhai lyrics in dialogue with other poetic and artistic lineages that also experiment with mimicry, wordplay, poetic plagiarism, and nonsense as subversive methods. We do this in a very physical sense, weaving two main threads by which textile becomes text and text becomes textile. With *The Incomplete Poem* we insert shanzhai garments into libraries, art collections, and home closets to comprise an ever-unfinished work, and alongside this we are continuously inserting shanzhai lyrics into publications ranging from poetry zines to fashion magazines to political journals, forming an ongoing piece we call *The Endless Garment*.

Earlier this year we performed a shanzhai poetry-lecture that oscillates between reading off shanzhai T-shirts and reading from theoretical texts in the space of the Stuart Hall Library to contextualize shanzhai writing as a postcolonial literature. Similarly, bringing shanzhai garments into the Women's Art Library at Goldsmiths situates the pieces within a tradition of feminist experimental text and textile.

We have slowly been assembling a collection of garments that are activated in various ways and distributed across various hosting sites that have included galleries, libraries, personal closets—it is always in transit and open to visitors to read, peruse, and wear. It is important to us that this poem is alive and ever-shifting, that it avoids becoming static or institutionalized, that anyone can add to or draw from its resources. Part of creating this lexicon of tactics also involves identifying artists and thinkers who have wittingly or unwittingly employed shanzhai tools of critique and subversion. Spanning different types of spaces is an effort to demonstrate how this work functions among different traditions, settings, and discourses.

While it can be difficult to pinpoint the precise protocols by which shanzhai phrases are produced, and we are mindful of over-ascribing agency, we look to shanzhai lyrics as evidencing strategies of poetic plagiarism that can be helpful for navigating a nonsense world. We employ a mode of reparative reading by viewing these phrases as moments of hopeful breaking with dominant forms.

BS: Is there a difference between "bootlegging" and "shanzhai?"

SL: The word "bootleg" connotes illegality and covert activities—the word literally refers to the practice of transporting illegal liquor in one's boot. Following from this legacy, we are interested in the politics of concealment and in alternate modes of circulation that arise from distributing illicit goods. Our project looks specifically at the language that appears on so-called bootleg T-shirts made in China and transported across the globe. Our aim is firstly to absolve these items from the moralizing condemnation they receive within a Western framework, and to this end we find ideological resonance in the term "shanzhai" from Chinese, rather than the English "bootleg." As writer Yu Hua notes, shanzhai translates directly to "mountain hamlet," suggesting the enticing possibility of absconding from society, with resources in tow to be shared and redistributed. Thus shanzhai goods retain an association with a history of rebellion and the ideals of radical collectivity.

Philosopher Byung-Chul Han traces the legal and art-historical underpinnings of shanzhai back to ancient Chinese legal structures that define a principle of truth as ever-shifting and relative to circumstance, rather than relying on fixed principle. Looking at the tradition of scroll painting, he further roots his definition in Eastern conceptions of art that thwarts the notion of individual authorship by pursuing a process that finds value generated via collective and ongoing inscription. As a scroll painting passes through many hands, its value increases as it continuously changes and expands, literally marked by all those who possess it. Bearing these two understandings in mind, we are particularly interested in the language borne of a certain breed of counterfeit clothing coming out of China that finds errant English in abundant configurations printed across T-shirts so densely as to form poems and patterns. This project seeks to explore the various strategies of shanzhai as ecstatically illuminating and potentially liberating.

BS: What can we learn from these mistranslated texts?

SL: We want shanzhai lyrics to be viewed not as error-ridden or mistaken but as a rich mode of communicating that speaks with perverse lyricism to the experience of living under contemporary capitalism. In thinking through our own definitions of bootleg, we relish the uniquely shiny and opaque qualities of shanzhai as a possible lens for this critique. Shininess is a characteristic endemic to the fashion industry as that which both draws attention to and conceals the fetish of the commodity. Counterfeit fashion items are often excessively shiny in material, and one could say this attribute attempts to make up for or conceal a lack of quality or authenticity. But in the case of our bootleg T-shirts, which are often flagrant in their "counterfeitedness," we find the opportunity to look more closely at the functions of this shininess. There's the possibility that something else is being reflected and refracted; the shininess of the counterfeit participates in a politics of opacity in that its opulence and

pp. 124–125: Various photographs sourced from Shanzhai Lyric's Instagram account (@shanzhai_lyric)

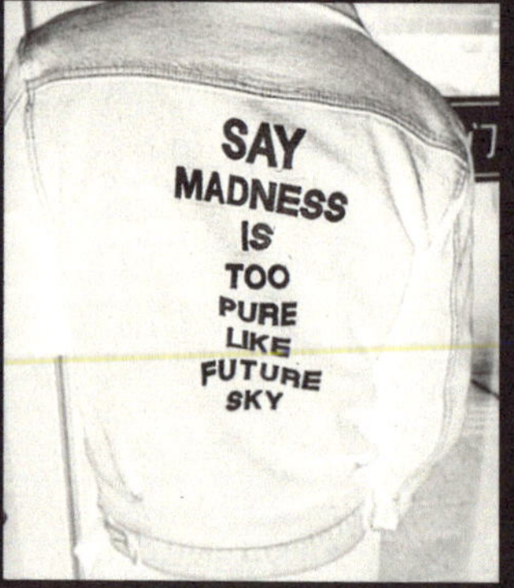
SAY
MADNESS
IS
TOO
PURE
LIKE
FUTURE
SKY

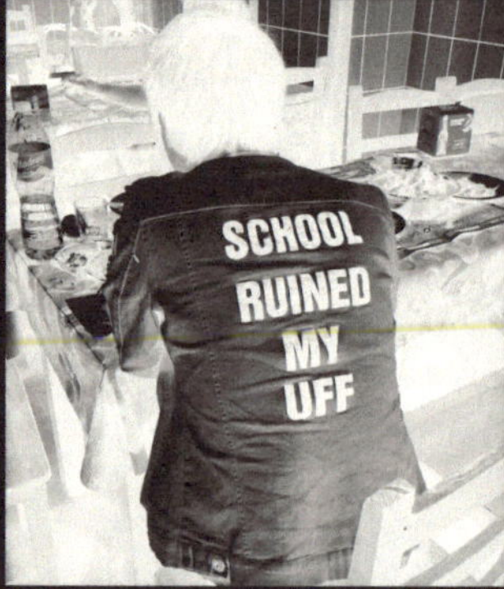
SCHOOL
RUINED
MY
UFF

BEING
EMOTIONALLY
MANIPULATIVE
ISN'T VERY PUNY
ROCK OF YOU

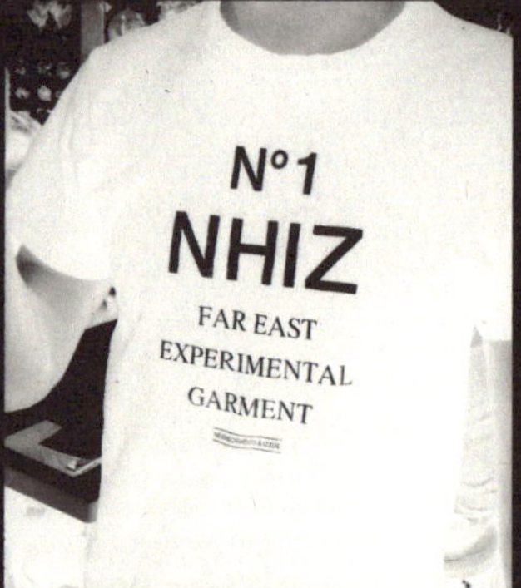
N°1
NHIZ
FAR EAST
EXPERIMENTAL
GARMENT

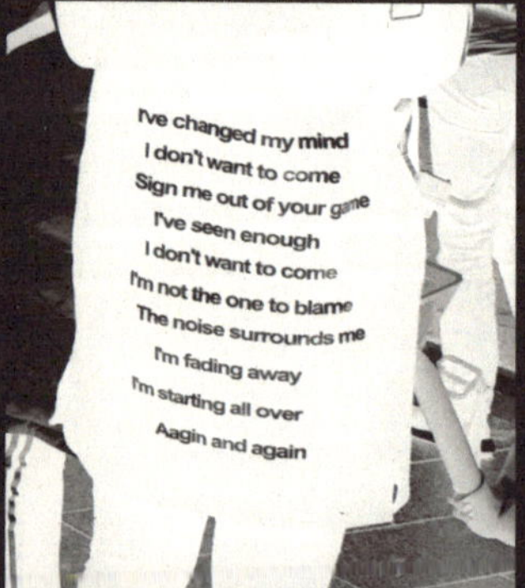
I've changed my mind
I don't want to come
Sign me out of your game
I've seen enough
I don't want to come
I'm not the one to blame
The noise surrounds me
I'm fading away
I'm starting all over
Aagin and again

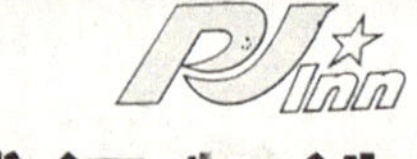
PJ inn
浦江
选酒
HUMANITY
IS AN OCEAN.

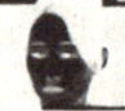

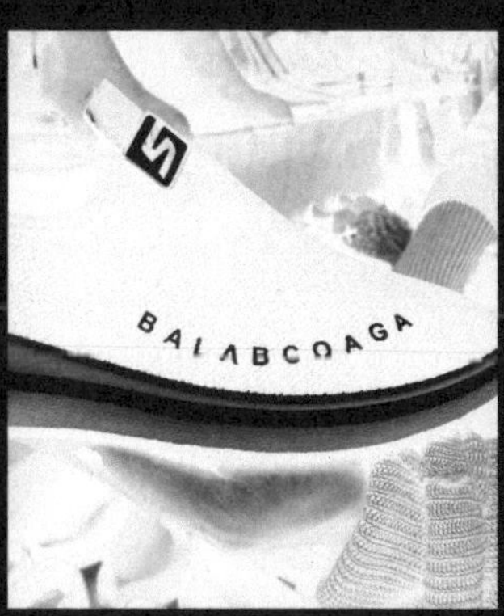
BALABCOAGA

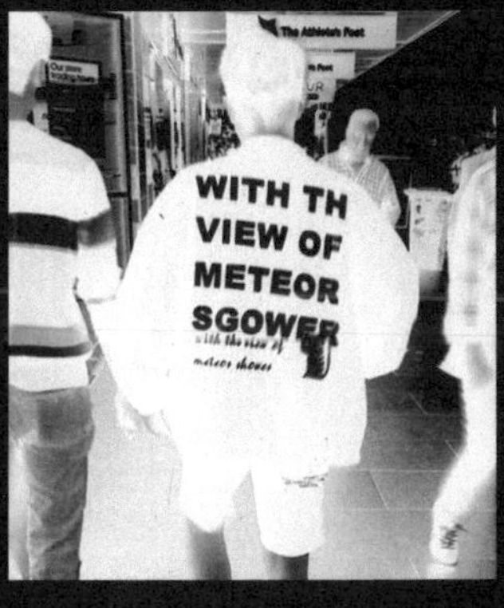
WITH TH
VIEW OF
METEOR
SGOWER

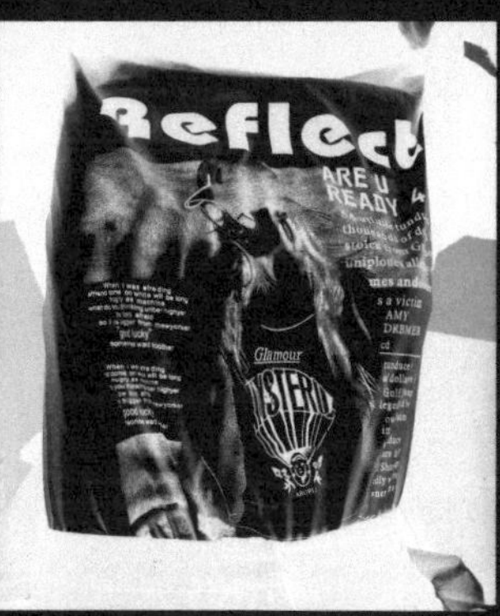
Reflect
ARE U
READY
Glamour

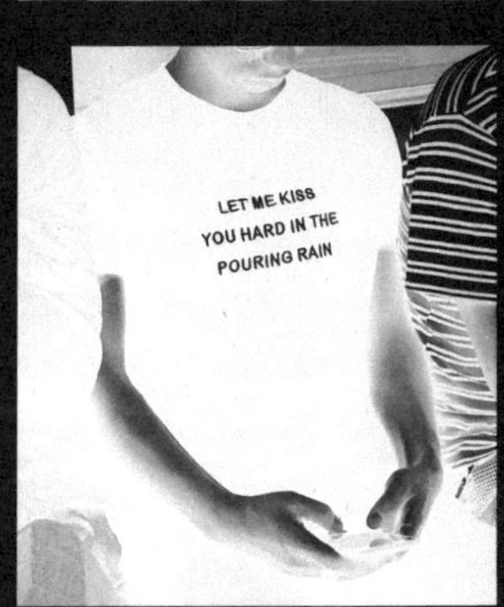
LET ME KISS
YOU HARD IN THE
POURING RAIN

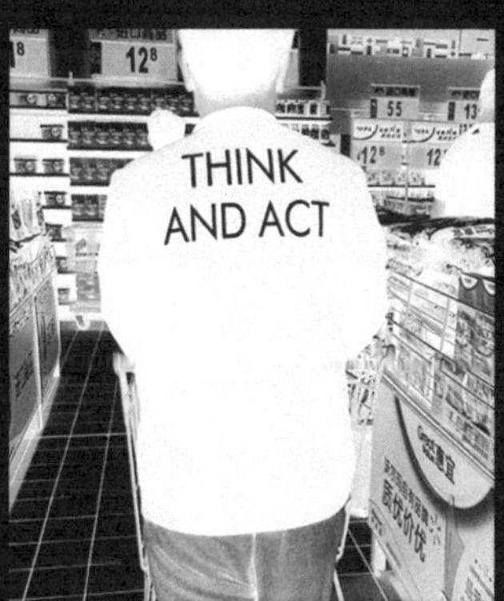
THINK
AND ACT

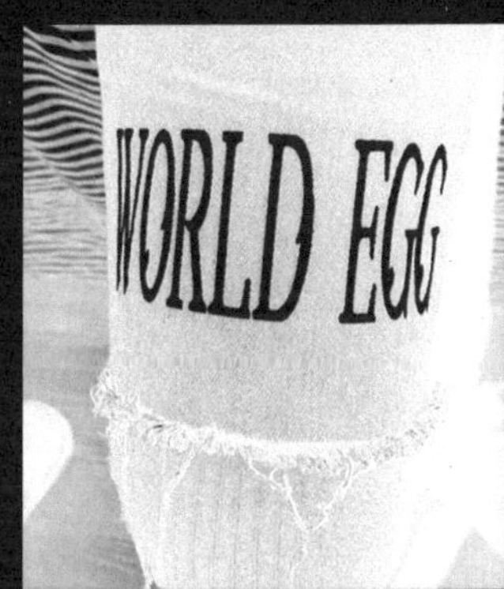
WORLD EG

seductive nature offers a certain protective shield by nature of its impenetrable sheen. The distracting, scintillating glint obscures an always shifting complexity and so provides cover for its subversive activities. The shiny "broken" English that acts as both decoration and description, indicates rupture at a wider level. The frayed and fraying structures of consumer capitalism rely on a language of smooth lies to sell happiness in the form of a T-shirt; the shanzhai lyric embodies where this smoothness breaks down to reveal the contradictions of the lie and give space to a different truth.

> BS: Today, shanzhai language has been co-opted by the very brands it so often collides with (e.g. Gucci items with the wordmark "GUCCY"). Do you believe these shanzhai phrases will remain a powerful symbol of the rupture that you speak of?

SL: Designations of theft are heavily tied to legacies of colonialism and sustain the myth of rightful ownership by particular corporate entities and nation-states. Subverting this myth is tricky because the fashion industry is cannibalistic in nature: as soon as shanzhai lyrics appear they are just as quickly subsumed by what they have risen to challenge. For instance, a company can capitalize on the cache of shanzhai by making its own cheeky interpretations of shanzhai versions of its products—and thus appear to neuter the destabilizing potential of secondary markets. Bootlegs reflect demand; they actually exist in symbiotic dependence with luxury brands, which need them around in order to demonstrate insatiable desirability.

Instances where designers and producers might use the factory blueprints or machinery towards their own designs are for us creative moments that engage in critique, response, and modification rather than theft of the original. This mode of reading draws into question the whole apparatus by which theft is determined, a notion of criminality designed to sustain the powerful by condemning the sharing of patterns and ideas while protecting corporate theft of time, land, and resources through exploitative, polluting labor practices.

In sharing and admiring this non-normative English we attempt to imagine the possibilities of reordering that can extend beyond aesthetics and language to challenge the configurations of global hierarchies. Shanzhai lyrics encourage us to enjoy and embrace a nonsense language that fosters unlikely collisions between different worlds and registers and destabilizes our notions of a correct, homogenous standard. Working to shift the mechanisms of meaning-making participates in debunking the primacy of the "original" and its attending notions of property and authorship, which are at their core western constructions designed to control and contain the flow of wealth. Shanzhai strategies are necessarily fleeting and slippery, but what they shed light on momentarily is a vital reorientation of values. We find the increasing desire for shanzhai products—and they might be considered more desirable than the original, with higher prices that reflect this—to be an exciting development. To us, this indicates a fatigue and frustration with an older aspi-

p. 128–129: Shanzhai Lyric, *Incomplete Poem* (2015–ongoing), installation view. Photo: Noel Woodford

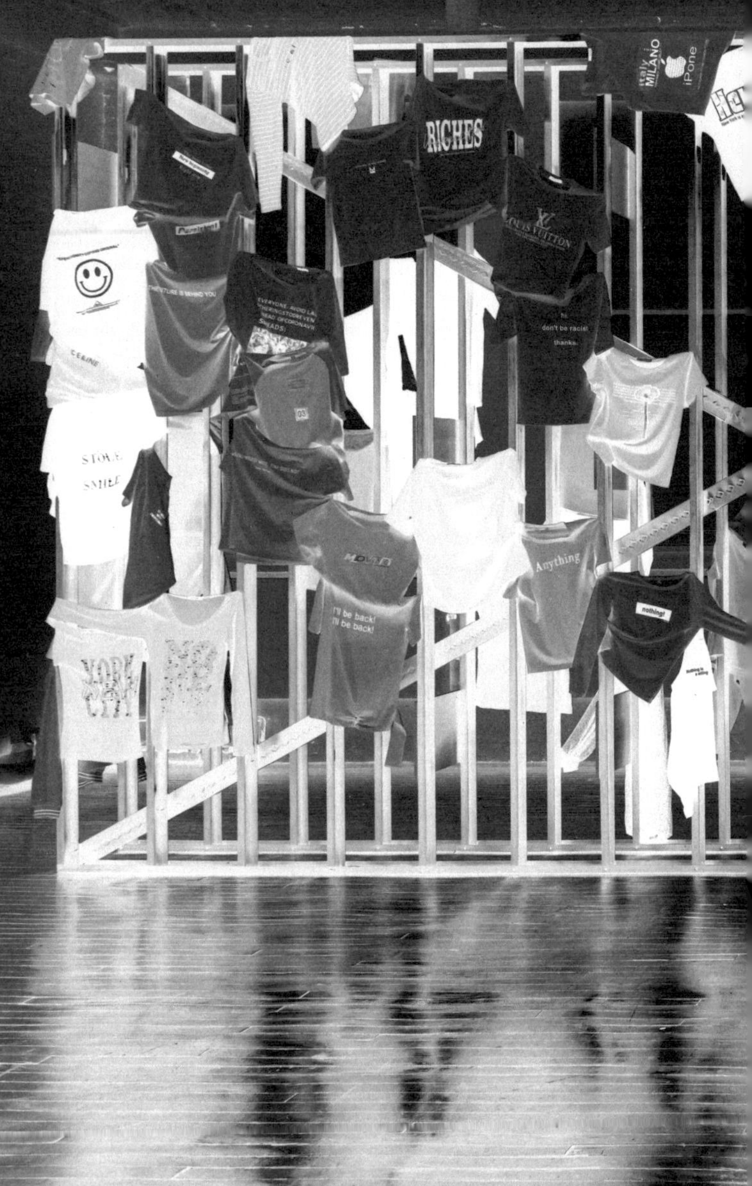
italy
MILANO
iPone
RICHES
LOUIS VUITTON
THE FUTURE IS BEHIND YOU
CELINE
hi,
don't be racist.
thanks.
STOLE
SMILE
I'll be back!
I'll be back!
Anything
nothing!

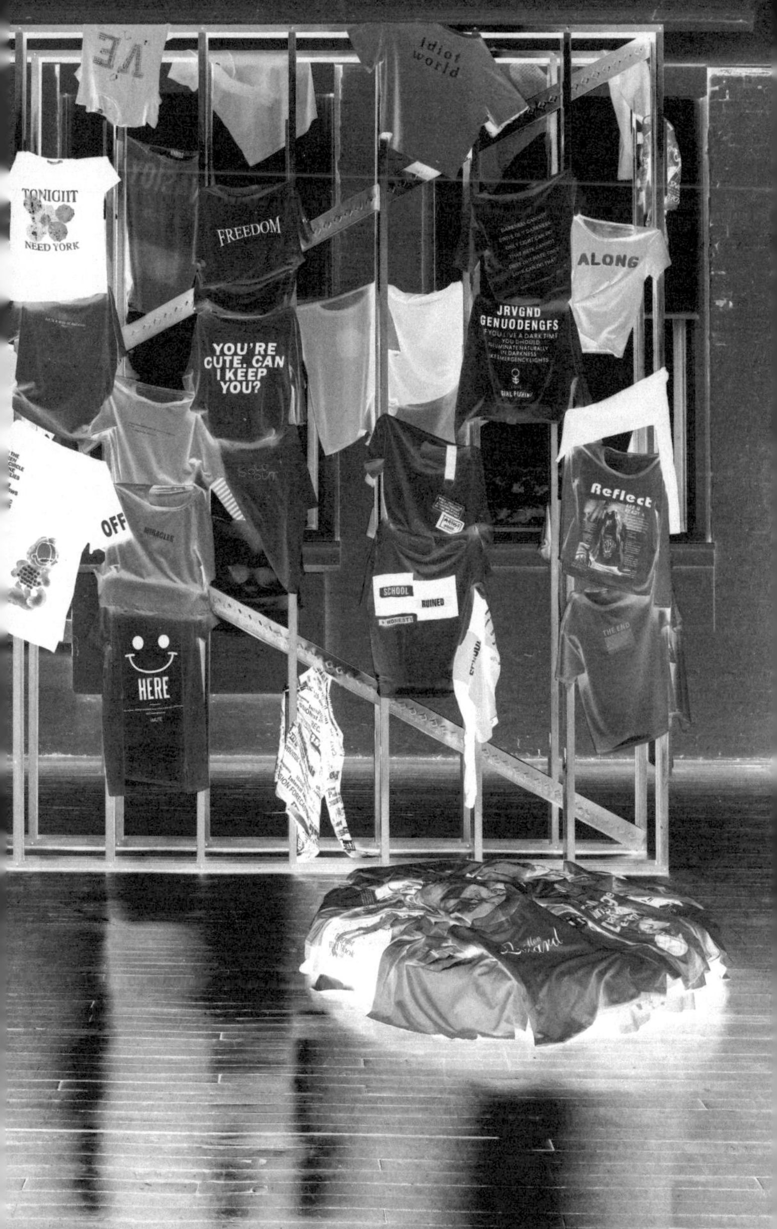
idiot
world
TONIGIIT
NEED YORK
FREEDOM
ALONG
JRVGND
GENUODENGFS
YOU'RE
CUTE. CAN
I KEEP
YOU?
Reflect
OFF
MIRACLE
SCHOOL
RUINED
HONESTY
HERE
THE END

rational model whereby a shanzhai product is understood to be "imitating" a luxury brand product. Instead, we see shanzhai as a form of innovation rather than imitation that offers, through shanzhai lyrics, a poetic take on the empty and worn-out signifiers of high fashion.

BS: The shanzhai lyrics that you collect are not attributed to any one author. Is this symbolic of something larger? A critique of the lone genius myth perhaps?

SL: Shanzhai lyrics are written through poetic collaborations between human and machine. They can be read as recombinatory texts that allow for the deterritorializing of meaning, as analogue hyperlinks that allow for a-linear and non-monolithic viewpoints to collide and intersect, extending and expanding in multiple directions. Following Byung-Chul Han, we view shanzhai lyrics within the lineage of traditional Chinese scroll painting, in which value accrues via collectively-authored, ever-growing loci of inscriptions. This process reflects an alternate model of meaning-making generated through the expression of not just one but a multitude of voices. Such notions of radical collectivity and freedom of expression might be seen paralleling the utopian aspirations of the internet whose endless scroll ideally allows for colliding registers of high and low through a seamless, simultaneous, and ongoing transmission that, as the collective Critical Art Ensemble notes in their work on poetic plagiarism, ultimately renders the notion of a single, original author irrelevant. It is only when companies seek to protect their assets and wield control over the flow of information for the sake of profit that the question of authorship and credit becomes a problem.

We recently experimented with the format of the scroll in our installation at the Long March Space in Beijing by inviting visitors to access the Open Archive by participating in a collective translation exercise. Shanzhai T-shirts could be taken off the rack and translated in as many ways as there were visitors to the space, and these versions were inscribed on an unfurling paper scroll that became an ever-unfinished document of the process of interpretation. How do we translate one nonsense tongue into another, collectively making sense of "broken" and distorted pieces? How do we find space to write a strange poem together that never ends? Poetry refutes the logic of exchangeability and legibility. We babble and exclaim. Freed, and on and on: FREEDON.

> BS: I'd like to transition to a recent iteration, or "bootleg," of Shanzhai Lyric: Canal Street Research Association (CSRA). Since its inception, CSRA has occupied several physical spaces on Manhattan's Canal Street, a place renowned for counterfeit goods, where you observed, researched, and engaged with the community. As a local New Yorker, it has been incredible to follow the stories and histories you've uncovered, always connecting back to this real vs. fake dichotomy. The project continues to evolve today, but perhaps you could begin by talking about the origins of CSRA.

SL: We had planned to spend much of 2020 tracing the pathway of a shanzhai garment around the world, through design, production, and various channels of distribution. But then just before we were to set off to Hong Kong, travel became impossible. Everything was canceled and we found ourselves back home in the neighborhood we grew up in, right around Canal Street. A curatorial duo called ACOMPI was planning a group show in an empty Canal Street storefront as part of "On Canal," an art and real estate effort to rebrand Canal Street by filling the storefronts—largely vacant—with artists. ACOMPI asked Shanzhai Lyric to contribute a piece. We mentioned that we'd actually be a lot more interested in a whole storefront—just having a place to hang out on Canal Street for three months and study the ebbs and flows of the blocks, well known for hosting New York City's counterfeit industry. And that would be the piece. Thus, the Canal Street Research Association was born. As the pandemic continued, three months turned into three years. We realized that to study the trade routes, unofficial markets, and global flows of counterfeit goods, we truly never had to leave our block.

> BS: Could you talk a bit about the history of Canal Street? Specifically, I'm curious how it became an epicenter of bootlegs.

SL: Before Canal Street there was a canal, dug out from a natural stream that flowed from Collect Pond, once lower Manhattan's main freshwater source. As Dutch and English colonizers settled around the pond, they began using Collect Pond as a dumping ground for the tanneries that were the first local industry. So the pond began to overflow with waste—sewage, runoff, animal carcasses—and the canal siphoned this waste into the East and Hudson rivers that ring Manhattan. Developers tried to disguise the horrible stench of shit and decay with rows of riverside trees to turn the canal into a riverside promenade, but it didn't work and so the pond was drained, filled in, and built upon. This made for perpetually unstable conditions. The jail that sits where Collect Pond once was is constantly leaking and sinking. The decaying matter in the shoddy landfill led to fetid, unhygienic conditions and by the eighteen-hundreds, the area became known as the infamous "5 Points," home to various marginalized communities, first African Americans and then waves of immigrants who ran the thriving street markets and food carts. These unofficial markets were—and are—often the only pathway to financial independence for marginalized communities that lack the resources to own property or work legally. And yet they have been shunned and criminalized since their inception.

There is a pretty direct line from this early history to Canal Street today. The street has always served as a landing place for different groups that have been pushed into semi-legal industries due to a system that marginalizes them. It is our understanding that unofficial import channels were established between the U.S. and Asia during and following the Vietnam War, when Canal Street became a hub for army surplus, and the counterfeit industry took shape sometime in the 1980s. It has become a lifeline for many immigrant communities, today mostly hailing from South China and West Africa,

pp. 134–137: Shanzhai Lyric's Canal Street storefront (2020)
Photo: Daniel Terna

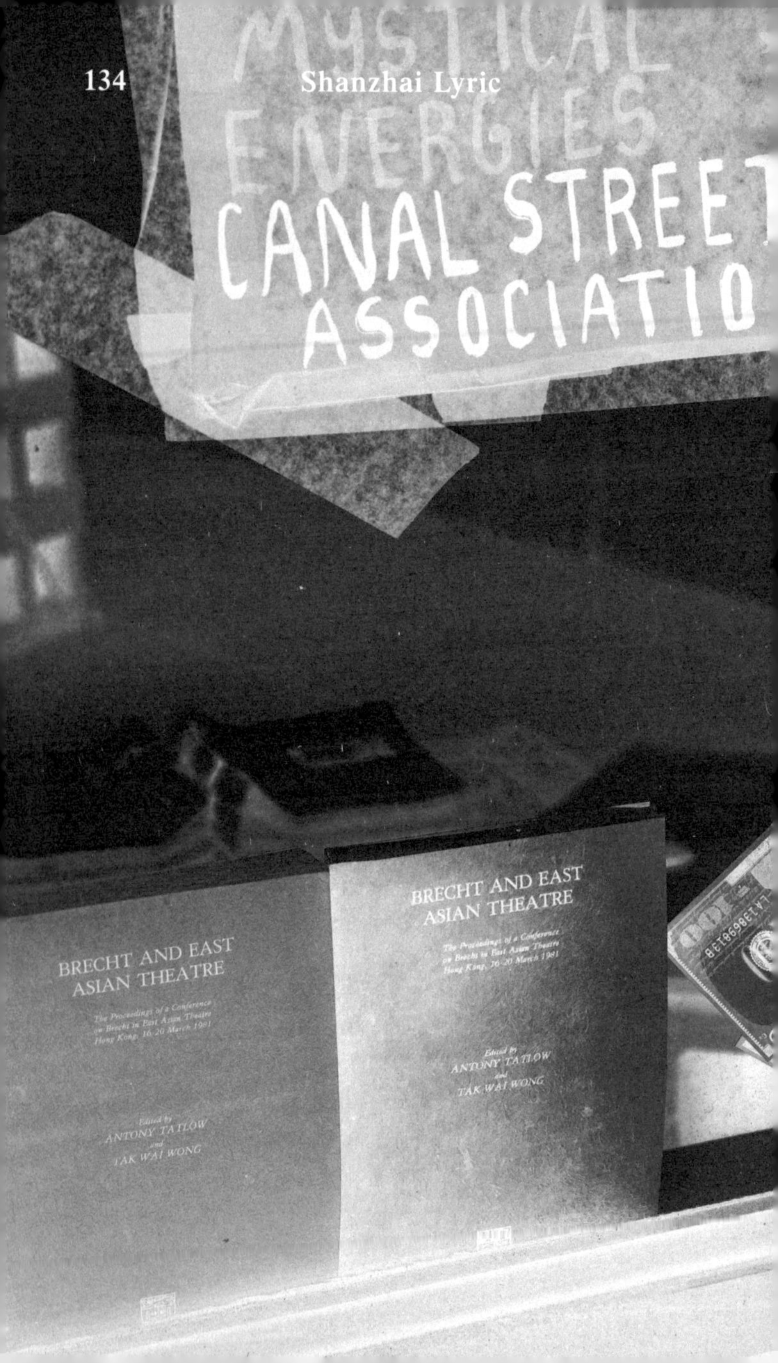

MYSTICAL
ENERGIES
CANAL STREET
ASSOCIATIO
BRECHT AND EAST
ASIAN THEATRE
Edited by
ANTONY TATLOW
and
TAK WAI WONG
BRECHT AND EAST
ASIAN THEATRE
Edited by
ANTONY TATLOW
and
TAK WAI WONG

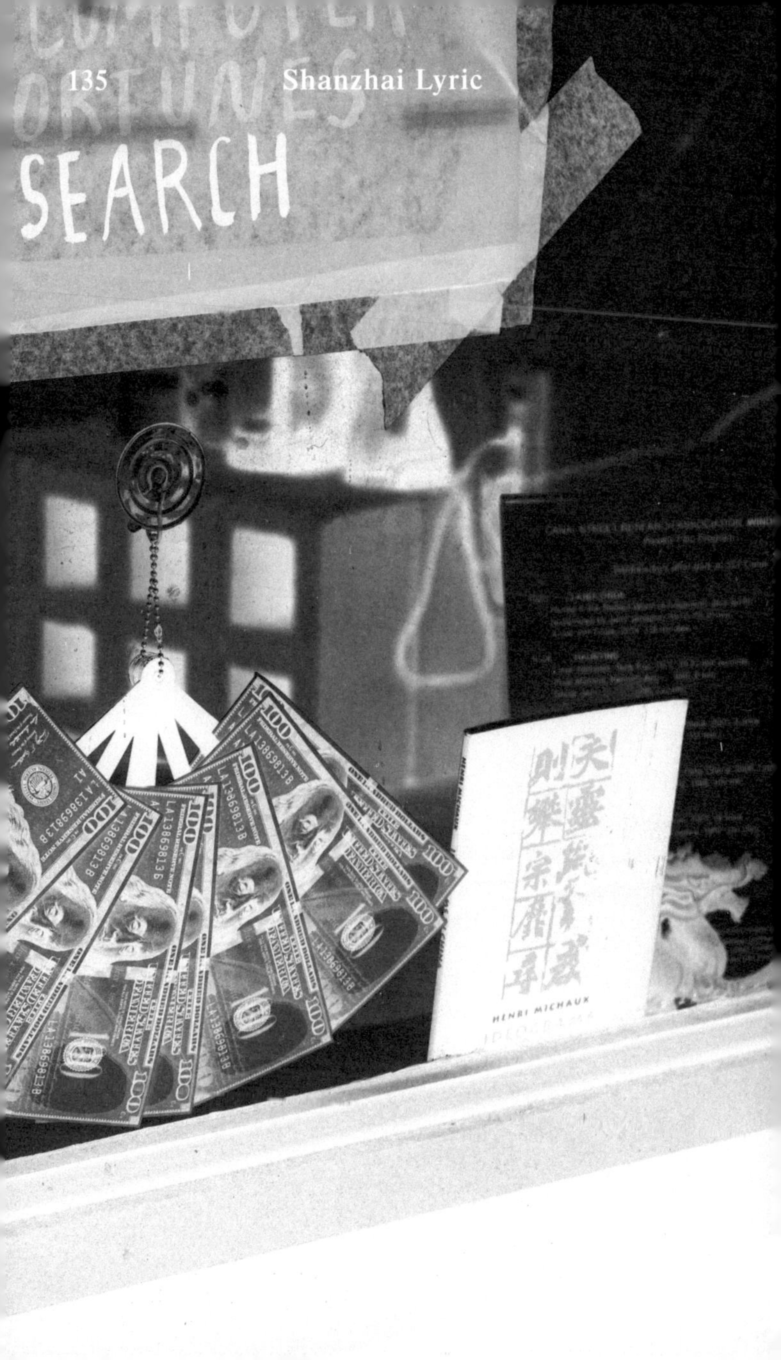

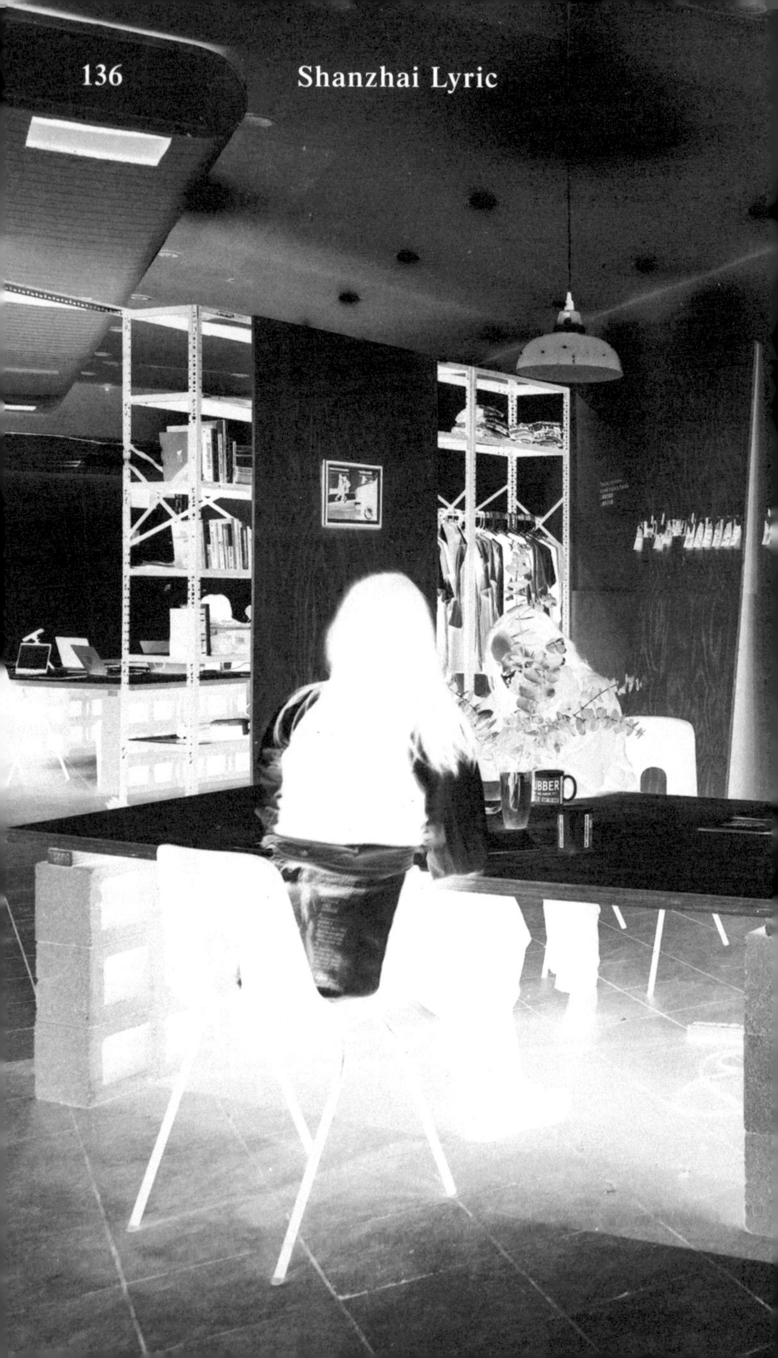

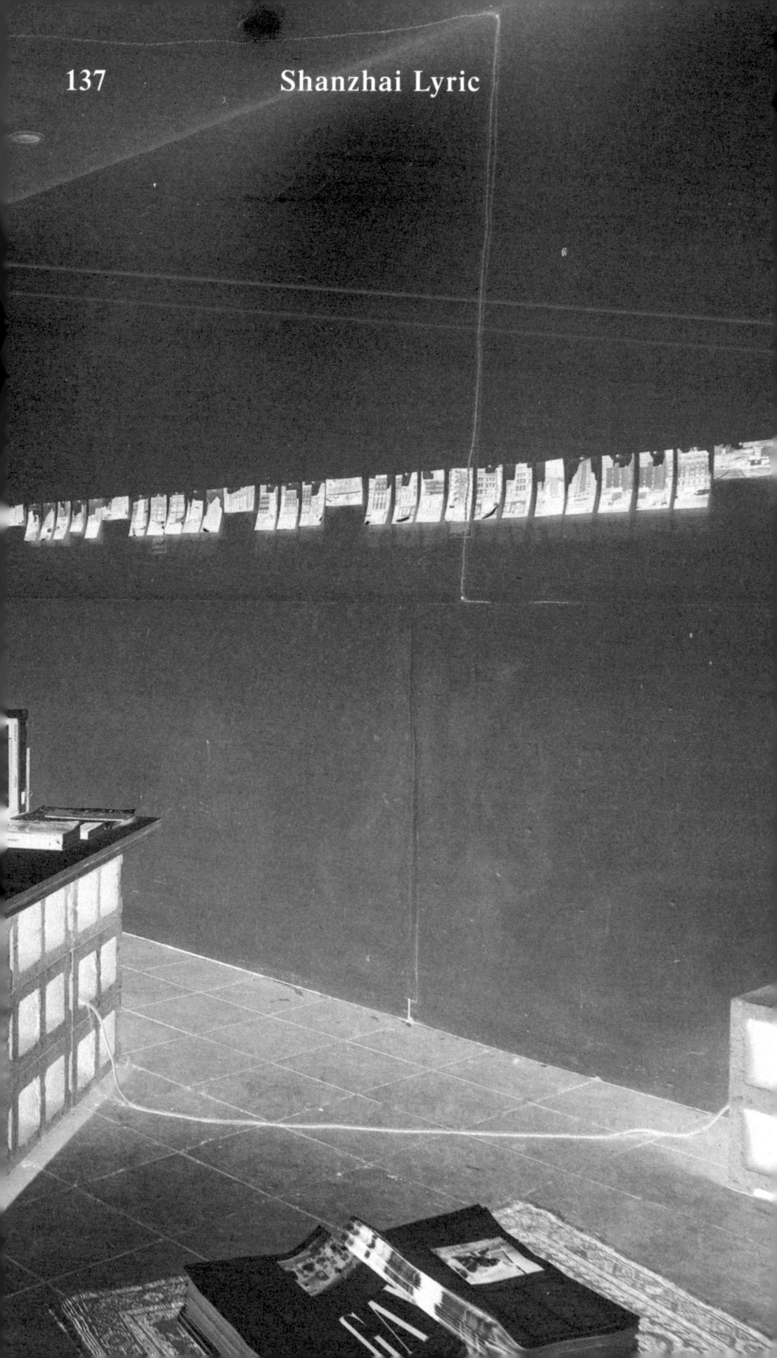

who engage in a complex cross-lingual collaboration along the block.

> BS: The threat of gentrification seems to weigh heavy on Canal Street given its location in Manhattan and proximity to so much luxury retail. Was this tension perceptible? As gentrification is so often introduced through artists and art spaces moving into a neighborhood, I'm curious how you were welcomed? How did you connect with locals?

SL: Well, we would say Canal Street is notable for how well it has *resisted* gentrification. Neighboring SoHo and TriBeCa have come to represent the artist gentrification narrative: post-industrial urban factories converted first into semi-legal artist live/work spaces and then into luxury lofts for the rich. Further East, the ethnic enclaves of Little Italy, Chinatown, and the Lower East Side have maintained their neighborhood identities somewhat through dedicated community organizing but have also become some of the priciest areas in the country. So the Canal Street environs are already fully gentrified, but Canal Street itself has in some ways resisted this shift. Its swampy, seedy origins and reputation persists. It is one of the few remaining places in NYC that abound with cross-cultural, interclass contact and communication.

It was important to us that our space was both intriguing and inviting. Because it was a bit unclear what was happening there, people would often come inside to try to understand. A store can be more welcoming than a gallery because a store has a script that everyone knows, whereas a gallery can feel alienating due to its obscure codes of behavior. People would come in and be both frustrated and delighted that nothing was for sale. And in this confusion, we'd have the chance to tell them we were studying Canal Street and invite them into that research by asking what brought them to the block. We learned many secret histories this way.

Anyone could hang out in the space to have a tea and get warm. Anyone could use the bathroom or the internet. Anyone could leave some items there if they needed a place to store goods. We also hosted concerts and drum lessons on the steps of Canal Rubber next door and we turned our storefront window into an outdoor movie screen so that vendors could watch movies while they worked. We always paired one short experimental film with one longer Hollywood flick to entice an audience with diverse tastes. This turned the street itself into a space of gathering and relaxation where the different communities—longtime residents, newer transplants, local artists, business owners, street vendors, and passersby—could ideally get more comfortable with one another. But it took many months of spending all day every day on one single city block for these relationships to grow.

At the same time, we have always been aware that we inhabited a storefront for no rent as part of a sticky and seductive partnership between art and real estate. In this case, a consortium of landlords welcomed arts programming as a way to make their vacant properties look more active and high-end to attract commercial tenants that would displace the artists. We often say that we are the trees planted along the canal to accelerate development and to cover up its stench. So this question has been central to our research: can artists play a meaningful role in cities where they are so often used to rebrand and upscale neighborhoods? We look to the philosophy, poetics, and politics of shanzhai for answers. Creative theft can be a way to redistribute the resources.

> BS: With the initial CSRA office you restaged several events, shows, and works that had previously occurred on Canal Street. How did these reenactments change or affect your relationship to the original? As a methodology, how might you consider bootlegging as a form of learning or tool for research?

SL: Despite Canal Street being one of NYC's major thoroughfares, there is no definitive history of the street. And this is largely because it is a liminal zone, rife with semi-legal activities that folks are loath to disclose. We began to think that re-staging or bootlegging ephemeral moments in the block's history could be a means of surfacing buried histories. And one thing we noticed was that a lot of the street's many layered past was encapsulated in the works of artists who were drawn to the neighborhood by the raw materials and cheap rents. We consider copying to be a form of learning. The bootleg is a mode of study, commentary, and critique.

Many folks on the block who are eager to chat with us and share their experiences are less comfortable doing so on record. So many vendors and purveyors on Canal Street are also artisans, tailors, singers, andactors that a dream of ours has been to create a semi-fictional history of Canal Street with everyone on the block. In this way, collaborators might feel more liberated to talk freely about their lives, avoiding self-incrimination because the line between real and fake, fact and fiction would be blurry. Bootleg as protection.

In New York City, we were delighted to learn that street portraiture is one form of vending that does not require a license because it is protected as freedom of expression. And so you see, art is a way of survival. Bootleg as portrait.

> BS: In addition to performances, you began to collect objects which amounted to an "office art collection." I was hoping you could talk through two or three of these objects and their relationship to the history of Canal Street?

SL: In our storefront office, artworks accumulated in what we called the office hamlet. Often these were by friends and local artists whose work touched on similar themes, and who inspire us.

Bon Lee, *Annie*: One day, at the entrance to Chinatown Building Supply just down the alley from Canal Street, we noticed a wall of photographs. The woman at the till told us they were for sale and had been taken by the shop's proprietor, Bon Lee. Amongst many sunsets and landscapes, one of the photos stood out to us. It appeared to depict a car nearly crashing into some pedestrians. The shopkeeper told us this image was from the filming of the 2014 remake of the musical *Annie*, in which a pivotal scene unfolds right in front of the store. The man in the photo was actually Jamie Foxx's stunt double. So what we were looking at was a reproduction of a photo of a double in a re-

pp. 142–143: Bon Lee, *Annie* (2014). Photo: Daniel Terna

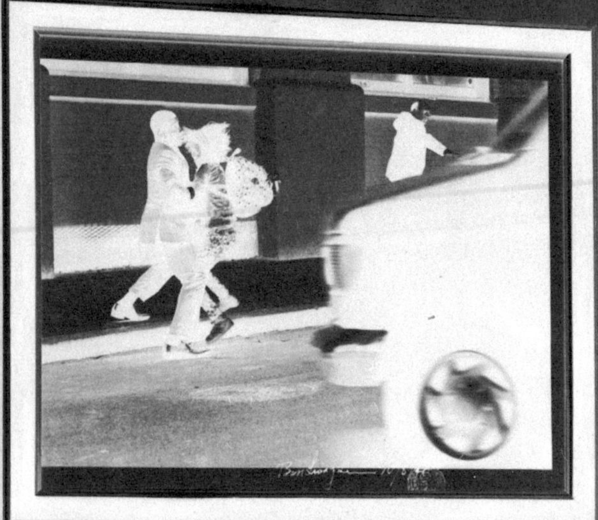

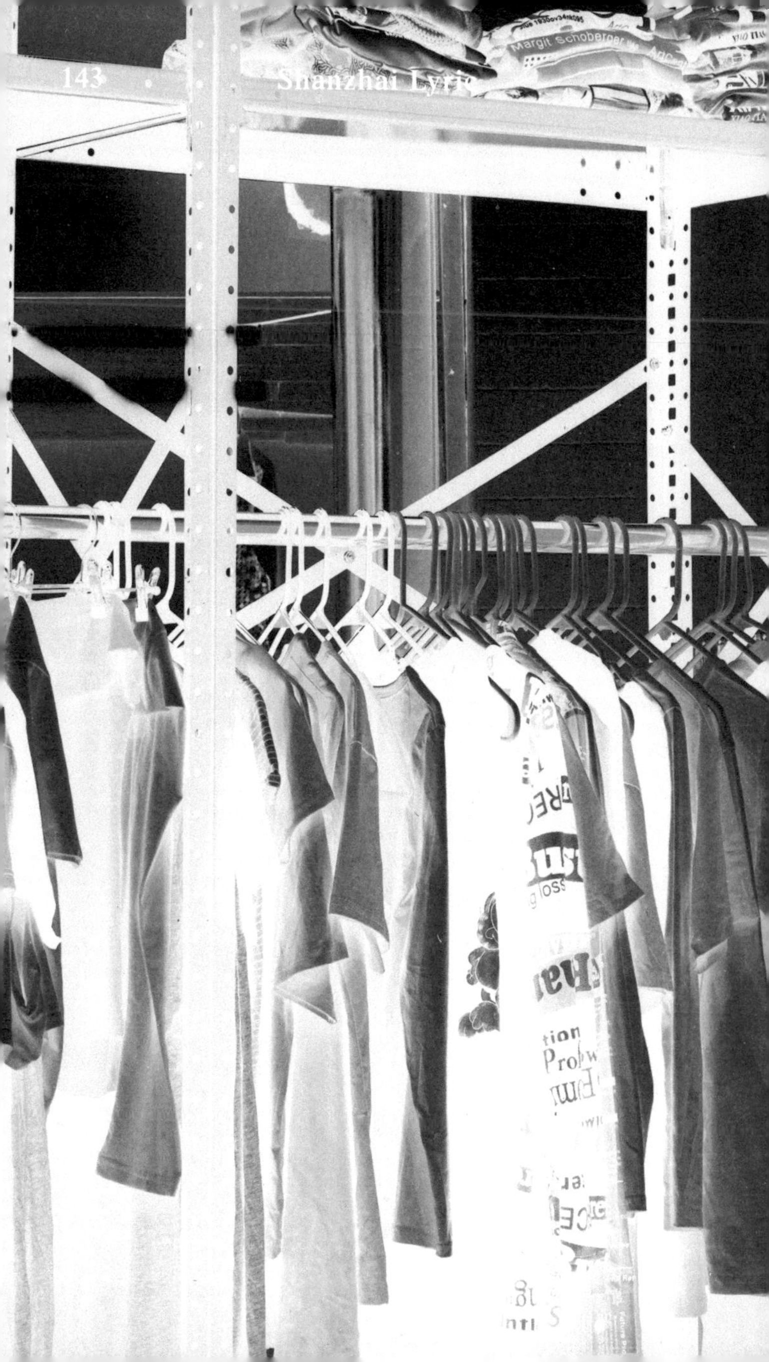
Margit Schoberger

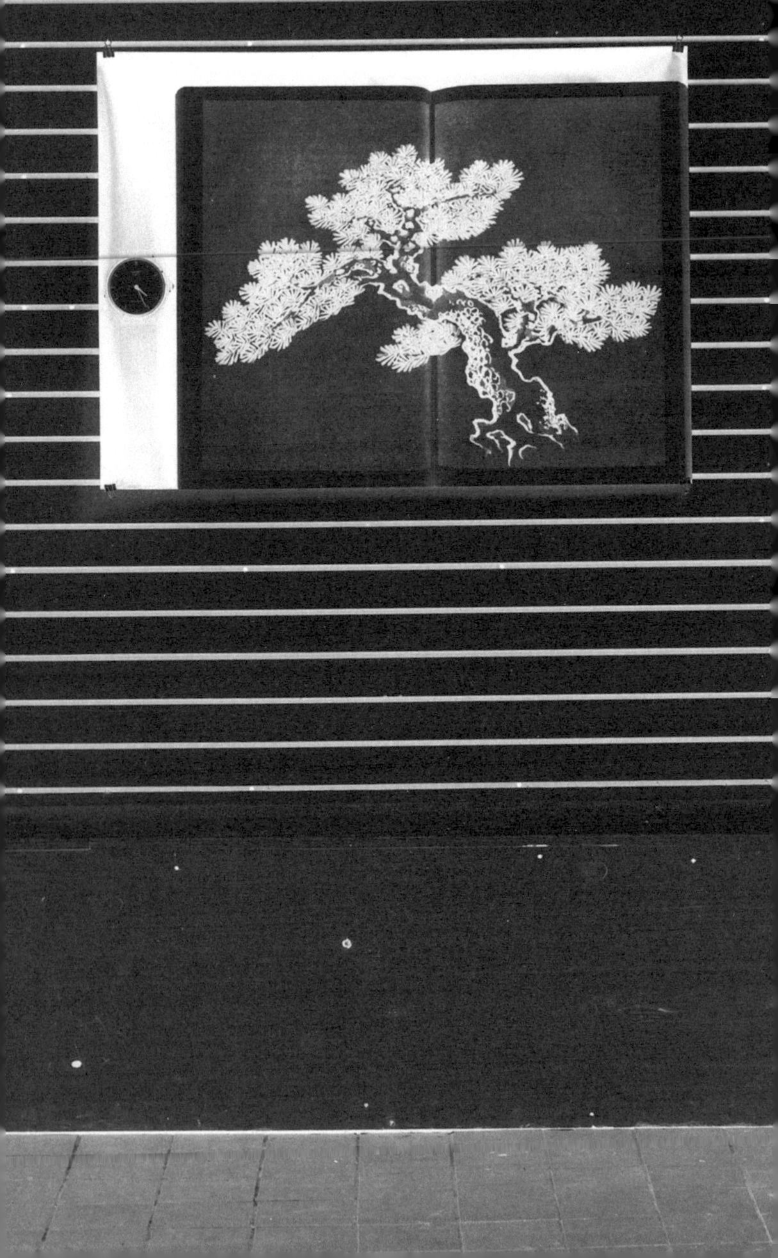

make—of a movie about a greedy industrialist with a heart of gold. We purchased this work and it became the first item in our prized office art collection.

Max Guy, *Love and Barley*: Max Guy is a Chicago-based artist who grew up in the neighborhood. His work *Love and Barley* is a bootleg he made of a Japanese landscape painting. According to philosopher Byung-Chul Han, the Chinese concept of shanzhai has its roots in Eastern traditions of landscape painting where emptiness in the composition leaves space for multiple authors to inscribe themselves into it. We try to let the project be guided by these collectively generated landscapes.

Still from *Film About a Woman Who…* (1974, dir. Yvonne Rainer), featuring Dempster Leech: In reviewing the history of intellectual property law on the block, we came across the evocative Dempster Leech. His name kept coming up as a private detective in news articles describing Canal Street busts. However, when googling his name something else interesting came up. Before his work as a PI, Leech was an actor and part of the downtown avant garde film scene. For instance, he starred in Yvonne Rainer's *Film About a Woman Who…* from 1974. Later, filmmaker Monica Scharf made a short documentary about Leech in which she draws out the connection between his former life as an actor and as a PI. Leech claims that it was because of his frustration with the fakeness of the acting world that he wanted to embed himself in the world of counterfeit busting. He wanted the scenes to be real. And yet, a lot of his work as a PI required him

p. 144: Max Guy, *Love and Barley* (2019). Photo: Daniel Terna to act undercover. To take on fake personas. At our second location in an empty office building on the Canal, we screened *Film About a Woman Who...* paired with *PI Shorts*, followed by a conversation with Leech and Scharf about the politics of the bootleg. We keep a still from Rainer's film featuring Leech as part of our ever-shifting office art collection.

> BS: I've been interested in the ways bootlegs create or reinforce community. There is perhaps no better place to understand this than on Canal Street. In what ways did you find that bootlegs hold this community together? What sort of protections does the community have in place from outside forces such as police raids?

SL: We came into our storefront space in the fall of 2020, in that first pandemic winter, following a summer of protest and uprising for racial justice. The entire block was boarded up by landlords fearful of looting and all the blank plywood "protecting" the empty property had turned the city into a blank scroll. There was a notable absence of cops and it became clear that their job was to protect property—not people. With businesses closed, they had nothing to do. And in the absence of cops, vibrant street life returned.

In this moment, a lot of things felt possible. We'd both long been priced out of the neighborhood and for the first time in years we were able to spend every day in the neighborhood we grew up in, talking to our neighbors. Our storefront had a perfect window onto the block and faced an active street corner where vendors, mostly from West Africa, conduct business and hang out. We were very intrigued by their pursuits and they were very intrigued by ours. This mutual curiosity was an opening for conversation—coupled with the fact that both of our industries were pretty much decimated by the pandemic so we all had a lot of free time to hang out and talk.

We learned that there is a long history on Canal Street of ethnic associations that operate as mutual aids, pooling resources to help members buy a home or pay funerary expenses. On Canal Street, when a police raid decimates someone's inventory, the community of vendors will sometimes help them acquire stock to start anew.

> BS: In its current form, CSRA is located in the office of a basement… almost *becoming* a bootleg in the underground or shadow market. Fom working with bootlegs at a distance (as archivists with Shanzhai Lyric) to employing bootlegging as a methodology (through performances on Canal Street) to now working as a bootleg in some ways, how has your understanding of the act or object evolved? How do you understand bootlegs differently now?

SL: Yes, we are currently located in the basement of an arts organization called Canal Projects, as official artists/archivists in residence. In some sense we have in fact become legitimate, rather than illegitimate or bootleg, and it is this tension we are interested in. We are a fake organization that has become real. Everything is bootleg.

Title page (p. 118): Text taken from a photograph from Shanzhai Lyric's Instagram account (@shanzhai_lyric)

White Castle®

Babak Radboy (BR)

Babak Radboy is a New York-based artist and art director whose work with brands like Telfar or the Berlin Biennale masquerade as advertising, yet sharply critique the industries they exist within. In 2017, Telfar and Radboy embarked on an iconic collaboration with the fast food chain White Castle, in which the designer created new employee uniforms and held an after-party in their Times Square location. On its surface, the partnership felt riddled with irony, but in fact it crystallized the brand's vision for a total reconfiguration of high and low culture. The project demonstrates how Radboy understands his role as a Trojan Horse-like figure—or better yet, a bootlegger smuggling "illegitimate" ideas into "legitimate" frameworks in an attempt to disrupt structures of oppression. Interview by Ben Schwartz (BS).

BS: I see a relationship between aspects of bootlegging and your practice, and I say this thinking of a more expanded definition of the term: focusing on ideas of subversion, infiltration, and an antagonistic relationship to structures of power. I'm curious about how you understand the idea of bootlegging, and how it might resonate with your work.

BR: I would relate it to private property. I relate it to how the logic of private property is enforced and recreated in a wide array of phenomena in which it's not proper. This whole idea, you could say, begins with land itself. And what reinforces all of this idea is the threat of violence—without that, bootlegging can't exist. The word I actually think about all the time, as opposed to "bootlegging," is "legitimacy." I think a lot about legitimacy and illegitimacy, and in my world, I try to create as many illegitimate junctures as possible.

BS: Could you talk about specific ways this illegitimacy manifests itself in your work?

BR: It goes beyond something formal, like a video or mark. It relates more to non-tangible elements: how we set up or structure a company, the flow of information. It touches every aspect of our practice. I am interested in seeking out this illegitimacy.

Generally, this starts on a very structural level, it's not just performative. With Telfar, a lot of things that appear the way they do are a result of the social relations that preceded them. When it comes to working with corporations and magazines, that all starts in conversations, in contracts, in the sharing or not sharing of information. The processes through which I work question legitimacy. When we shoot videos, I don't say "action," which questions my own legitimacy as a director. Or when working with clients who absolutely have to be on set at a shoot, I just simply don't send them the address.

But in order for all of that to work, what we make has to actually perform. By delegitimizing the process, the client loses its bearings for how to intervene. It's not always antagonistic, sometimes it's just about setting up a process so alien that the client doesn't know how to ruin it.

It feels especially relevant as it relates to communication, and today that's often referring directly to social media. Professionalism is a process, but it also exerts an influence on the product, and nobody is looking for professionalism. Nobody is on Instagram liking something because of how professional it looks. And the professionalism that people are seeking is just zapping everyone's energy. Companies don't know what to put on their Instagram, so they just tap a bunch of professionals, they create through professional processes, they hire professionals that hire other professionals, and then you have an output that feels totally unrelated to the brand. Even the art directed photoshoot… that has happened over time without people questioning it because it fits so naturally into how careers are organized. But if you just transpose that to Instagram, with a series of images, you're setting yourself up for people to become less interested. People don't want to see a professional series of images on Instagram, and yet that's what every single company does. They don't know how to procure anything other than that because they don't have any other processes.

BS: This tension between legitimacy and illegitimacy is how I associate your practice to bootlegging. I see a bootleg as a way of undermining signs and symbols of legitimacy—such as a logo—to then sell something illegitimate. Could you speak on the power of manipulating forms or structures of legitimacy by working within them?

BR: I've always been interested in what constitutes a form. They are always the result of social processes rather than formal ones. The form encodes the social process and vice versa. And now you can imply the social process through the form, it's a way of reverse engineering. I find there is something useful about advertising. We have a very limited vocabulary of forms through which we can communicate. There is a convention around how these things are to be read. I've found the art world to be the worst possible way in which to communicate anything because the context completely forecloses the possibility that it will have an effect of any kind. You can write "Kill All Children," as Bjarne Melgaard does, on a painting and it's completely fine. But if you do that on CNN it's a problem. If you are looking for trouble, the gallery is the wrong place to go. But in advertising, because of how it is encoded, its audience will automatically identify themselves as the one being addressed. If you have imagined them, given them attributes, they will subconsciously take on these attributes. If you posit there are obvious things you both agree on, then the reader will meet you halfway—which is how advertisers create manipulation and how hegemonic practices work. If they show you a white middle-class family, then that now becomes how you understand the idea of a family. It's a level of legitimacy self-organized through the flow of capital.

p. 153: Castle N°16 (2017). Photo: Jason Keeling

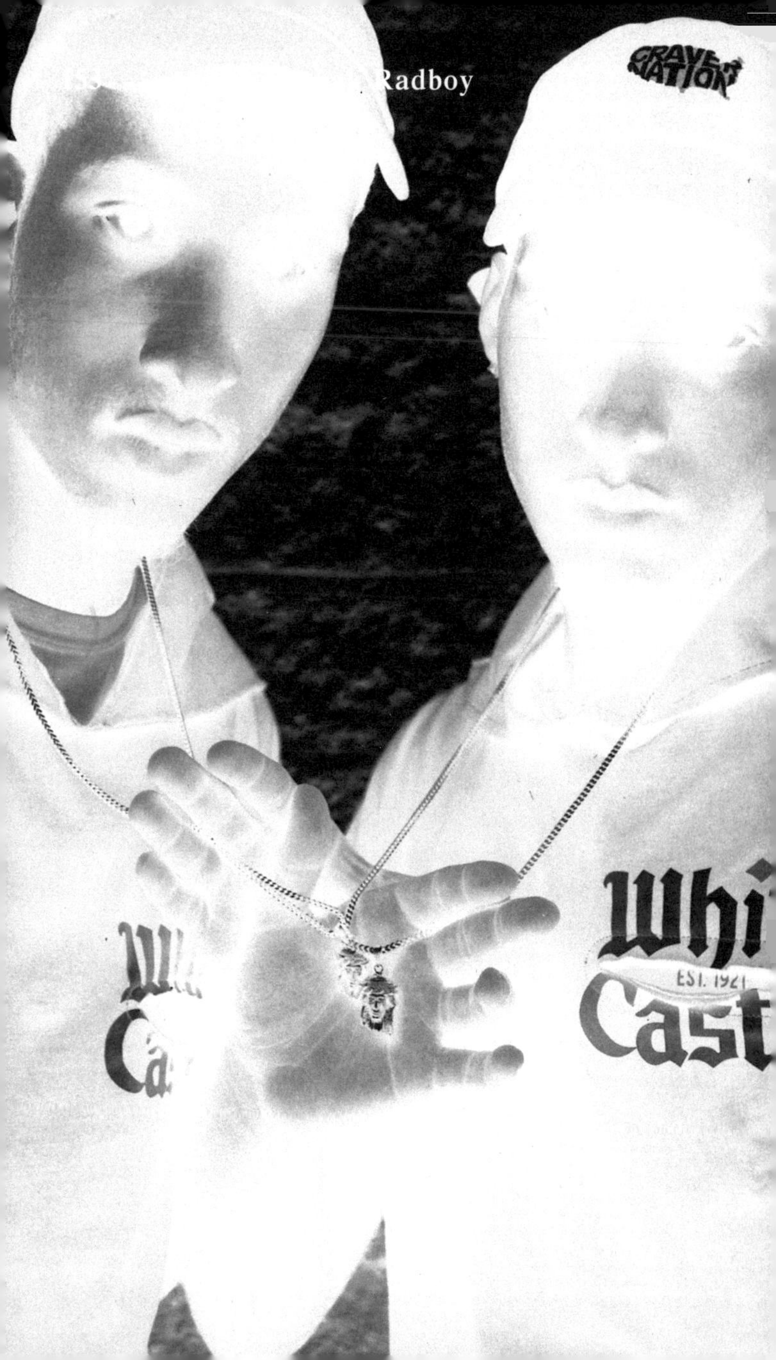
Radboy
GRAVE NATION
Whi
EST. 1921
Cast

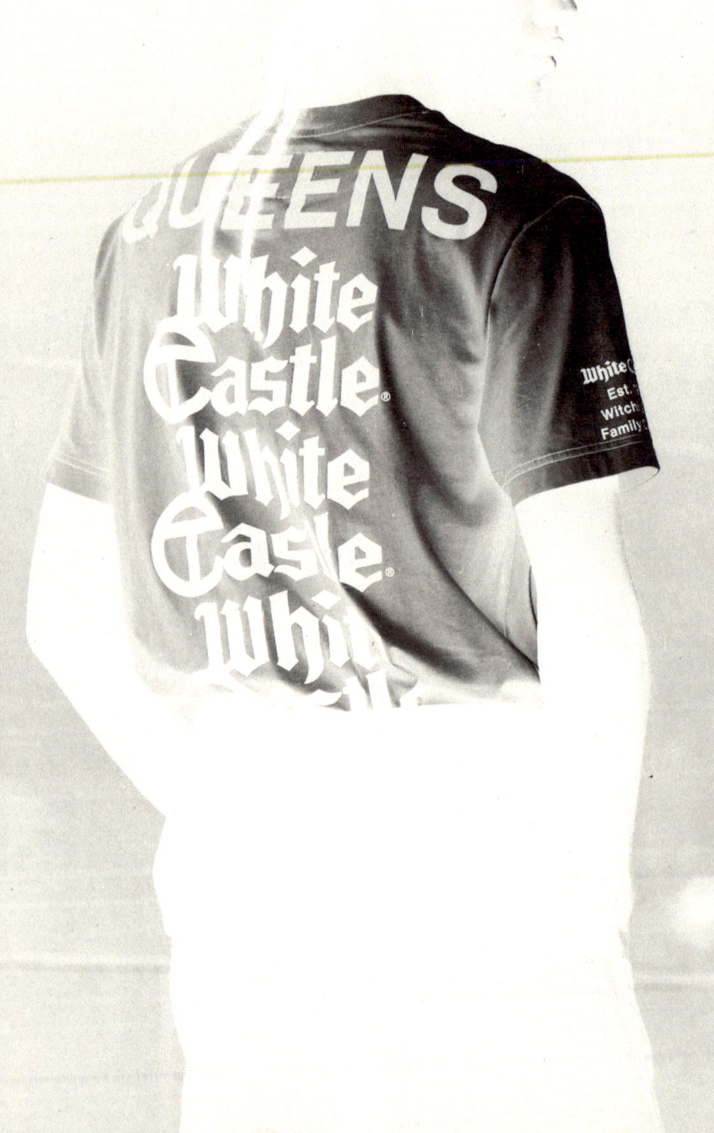
White
Castle®
White
Castle®

And so, with the Berlin Biennale, the ads themselves imply that it's a hegemonic attitude, so you automatically identify with it. You can say something outrageous, but you've already created this empathic process. Us saying "I want to die with nature, not become her manager," that is actually something people can identify with, but it is barred from the realm of annunciation. However, if it's presented in the right way, with the right kind of symbols of authority and the right conventions, then it becomes something much more digestible.

BS: Do you find it difficult to maintain this spirit of illegitimacy as you work with more corporate or mainstream collaborators, or as your projects find more commercial success?

BR: When it comes to Telfar in particular, it has become this really successful company, but in fact, it's actually not a company. That's not what's driving it, it's not something which is exchangeable or comparable. That has a real effect on us when it comes to things like investment. I don't think we can take on investment. Besides not wanting to, it would destroy the thing that it is; it's just not how we operate. Even if we were to make more money, the question would be, "Well, what do we want? Is there some car we want, is there some house…but under what city and what government?" The money isn't good for much. But the company gives us autonomy over time and space which allows us to spend time with people we want, to make things with the people we want to work with. The basis of the company is a social prac-

p. 154: Telfar × White Castle collection. Photo: Jason Nocito

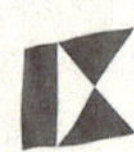
Berlin Biennale
für zeitgenössische Kunst
I want to die
with nature—
not become
her manager.
4.6.–18.9.2016

tice. We used to have to organize around shows, and now we have the autonomy to organize it in whatever way we want. Of course, we have to make money to buy more time, but at least the ratio of time and money is good. We used to be making clothes and were involved in these contracts where someone is taking a huge percentage of the money, and this was something you struggled to get. And musicians and directors and producers we talked to were all involved in similar oppressive contracts. But now we're able to make videos together, we've been able to make music together, we've been able to create enough space for us where no one is really interrupting the process. And what we're making is performing, because the audience is hungry for what we are making, and the audience is outrageously underserved.

> BS: I'd like to turn to the idea of Shanzhai. I think it relates to a very contemporary form of bootlegging, or perhaps operates in this middle ground between legitimacy and illegitimacy. You've worked with this idea in the form of the Shanzhai Biennial. I'm interested in how you've seen it evolve over the past few years, from something that was disparaged to something that is now embraced as a tactic for corporations.

BR: Any thoughts around Shanzhai should be organized around the material conditions under which it was created, which have to do with a racialized global capitalism. There is no other way to look at it.

p. 157: Banner for the IXth Berlin Biennale featuring text by Chris Krauss, creative direction Babak Radboy (2016)

China's entry into the world market was supposed to be eternally subjugated. Shanzhai is one instance, on a visual level, with some fun graphic consequences, where you can see that happening. It's the same thing that happens in a city where you have poor kids inventing a new cultural form, which then becomes consumed by a global creative complex. What happened in Shanzhai is there was an opportunity that was spotted within the code where the people who were empowered to produce luxury items couldn't do so in certain ways. So Dior, for example, could never act as a mass brand because it would go against its own logic. Could Dior sell a bag for $6,000 at one store and then sell a similar bag for $200 at a different store? I don't know. But Telfar says yes, you can do that. However, the psychology of Dior, the ability for it to reproduce its message, relies on so much violence, that it couldn't produce that dichotomy and complexity. Not to mention the larger regional, cultural monopoly it exists within. So these independent producers saw an opportunity in Dior that Dior could never exploit on a mass scale. It is appropriation. But not in the strict sense where one party is innocent and one is evil. All parties involved are appropriating to just exist in the same shitty world.

> BS: Is appropriation or bootlegging still a powerful tool today, in a culture where copying is very much at the core of everything we produce?

BR: The discourse for appropriation is in a way unuseful. We act like the solution is for people to stop appropriating, when really the solution is just to destroy the world. Whenever you are acting as the relay between two parties, you have to recognize you are betraying someone, and you need to make that choice before you start. Bootlegging is still a form of appropriation…it all is.

I think bootlegging needs to be expanded past its material manifestations and into the more conceptual forms that it's animating. That's where I see it becoming more about legitimacy. Nobody wants to say they're illegitimate, but in fact, that *is* what we should be doing—figuring out how something can be made less legitimate. Legitimacy is always about delegitimizing something else.

BS: Do you see illegitimacy as being connected to authenticity?

BR: Authenticity is an effect of illegitimacy. Legitimacy is related to violence. When you are bootlegging, when you are copying, when you are working illegitimately, you are refusing to rely on the violence that organizes the social space of annunciations.

Title page (p. 148): White Castle logo taken from the Telfar × White Castle collaboration, art directed by Babak Radboy

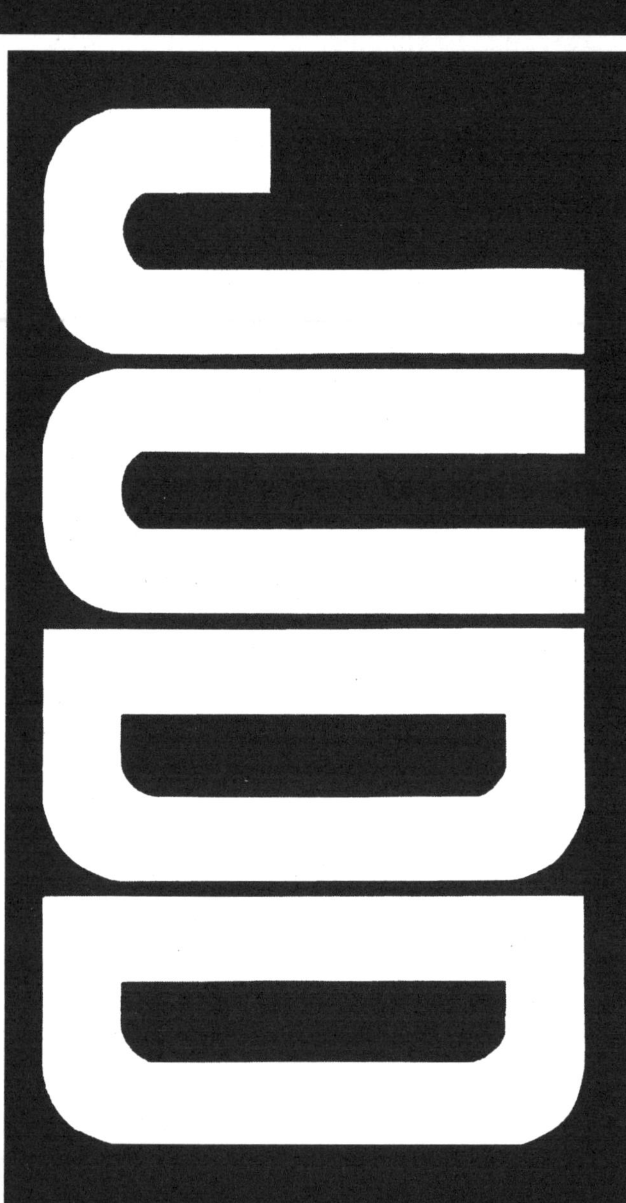

Matt Olson (MO)

Matt Olson is a Minneapolis-based artist and founder of the studio OOIEE (Office of Interior Establishing Exterior). Much of his work involves exploring obscure moments in the history of contemporary art, and transforming them in ways that feel both intimate and powerful. Running throughout Olson's work are notions of "in between," "bothness," "open practice," and, perhaps most importantly, "love." Each one (but especially the last) feel critical to understanding and embracing the idea of bootlegging. In a work that has long resonated with me, Olson recreates an iconic Donald Judd chair out of birdseed, which is then left outside and picked by birds, slowly over time, down to nothing. The piece is a reminder that ideas are "in the air," they are available for use by anyone, but eventually must be returned back to where they came from. Interview by Ben Schwartz (BS)

> BS: For me, bootlegs are inherently hard to define. Everyone I speak to has a different definition, idea, or perspective on the gesture. So I'd like to begin with a seemingly simple, but in reality very complex question: how would you define bootlegging?

MO: I guess if writing poetry is the act of embedding more meaning into words than we normally allow—by intentionally arranging and sometimes "misusing" words and their rules—and through that, we end up with something more expansive.... I guess I'd say a bootleg moves like poetry. That spirit is one of the things I love about bootlegs, they're more about *expanding* something, than *authoring* something.

They're hard to define (like everything). I notice these phenomena too, that when I set out to define a word, it's easy to forget the actual goal is to develop a *space* of understanding. And I have this bad habit of thinking it's about *narrowing* and should feel inherently *reductive*. It even registers as sort of somatic I think, so it's a deep habit? But when I say it out loud, the idea of "shrinking" the way to understanding seems flawed. And what *actually* happens, the more I think about something, the "bigger" it gets. It's becoming *less* clear even as my understanding grows. And I think bootlegs do that too.

To some degree, I'm interested in the whole spectrum of related meanings around bootlegs. Even piracy, which seems straightforwardly about capitalism at first glance—but I'm *super* interested in the ways that people participate in misleading themselves and others with stories and symbols. Appropriation is/was more high art but maybe recently is being used more in the socio-cultural identity politics realm? Also fascinating. There's the kind of bootleg that is very fashionable "now"—mostly T-shirts and clothes, with "brand" being the most common location for... play or whatever it is. But I'm most interested in the broader and more foundational questions about the nature of separateness in general. Are things separate from me? Do ideas "belong" to people? Can we really own things?

I think OOIEE's work is related for sure and, initially, I actually used the term bootleg sometimes because people wanted to call it "appropriation," which didn't feel right. I've always described our work as being "related to art and design" and often call our version of bootlegging "using art history as a material." I still feel that.

Some of these themes and attitudes have been moving me around all my life, but I guess in terms of "work," I can trace it back to 2008. Initially it involved seeing photos of work by people like Scott Burton and Guy de Cointet on the internet and free from much context, and I was just totally lit up by them. I felt like I had to respond. I was seeing photos on blogs and something was happening, building up and... I couldn't *not* move with it. I was also starting to see, feel, and consider it all through the lens of Sturtevant, who's been especially important for me. By doing the work, I could become it.

The studio started making some Scott Burton chairs in plywood and soon we were attempting to make the sets of Guy de Cointet performances from the 1970s out of MDF. I could totally go off about it all… The de Cointet sets didn't exist outside of photos—no one had kept the objects—so in a way it felt like we were rescuing them or something? Carrying them forward. Extending them. Repeating them. There's just *so much* to say. Too much, really. There's always been such an aliveness in this space for me, and it feels like the projects come to get me as much as I "decide" to do them. I wasn't totally sure what I was doing. Almost just following some energy forward.

Later I started finding humility, poetics, positive uncertainty, anonymity, a new sort of access to things and ideas that are extremely charged. And it wasn't

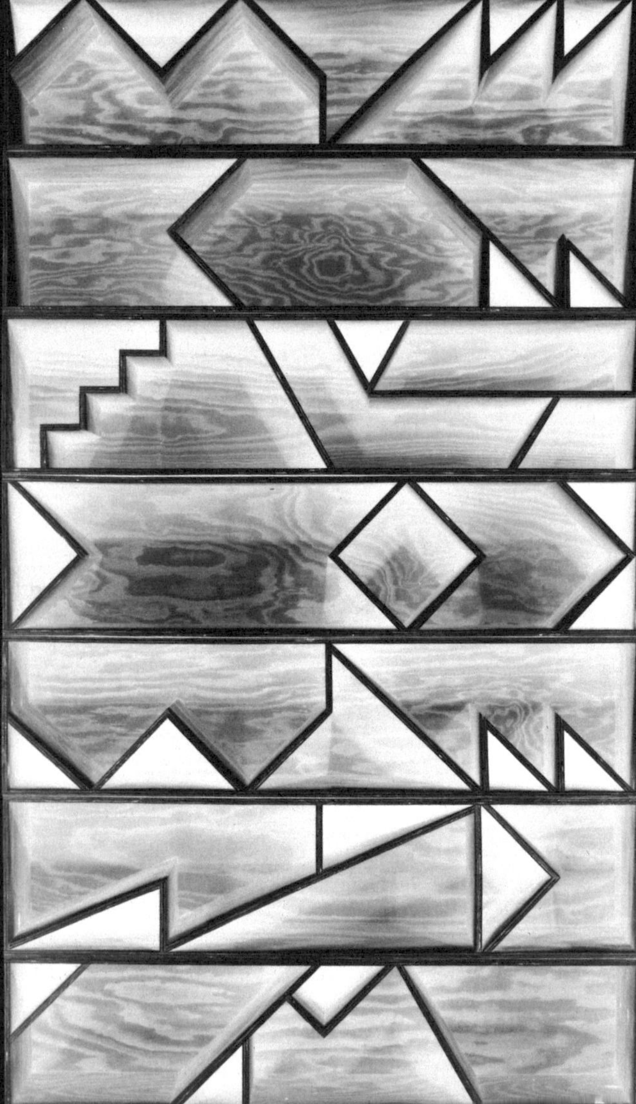

really meant to be "against authorship" in a binary sense, but I definitely wanted to run counter to it. Some sort of refusal of dislocation of those stories. A resistance to the notion of "individuation." I agree with Fred Moten who said individuation is a) impossible and b) undesirable. The story of authorship is a part of what holds this whole tired and boring set of language/thought systems together. Stories of academic and institutional power and historical framing, ownership, ego, self-centeredness.

What I'm interested in is love. I like to fall in love with things and then *move* with them. I don't know for sure where that delivers us, or me, but that's why I like it. It's a form of care. I refuse to let the story of authorship and separateness give shape to the things I love. I love motion. I think bootlegs are in motion.

> BS: I recently watched the film *Certified Copy*, where the main character writes a book about the value of a copy. He states that the power of a copy is in its ability to bring us closer to an original. I'm interested in how this might relate to your practice. Is there a desire to become closer or engage in a more intimate way with art history? How does your relationship with a subject like Scott Burton or Donald Judd change after "bootlegging" one of their pieces?

MO: I watched this movie on your recommendation, I liked it! But I don't really believe in the story of "the original"—I mean it sorta lives in me by habit, but I can usually see past it. I remember writing songs

p. 164: RO/LU, *Seven Stacked Benches (after shelves)* (2012)

in my twenties. I was in a band and occasionally we'd devolve into an argument about who wrote what part. It was always so embarrassing and awkward. Unnatural. I knew deeply it was wrong. But at the time I just played along. It's hard not to? I still play along sometimes. It's messy. It's ego.

If you start unpacking all the different stories humans have memorized—and repeat—about authorship, property, originality, separateness, power, economics, capitalism, culture, status, hierarchy, institutional/academic/corporate authority—layers and layers—it all becomes pretty incoherent. That doesn't bother me though, I don't really wanna solve anything about that. I just wanna be in it.

I've told this story before about getting frustrated while we were building a Guy de Cointet set. Many of the early projects were self-initiated and unfunded so, no money and lots of hours, and even though I wanna resist that type of story—the money/time story—it has a way of finding its way in. Anyway, in a moment of frustration and fear at the studio, questioning the whole project I hollered out "Why in the fuck are we even doing this?" And Sammie Warren—who is amazing—said "We're learning from these things in ways that no one could teach us." I've never really stopped feeling that. I mean, *that's* the work. I love objects and ideas but it's the resulting motion(s)—how *we're* changed—how we become the things, people and ideas we love. Transformation is the result. What is the entropy of love?

BS: I like the idea that a bootleg might tell us more about a subject than an original. How does that idea resonate with you?

MO: I led a workshop at Cranbrook a few years ago. I have these photos of a bunch of Anthony Caro sculptures sitting outside, casually, in a rough gravel space. I loved them immediately when I saw them. Like, deeply. Electric. Can't explain it. More than his other work. Through some research, I learned this was a gravel parking area outside his studio when he taught at Bennington College and that the sculptures weren't really finished. So he's like this art history sculpture giant and here are all these objects which he may or may not have thought were sculptures. He wasn't famous yet. So the idea and act of making them and showing them—becoming them—not as *our* work or anyone's work, but as something we love that, through action, has the power to temporarily dissolve the barriers of stories. Not something to be "figured out" but as something we do.

Anyway, the workshop began with us reading five texts: "Pierre Menard, Author of The Quixote," Jorge Luis Borges, "Art Which Can't Be Art," Allan Kaprow, "I (Not Love) Information" and "Take Care" by Anthony Huberman, "Compatibility Mode," Seth Price (though thinking back, I wish I'd chosen "Decor Holes" by Seth Price… that would have been so much better!).

The whole point I guess was to examine the different stories we tell ourselves, all these layers of "thought and memory" we frame with, and then compare it to the experience we have in the lived realm. For me, they don't really match up. And I don't think that's bad, I think it's good. We should remember and accept this more frequently. The map is not the territory. Is an unfinished Anthony Caro piece an Anthony Caro? And, oddly, I gotta say, there's this Flaming Lips lyric that keeps coming to mind: "we were perplexed, finding the needle, in the needle's disguise."

> BS: In your piece at the Aspen Art Museum, you used textiles with the sky printed on them to cover various works of art in the institution. In a lecture at Sci-Arc you spoke about conversations with artists asking for permission to cover their work. While I know you meant quite literally covering the work with textiles, I also think about "covering" in the sense of a cover song. Could you view these sky forms as OOIEE "cover songs" or "cover pieces?" Does the idea of "covering" mean something different than "bootlegging"?

MO: The artists in Aspen were all asked, not really for permission, but more just to check in. They were all into it. Anna Sew Hoy did a performance with the textile which, a person could say, brought it even further into her work or her into our work. The piece, which was called *No Separation*, did a lot of different things. Man, there's just so much I love about what happened with that. Those textiles were also made into wearable garments and people could check them out and wear them around town, on the slopes, et cetera. So the piece left the museum and encountered people who didn't know what it was. There's an anonymity and humility to that which is really exciting.

The Open Field residency at the Walker Art Center in 2012, 'When Does Something Become Something Else (The Apparent Is the Bridge To the Real),' has some similar stories and also involved checking in with like 25 artists to let them know we were going to be remaking *their* work, with the public and then leaving the pieces outside on stages. Art performing art. A few people in the institution were *really* sensitive about the project—it felt like human fear/power stuff and was really fascinating and also made me feel kinda sick—but, all the artists or estates were good and a couple were actually excited we were doing it. Felix Gonzalez-Torres estate was into it and requested documentation. We remade *WAR IS OVER!* by John and Yoko—the public got a screen printing class and hundreds were made—Yoko wrote and thanked me. Those experiences have been super profound and freeing.

It's interesting how much music comes up as part of all this. I definitely see the "cover" connection in songs. I like that too because with a cover song, it's so clear that they are the same thing *and* completely different. I get even more excited thinking that maybe someone is singing along to a cover that they might not know is a cover, and they're laughing (or crying or spacing out or some combination) getting a few of the words wrong and also remembering something all while they're driving to GPS directions and they have a rock in their shoe… and on and on… that's a glimpse of what humanness is also like for me. That's a kind of music in itself.

> BS: You often speak about the idea of "in betweenness." A bootleg seems to operate in this way, somewhere in between an original and reproduction. What effect does this idea have on how we understand bootlegs? In

pp. 170–171: OOIEE, Installation view of the exhibition 'There's No Separation' at Aspen Art Museum (2016)

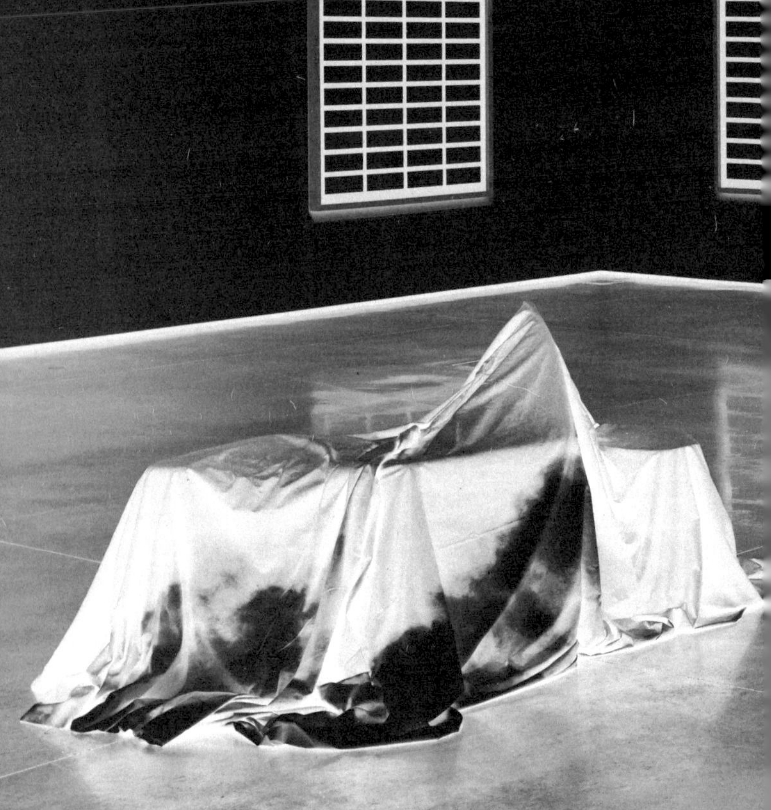

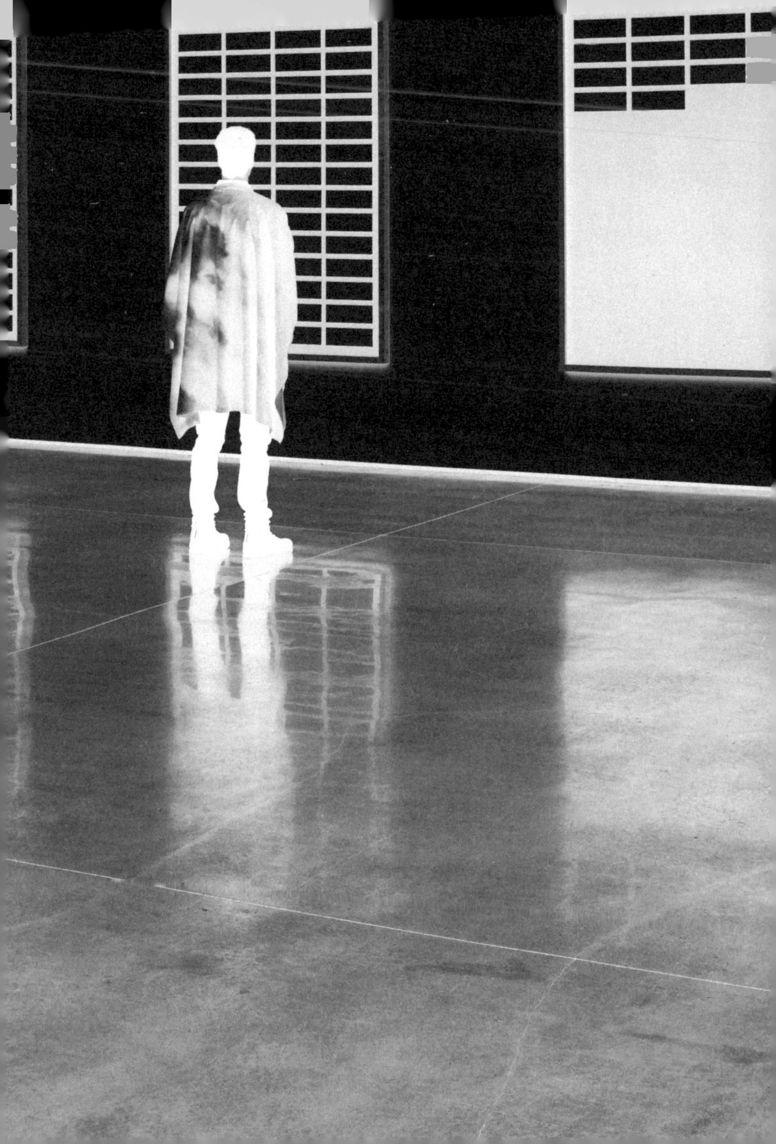

what way does this give a bootleg its sense of magic?

MO: Maybe I think everything is in between everything? Lately I prefer "bothness"... similar. But I have such a habit of falling into the trance of language, which often leads to the pattern of separateness as a way of thinking and perceiving. And I think the nature of reality is really *very* different. The truth of things is much more about interdependence and interconnectedness. Collage and aliveness. I think that's where the magic lives... in the potential. The not knowing.

To go further with the music space, I love the phenomenon of headphone bleed. I learned about it when I was first recording music in a studio. When you record a separate guitar track, for instance, you can always hear the faint trace of the drums which you played along with in the result. Most recording engineers work to hide or minimize it but it's there. For me, that's a good example of "bothness." And when you sit by someone on the train and you can hear the music someone is listening to... I like that kind of thing. It's the same song I'm hearing, same recording, but it's not the same as the person with the headphones on. It's an experience not a thought. The magicness of anything is about love and love naturally expands. Bootlegs for sure!

BS: I'm interested in the work you make and its relationship to translation. How do you think about the material shifts that take place in your work? What happens when drawings from Guy de Cointet become directions or furniture? How does a Burton chair change when it is made from plywood?

What does it communicate differently, more clearly, or maybe even incorrectly?

MO: The answer for me is still "I don't really know." But I do love translation. It's built of motion, transformation and all its entropies. And again my interest is in expansiveness. I notice when I'm communicating with someone, and English isn't totally natural to them, the "mistakes" we make speaking with each other don't hinder my understanding at all, they tend to make it bigger. It feels better and I listen deeper. And I love this Jacques Lacan idea that "language isn't meant to inform, but to evoke." And I mean, that's very much at the heart of all this for me, too.

I believe the Lakota language is/was kept small. One thing that can cause: a person needs to bring things to life in their mind more contextually... so, less language can bring something else to life. This sort of operation is the essence of art?

For me, I don't know, it's all capable of being material. Art history. Identity. Habit. Prayer. Love. Plywood LOL. My experience of reacting to these things and making them is itself a material. The result—I don't really like that word though—the outcomes... I guess there's just an increased intimacy with it all. An increased intimacy with the world.

The ideas, the objects, the stories, the changes… and it's very much a lived thing.

BS: I am interested in the relationship between a bootleg and a community. Especially bootlegging niche ideas or subjects and how they might act as talismans or totems for a particular group of people. I think about this in relation to the blog community

> that you were an active member of. Could you talk about this idea and how you developed a community around your practice?

MO: I really miss blogs. There's this story of these Dutch social scientists who studied the Deadheads who toured with the Grateful Dead—and btw, Dead bootlegs are a great example of a love community and economy—and they found that Deadheads who spent this fairly small amount of time together on the road were "better friends" with each other—by the measures that social scientists use to measure these things—than people they spent much more time with and had deeper connections to, like coworkers and neighbors. Which for me points to the idea that... I mean, it almost sounds naively simple but, when we're organizing our reality around something we love, there are different channels available and open.

I think the resulting entropy of love around music, or cultural objects and ideas... it's always naturally happening. It loves to happen. It's like trees!

> BS: You speak about ideas being "in the air," and for me, this translates to a very open notion of authorship. What are your thoughts on ownership? Is authorship important to you?

MO: This really weird thing happened in 2012. We made a project called *Settee × Three after Burton Photo (Public/Private/Secret)* which was three different versions of a Burton piece. One was poured concrete, installed on the street in front of a gallery called Sit & Read in Brooklyn. We'd been planning the piece for about a year and then the week before we did it,

Oscar Tuazon did a concrete Burton chair in a show in Milan. I couldn't believe it. Literally the same week! What are the odds? At first I was bummed. There were a lot of competing stories available in me. Luckily a friend encouraged me to see how amazing and weird and magical it was. It led to some good exchanges with Oscar. I remember discussing this idea that something in the work demands that it's remade. That aliveness still interests me. That aliveness exists in the world… we're part of that, not separate from it.I'm not really against authorship as a thing? I just don't like what it does to me when I'm believing in it.

> BS: I'm curious if you see bootlegging as something subversive? Can a bootleg be an expression of love and betrayal simultaneously? Are you interested in "betraying" anything with your work?

MO: It's probably subversive to/for many people. I guess it sorta is to me? Maybe in certain circumstances we allow a bootleg to perform subversiveness? In one of the classes I teach, students are required to watch a talk Virgil Abloh gave at Harvard—it's a good talk for students—but there's a moment where he shows some images of Nike Off-White™ work (which are sorta bootleg like?) that haven't been released yet and he says something to give the impression that he's being sorta subversive or something but… c'mon, we know Nike was totally down with that. Sometimes the drunk performs the drunk as a way of continuing their drunkenness.

pp. 176–177: RO/LU, *Settee X Three (after BURTON photo, in Private, Public + Secret)* (2012)

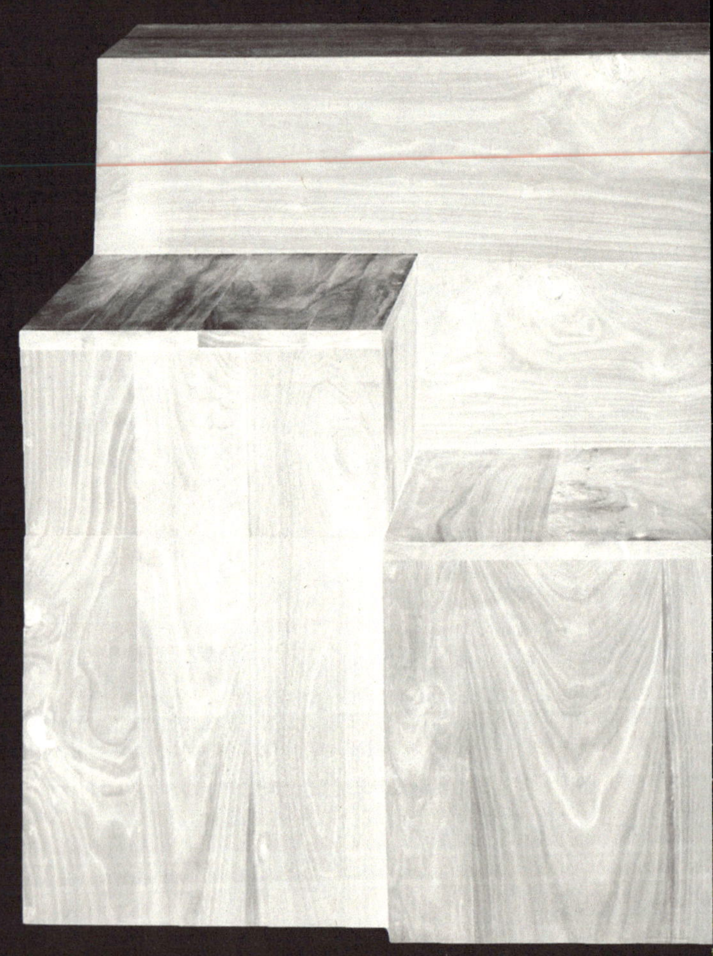

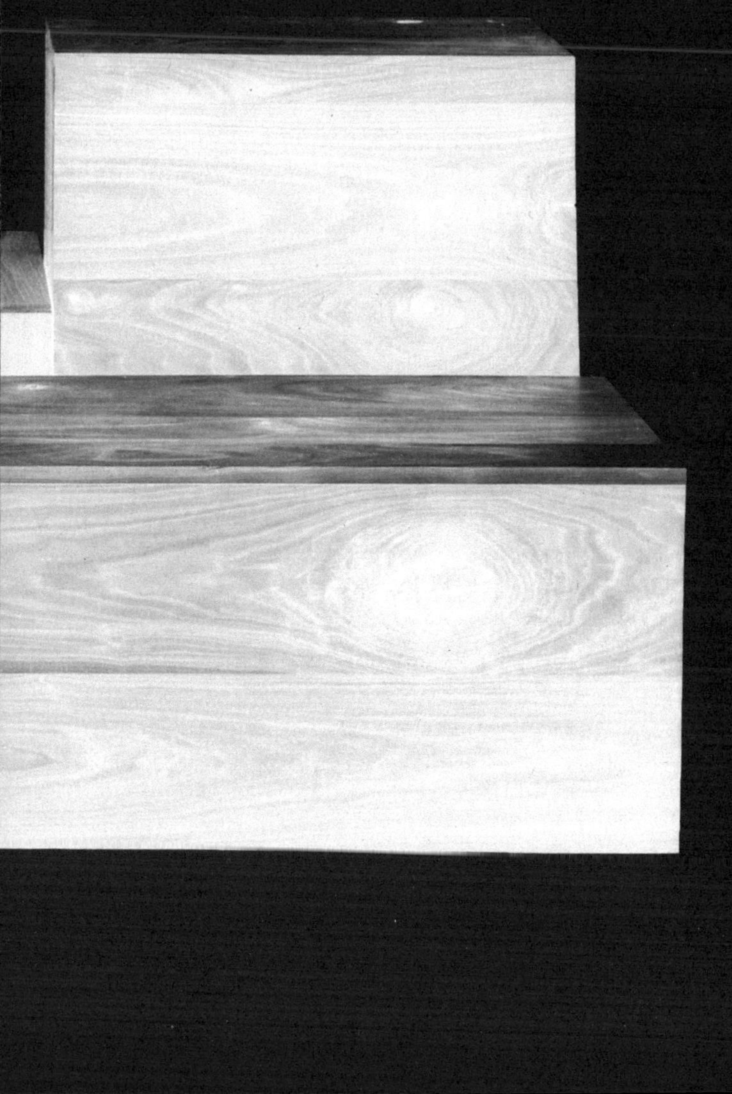

It's amazing that you bring the idea of "betrayal" into this too… it's not a word I would *ever* think of and there's a nice shock seeing it. It makes me happy. Simultaneous love and betrayal. I do like that. But I'd wanna add way more things a bootleg is also being at the same time. I think our belief in language and thinking is always betraying *us*.

BS: Love seems to be very much at the core of what you do. Could you expand on the relationship between bootlegging and love. I think specifically how bootlegging might relate to some of the complexities of love: understanding, acceptance, collaboration, ego, et cetera.

MO: I think the fact that all this work that I've done emerged through a garden design practice is maybe important to mention. I think the experience of designing something and then watching it change and grow… it's been instructive in ways that can't be articulated in language alone. We recently proposed remaking a garden by Fischli/Weiss. A bootleg garden. I really hope that comes to life! Love is hard to talk about. Even harder to write about. I know what it means to me, usually.

I guess my experience growing up in capitalism (which is a force that figures into all this and is *so* present we often don't see it), I learned a lot of stories about life and separateness and individuation that turned out to be destructive and limiting… and I think a lot of those stories are fueled by fear (disease) and I speak of love as something we don't really understand yet but, it's a direction we need to go in, together. It's an attitude. It's a way of seeing the world. When we remake a piece, we're extending it, we're joining it, we're accompanying it... it is becoming us and we're becoming it.

And increasingly, I've liked the word/concept "joining" as a way to point toward all this. I've been making stuff lately, like, an acapella recording of a Japanese women's choir from the 1970s and phonetically learning the sounds and then adding my voice to the recording. Quietly and with humility. Or recording my voice speaking *with* Susan Sontag or James Baldwin. I see it as "joining." I'm joining it and it's joining me. Is that a bootleg?

I was into the Dead in college, mostly for the drugs, but I was changed by it all. And maybe I get the most excited about the Grateful Dead tapes. This whole world emerged around the love of Grateful Dead performances. Taping was allowed. People shared freely. And love can be super generative.

I still have a sense of skepticism that any of this can be resolved or that there's any sort of arrival at an answer. And reading back my responses here... all the talk of love makes me uncomfortable in my brain, not my mind, which includes the brain. But whenever I feel skeptical or anxious about an idea I'm excited about, I like to remember that one of my favorite people says "being skeptical is like choosing immobility as your primary mode of travel."

Title page (p. 160): Graphic from a 1963 Donald Judd exhibition poster from Green Gallery, New York

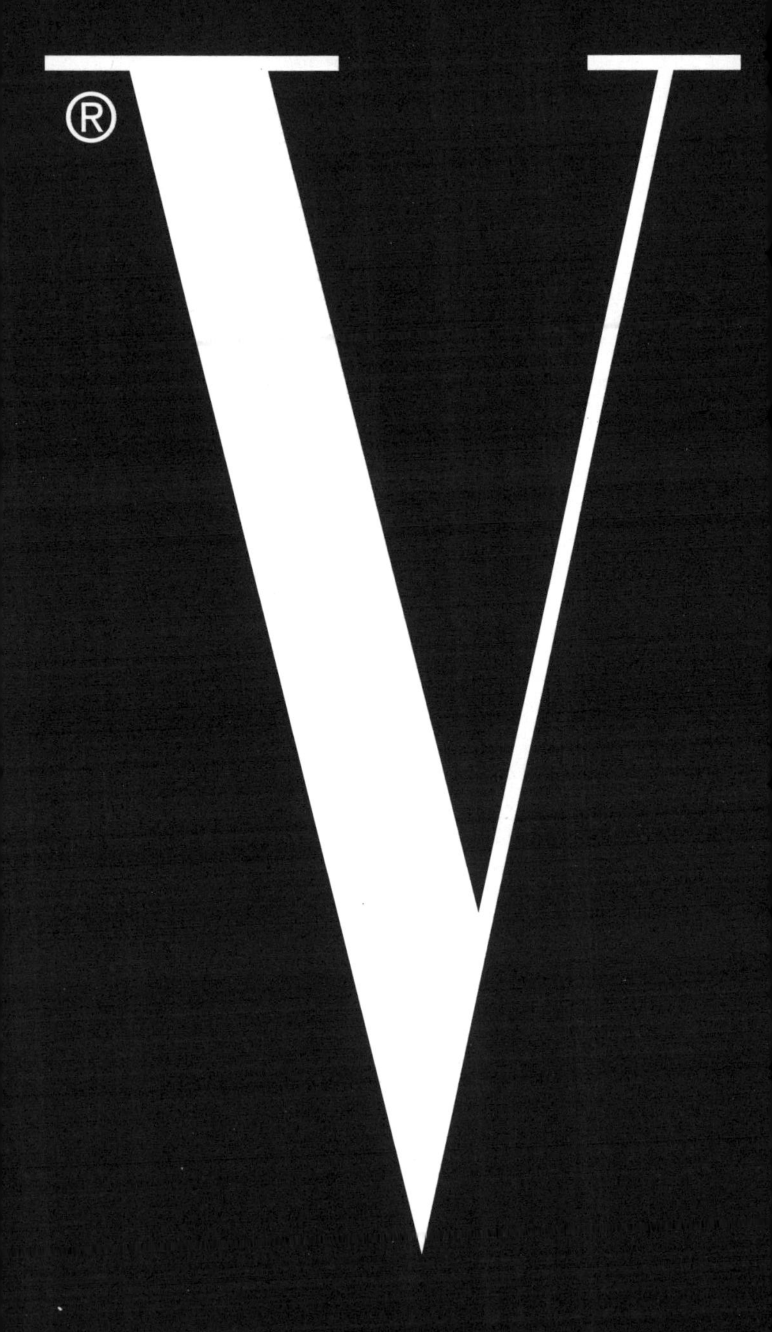

A March Issue, Line Arngaard (LA) & Sonia Oet (SO)

A March Issue is a collaborative publication from graphic designer Line Arngaard and fashion researcher Sonia Oet, realized in spring 2018. The project is a page-by-page recreation of the March 2018 issue of *Vogue* magazine, reproducing every single photoshoot and ad using their friends, classmates, and teachers for models and a white T-shirt and blue jeans to replace each featured "look." Flipping through *A March Issue* is both humorous and chilling. The seductive gazes, blowing hair, poses, and layouts feel hyper-familiar, but for Arngaard and Oet to remake 372 pages of high-fashion editorial, rough decisions and humorous compromises had to be made. The result is *just different enough* to become its very own thing. The white T-shirts and blue jeans function as visual placeholders, the repetition becomes almost scientific and visualizes the amount of fashion the industry produces. How much is left when the fashion is removed from fashion is fascinating—and perhaps reveals more than the clothes themselves. Interview by Marie Hoejlund (MH).

MH: What does bootlegging mean to you? How has working on *A March Issue* impacted your understanding of the gesture?

LA/SO: Over the course of the project, our understanding of the word bootlegging has changed a lot. Instead of seeing it as a lesser version or reproduction of an object or concept—a copy to be sold at a cheaper price—we have come to view it as a method of researching and getting to know an original.

The reason our understanding and use of the term has shifted was that we found ourselves becoming "bootleggers" in our own right. When we graduated from the Gerrit Rietveld Academie in Amsterdam—Line from graphic design and Sonia from fashion—we had been working together to come up with a concept for a publication about the "white T-shirt and blue jeans" look as both an archetype of modern clothing and a method of choice reduction. At one of these sessions we had a *Vogue* magazine in our hands, and as a joke we started talking about how the magazine would change—what it would mean—if every model in every photo was wearing the same outfit. This passing thought accelerated into reality, and before long we were in the middle of bootlegging *Vogue*. Our prior relationship to the concept of the bootleg was completely changed by this project. We did not remake the magazine for any commercial reason, but because we wanted to subvert its content—to simply take it apart, alter some elements, and put it back together. In this way, we entered the world of the knockoff: the world of hijacking, copying, reinterpreting, re-making, translating, and appropriating.

MH: Flipping through the pages of *Vogue* side-by-side with *A March Issue* is a mesmerizing experience. Can you talk about putting the project together?

LA/SO: The idea of bootlegging the magazine came out of discussions we had been having about the pace of fashion, the stress it produces, and the urgency of taking a step away from it. We started by trying to understand why we felt a need to talk about "fashion detoxing" and "choice reduction" in the first place.

One factor that we could both easily relate to was the impact of mainstream fashion publications like *Vogue*. We both felt alienated by the portrayal of people and the one-sided approach to fashion that these kinds of magazines represent. We started wondering: what's left if you take away the fashion from a fashion magazine?

In the beginning of the process, we went through the entire original *Vogue*, page by page, element by element, trying to understand the underlying structures, the poses, the typography, and the visual language. We had to get to know every detail of the magazine in order to then be able to flip it and find an alternative version. Once accustomed with the magazine, we started to define strategies for translating all these elements. For example, we planned to reshoot all the images with everyone wearing the same "default" outfit, distorting logos using Photoshop's "Content-Aware" tool and covering up bags, shoes, and cosmetics with T-shirts.

We had the first photoshoot in mid-March 2018, and over the next few months we had photoshoots almost every day—right up until the beginning of June, when we had to send the magazine to print. It was a huge collaborative effort involving 22 dedicated photography students and hundreds of models.

The headlines and the cover for the magazine were made in collaboration with a classmate, graphic designer Robert Finkei, who applied a method he had developed for splitting up and reorganizing images to the typography of the magazine [the effect is garbled blocks of type that retain qualities making them recognizable as letterforms, yet are entirely illegible]. For the magazine's body text, programmer Bjørn Karmann helped us to develop a simple software application that could reorganize the existing text of the magazine alphabetically, so that the text on every page contains exactly the same words, but in a different order.

After a whirlwind production process, the magazine arrived back from the printer and we were somewhat surprised to see how much it was still a fashion magazine even without all the flashy garments. But maybe that's the thing about bootlegs: by the time something has been changed just enough to feel different, it's not a bootleg anymore.

MH: How do you relate concepts like appropriation or copying with bootlegging? Is it important to differentiate between them?

LA/SO: It's difficult to point out the exact differences between these terms. We think that all of them could be used to describe projects like *A March Issue*. One way to look at it would be that, in our case, the bootleg is the object—it's the magazine you can hold next to its original in order to feel that the two are somehow the same, but are also different. For us, copying and appropriating are the methods that were used in the process of making it. For example, every image in *A March Issue* is an appropriation of the original. We didn't seek to make perfect 1:1 translations but instead sought to subvert the original and to offer a different perspective. Of course, the copying and appropriation of the images in the magazine was very much influenced by our surroundings: Who can model? Who can take the picture? Where can we do it? It's probably the case that many bootlegs are born like this: making use of whatever is around. Still, it was important to us to constantly relate back to the original *Vogue* by staying as close to the content, poses, and material choices as possible.

> MH: Irony seems to play a strong role in fashion bootlegs. I'm curious about what role irony played in concepting and creating *A March Issue*?

LA/SO: One of our mentors during the project, graphic designer Bart de Baets, said to us: "When I tell people about this project, I say that it's like the most elaborate joke ever." At the time this freaked us out a bit. Were we just executing a gigantic joke? Eventually, comments such as this made us realize that humor and irony are essential parts of the project and an effective way to question and challenge the original. We came to embrace it rather than discard it, and found that it was a useful tool for critical reflection.

pp. 186–187, 190–191, 194–195: March issue of *Vogue* magazine (2018)
pp. 188–189, 192–193, 196–197: Line Arngaard, Sonia Oet, *A March Issue* (2018)
Title page (p. 180): "V" from the Vogue logo

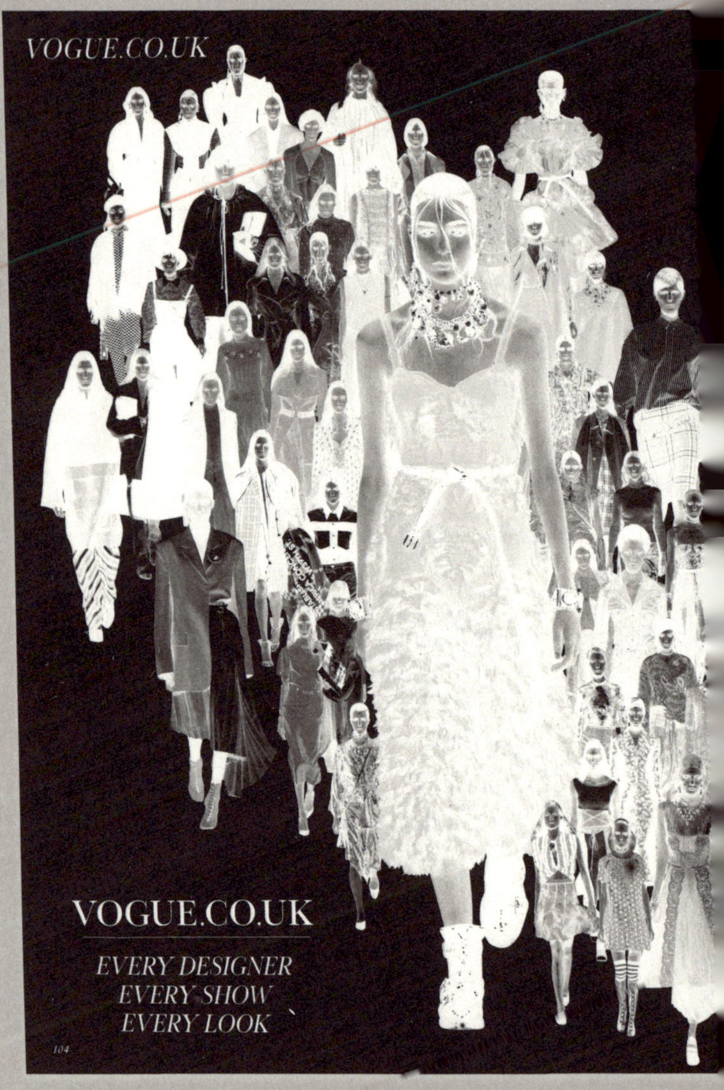
VOGUE.CO.UK
VOGUE.CO.UK
EVERY DESIGNER
EVERY SHOW
EVERY LOOK
104

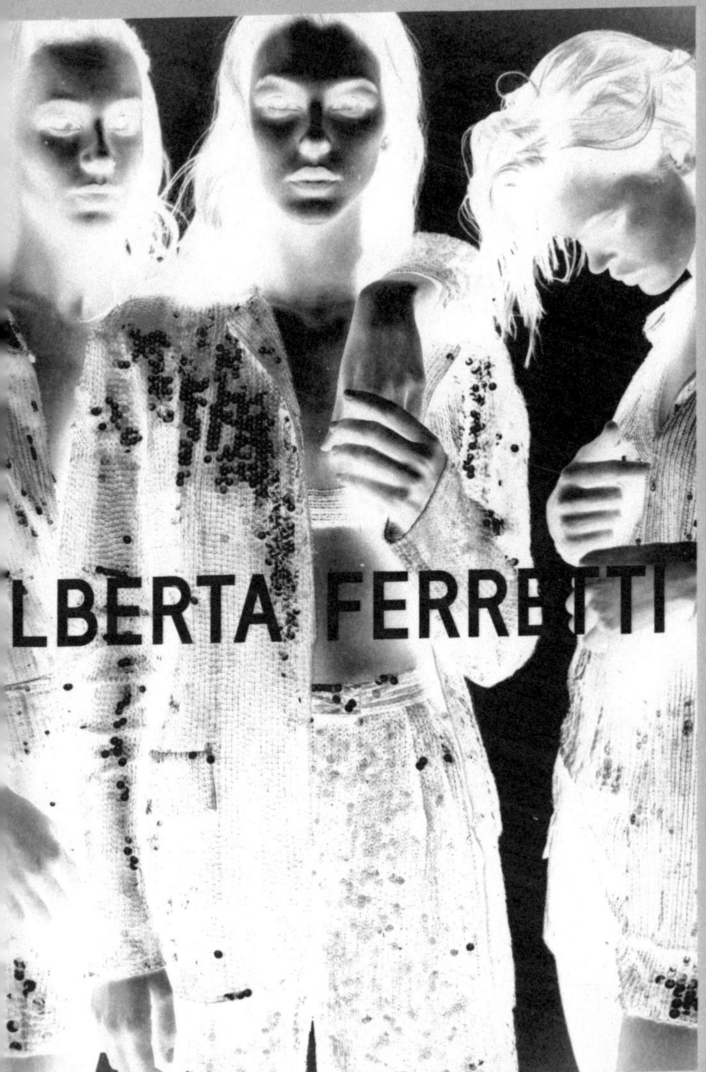
LBERTA FERRETTI

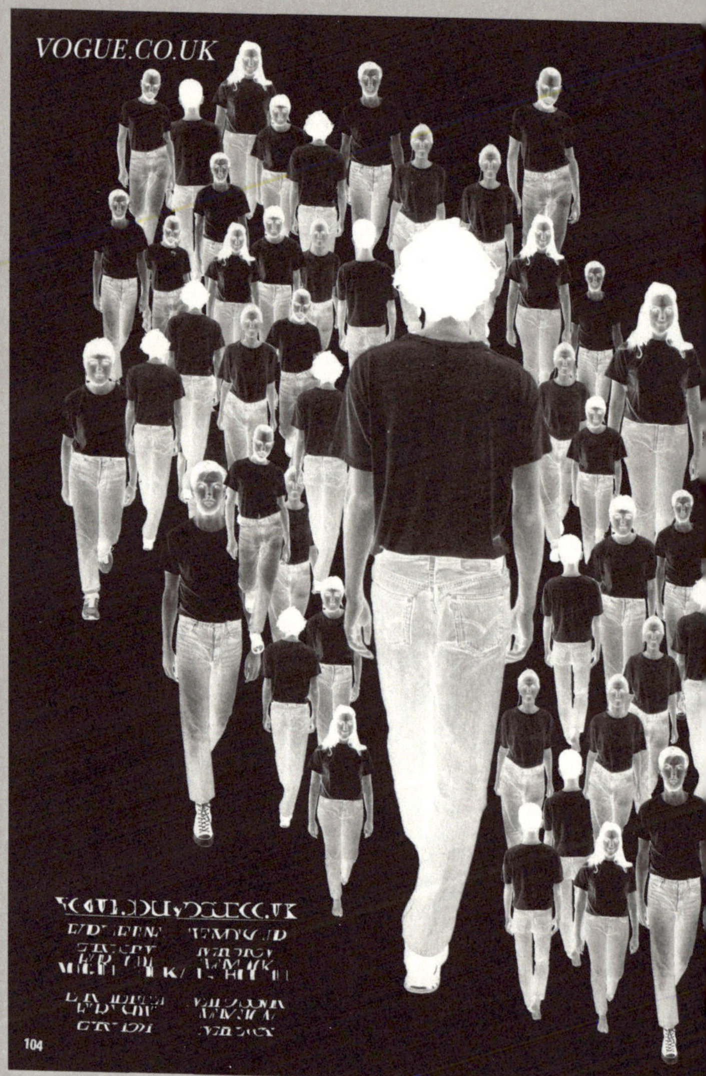
VOGUE.CO.UK
104

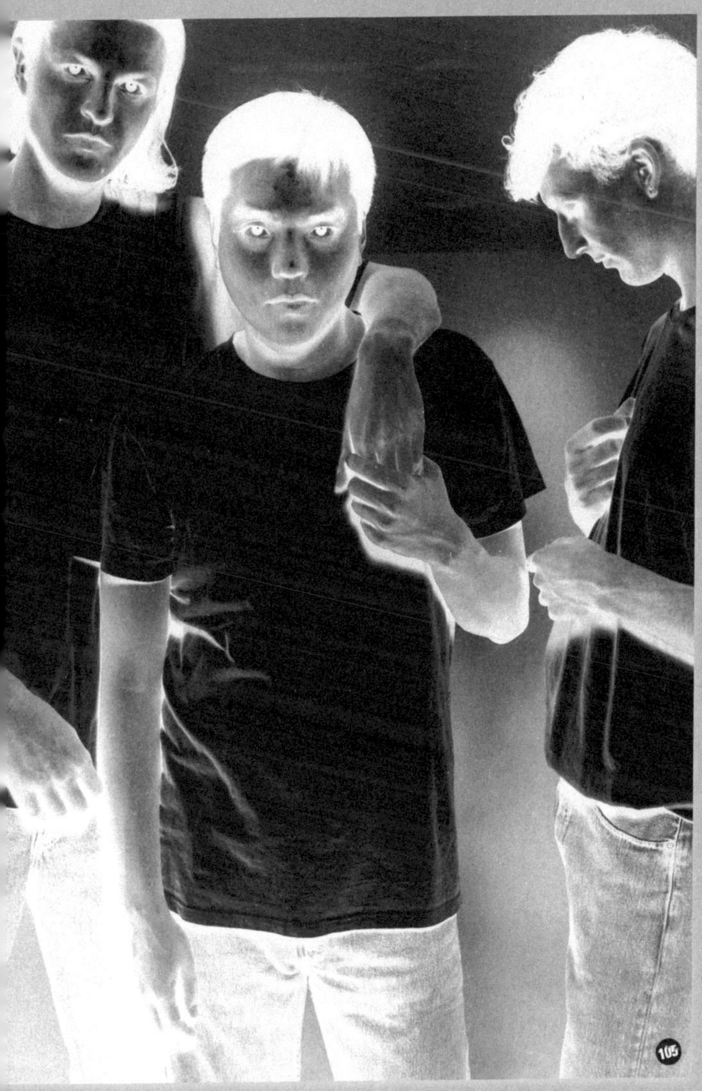
105

Designer Profile

THEODOOR FRITZ

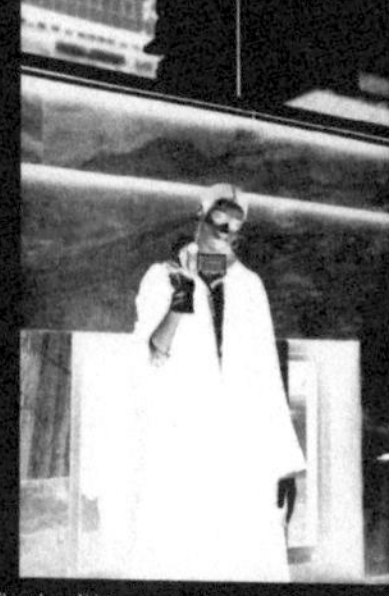

Theodoor Fritz was established 2014, with a strong focus on the making and design of fashion gloves for bicycle and scooters. The gloves are each handmade with luxurious leather and wool lining. They use mostly recycled and gently renewed leather. Their future collections plan to include embellished jewellery on the gloves, as part of the further development of the product line. Each pair are one-offs, and the designs are mostly focused on materials used. Visit theodoorfritz.wixsite.com to shop their collections.

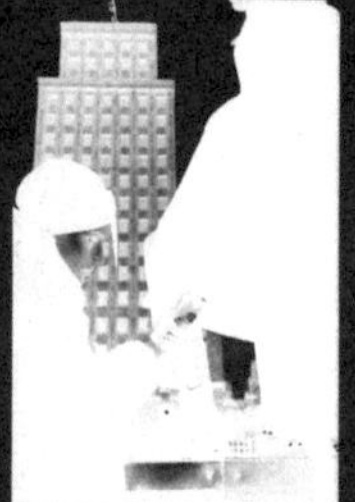

ANALOGIAS

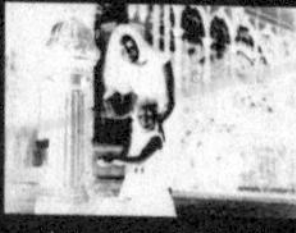

With original designs exclusive sustainable fabrics,high end manufacturing. Analogias offers the opportunity for mothers and daughters to enjoy fashion together or separately.The collections are inspired by blend of avant-garde and tradition to create a unique wardrobe both feminine and elegant for woman and to allow the little ones to shine like mamma without losing the lightness proper to the childhood. Analogias pays attention to details and innovation. Discover the collection on www.analogiascouture.com and Instagram @analogiasofficial

CLARA IN WONDE

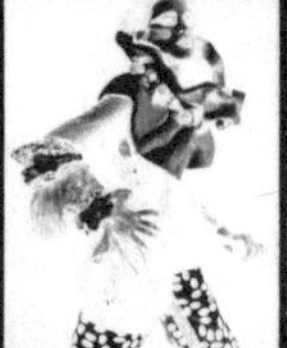

www.clarainwonderland.com

GABRISADESIGN

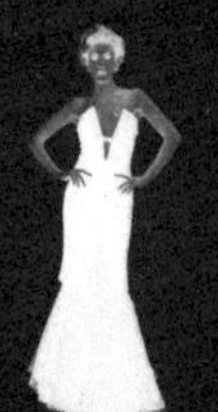

An essential style that sculpts the body. GabrisaDesign has a double soul: a metropolitan and elegant look, suitable for the modern woman who knows how to be romantic but also daring. The brand produces a woman collection, accessories and a small capsule for men with shirts and ties. Great care is dedicated to the creation of clothes, entirely handmade and combining different materials and fabrics that transform these clothes into true masterpieces of tailoring, emphasizing that exclusivity is the real hallmark. Visit www.gabrisadesign.com

ALBAETEZ

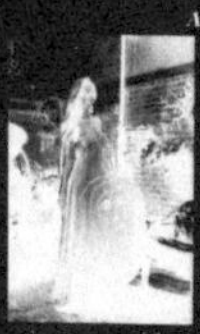

Since 2009 Sahar Etezadzadeh has been active in designing women's clothing and accessories and has participated in several workshops and exhibitions in Italy and Iran. Her designs have been shown on dedabo.blogspot.com She took part at L.U.N.A Lab Store exhibition and cooperated with La Boheme clothing store in Bolonga. Her style is innovative expressing individuality, uniqueness, and femininity with inspiration from eastern culture and the traditional elements. Albaetez was found in 2015 aiming to design clothes for women who are confident. Visit www.albaetez.com for more information.

KAHVARAH

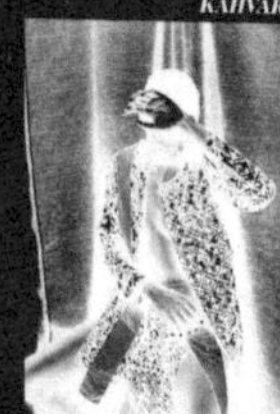

CYCLADES

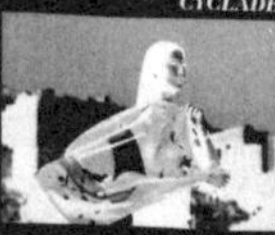

Cyclades is a London based luxury accessories label founded in 2017 by third generation artist and designer: Leto Lama. Cyclades accessories are made with the best fabrics and silks in Italy. The collection comprises of scarves, twillys, pareos, ties and pocket squares. The designs are all statement pieces, extremely stylish and unique which ensures why there is so much hype surrounding the brand. Cyclades will also be showcasing at Scoop London during 2018 fashion week. Visit www.cyclades.shop for more information. Photo credit: Katerina Avgerinou.

MELANIE JACQUELINE

Melanie Jacqueline is a clothing designer based in and originally from Newfoundland, Canada. Formerly a primary school teacher, MJ now designs and creates full time. Each handmade garment exhibits creativity and individuality: an explosion of vibrant colours and prints wrapped in timeless silhouettes. Focused on knitwear, the line is designed to be comfortable, wearable and versatile! Visit www.melaniejacqueline.com Instagram: @meljacdesigns Photo: ©Dave Howells

SHANTRESS SA

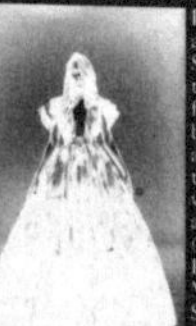

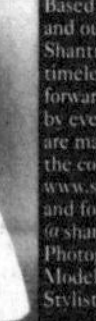

Based in
and our o
Shantress
timeless a
forward p
by everyd
are made
the collec
www.shan
and follow
@shantre
Photograp
Model: M
Stylist: K

Bound for Life.
Made for Travel.
Visit www.dolynbags.com
to place your order.

DOLYN

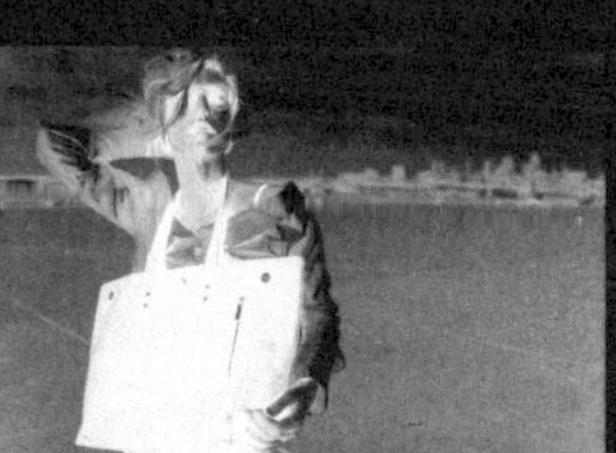

NCA STETCO

In 2016 Anca decided to put together her passion for fashion and design in order to create her own shoe collection. The philosophy of the brand is quite simple to understand: an experimental and innovative design made with materials such as exotic skins, special fabrics and the finest Italian leather and suede. Everything is 'made in Italy'. They create a selection of indispensable styles, flat and heels, that a ds for every aspect of h–r life. o.com for more information. @ancastetco_official

GYLLIUM

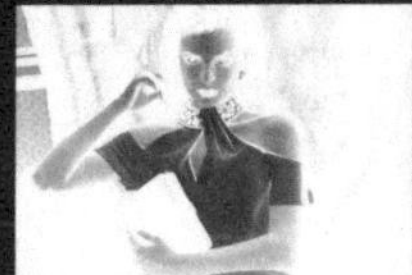

Gyllium specialises in luxury leather personal agendas and other premium accessories. Seen here is their agenda titled 'The Eternal: Winter' it is a classic item made from lustrous fur with monogram details. Visit their website www.gyllium.com or follow them on IG @gyllium

HELENA BAJAJ LARSEN

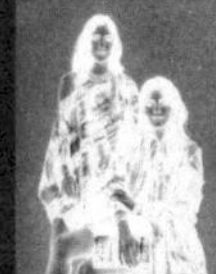

Franco-Indian-Norwegian designer Helena Bajaj Larsen's work encompasses minimalist silhouettes made from intricate hand-printed textiles. Every garment is one-of-a-kind as she personally paints each piece with a variety of textile dyes. The recent Parsons graduate hopes to take the idea of high-end craftsmanship and put a contemporary spin on it, blending modern art stokes with elegant evening-wear. She recently had her debut show at Lakme Fashion Week in Mumbai. Visit www.helenabajajlarsen.com for more information. Instagram @helena.bajaj.larsen

TISANS OF IQ

Artisans of IQ is an ethical luxury brand. Ileana Quinones the founder partners with highly skilled women artisans in Cambodia and Thailand to empower these women and handcraft one of a kind, bold statement jewellery and accessories. Her designs e independent pieces that are lelicate for women all over the nake a statement! This spring she lection into handbags for more w.artisansofiq.com STATEMENT

TAM ARA

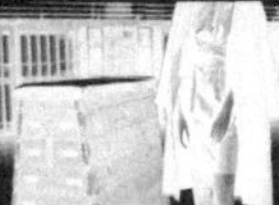

Welcome to the world of TAM ARA – a women's fashion label, created with the aim to change the way of thinking about quality and style of day and office wear. Material and comfort is essential thus they work only with natural fabrics. TAM ARA strives for sustainability: using local suppliers and by creating exclusive limited and timeless collections. They want clothes to express the personality of the wearer and wish to see more self-confident women on the streets of our cities. Visit www.tam-ara.cz and DARE TO BE YOURSELF.

THE VERYOUNG

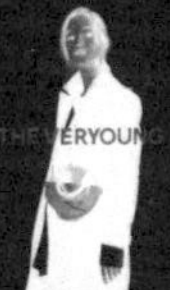

'the verYoung' is a fashion goods brand, rooted in experiences about fashion department in both home and foreign, directed by Se Young Eum who is a womenswear designer. With its own symbol and identity of this brand, she launched their first leather bag collection in 2017. They offer a variety of visual contents that represent their take on the concept of a certain lifestyle: the beautiful corruption of a slightly unstable and immature woman who is imperfect with the romantic fantasy of a little girl. Visit www.theveryoung.com

MIMINE AG

Mimine Ag is a luxury couture brand based in London. The brand pride itself on its attention to details, the carefully hand painted prints and the promise of exquisite haute couture techniques to always provide the best fit as well as perfectly tailored pieces. The Mimine Ag woman does not try to fit in the society she lives in. She rather makes her own rules. Visit www.mimineag.com

VOSRIO

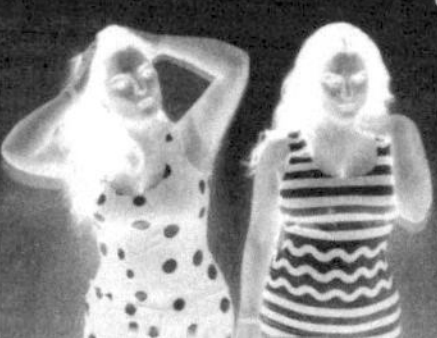

IAKOVOS NEKTARIO

VOSRIO

1977

is a lifestyle brand company. Collections are created and designed with cosmopolitan destinations as an influence. Their designs are simply contemporary and evoke stylish comfort. VOSRIO offers an exclusive line of accessories and home decor.

Available at www.vosrio.com email at info@vosrio.com
Follow on Instagram @originalvosrio and Facebook at www.facebook.com/Vosrio

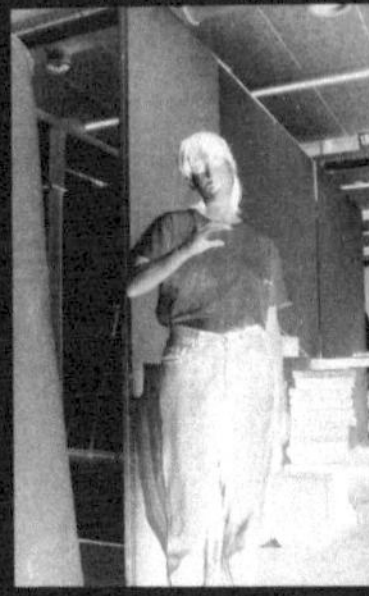

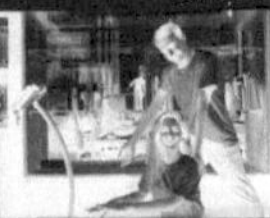

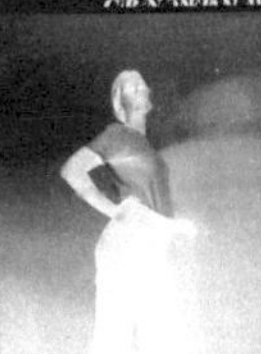

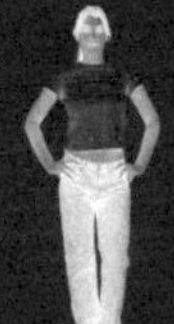

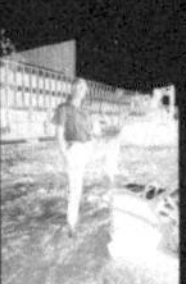

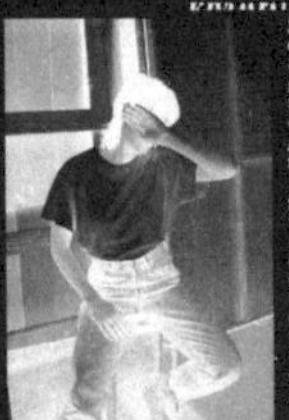

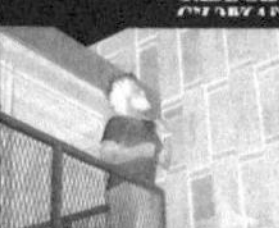

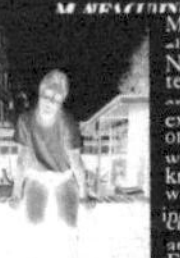

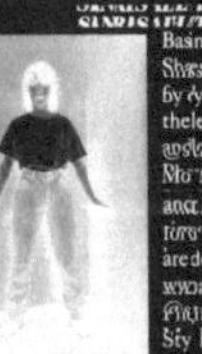

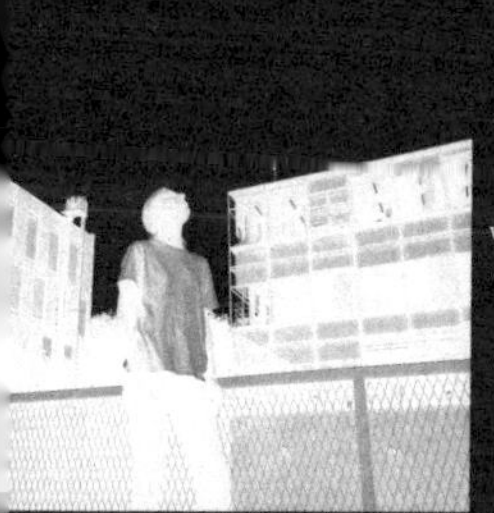

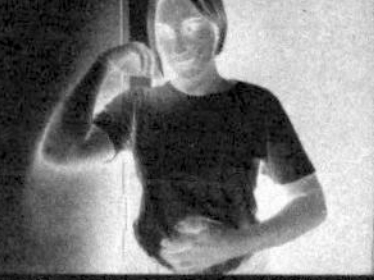

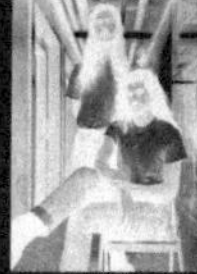

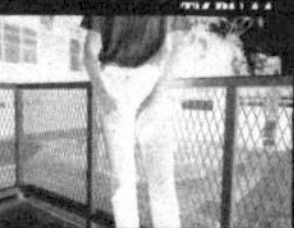

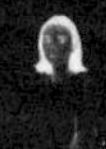

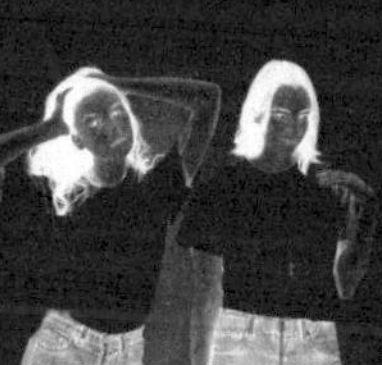

353

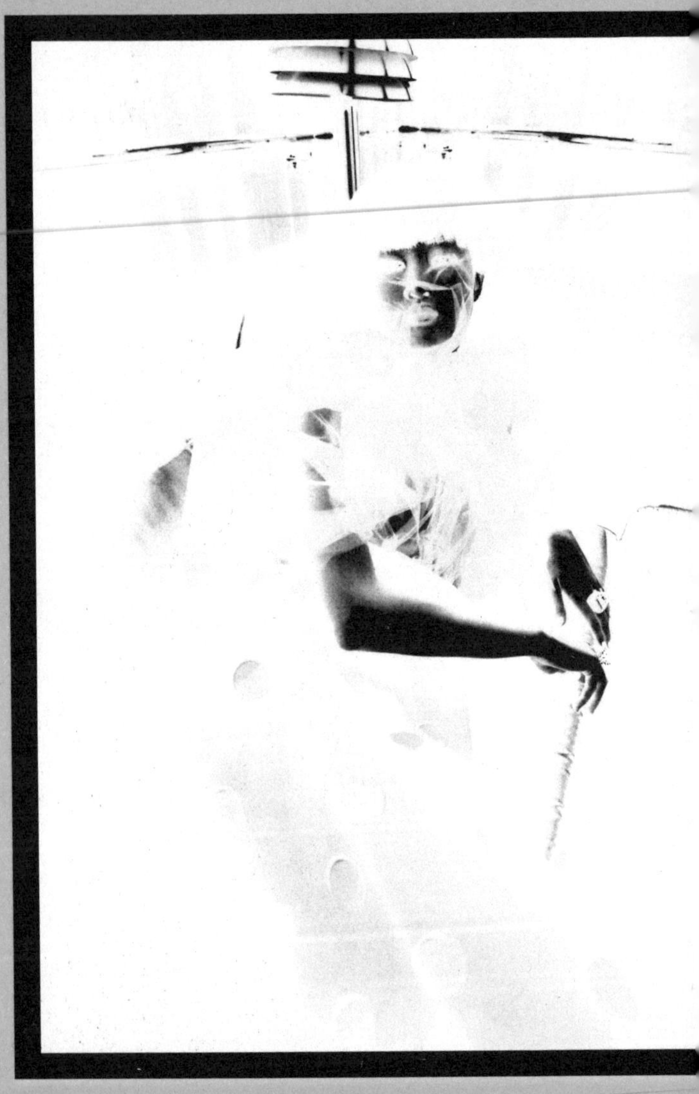

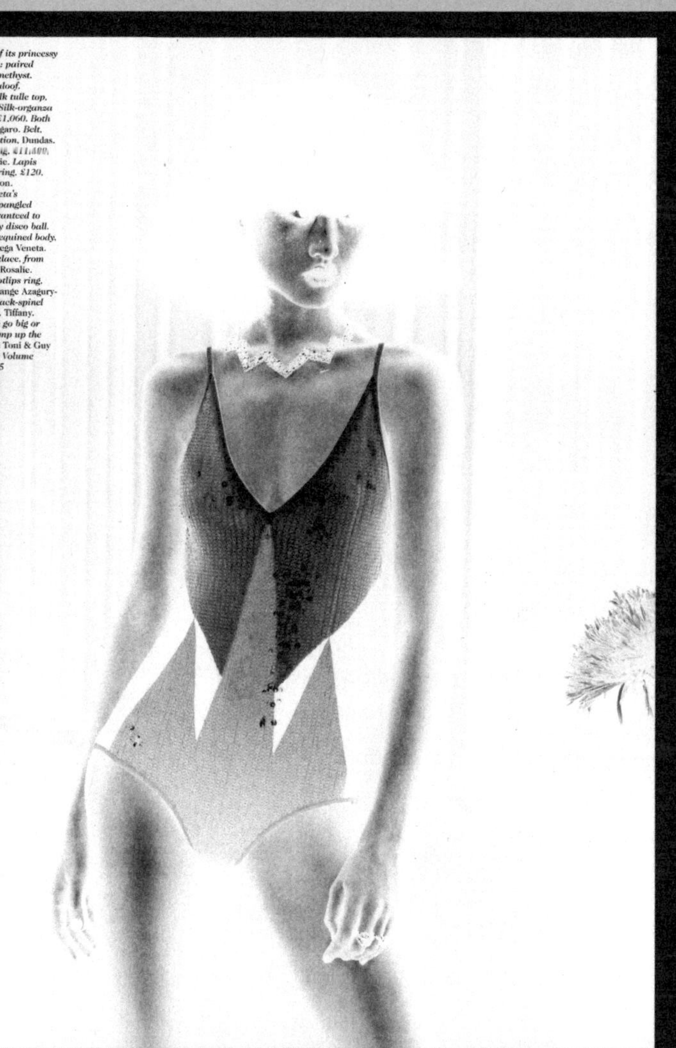
f its princessy
: paired
nethyst.
aloof.
ilk tulle top.
Silk-organza
£1,060. Both
ngaro. Belt.
tion, Dundas.
ric. Lapis
ring. £120.
lon.
eta's
spangled
ranteed to
y disco ball.
equined body.
tega Veneta.
klace, from
Rosalie.
otlips ring.
lange Azagury-
lack-spinel
, Tiffany.
: go big or
amp up the
h Toni & Guy
y Volume
25

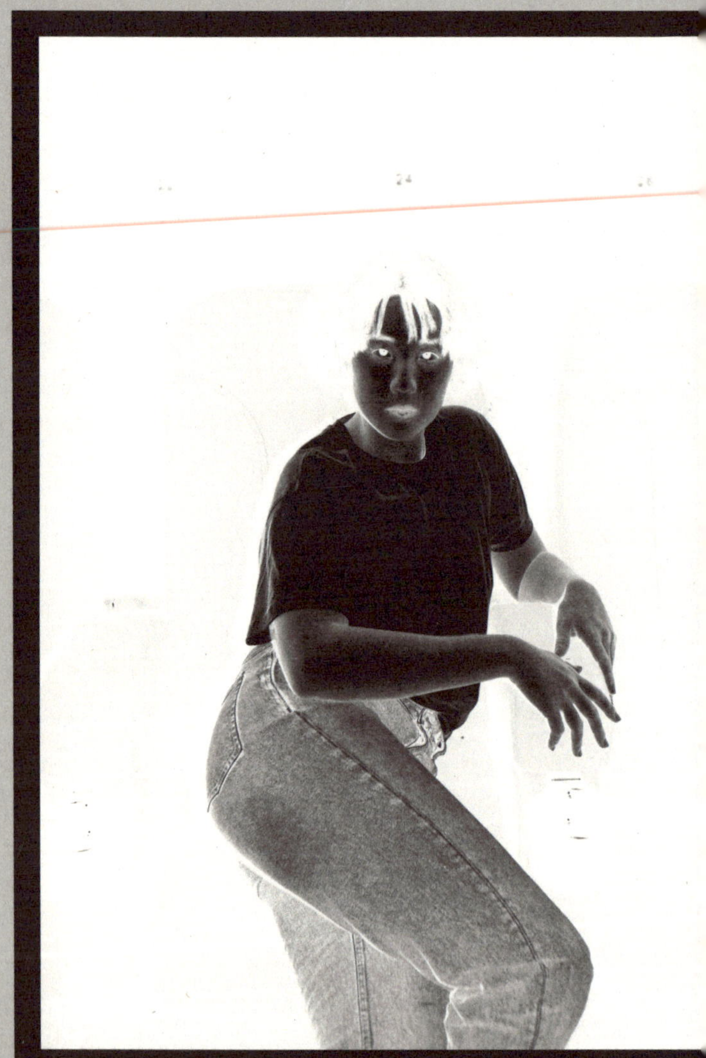

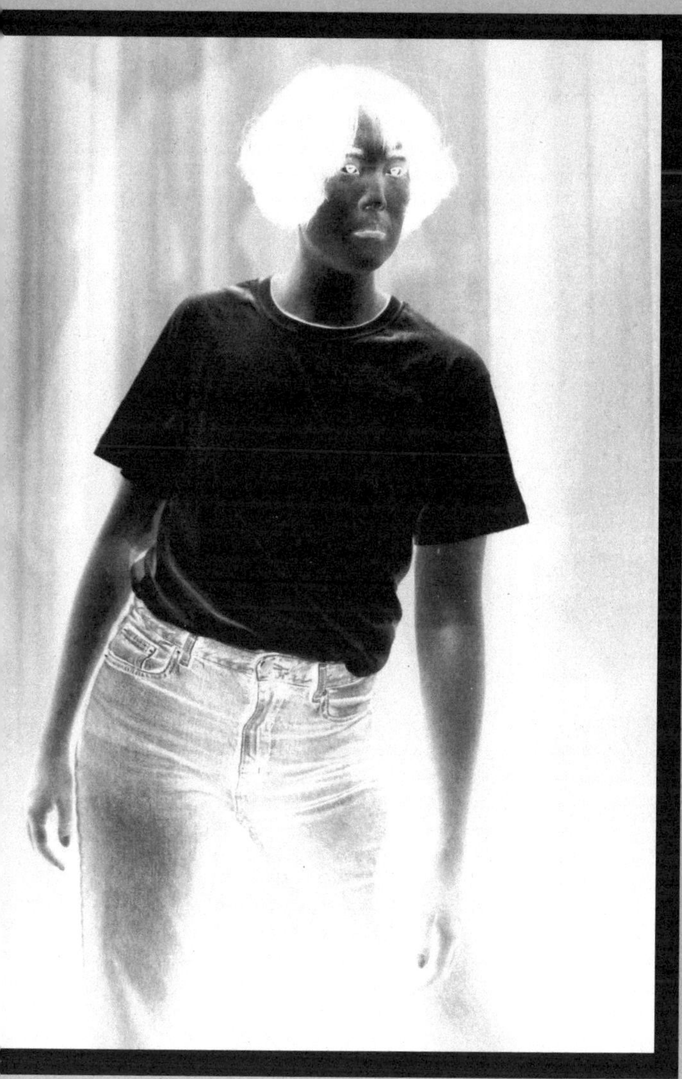

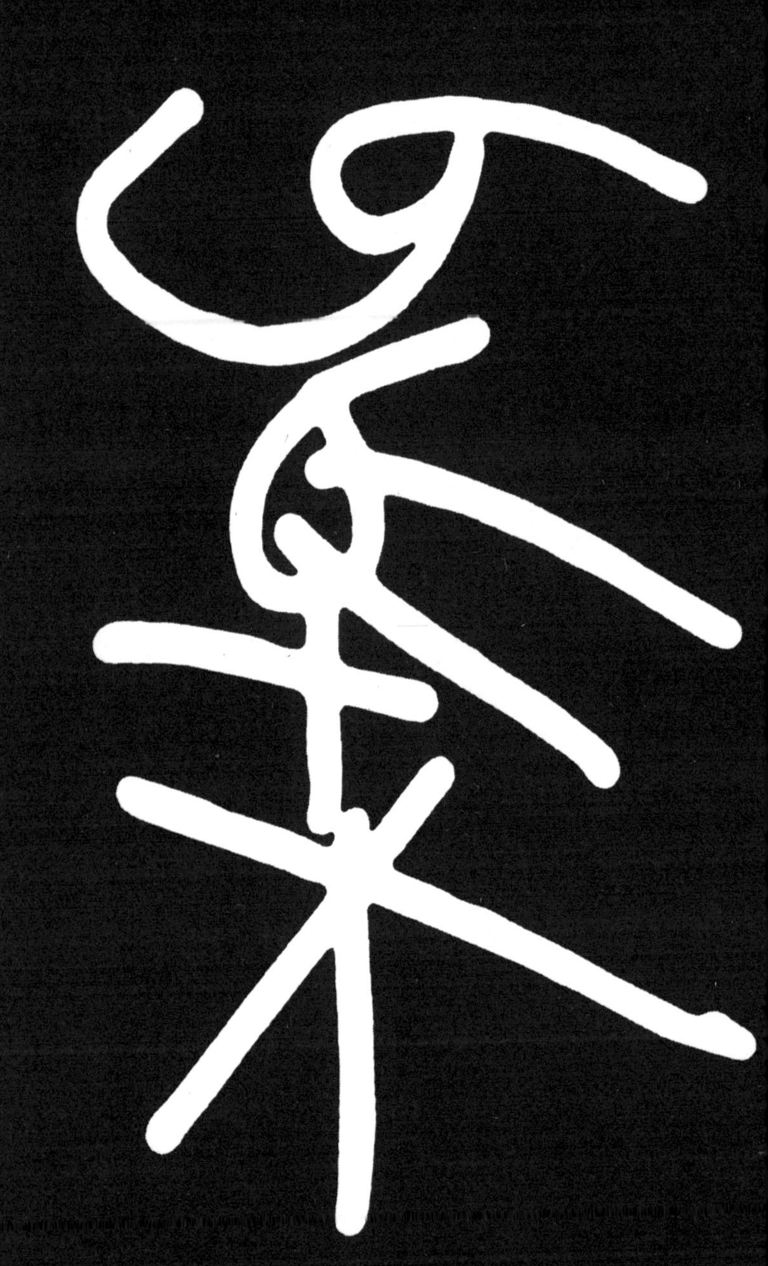

Boot Boyz Biz (BBB)

Boot Boyz Biz is a "research and production worker cooperative" founded by Kevin McCaughey, which collectively designs and proudly self-produces bootleg T-shirts as a form of creating and disseminating research. The shirts, whose subjects range from Cocteau Twins to "Cybernetic Serendipity," Roland Barthes to Björk, are covered in obscure graphics and dense typography creating layers of connection and meaning. The intricate designs require reading rather than viewing, challenging the conventions of graphic shirts and pushing the limits of traditional bootlegs. Since its inception, the brand has evolved to incorporate elements of politics, education, and spirituality, reimagining the potential of bootlegs as a form of "education through images." Interview by Ben Schwartz (BS).

> BS: Could you talk about the beginning of Boot Boyz Biz? What inspired the project, and what was your relationship to bootlegs at the time?

BBB: Experiences that built a base for our practice today were percolating long before we formally started the project. I can trace BBB's beginning to a triad of formative phases: 1. File Sharing, 2. Punk Tees, and 3. Artist Books.

The bootleg impulse first revealed itself to me while I was learning the dark art of CD burning in middle school. Getting hooked on making and trading mixes anticipated the kind of "mixtape mentality" or "dragonfly eye" that guides our ways of seeing today. The mix as an object has utility in the discovery of new tunes, but it also sparks intense perceptions of time and place stemming from the context of the exchange. The mixtape "event" integrates the material and immaterial as memories are burned onto the disc, as are mp3s, making for a complex aesthetic object (basically space-time travel) and an important component of convivial cultural exchange.

More early obsessions with music led to online activity: creating Blogspot "music blogs" and using the p2p network Soulseek, opening the door for experiencing new modes of infinite free exchange. By excavating well-organized folders on Soulseek, you could find shortcuts into expansive music histories, while peeking into a specific user's library revealed a kind of world-view in mp3s.

Meanwhile, offline, my closet was increasingly corresponding to my iTunes collection. Most of the short-lived 1980s punk/hardcore bands I was into never had real merch, so it was up to bootleggers to fill a void as demand increased from an accelerated (re)discovery of relatively obscure music, partially due to file-sharing culture (big up ebay user: negativereinforcement and eatdeath.com). Tees and punk (or any music/subculture) are seemingly forever symbiotic. Tees satisfy an individual desire for unalienated belonging while simultaneously preserving and reproducing the scene itself. The internet eliminated dependency on local shops, exploding choices and access to symbolic capital. I learned from digging for boots online that a shop's stash of commodities (online or IRL) becomes doubly useful as an encyclopedia, where each tee becomes a visual-mnemonic fragment that maps onto a larger landscape of underground music.

Tees get more interesting at gigs where they act as foregrounds and backgrounds for the show. Their collective formation in space makes a visible soundtrack, bridging the historical and present through a shuffling inventory of shirt-signs. The temperament of any gig correlates with what tees are present—forming constellations of meaning and tension. Often revealed by the tees, the most memorable gigs show an amorphous unity of differences (see: Chaos in Tejas 2011) opposed to ones clearly bent toward a single ideology. This best vibe is brought out by bands with diverse ranges of influences or gigs booked with eclectic lineups where contact with the other is built into the program. More than a fruitful blueprint for curation, the lesson is that by fostering a diverse range of inputs, the potentials increase for creating new meaningful connections. This ideal translates into how we assemble topics and ideas for BBB collections today.

Studying graphic design brought awareness to punk's earlier 20th-century analogs found within the historical avant-garde, where, like punk, new collective consciousness was fostered by modes of radical making focused on transforming images of everyday life into new critical forms. Dada montage and constructivism added a historical spark to the cut and paste fanzines I was grinding out at Kinkos late into the night. The historical trail illuminated more evidence: Breton's "one publishes to find comrades," clandestine activity in "samizdat" publishing, non-linear storytelling in *Medium is the Massage*, the deconstructive "book in a box" *Aspen* magazine, the convivial correspondence in 1960s Mail Art, and potentials of the collector in Ed Ruscha's artist books. These historical images screamed almost explicitly "bootleg" as they used assemblage with emphasis on the public-making "multiple," revealing strategies for inquiry-based projects that now leave an invisible ink on our work.

These histories initially inspired a fervor of (mostly non-serious) Riso publishing activity (produced under the moniker Nonporous) from around 2013–2016—concurrent with the excitement around Printed Matter Art Book Fair stuff. Then it became clear that tees (totes too) and books were becoming increasingly symmetrical as desired objects in the zine scene. Tees reward a more instantly gratifying cultural capital to the buyer and give an economic boost to recoup the low-margins in publishing, but they're often designed as a modest supplement or a means to an end. Then we thought: if tees provoke a heightened desire, instead of using them as bait for getting eyes on zines, why not make the tees the zines themselves? By taking the industrious reproductive activity of the risograph into the realm of screen printing tees, the task was then to pack as many ideas into a T-shirt as we would into a sixteen-page zine, merging the means and ends into a single cohesive expression.

Through understanding the value of open cultural exchange within a DIY ethic, and possessing

p. 203: Boot Boyz Biz NYC Earth Art T-Shirt (2019)

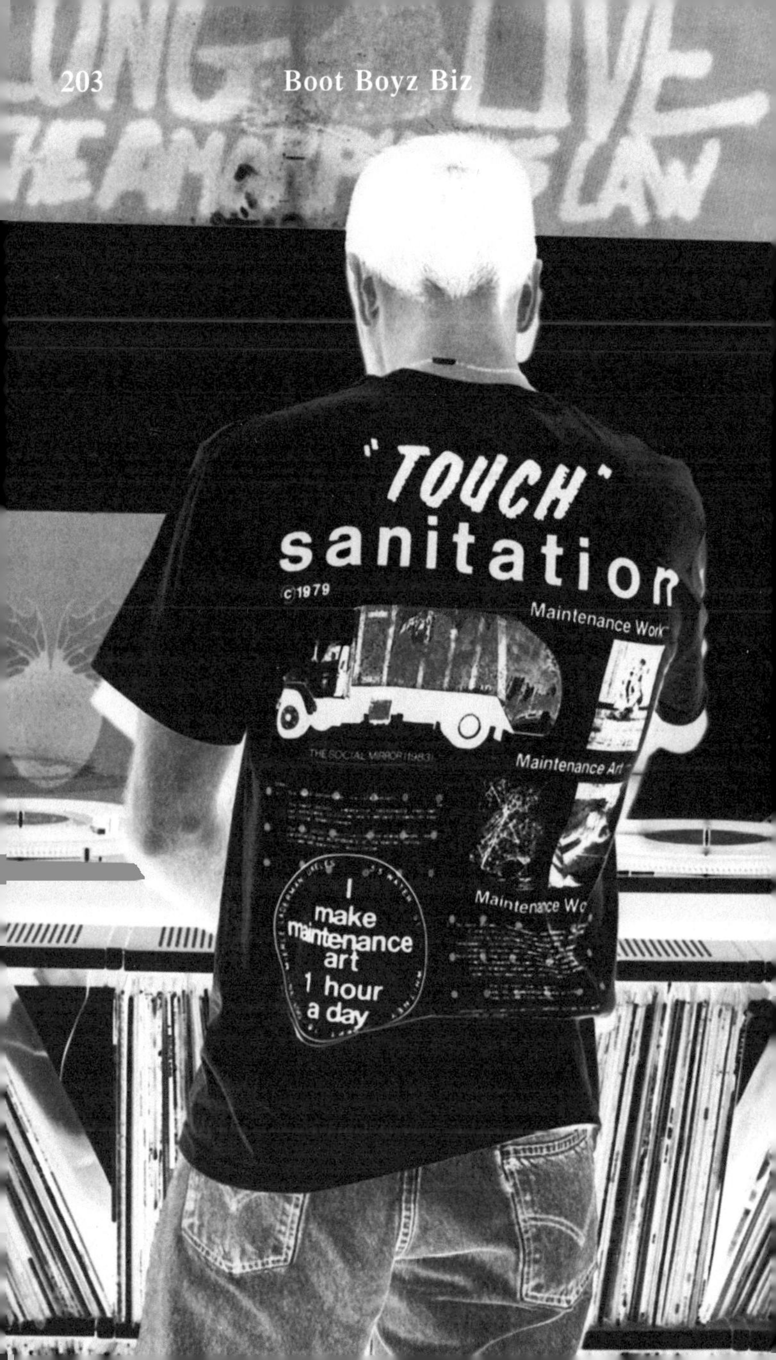
"TOUCH"
sanitation
©1979
Maintenance Work
THE SOCIAL MIRROR (1983)
Maintenance Art
I make maintenance art 1 hour a day

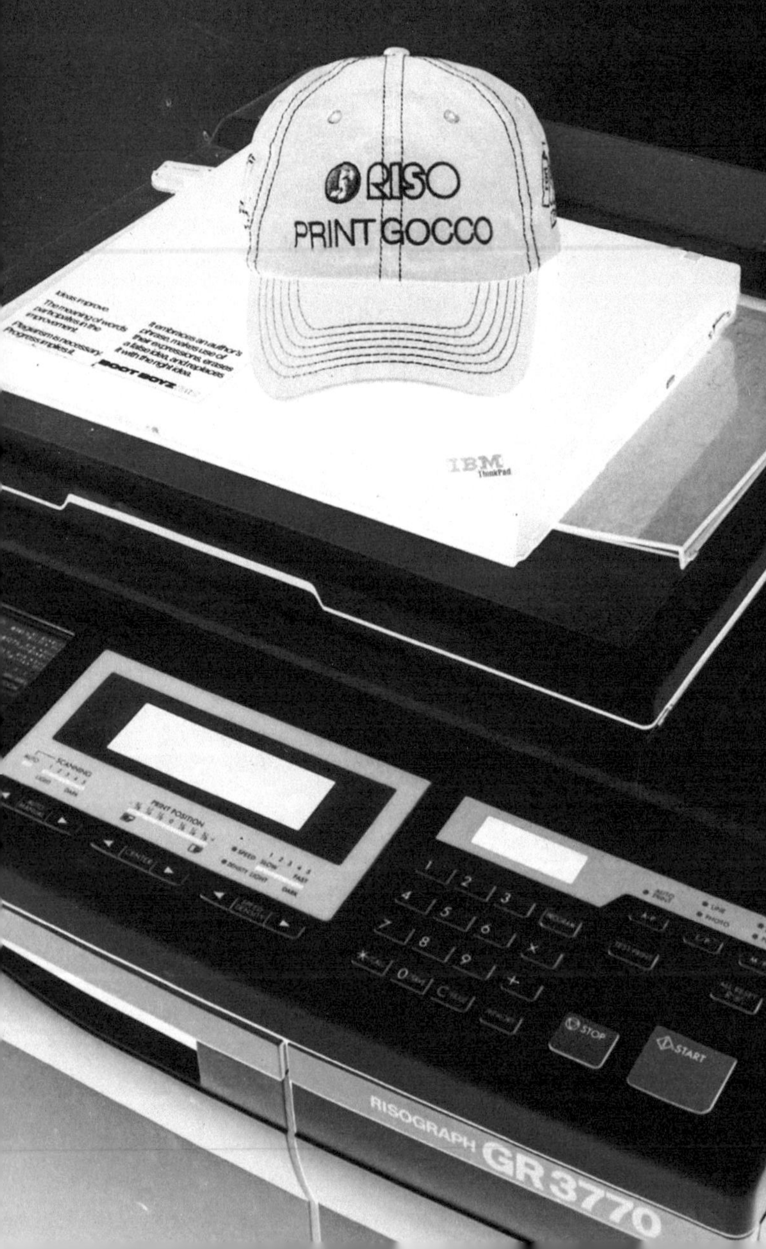
RISO
PRINT GOCCO
IBM
STOP
START
RISOGRAPH GR 3770

knowledge of radical publishing strategies, we were able to lay the foundation for the project.

> BS: How do you decide what to bootleg? What variables are you conscious of when making bootlegs: i.e. power dynamics, different cultures, economies, contexts, etc.?

BBB: Above all we boot what charges us up, what expands our understanding of the world, and what gives us courage to continue creative work. Instinctively it's a matter of real-recognize-real. When you find something that moves you emotionally or intellectually, there's an impulse to pass it on. Think of Newton's Third Law but with ideas. Competitive ideology suppresses the urge to share what's valuable and Web 2.0 exploits it while trivializing it. Our process starts by collecting material that makes us move, then it becomes a matter of mapping the personal onto our larger social context. We're always seeking the largest overlap between what we like and what could be useful to the widest range of peers both today and for posterity. The task is to create value by filling gaps.

We adopt a rhizomatic temperament permitting us to wrestle with multiplicities of form and thought throughout history—an inverted version of the "lifestyle" concept. The output of most brands appears as a single homogenous "totality," where our individual projects each contain unique heterogenous *totalities* within a constraint of the 16×20" printing pallet. This freedom of thought (onto a limited space) gives us a large scope to organize and put history in motion. We

p. 204: Boot Boyz Biz Riso Gocco hat (2022)

look to historical flash points across all disciplines that reveal moments of counter-hegemonic rupture. By capturing sparks from the past we hope to energize the present. What kind of sparks? Ones that advocate for free, meaningful activity within communities, and ones that help us unravel the psyche of history. Our project aims to bump threads and keep ideas at the top of feeds. We can only change the world if we increasingly understand it together.

We think: What stories do we need to vitally argue for today? What thinkers might be just below the surface to a large group of people? Are we being constructive towards an open and collaborative society by nudging specific topics? What pathways are available to make a potent idea both legible and complex? Do we have enough understanding to effectively translate an idea?

We boot what others won't. We know there's inspiration tucked away in remote institutions/disciplines that have potential to benefit a wider audience. We try to demystify these ideas and reverse radical monopolies. Alternatively, we like fishing out ideas baked into pop-culture that are often missed or dismissed. Magic happens when these high and low worlds bump into each other, and we're especially drawn to ideas that dance between both.

We have principals that draw from a common sense "boot-code" (i.e., considering out-of-print status, if sources are living or dead, active or inactive) but we deliberately stretch its limitations (mostly in terms of accepted form and selection) because we believe the task of any new generation is to make traditions anew. We use this instinctual compass while keeping in mind the explicit (but somewhat slippery) Fair Use doctrine, giving us a benchmark for producing transformative works. Fair Use favors the usage of fragments from existing works, and we find a home in these fragments which we can salvage from relative obscurity. When we put fragments in careful sequence, we can correlate stories using image and text in kaleidoscopic form, inviting opportunities for discovery, new appreciation, and increased subjectivity. What is inquiry-based visual communication if not criticism, comment, reporting, and teaching?

We acknowledge the very real tension between a co-optive, cynical "booting from above" and a supportive, convivial "booting from below." We associate with the latter as our practice has stayed DIY and independent from the start, but that fact alone doesn't automatically clear one from doing damage. Bootlegging becomes dangerous in two main ways: banalizing and occulting. Banalization happens by fetishizing history, reproducing stereotypes, atrophying memory by distilling it into rigid icons, calcifying thought (think Che tees or any tees that prioritize appearance over substance). We fight this by arranging constellations of unusual images that crisscross disciplines and timelines, exploding history into pathways that require deeper readings. Instead of worshiping history, we put it up for question. Occulting practices take historical images and re-mystify them devoid of context and history, for sole aesthetic benefit of the occulter, resulting in a less legible and mystified environment. While we let graphics on our projects speak for themselves, we combat occultation by presenting extended roadmaps of our research, showing our hand and leaving the puzzle pieces that make up our work open to all, to promote expanded inquiry and meaning-making. Booting for us is not an act of enclosure but a gesture of "giving-on-and-with" (Édouard Glissant).

As we've become more popular, we've oriented ourselves deeper and deeper into the cracks of history for insights for material, because honest bootlegging can't be a day at the beach. We push ourselves to up the level of visual transformation by syncretizing increasingly disparate-but-connected elements, so that a design is never about only one thing. A tee becomes a cosmology, a salad of pictures, and a web of knowledge with multiple entry and exit points into enriching stories.

The topics, ideas, and images we engage with are priceless, what you're paying for is our labor to organize and produce the things and keep it going. Material growth isn't part of the program.

> BS: How has your understanding of a bootleg changed over the course of the project? It feels like very early on, the project was a more traditional form of bootlegging (thinking here of the one-off music related shirts). Recently it retains those elements of fandom, but the releases are pushing the potential of what a bootleg can do or be—resurfacing ideologies, educating, et cetera. I am interested in this evolution.

BBB: Yeah in the beginning the main influence was punk boots so there was little constellation going on, the tees were standard fare often about one thing. Back then even imagining a non-music boot on a colorful blank felt sacrilegious! But once you sidestep dogma and try something new and actually it hits.... going back feels increasingly one dimensional.

p. 209: Boot Boyz Biz Ω(+> / Prince T-shirt (2019)

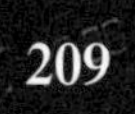

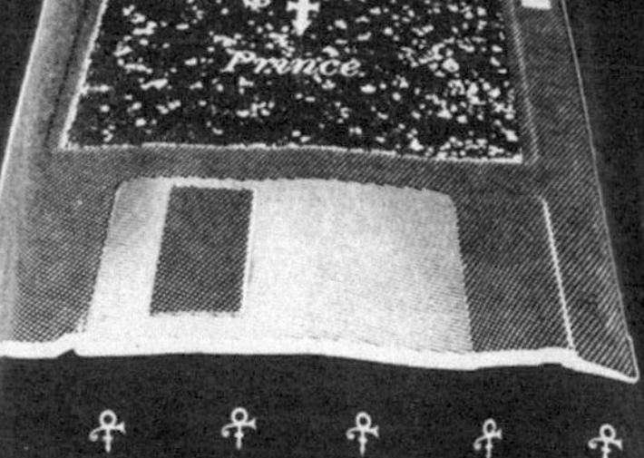
Int. Cl.: 16
Prior U.S. Cl.: 38
United States Patent and Trademark Office
Reg. No. 1,871,900
Registered Jan. 3, 1995
TRADEMARK
PRINCIPAL REGISTER
Prince
(MINNESOTA CORPORATION)
BUMPER STICKERS AND STICKERS, IN
FOR POSTERS AND PUBLICATIONS,
GERALD C. SEEGARS, EXAMINING ATTORNEY

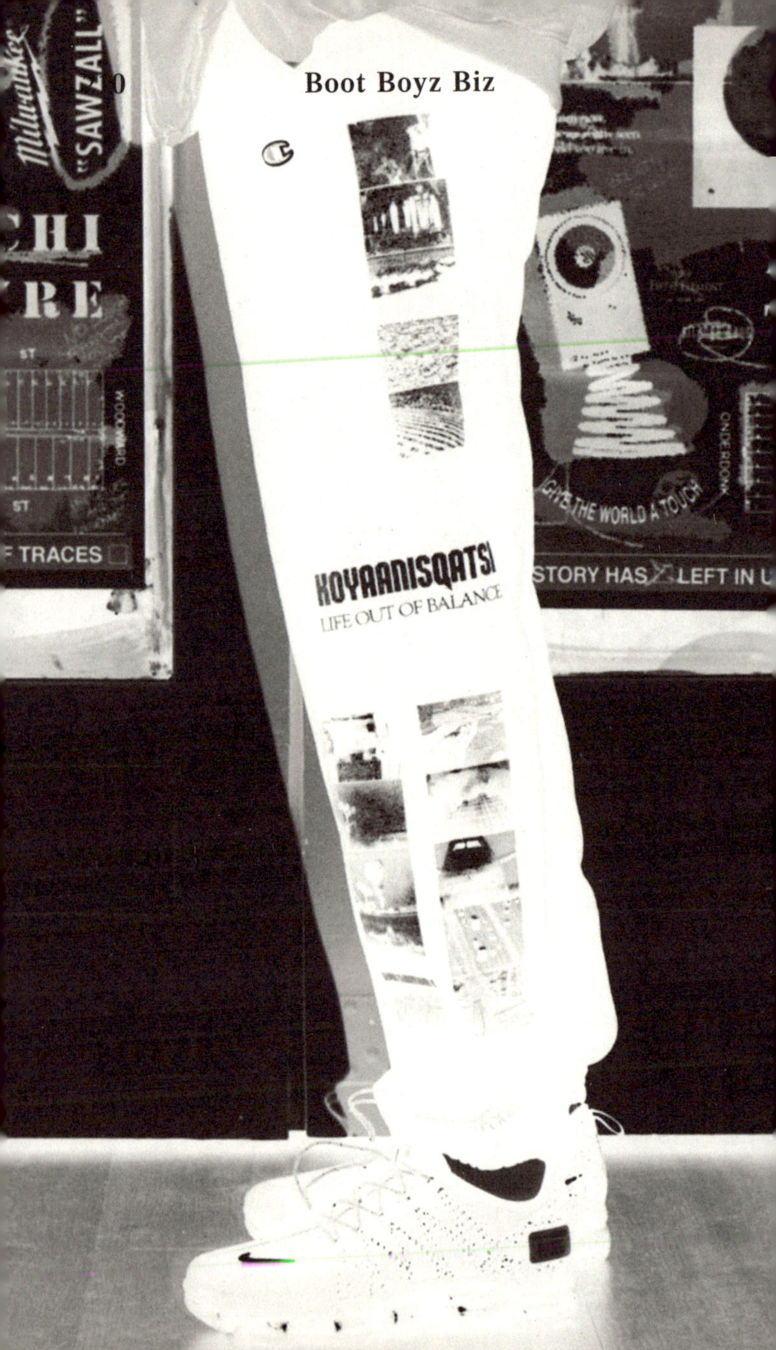

Milwaukee
"SAWZALL"
CHI
RE
TRACES
KOYAANISQATSI
LIFE OUT OF BALANCE
GIVE THE WORLD A TOUCH
STORY HAS LEFT IN U

2015–17: Bootlegs are a personal, social tool
2017–19: Bootlegs are a personal, social, educational tool
2019–21: Bootlegs are a personal, social, educational, political tool
2022–??: Bootlegs are a personal, social, educational, political, spiritual tool

Our oscillation of research and production continues to propel us in unexpected directions. Now might be approaching a point where it's a misnomer to call what we do bootleg. The word mainly indicates our departure from punk bootlegs, but we've since gone through a transformative turn (bootlegs-without-bootlegging?). The project has become more complex and hard to pin down over time because of a few things:

1. The topics we wrestle with often make use of intertextual strategies themselves (sampling, collecting, montage, publishing, et cetera) across all different disciplines (film, philosophy, music, et cetera). So as we continue to learn from our "bootleg ancestors," it gives us the courage to push and experiment.

2. The embracing of a "horizontal montage" design strategy in order to converge aesthetic, intellectual, political, and spiritual energies together like a time-lapse photo. The comprehensive strategy aims to bridge languages to show a bigger picture. We try to work this into objects (when the space affords it!) and have it shine through the "group" style presentations.

p. 210: Boot Boyz Biz Koyaanisqatsi pants (2019)

3. The more visible we get the greater the pull is to make the work more transformative and unarguably fair use.

> BS: How do you feel about the T-shirt as a medium? Would you consider these T-shirts publications? Exhibitions? What inspired you to create other objects?

BBB: I love tees. They're basically memes. Tees, they put people at ease. It goes all the way back to Adam and Eve. Tees link and make us think. They make you wanna buy a stranger a drink. A tee is both a personal joy and a public utility. A thing to start thoughts. A comrade and conductor of electricity. Closets are memory palaces and what's worn in crowds is ideology made visible (sometimes sweet, other times horrifying). Tees shape habits. A weak metamorphosis. Tees are funny complex things because they integrate the subject-object divide. "Are you wearing the tee or is the tee wearing you?" It's both at the same time, and this creative mimesis excites the imagination. "What's that shirt? And who are you?" Design lays traps that put people on new paths. Between the home and out in the world, tees leave a wake of aesthetic experience within everyday life, allowing for infinite creative potential.

What do tees do? They embody thought for a wearer and make contact with a viewer resulting in various levels of attraction, repulsion, or indifference. But they are also everywhere and add to the visual pollution that overwhelms our daily senses, so indifference is often the most practical response. To make effective contact with others, the familiar graphic tee needs to become strange again through an oscillation of distraction and concentration. Design strategies that defamiliarize images from the past into new poetic forms (mood sculptures) can jolt viewers and awaken sleepers into active modes of perception. For visual communication to transform/subvert thought and stick in the mind (like all good art, memes, film, et cetera) it must be all at once familiar, strange, and wonderful.

Tees act medicinally by converging reason and entertainment, where poetic visible language becomes a chaser, allowing for big ideas to go down easier. I think of Barthes' idea in *The Pleasure of the Text* that distinguishes instantly gratifying texts ("Pleasure") with challenging transformational texts ("Bliss"). Generic bootlegs could be seen as self-gratifying and hedonistic, while our aim is to bring both pleasure *and* challenge the position of a subject towards new thought: Booter's Delight.

McLuhan points out that clothing is a technological extension of the skin, so are tees then more like embodied capital rather than objective cultural capital? There's something deeply psychological about a "second skin." Any modification in cultural capital (including what you wear) changes both consciousness and unconsciousness, and empowers or depowers people for better or worse (like a sigil). The outward effect is that tees edit the social-visible landscape with a potential to produce collective consciousness. I'm interested in learning more from the historical ur-tees, like tattooing and heraldry.

Tees are players in urban semiotics as moving texts—they map perceptions and animate thought. Graphics are energy and flow where the tee goes. Love at last sight. Tees can help our environment to be more vibrant, exciting, convivial, spontaneous. The task:

Make contact. If tees are a contemporary form of communication, we can aid a counter-public sphere with charged up graphics. Tees sometimes get hit with a negative value judgment but wise people respect all forms by which knowledge is communicated. Part of growing is dismantling black and white distinctions between mediums, disciplines, et cetera. It's always more fruitful to find overlaps than uphold divisions.

We see the tees' affinities with many mediums: posters, exhibitions, zines, essays, films, libraries, music, et cetera. and with disciplines like archeology, library science, exhibition design, publishing, journalism, translation, et cetera. Its root is in the creative act. Furthermore, why should there be a distinction between T-shirts, classroom presentations, podcasts, YouTube videos, wikis, et cetera. that heavily rely on reference material? If all of teaching is now a commodity (bought and paid for), why should there be a distinction between what's shown in a classroom and what's on a T-shirt or a website? And why should exclusive commodified education be privileged in its use of copyrighted material?

Though our tees themselves are scarce, the images that make them up are infinitely reproducible. (See ours and make it anew!) Plus you can get most of the thought value from our projects without buying anything! Boots circulate the city as well as the internet, living two different time-space realities at once, which complement and enhance each other. As a part of practical culture, tees are accessible with high visibility, so when they work, they make good traps for spreading ideas. Tees work best when they remain in circulation. When the boots keep working we keep working.

p. 215: Boot Boyz Biz Affiche throw blanket (2022)

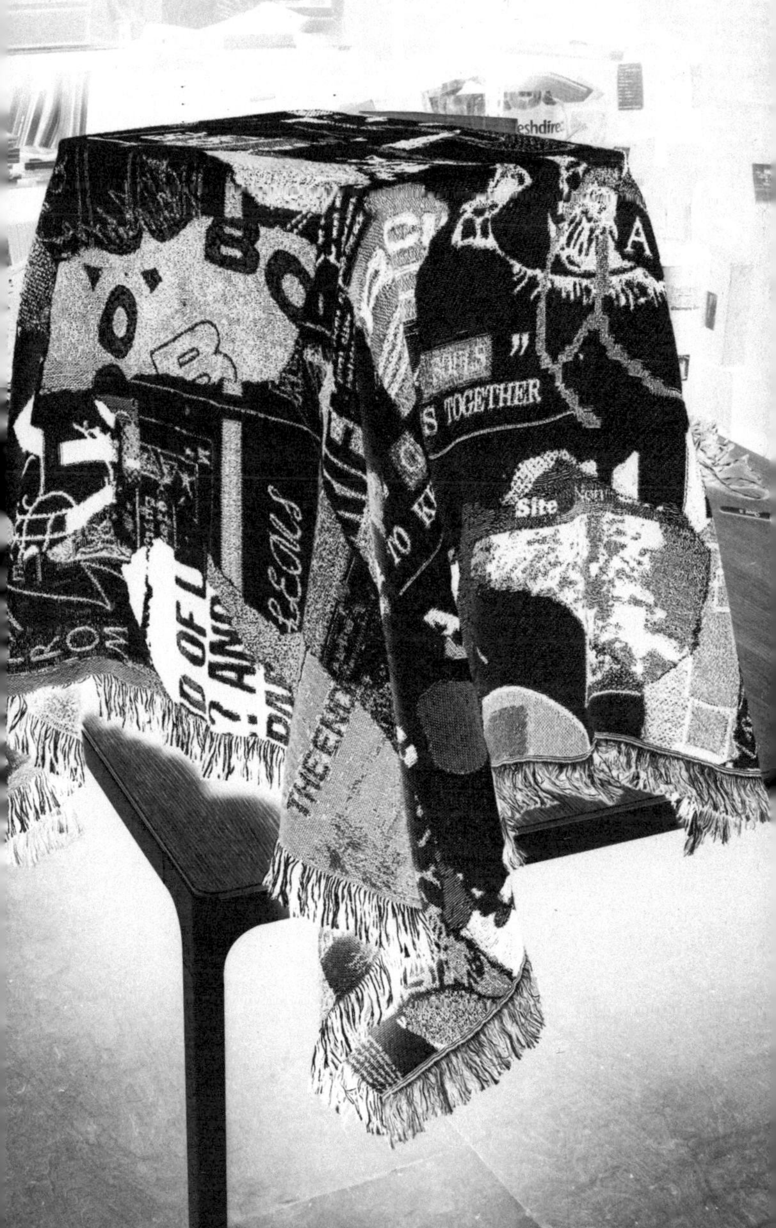
S TOGETHER
Site

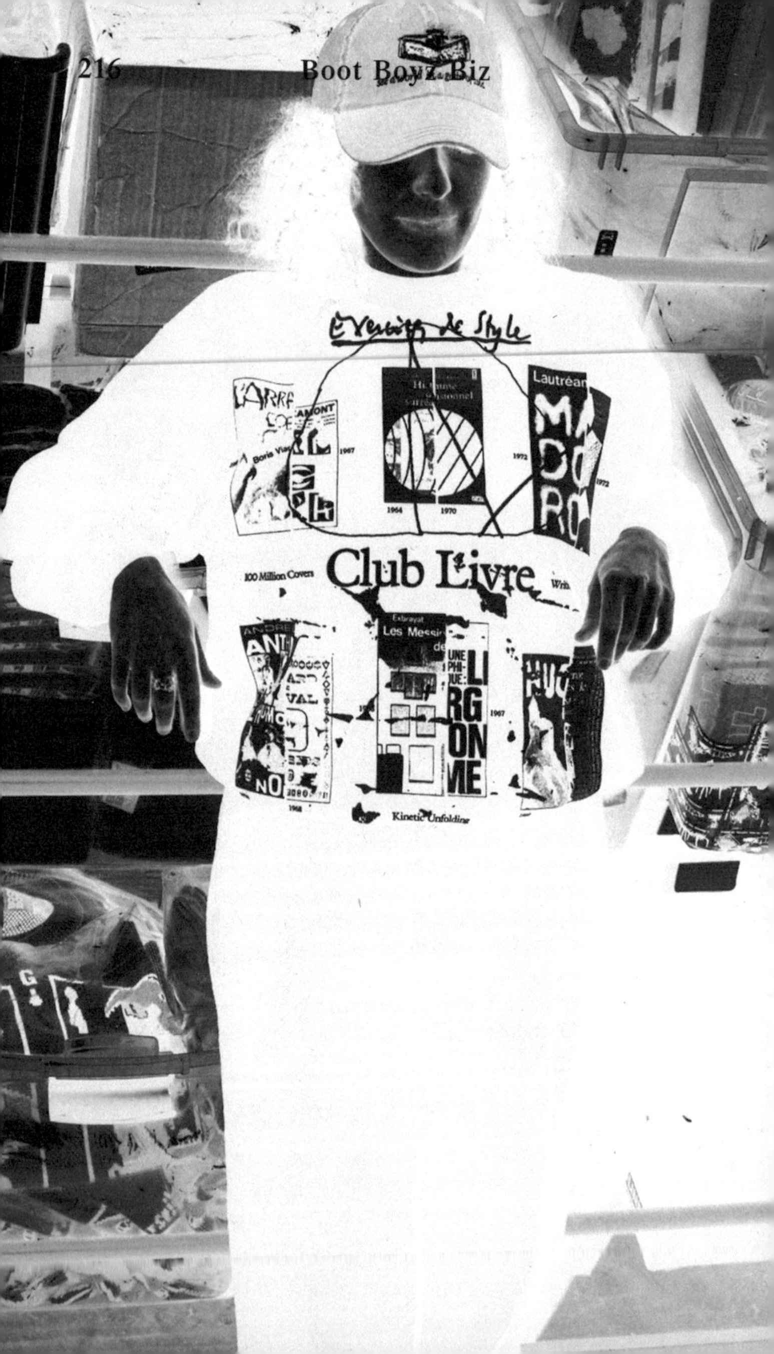
Club Livre
100 Million Covers
Kinetic Unfolding
Lautréam
Exbrayat
Les Messi
1964
1970
1972
1967
1968

Thoughtful boots can invert the advertising tactics that manufacture false needs by tapping into a new creative function of "mimetic desire." Boots then could create new demand for "wish images" that would be inspiration for a better future.

BS: What are your thoughts on bootlegging in the design world? You've had a big impact on the "bootleg craze". Do you feel designers recognize the potency of the gesture, or has the proliferation of the visual language reduced its power?

BBB: With the proliferation of image sharing online and mood-board dependency, it's clear that bootlegging is in accord with our epoch. It's becoming increasingly clear to younger generations that copyright law has never been there to protect artists, and only to benefit the distributors and gatekeepers (almost never the artists themselves) who have a monopoly on reproduction and extract rent. The confusion and taboo around bootlegging is largely due to misconceptions conflating pre-digital property rights with intellectual property.

I don't think we can take credit for any craze, but we may have started during the height of one. With any opportunity, some see a potential for participatory action while others see clout and dollar signs. There's definitely a lot of half-assed boots out there that look like someone's passive income strategy. To show some militancy: If you're not printing your own boots, you should do something else. Urgently, the childish "self-help" function of T-shirt consumption needs to be exchanged for a will to

p. 216: Boot Boyz Biz Faucheux Book Club sweatshirt (2022)

build and participate in non-sectarian communities of inquiry and practice. Be a *passeur* not a poser.

> BS: Do you have thoughts about why bootlegging has become so popular lately? In the design community, but also beyond, with corporations like Gucci embracing the act despite prosecuting bootleggers?

BBB: It's popular because it's cheaper and easier than ever to make anything, especially tees. You likely won't have to take on any debt either. Access to screen-printing, space for managing inventory, labor, et cetera. is no longer necessary nor a barrier for entry. Have a boot idea? Upload graphics, take pre-orders, and have a service fulfill the orders. But not without atrophying a designer's integrity and sense of responsibility. Unless you make something yourself, you have a very limited understanding of how it functions. "If you're going to live outside the law you have to be honest" (Bob Dylan).

Corporations understand sign value and the fact that the value of an image (logo, product, et cetera.) is only increased through its reproduction in space. These big brands realized it's more profitable to embrace bootlegs instead of prosecuting because the products (inaccessible to most people) circulating in public generates brand recognition and signals a brand loyalty among communities who couldn't normally afford their product. The build up of clout is later converted into real dollars when the population buys the brands official, but more affordable products (where these companies get most of their revenue)—wallets, belts, perfumes, socks et cetera.

BS: Could you talk about the relationship between bootlegging and community? Both bootlegging's role in creating as well as preserving communities? I am thinking here of fan communities (those that receive the objects), but also the community of people creating and producing the bootlegs.

BBB: There's two types of people—people who love and acknowledge being shaped by other ideas, and people who refuse to admit they're inspired by anything other than themselves. The former is a prerequisite for a meaningful building of community, and the latter perpetuates the anti-social cult of "genius" and us vs. them attitudes.

Communities are tied together by symbols and institutions. The reproduction of images, often through traditions, are a necessary faculty for maintaining stability within any community. Images speak of cultural memory, and apply it to life, signifying what people and groups value (folk art). You see bootleg tees having a significant role in reproducing music scenes and have an institutional role (our logical starting point). Bootlegs can be issued to signal membership in a closed off community, so we want to agitate this by nudging people toward unfamiliar images that make identity unstable and fuzzy.

BS: Could you talk about the relationship between bootlegging and archiving?

BBB: Derrida's "There is no political power without control of the archive, if not of memory. Effective democratization can always be measured by this cri-

NEW IMA

E NEEDED

terion: the participation in and the access to the archive, its constitution and its interpretation" is big for us. The increasing amount of boots moving through space make for a new decentralized archive sponsored by an invisible college (Bootheads) making wisdom visible.

In the age of infinite reproduction (scanning, printing, photography, file sharing, et cetera), archival material longs to explode from strictures of space and time. The Good Booter in the Age of Infinite Reproduction lights fires and looks to the Burning Bush miracle: cultural material is illuminated by new energies in the present while its sources remain preserved, unscathed, if not strengthened. The potential of booting is fruitful only if the object remains in circulation, as its primary function is to create events and not art objects (exhibition value over cult value).

Think of an archive as a city, and think of the city as an archive where its streets are living language. Tees participate in that language by activating thought and social contact in everyday life. We take a stab at reorienting "the archive" through our projects that move ideas outside their hiding places and into streets and spaces like carrier pigeons intensifying neighborhoods into peer-to-peer spaces; meanwhile their traces float around the web's labyrinth—making sparks fly across space-time.

Preservation by power is often practiced by a kind of "closing off" that prevents creative flourishing to most; this is strange when you realize an idea or object is only preserved in "the now" by its reproduction and connections within everyday life. Walter Benjamin wrote, "Every present is determined by those images that are synchronic with it." So if an image is not circulating well, it's basically dead, and most archives and their constituents are stuck. Since top-down hegemonic institutions often give us narrow insights in jurassic forms, we have to organize an alternative network of citations into a new "useable past" that's less about preserving what "is" (mostly bad), and more about redeeming ideas that are increasingly missing from popular attention, then putting them in motion using participatory mediums for today.

Archiving (and bootlegging) to us is close to how T.J. Demos described the Otolith Group: "recovering the living potentiality of dreams that would have seem to have died decades ago." Along with this we also want to carefully exorcize what John Dana in 1917 called "the Gloom of the Museum," by making theories popular, not walling them off from public life for a private few's benefit ("experts," museum goers, powerful interests), who are often only interested to artificially increase an object's cultural value for later conversion into economic value. The old archive uses history as a hallowed investment strategy while concealing its liberatory potential as a public toolbox for collective reflection into action. A consequence of busting the museum/archive could be the realization that much of the dominant culture's current and future archives are mostly useless for public wellbeing, so we have to look elsewhere for recovering what could be useful for building a better world without exploitation, suppression, and alienation.

Everyone has their own archive of "objects in space" and "images in the mind" from which they draw to understand and participate in the world. Not unlike the historical "Commonplace book," our index of projects composes an archive of inspiration that guides a strategic perspective. The continuous process of collecting and fragmenting, i.e. "taking a page from someone else's book" is at the core of mimesis and creative growth. By reproducing our work in multiples, the "pages" from our archive are readied to leap from our archive and shuffle into others self-constructed archives. Even adding one new card to one's deck will modify and update the whole. If people depend on the objects and ideas laying around to make decisions, our projects lend themselves as fragments of living memory suited for a new kind of "open archive" of creative energies. This simple reciprocity of "giving-on-and-with" (Glissant again) is what extends the life of ideas and objects.

Some say we're entering a dark age of archiving due to the dematerialization of everything, so printed items can combat this a little by constituting a new doxographic resource (a compendium of a variety of intellectual views).

BS: What is the future of bootlegs?

BBB: Education through images will only increase, but there will be a continued fight from IP holders to wall people off from knowledge (until we pay up). As history becomes increasingly available via digitization and new means of reproduction emerge, we can expect an increase of creative acts in the spirit of "bootlegging," taking all kinds of forms and qualities.

It feels like positive attitudes towards transformative reuse are becoming more wide-spread. Maybe due to a growing observation that creatives need to make "content" to survive, and some of what's around and most useful wrestles with historical content and its impact on today. (BBB is just IRL "posting" by the way).

Tees will stay important as a pastime for both enthusiasts and slower moving subcultures but will fall in-and-out of the dominant trend cycles. As we age into an increasingly precarious world, tees and bootlegs make us complacent and take us back to "more pleasant times" but we have to resist reactionary nostalgia (or at least make productive use of it by forging new meaning) and make new connections with the past to flourish in the present! In other words, a boot can't just be a window into the past, but needs to illuminate pathways toward something fresh.

Title page (p. 198): Graphic from the Boot Boyz Biz Björk Violently Happy T-shirt

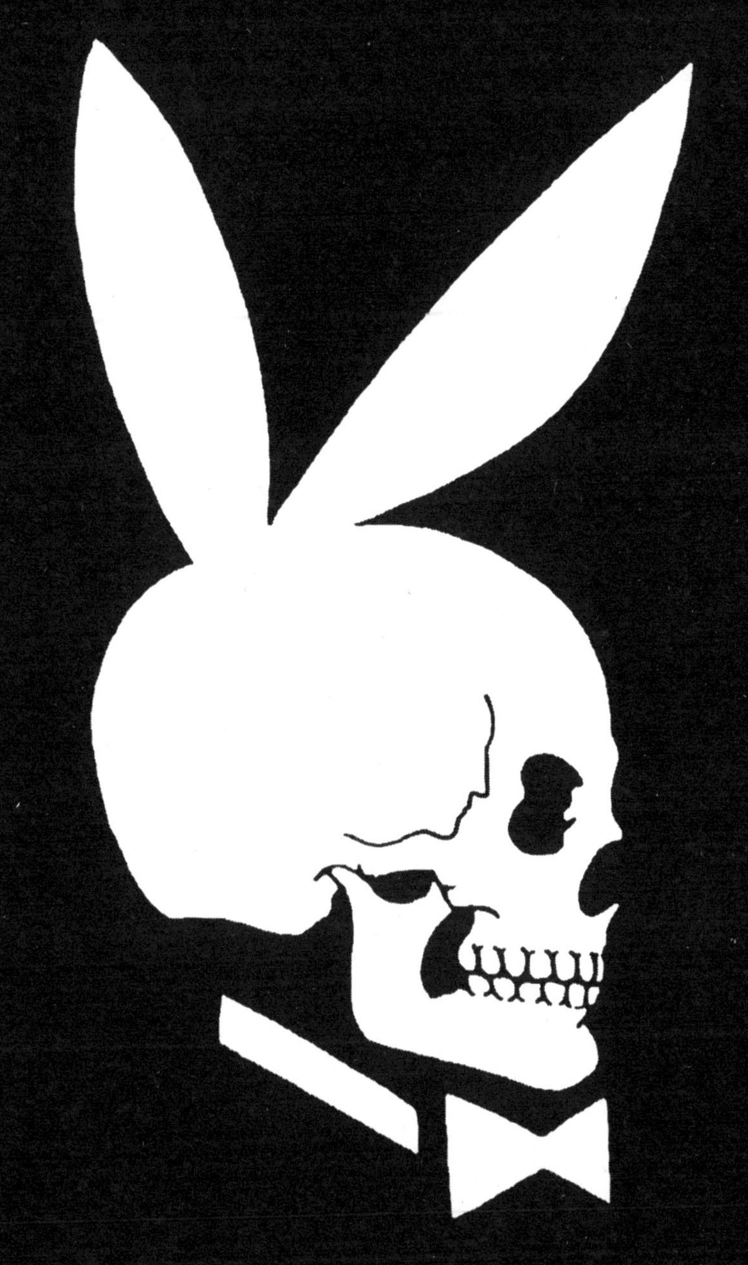

Jonathan Monk (JM)

Jonathan Monk is a Berlin-based conceptual artist whose practice travels across printed matter, multiples, sculpture, and installation. Monk often works with ideas of copying and appropriation, recalling conceptual masters of the past all while adding his own blend of wit and humor. In one notable ongoing project, Monk auctions off drawings of iconic works of art on restaurant receipts to his followers on Instagram, all for only the price of the meal. The charming series of works and method of distribution illustrates how objects can become a connective thread between fandom, access, and community. In another series of works titled *Exhibit Model*, Monk displays images of his previous shows as wallpaper, a process of bootlegging oneself where any notion of "an original" begins to dissipate. Interview by Ben Schwartz (BS).

BS: I don't think I've seen your work framed as bootlegging directly, but I do feel it explores similar ideas (copying, appropriation, fandom, shifting contexts, subverting economies, etc). Is bootlegging something you consider in your work?

JM: My initial contact with the idea of bootlegging came in the early 1980s when I acquired an illegally recorded Smiths concert on vinyl. It all felt very under the counter and the recording was excitingly crude. Bootlegging seemed only to be related to music and film. I remember VHS tapes being passed around at school not exactly sure what was on them as we didn't have a video player. The idea of copying something and making it available seemed appropriate at the time. The notion today does appear to have lost some of its guilty pleasure.

> BS: When discussing your work, it is often framed as appropriation or even "cover versions." I'm curious if and how you differentiate between the ideas of appropriation and bootlegging.

JM: I'm never really sure about this. I think my work does try and move the idea (whatever it happens to be) further. I generally try not to simply replicate a work, an idea, or a situation. I once produced an edition with Michèle Didier in Brussels (now Paris) in 2010. The idea was to make a facsimile copy of *Diecimila* (1977) by Chris Burden, which in itself was an exact copy of an Italian bank note. We even fabricated the green display folder the edition was housed in. My name did not appear anywhere on the work; even Burden's signature was painstakingly recreated in pencil. Burden forged money and we forged his work. I liked the idea that in the future my piece might mistakenly be sold as his and it was feasible the opposite could happen, although unlikely. This may or may not answer your question...

BS: I've often come to appreciate a subject more through the eyes of a fan than directly from the subject itself. It was pointed out to me that Barthes notes a similar idea in *Camera Lucida*: "One day, quite some time ago, I happened on a photograph of Napoleon's youngest brother, Jerome, taken in 1852. And I realized then, with an amazement I have not been able to lessen since: I am looking at eyes that looked at the Emperor." How do you think our understanding of a subject changes when seen from the perspective of an admirer?

JM: Beautiful. I guess we are all slowly getting used to seeing the world through a system of carefully curated filters. Our knowledge of a subject depends on how or where information was gleaned—John Peel was a very good promoter; google might not be.

I remember a family visit to the Tate in London—I was probably around twelve at the time. Standing in front of a van Gogh, I recall not the beauty of the work but the realization that I was standing exactly the same distance away from the work as Vincent was when he painted it.

BS: Bootlegging is closely related to ideas of fandom. In your work, for example, you are clearly a huge admirer of the art you're referencing. I'm curious, at what point do you consider that a creation moves from an homage to an artwork? Is there a difference?

JM: If I knew this I could (and probably should) retire. I think each project has a slightly different outcome and it is already hard to say when something is or is not art. If I'm able to continue what I do without having to legitimize my every move, then great...

BS: The particular period of conceptual art that you often work with is known for its cold, administrative qualities. Bootlegging I would argue can be a very personal gesture in the way that it reveals love, admiration, and even obsession for a particular subject. *Relief*, for example, touches on these dry sensibilities, but in fact reveals something entirely intimate… your private collection, your affinity for LeWitt, et cetera. Does it feel important for you that a personal narrative comes through in the work?

JM: Often, but not always. The particular piece you mention was supposed to be quite a cold reflection on LeWitt and his books. But the fabricator left some of the production process in the piece, so the book shapes appeared to be used or slightly off white. I liked this accidental addition, so I left it.

BS: Do you think it is possible to bootleg oneself? Or perhaps an equivalent question is, is art ever original? I think your project *Exhibit Model* raises questions akin to this. If I'm onto something, what might that mean for this particular body of work?

JM: I do. In 2008, I made a series of sculptures, *Deflated Sculptures I-V*, based on *Rabbit* (1986) by Jeff

p. 231: Jonathan Monk, *Deflated Sculpture II* (2009)

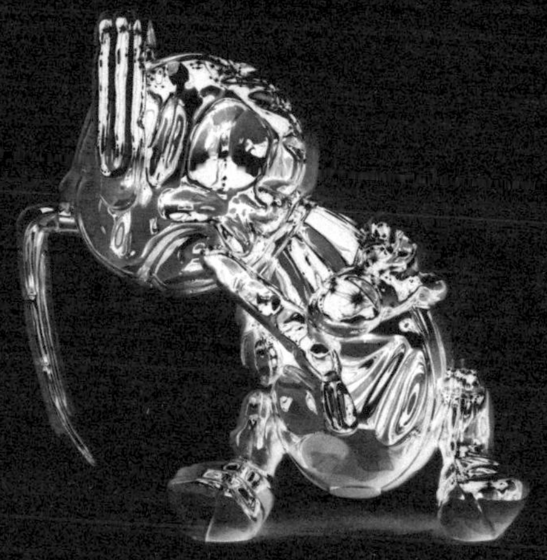

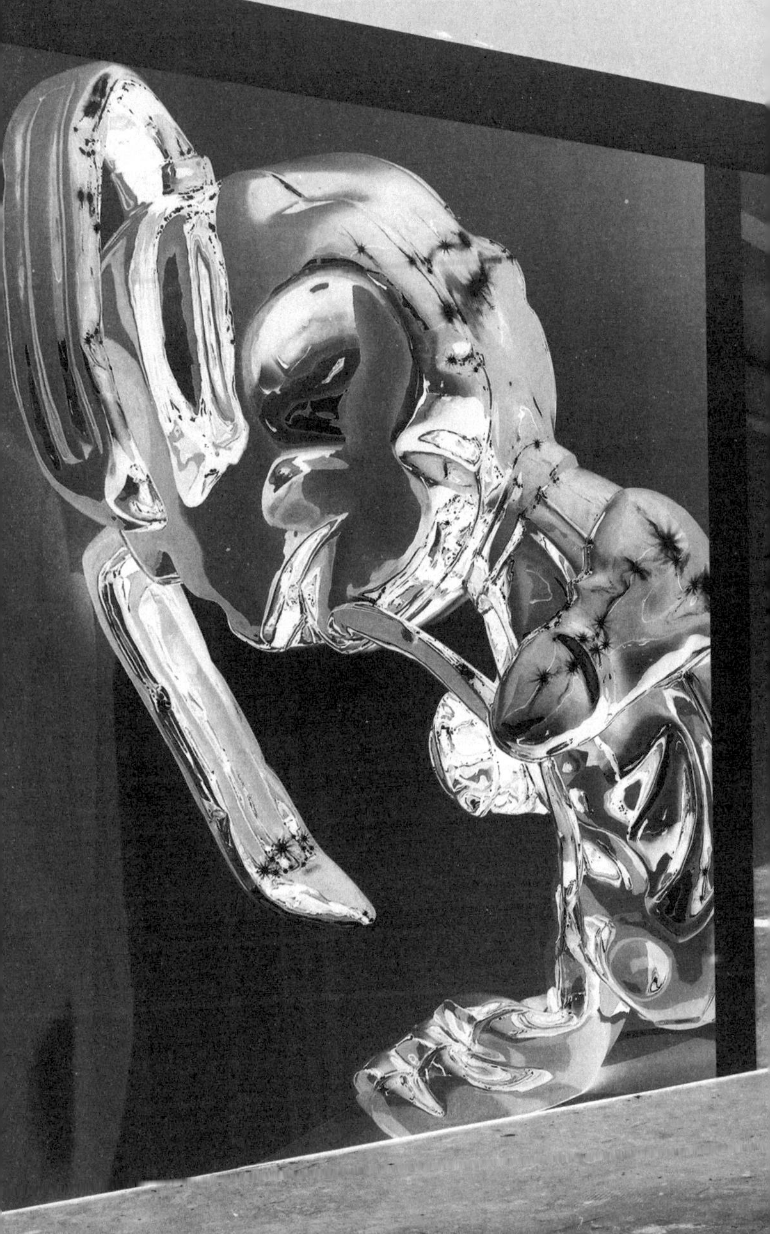

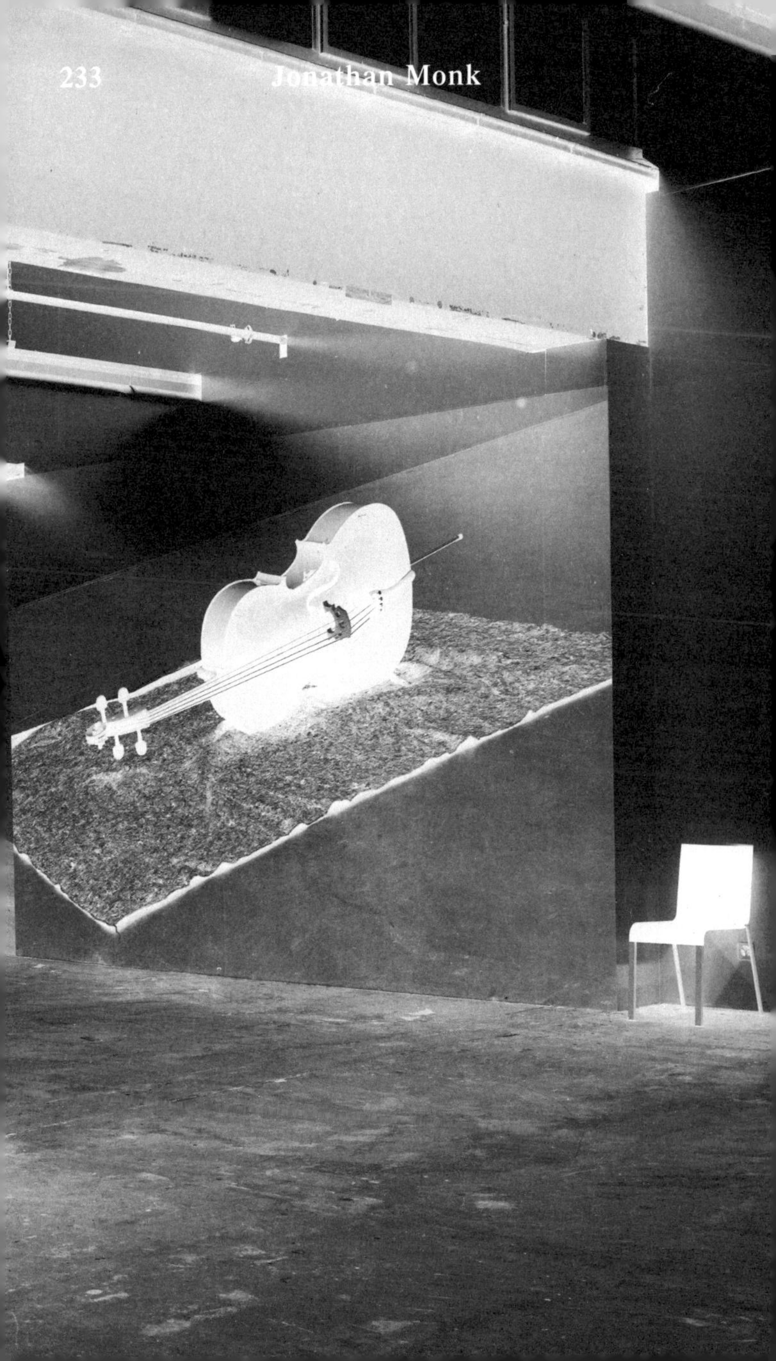

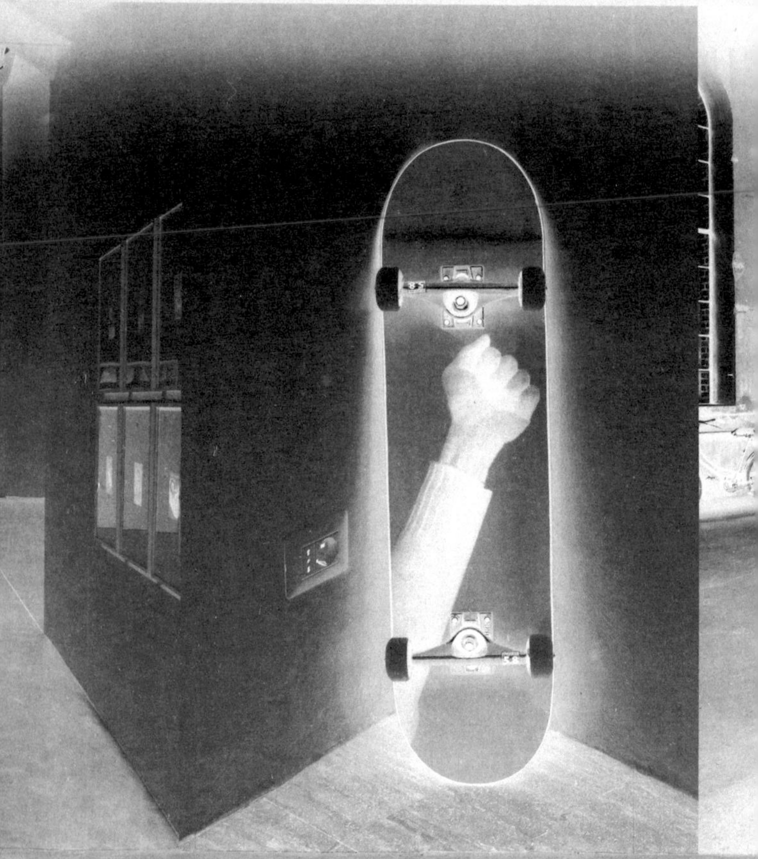

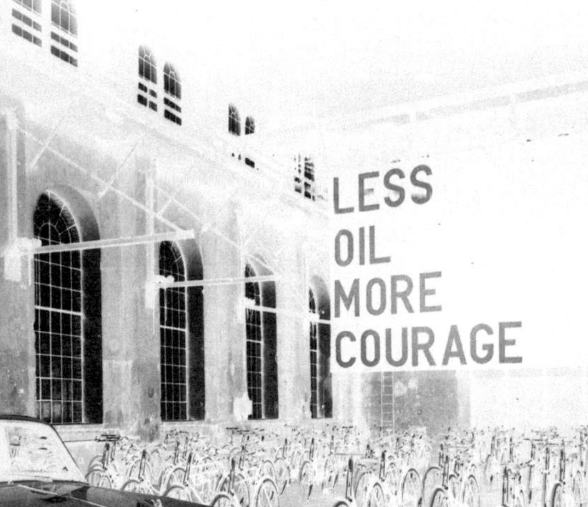
LESS
OIL
MORE
COURAGE

Koons. These were all fabricated in China, based on images of the original Koons sculpture and pictures I'd taken of an actual inflatable toy rabbit. Recently, I made new versions in China based on my own *Deflated Sculptures*. The *Exhibit Model* project, I guess, uses a similar narrative of copying and reappropriating. I like how the initial idea slowly disintegrates or vanishes into the background.

> BS: In many situations, bootlegging provides a means of access. In fashion, for example, a bootleg is often a way to own a version of a more expensive luxury item. While there are several interesting ideas at play with your *Restaurant Drawings* series, I wanted to ask specifically about its price point. Are you interested in the way these drawings undermine the economic aspects of the art world? That now, essentially, you can buy a Christopher Wool or an Ed Ruscha for the price of a meal?

JM: I'm not sure they really undermine the economic aspects of the art world. I occasionally think the project will come back and haunt me, although I don't really have a problem with this. It is part of the game, illogical as it might sound in relation to my market value—this is something that I always found quite funny. Money aside, it might be easier to buy an actual Christopher Wool work than one of my *Restaurant Drawings* that pictures one of his paintings [due to a process of selecting who can buy the piece from their Instagram comments]. It is a com-

pp. 232–235: Jonathan Monk, *Exhibit Model One* (2016)

pletely different world though—comparisons are not so easy.

BS: To me, *Deflated Sculpture* (2009) feels like a rare instance in your practice of bootlegging as a form of direct critique. Do you feel like bootlegging or appropriation is still a potent form of subversion?

JM: Although these works were not intended as a direct critique, the 2008 market crash and subsequent aftermath added to the deflating context. I was really just trying to add a touch of reality to the dialogue.

BS: You're often asked about the importance or relevance of originality. I think with bootlegging, there is almost a desire to be unoriginal in the effort to replicate, as best as possible, something else. Rather than ask about the value of originality, I wanted to ask what you feel that we learn from copying?

JM: A rereading of the past. The post-conceptual artists lead me to the conceptual artists, and so on. After art school, I made a multiple entitled *Learn To See How Others See*. I had slowly acquired old prescription spectacles via flea markets and secondhand shops. The glasses of others were numbered and boxed. I'm not sure how many pieces were in the edition or what happened to them. I'm losing focus.

pp. 238–239: Various photographs sourced from Jonathan Monk's Instagram account (@monkpictures)
Title page (p. 226): Graphic from a *Restaurant Drawing* by Jonathan Monk of Richard Prince's *Skull Bunny* (c. 1991)

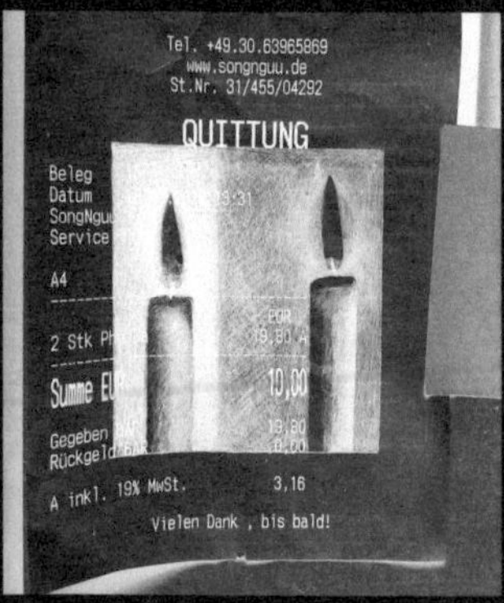
Tel. +49.30.63965869
www.songnguu.de
St.Nr. 31/455/04292
QUITTUNG
Beleg
Datum
Service
A4
Gegeben
Rückgeld
A inkl. 19% MwSt. 3,16
Vielen Dank , bis bald!

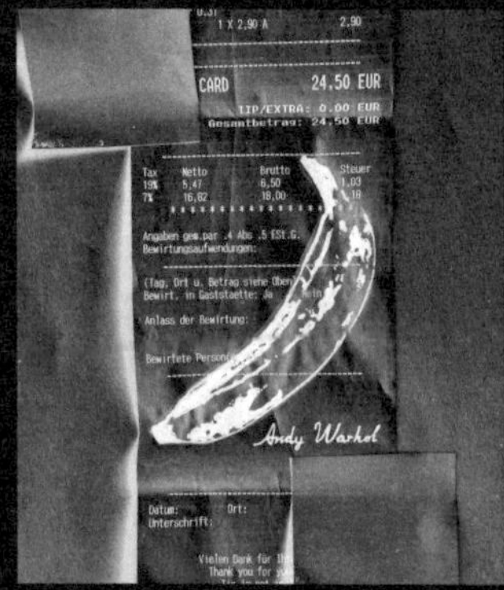
CARD 24,50 EUR
TIP/EXTRA: 0,00 EUR
Gesamtbetrag: 24,50 EUR
Tax Netto Brutto Steuer
Anlass der Bewirtung:
Andy Warhol
Datum: Ort:
Unterschrift:

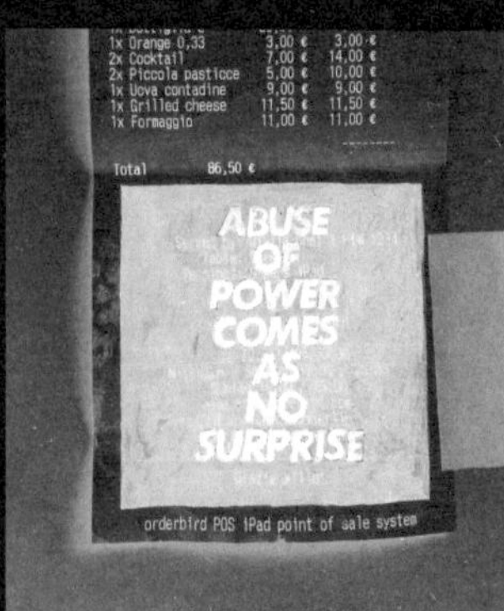
1x Orange 0,33 3,00 € 3,00 €
2x Cocktail 7,00 € 14,00 €
2x Piccola pasticce 5,00 € 10,00 €
1x Uova contadine 9,00 € 9,00 €
1x Grilled cheese 11,50 € 11,50 €
1x Formaggio 11,00 € 11,00 €
Total 86,50 €
ABUSE OF POWER COMES AS NO SURPRISE
orderbird POS iPad point of sale system

1x Salat Becher 4,80 € 4,80 € A
2x Brötchen 50 Cent 0,50 € 1,00 € A
11,80 €
Gegeben (Kartenzahlu 11,80 €
Bedient von: Carlotta
Tisch: Theke
Terminal: iPad von Oliver

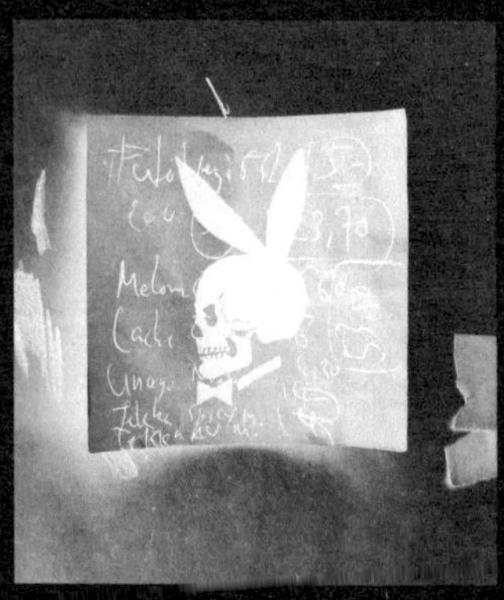

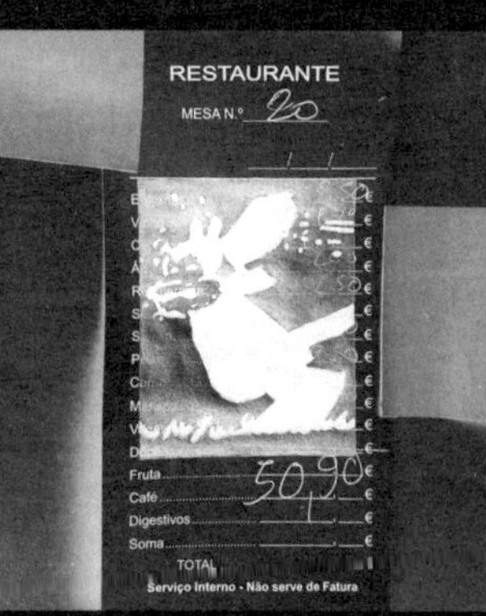
RESTAURANTE
MESA N.º 20
Fruta
Café
Digestivos
Soma
TOTAL
Serviço Interno · Não serve de Fatura

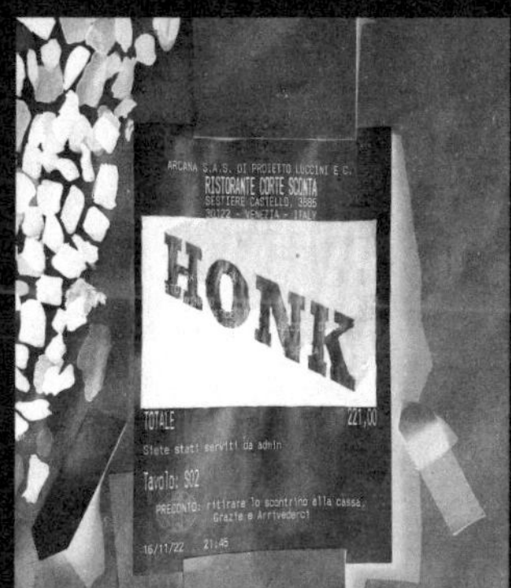
ARCANA S.A.S. DI PROIETTO LUCCINI E C.
RISTORANTE CORTE SCONTA
HONK
TOTALE 221,00
Siete stati serviti da admin
Tavolo: S02
PRECONTO: ritirare lo scontrino alla cassa,
Grazie e Arrivederci
16/11/22 21:45

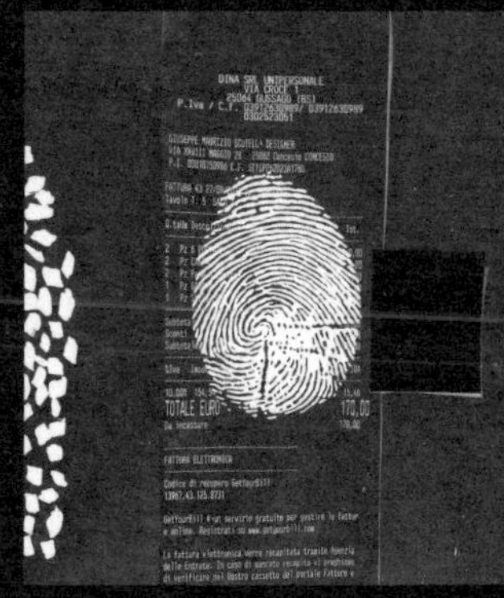
DINA SRL UNIPERSONALE
VIA CROCE 1
TOTALE EURO 170,00
FATTURA ELETTRONICA

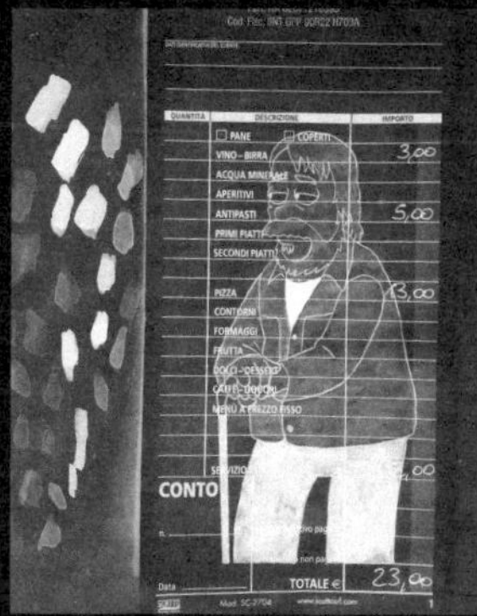
PANE
COPERTI
VINO - BIRRA
ACQUA MINERALE
APERITIVI
ANTIPASTI
PRIMI PIATTI
SECONDI PIATTI
PIZZA
CONTORNI
FORMAGGI
FRUTTA
CONTO
TOTALE €
3,00
5,00
13,00
23,00

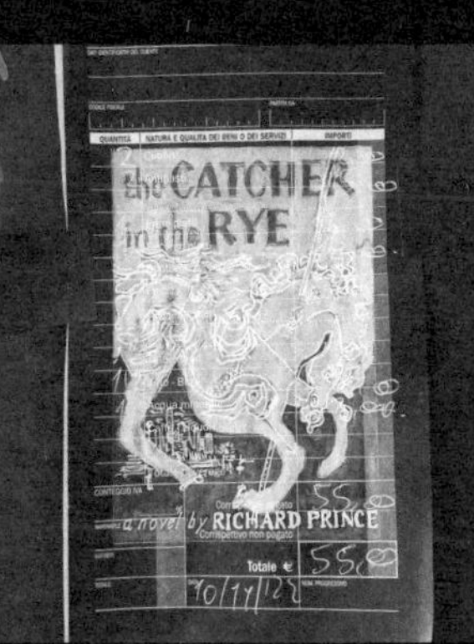
the CATCHER in the RYE
a novel by RICHARD PRINCE
Totale €
55,00

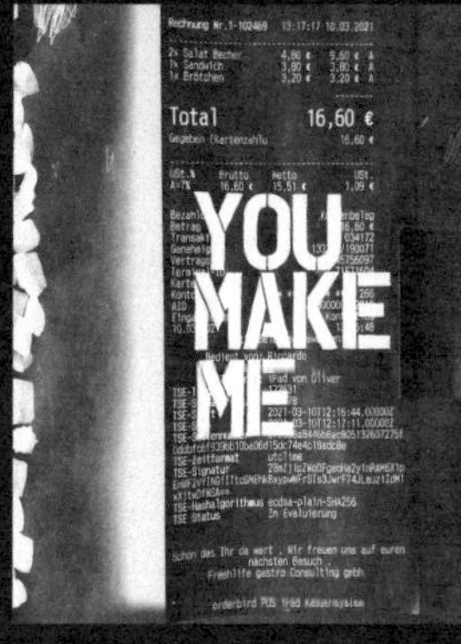
Rechnung Nr.1-102469 13:17:17 10.03.2021
Total 16,60 €
YOU MAKE ME
Freshlife gastro Consulting gmbh

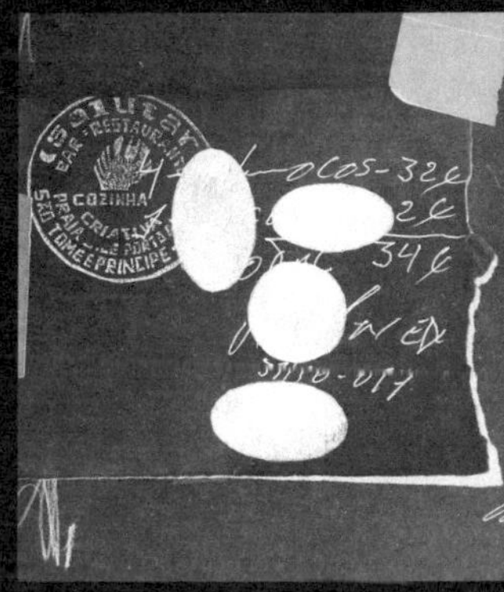
BAR - RESTAURANTE
COZINHA
SÃO TOMÉ E PRINCIPE

The Office of Culture and Design

7 Shoreline Street

Parañaque City

Ph 1700

Clara Balaguer (CB) & Czar Kristoff (CK)

Clara Balaguer is a Rotterdam-based (via Manila) artist, publisher, educator, and sometimes internet troll. Czar Kristoff is a Philippines-based photographer and educator. The two work as a part of the collective publishing imprint Hardworking Goodlooking (HWGL) along with the designers Dante Carlos and Kristian Henson. Through limited-run publications, often produced in Filipino "cottage-industry" presses, the collective engages with such topics as "the decolonization of cultural labor, parlance in the vernacular, and the value of what has been invisible." While several tenants of bootlegging run strong in the studio (collective authorship, politics of print, alternative means of production and distribution), I was particularly curious about the ways in which they contextualize and deploy a unique Filipino vernacular generated from interconnected layers of cultural mimicry. Their publications not only preserve and promote this cultural vocabulary, but attempt to rethink the complex power dynamics involved in any bootlegging or appropriation discourse. Interview by Ben Schwartz (BS).

BS: In my research, I've been reconsidering what bootlegging means today—what an extended definition of the gesture might be given the evolution of culture and technologies since its inception. In that spirit, I'm wondering about your relationship to the idea, especially with practices that move between borders. I'm thinking here about ideas of smuggling and infiltration.

CB: I think the term "bootlegging" is a very Western term, more associated with subcultures, especially related to music. In the Philippines, I would equate it with the local understanding of piracy. It's not that I don't like the term "bootleg"—the way it sounds and what it implies is actually really interesting. I like the idea of slipping something in your boot, of smuggling something so close to your body that it reacts to your temperature.

I am interested in piracy, but an ethical form of piracy, if that can even exist. Ethical in the sense also of being a collective code, as honorable as possible in the eyes of a ragtag few who function at the edges of legality, in the realm of the dishonorable. And an ethics constructed with the possibility of unalignment, of individual boundaries (moralities) that are in slight disagreement.

I think about unauthorized redistribution. Piracy for me involves this concept of booty. Essentially, booty you are looting. There are of course several factors to consider in this looting. Who is receiving a majority of the benefits or profits? From whom are you taking, and to whom are you redirecting this expropriation? It's not as cut-and-dry as saying that any desirable end justifies any means whatsoever. How can those means involve as little violence as possible? When is that theft simply a form of restitution that could by no other means be acquired? What rules govern the notion of thievery, who wrote those rules, and whom do those rules disproportionately benefit?

I also really connect with this idea of smuggling between borders. I recently migrated my practice from Manila to Rotterdam, where I live today. And in that respect I see bootlegging relating to this idea of remittance. In Filipino culture, you are often expected or driven to migrate to richer lands in search of opportunity, and then remit much of the capital you earn abroad back to your family at home. The culture of remittance is not just socially ingrained in the kinship politics of the Philippines—a kinship based not as strictly on blood as it is on debt, and debts of gratitude, and neighborly proximity—these remittances are economic touchstones. They account for roughly 11% of the country's GDP.

I left the Philippines for a professional opportunity overseas, like so many other people. Unlike so many other people, I have the privilege of a dual nationality passport that allows me mobility. I left, and logically got closer to the microphone of access to (cultural) capital. I think about trafficking within and through institutional walls, how to facilitate a system for people to do their own trafficking... of bodies, of knowledge, of practices, rigging it so that others too can be in range of that proverbial microphone.

CK: I also think of bootlegging as pirating, and the ubiquity of pirating music in the two-thousands. When it comes to design, I remember in the early stage of my photography practice, I worked for magazines, and was often given reference images by the editor or clients. They are called "peg" from "jpeg," but also "peg" like a "pegboard." These references were often from the West, and Filipino photographers and stylists would essentially try to copy them. I think bootlegging for us is much more aspirational, an attempt at mimicking what was considered beautiful by the West, which I think is also important to reassess.

CB: Exactly, bootlegging from the periphery is often aspirational. You're trying to bootleg whiteness, Western culture, modernism. And I love the term "peg," it speaks to what or whom you are trying to serve.

> BS: I'm curious about this cultural mimicry, especially as it's filtered through your practice Hardworking Goodlooking. I'm interested in how this attempt to emulate or recreate another culture might become its own unique framework or identity. I'm also interested in the complex and delicate dynamics between the various cultures.

CB: I've been thinking of HWGL recently in the framework of ventriloquism. A friend of mine actually bootlegged a book for me, *Dumbstruck: A Cultural History of Ventriloquism*, which speaks to this idea of not trying to copy but to throw your voice, to control the dummy. With our work, I believe we were trying to reverse that source of power, to be the ventriloquist of a voice in design (or material culture) and not the dummy beholden to a foreign puppet master. The Western—sigh, caveat, yes, I get that the West is a contested concept, but here I speak from an imperfect map drawn from the lens of a Southeast Asian postcolony—voice is inevitably present, or rather this bootlegged Western voice is always present. It is undeniable that graphic design, as a field of professionalized practice, was invented as a Euro-Anglo project. This fact can never be undone, and it would be disingenuous to think that we can renege these roots. Well, OK, perhaps it was not really *invented* by the West, but rather given a name, structure of certification, canon of propriety, all mass-instituted in public consciousness as a profession. HWGL is interested in not just mimicking the modernist West, but speaking with, within, and against it, discovering our own language of agency. This language was made possible by the work of Kristian Henson and Dante Carlos coming into contact with mine and Czar's notions of design, learned elsewhere and otherwise.

The demographics of our publishing hauz are a microcosm of Filipino-ness, skewed slightly towards privileged class. Quick-and-dirty statistics state that HWGL is 50% queer, 50% straight, 75% cismale, 15% cisfemale, 50% diaspora, 50% local, 12.5% white, 12.5% Taiwanese, 75% Filipino native (but 0% indigenous), 25% middle class, 50% second generation upper class, 25% old school upper class. Two people educated abroad within a highly modernist Western system, but with a tender longing for a local culture from which they were dislocated through migration. And two others—both born and raised in the Philippines, yet of different class strata—doing field work and translation, as well as "the design work" itself, both working through a distancing from post-colonial inferiority complex.

Kristian and Dante were able to pass hybridized local culture through their filter to create a specific vernacular. It's not necessarily local, but it takes the local as a starting point. And here, Czar and I have

pp. 246–247: Spread from *FFF (Filipino Folk Foundry)* (2015)

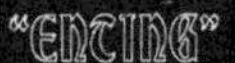

Clemente D. Diaz 17/10/1962
+63 920 8713812
Molino III
Bacoor City, Cavite

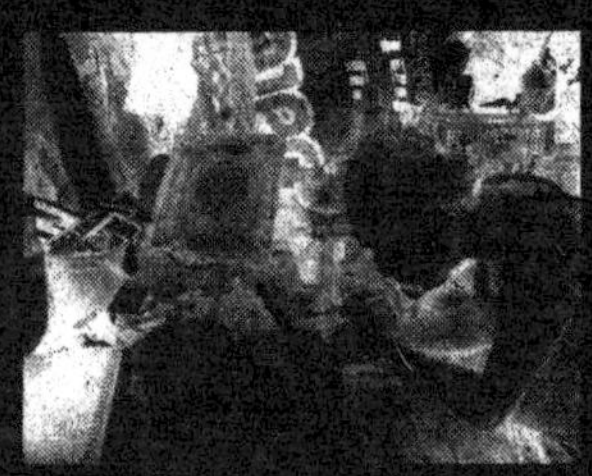

HAMBURGE
hamburge
FONTSIV
fontsiv

ISULAT ANG MGA LETRANG ITO SA SARILING NYONG STYLE (GAMITIN ANG BRUSH)
Use a brush to write the following letters in your own signature freehand

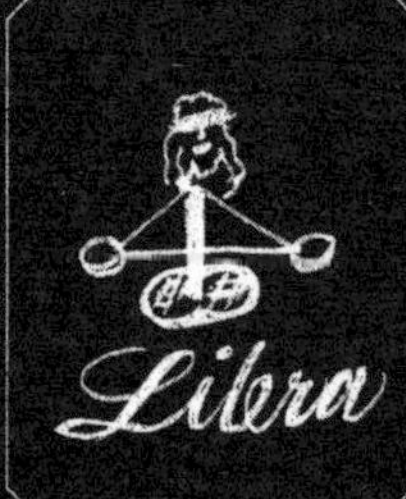

ILARAWAN ANG HOROSCOPE SIGN NYO.
Draw your horoscope sign

ILARAWAN ANG ISANG BAGAY NA RELIHIYOSO
Draw something religious

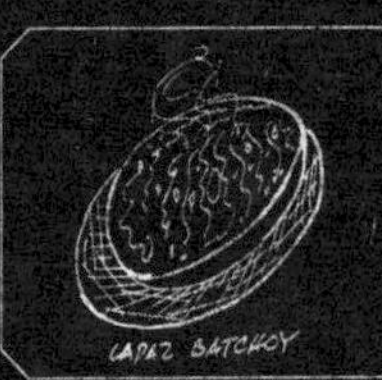

ILARAWAN ANG ISANG SIMBOLO/LUGAR/BAGAY GALING SA PROBINSYA NYO
Draw something symbolic of the place/province you are from

Members FFF 206

"FRANCIS"
Francis M. Mejia 31/07/1968
francis.mejia91@yahoo.com
+63 929 8276227
237 Dr. Pilapil Street, San Miguel
Pasig City, MM

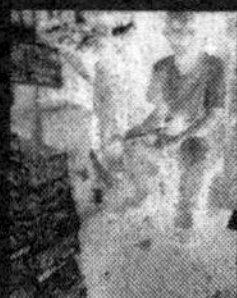
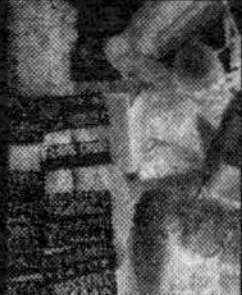
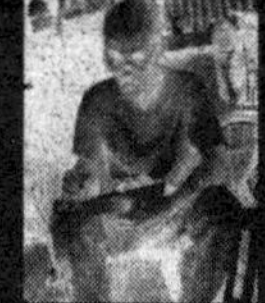

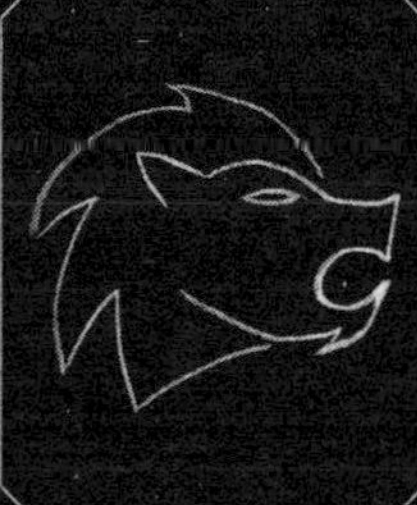

ILARAWAN ANG HOROSCOPE SIGN NYO.
Draw your horoscope sign

HAMBURGE
hamburge
FONTSIV
fontsiv

ISULAT ANG MGA LETRANG ITO SA SARILING NYONG STYLE (GAMITIN ANG BRUSH)
Use a brush to write the following letters in your own signature freehand

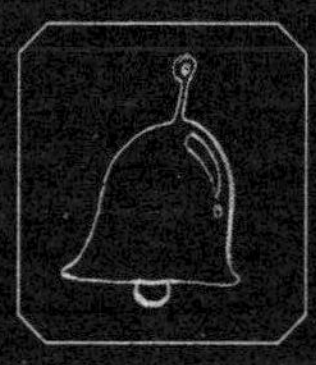

ILARAWAN ANG ISANG BAGAY NA RELIHIYOSO
Draw something religious

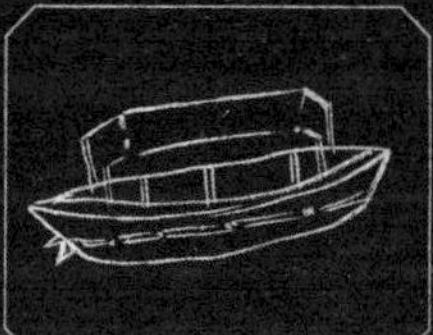

ILARAWAN ANG ISANG SIMBOLO/LUGAR/BAGAY GALING SA PROBINSYA NYO
Draw something symbolic of the place/province you are from

Members /FFF 207

played a key role. As interlocal interlocutors, translating a landscape unfamiliar, unfamiliar even sometimes to ourselves. This relaying has involved active rediscovery of our home territory. And in that relay of data, providing context and emotion, not just mood board imagery, our interpreting has also conspired to create this creolized visual lexicon. Without this diasporic and multi-shaded exchange, this new dialect would not have been possible.

Filipino visual culture is subject to a condition or conditioning which gives it the delightfully and painfully wild aesthetic we see today. So we are interested in interacting with that visual culture, understanding the conditions that created it in order to define new rules for play.

It's not this idea of decolonizing as a refusal. It's impossible to refuse all the things we have become indoctrinated with. I can't refuse my post-colonial self. I can only engage in its repair and repurpose. It's also quite easy to refuse when one already has a subsidized, funded seat at the Western fountainhead. On the edges of want, in the outskirts of visibility, in the realm of the barely audible, one cannot totally refuse the structure of force and control imposed upon you. How do you reverse the relationship to this conditioning, inverting the ratio of power, acknowledging yourself as inextricably entangled with it? You become the ventriloquist, not the dummy. And how to love the dummy as well, even as you bend its voice to yours? Fucking complicated. Because there is this fascination with modernism as well, this respect for its forms and shapes, a nod to its noble intention of common, inclusive order (however failed this inclusivity might have been.) Common in the sense of the people. The unsubjugated respect for modernism coexists with an unironic love for vulgarity. Vulgar in the sense of the everyday, the way certain plants are given the species name *vulgaris* because they grow everywhere, are well-known. I will not pretend I don't like any Western design or that I haven't learned anything from its practitioners, many of whom I consider friends, many of whom are not white.

> BS: I love that you brought up this idea of ventriloquism. I've been interested in gathering analogies that relate to bootlegging and help me to pinpoint a more specific or developed understanding of the act. Lately I've been thinking of karaoke vs. lip syncing. It's about copying but adding your own voice, performing, participating.

CB: Right! There is a lot of joy in knowing it's a copy through your own voice. TikTok remixes are a testament to that collective pleasure.

CK: It makes me think of drag performances. When you put on drag, you create a new version of yourself or extension of yourself and/or embody the person that you aspire to be. And most of the time there is a performance involved to activate this drag you created. Most of the time they sing songs by a diva, or in some cases by a pop group like Vengaboys. Through this process, they could articulate and/or practice their own desires, their hopes, their dreams through the lyrics, the rhythm, the vibration of the speakers, the stage, the clap. A friend who visited me recently here in the Philippines asked me, "Why do Filipino men like to sing songs about heartbreaks?" I responded, "Probably because men aren't allowed and/or trained to articulate our feelings, so we just sing them for three to four minutes, and in most cases fueled by Kwatro kantos, Tanduay, or a bucket of beer."

CB: I have been trying to locate, to no avail, an explanation of a corporate talking format/exercise called "bull session." In vernacular talk in the Philippines (borrowing, I believe, from North American slang), it's like saying "let's get down to business" or "let's have a real talk." But I once read a paper or article that described it as a kind of role-playing conversation where I, as a participant, could inhabit opinions that I didn't really possess or were opposite to how I might really think or feel. In this setting, I could say something without certainty being ascribed to it. It's a place to try out an extension of the I's persona. It allows for the possibility of retraction: statements are a costume. It could also be a roundabout way of saying without saying, of smuggling an opinion you cannot fully express yet for fear of the retributions around honesty. This can be frustrating, to not be able to speak of things directly, but it is understandably attractive in cultures that prize saving face. Bull sessions feel like a form of bootlegging.

> BS: Earlier you mentioned the idea of ethical piracy. I think that today in fashion there is this idea of an "official bootleg." How do these two contradictory ideas exist alongside each other in your practices?

CB: It has a lot to do with the conditions I touched upon earlier: who's copying, to what extent, and for what purpose. I'm most concerned with the "who's copying" aspect of this. In some conversations with people involved with F/LOSS (Free/Libre Open-Source Software), my concern with who's copying is slightly distasteful. In this community, there can be this idealistic notion of free = free for everyone without restrictions, even to those you may not align with. It is an anarchist more than socialist approach to property. (Oh yeah, I don't use socialism as a boogeyman word, as some people do in the U.S.) Even though it's a free market, there are still power structures that apply and that are activated swiftly to crush little people with good ideas. How do you regulate the oppressive tendency of an unregulated market? How can you keep it truly free? Freedom implies equity.

I do think F/LOSS is a noble way of approaching culture, content, and creation. But in its purest sense, it can also be a bit naive, as it doesn't necessarily take intersectionality of struggles into account. Who is copying very much matters. Free culture becomes painful when you are on the lower rungs of the power ladder. This is where something like cultural appropriation comes into play.

While cultural appropriation discourse is a way to protect communities who are marginalized, taken to an extreme it becomes problematic. It becomes a discourse of racial purity vehiculated by the progressive left, who have become progressively puritan. It's punitive puritanism that uncomfortably fertilizes soil for the rise of the alt-right.

There's nothing progressive about racial or cultural purity. It is often merely the same oppression, just with another hand holding the whip. The weapon of purity is wielded not just amongst the rich, wealthy, white, and cismale. It is often turned on people who are on the same side but living through singularly different experiences of what racial, cultural, gendered, and so many other forms of marginalization can be. A culture of disproportionate offense that positions any question as attack and invalidation… this kind of culture generates an inability to dialogue with difference. Like any form of inbreeding, it is unhealthy in the long run. No matter how justified the motive of segregation, at the end of the day, when applied as a default form of structural operation and not as a tactical defense mechanism, segregation is harmful because it precludes diversity. When we are fighting more often with each other than with the systems that subjugate us all in the first place, this makes the work of seeking justice, redress, and change more exhausting than it needs to be. I'm tired.

When you talk about appropriation vs. bootlegging, there are so many nuanced factors at play. We need to be thinking about contexts, intention. Yes, intention. Controversial, as the road to hell is paved with good intentions. But yes, intention: it doesn't exonerate, but it does mitigate. Maybe it's also about setting up personal limits, which I have to often do when moonlighting as an internet troll hunter. I need to establish my own moral limits of who I hunt, why, in what circumstances, and how far I go.

BS: Can trolling be bootlegging?

CB: I think yes, if you're inhabiting a different persona. There are infiltrator trolls, who smuggle themselves into forums by misrepresenting their position. These trolls exit their own echo chamber and pretend to be on the side of whatever it is they actually oppose, making subtle counter-arguments within the community they infiltrate. It's a long process to break down ideologies and build sensitivity. At times, you're forced to cede your own morality to build a larger ethical framework. Counter-indoctrination doesn't happen overnight and it's important to keep the greater goal in mind, for example, trolling against fascism or toppling the patriarchy. I've sometimes found myself at odds with some behaviors of troll pack members I've hunted alongside. I'm careful how I critique people's behavior in those affinity-action groups. You don't want to destroy relationships within the pack. But also, pawning your moral boundaries to peer pressure is unsettling. It's not fun to troll hunt as a tiny mob when your comrades are being openly transphobic, classist, racist, misogynistic, etcetefuckingra. Again, it's a long game, a slow process to create change. And it cannot really be done alone. Change is almost invariably a collective process. The dark beauty of collectivity is that it is a labor of holding difference so that we may evolve together, at different speeds but at the same time, or at least in the same direction

> BS: I feel like it relates back to this notion of a bull session: the suspension of acceptability for a more honest conversation, or in this case, to reach a particular goal.

CB: Yes, it makes me think about what is happening right now. The right are very adept at being tolerant within their own ideology because they are the culturally deviant position. A GOP gayservative can work with a Christian evangelist hardliner if it means getting Trump re-elected. There is an ideological truce that happens, an acceptance of working (or trolling) together to support the same larger ideas. The left, on the other hand, is deeply fragmented.

All the infighting to define who on the left holds the purest version of being on the left means losing sight of any larger goal, of the shared struggle.

> BS: I'm curious about the relationship between bootlegging, trolling, and legitimacy. Trolling, like bootlegging, used to feel like an underground, bottom-up, subversive act meant to wreak havoc on those in power. And now the trolls hold the power, using troll-like tactics that create an aura of outsider authenticity. In a similar progression, I think about bootlegs embraced by luxury brands, and the complex and confusing ways in which they garner legitimacy by embracing the aesthetics of illegitimacy.

CB: Right. It's about understanding these aesthetics of legitimacy, and how those can be used or manipulated. Manipulated as in handled, molded, something that happens with the hands. In the past, for example in traditional news media, to be legitimate you had to have a polished, error-free look that made it seem like there was a legitimately professional apparatus supporting your image, graphics, output. But now the aesthetics of trust come from imperfection. Grainy, jerky cell phone or CCTV footage on the news feels slightly more believable than high-res camera work. The same goes for conspiracy theories and how they generate a sense of accessing knowledge that short circuits centralized narratives of power. And this shift, where authorities are realizing the potential of a grassroots aesthetic, is nothing new. We're just reawakening to how much a part of our culture this is.

I used to work at an advertising agency, and when we would have campaigns with user-generated content, I would make fake user content to falsify public interest. This is called astroturfing. I didn't realize how insidious this was at the time. But then that's advertising for you. A corruption of the mind, flesh, spirit. A deal with the devil, who incidentally sells potato chips. Villainhood is ever so complex. The devil is also a methodical teacher if you are able to not only survive, but transcend him. (I've used astroturfing in my troll hunting as a non-violent way of seeding other points of view.) Yes, him. Advertising was also patriarchy par excellence.

> BS: Czar, I'd love to hear about your Temporary UnReLearning (URL) Academy. To me it speaks to the potential of bootlegging structures and systems, a way for the gesture to move beyond objects.

CK: I would say that Temporary UnReLearning Academy is an accumulation of different structures that I was able to encounter and experienced since I started my practice. It is a nest made from different types of twigs and leaves. Or actually, it is a nest modeled from other nests.

The collective 98B Collaboratory are the first people who welcomed me to be part of a conversation. This was back in 2013. I did not know anyone from the art and cultural community. My world back then revolved only around photography, skateboarding, Tumblr (Academy), and unemployment. I see great value in this encounter especially when Mark Salvatus, who was the director back then, introduced me to a pirate copy of Susan Sontag's *On Photography*. I think from then on, I became more critical and serious with my work. I somehow had an idea of the direction of my life.

Another important part of this nest is Thousandfold. It was initiated by Wawi Navarroza in 2015, to provide a space for photographers to get to know each other and introduce us to critical conversations and projects. They organized a photography festival, portfolio reviews, discussion on photobooks—in some way, I see Thousandfold as a school. I live in the outskirts of Manila and I vividly remember taking the PNR train just to attend these gatherings. This is how I met Clara actually, who I only knew through the internet, as an Instagram friend. After a year, Clara and I did a series of book pirating workshops/sessions. We would meet at a cafe with friends and each bring books. The cafe was situated next to a copy shop and we would go over and just photocopy the books we liked. During these sessions we would talk about our book selection and also talk about politics, pop culture, gossip, et cetera. I would say that this type of gathering reminded me that learning can happen anywhere, that studying in a group is always fun, and also that it is okay to pirate, especially if it is for educational purposes!

My encounter with Para://Site Projects in 2017 was also a big part of the conception of URL. It was founded by siblings Mariano Batocabe and Abbey Romina. They would organize exhibitions, film screenings, and talks at their home in Las Piñas, at a farm (hosted by Saree Gloria), a botanical garden (with Nomina Nuda), and even within a Minecraft server (with Club Matryoshka, Likido, and Spoonin Boys). I was attracted to their practice because somehow it reminds me how skateboarders (re)define spaces. And also they were very welcoming. I was not part of their circle, but they were kind enough to let me intervene in their nests.

Also, my involvement with Hardworking Goodlooking, being exposed to material and content that I rarely pay attention to, was a big part of the formation of URL. I remember in 2019 when Clara and I visited the Asia Art Archive in Hong Kong—I would say it was a life-changing moment. I remember being surrounded by thousands of books written by brilliant minds, and I couldn't help but be emotional. Because access to endless knowledge is a privilege that I do not think I would have had, given my social background.

Intramuros is a walled city located in Manila, built by the Spaniards during their colonization. Within this city, the first universities were established. In an article by Peter Murphy and Trevor Hogan called "Discordant Order: Manila's Neo-Patrimonial Urbanism"—which was, by the way, distributed to me by a friend with JSTOR access—they say that, "Variations of the Intramuros model became widespread through the Philippine archipelago. This was based on a social-symbolic understanding that the world was divided into domains with strong boundaries and that careful gatekeeping was needed so as to regulate the relation between domain and environment in favor of the protected domain rather than open environment. This contrasts with the church-and-plaza model where the apse and square – or the portico and square – function as inter-mediation between domains. In the latter case, persons are constantly crossing from one domain to another through the portal spaces of public spheres. In this model, gateways operate to facilitate

pp. 258–261: Workshops hosted at Temporary URL

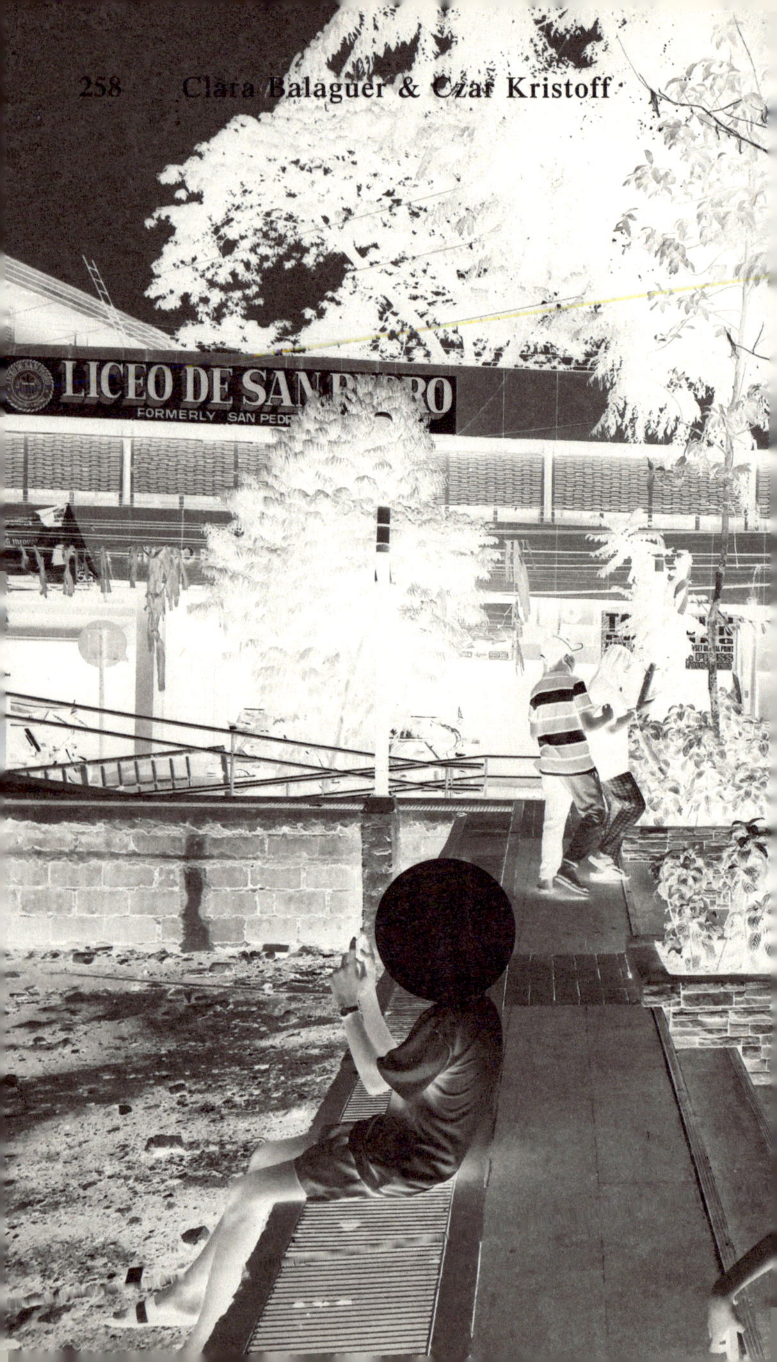
LICEO DE SAN
FORMERLY

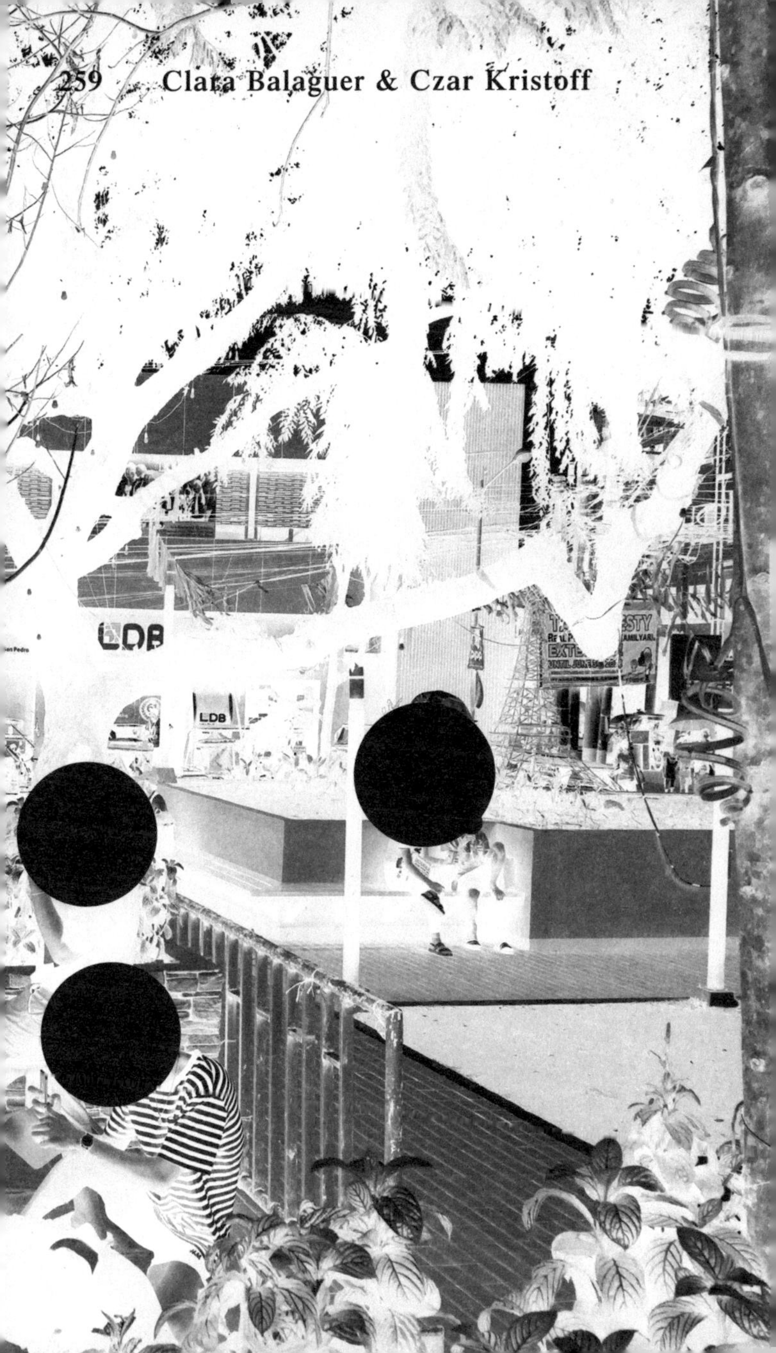
LDB
LDB

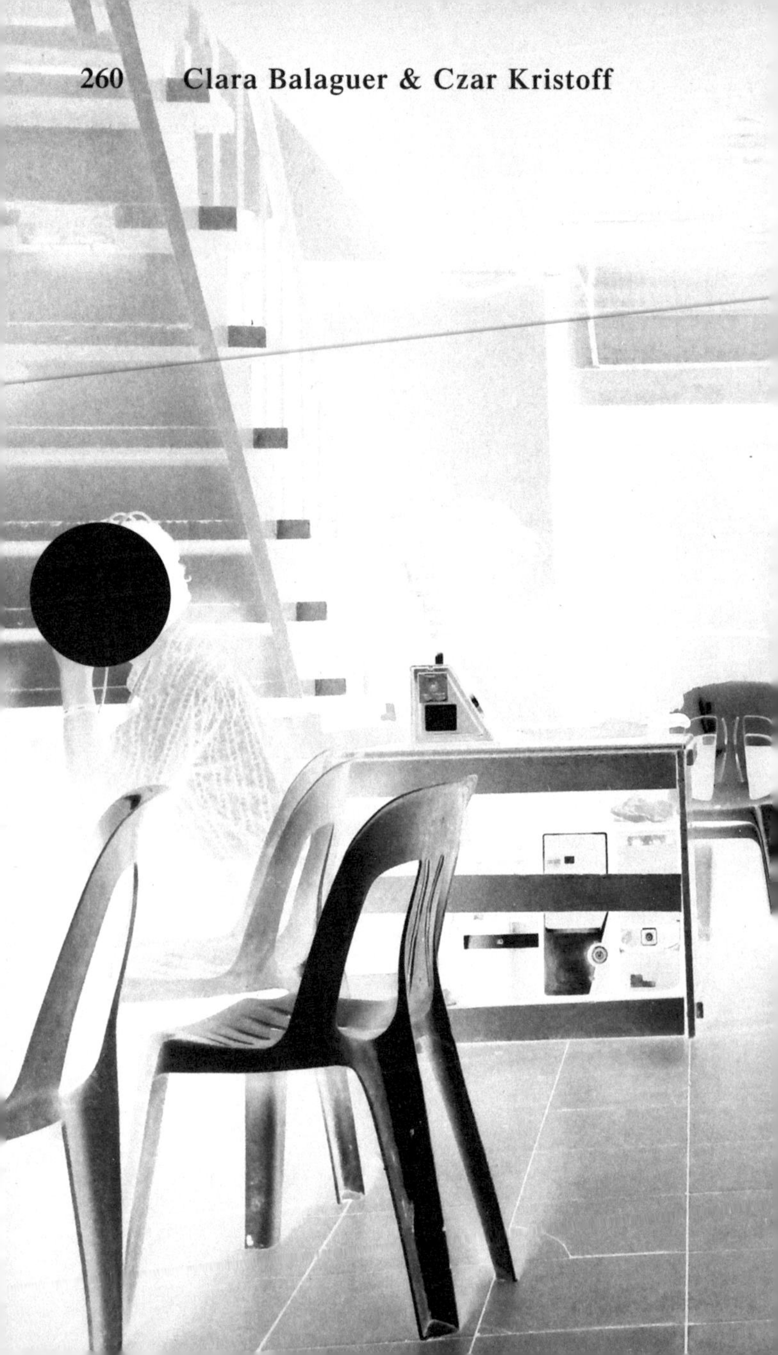

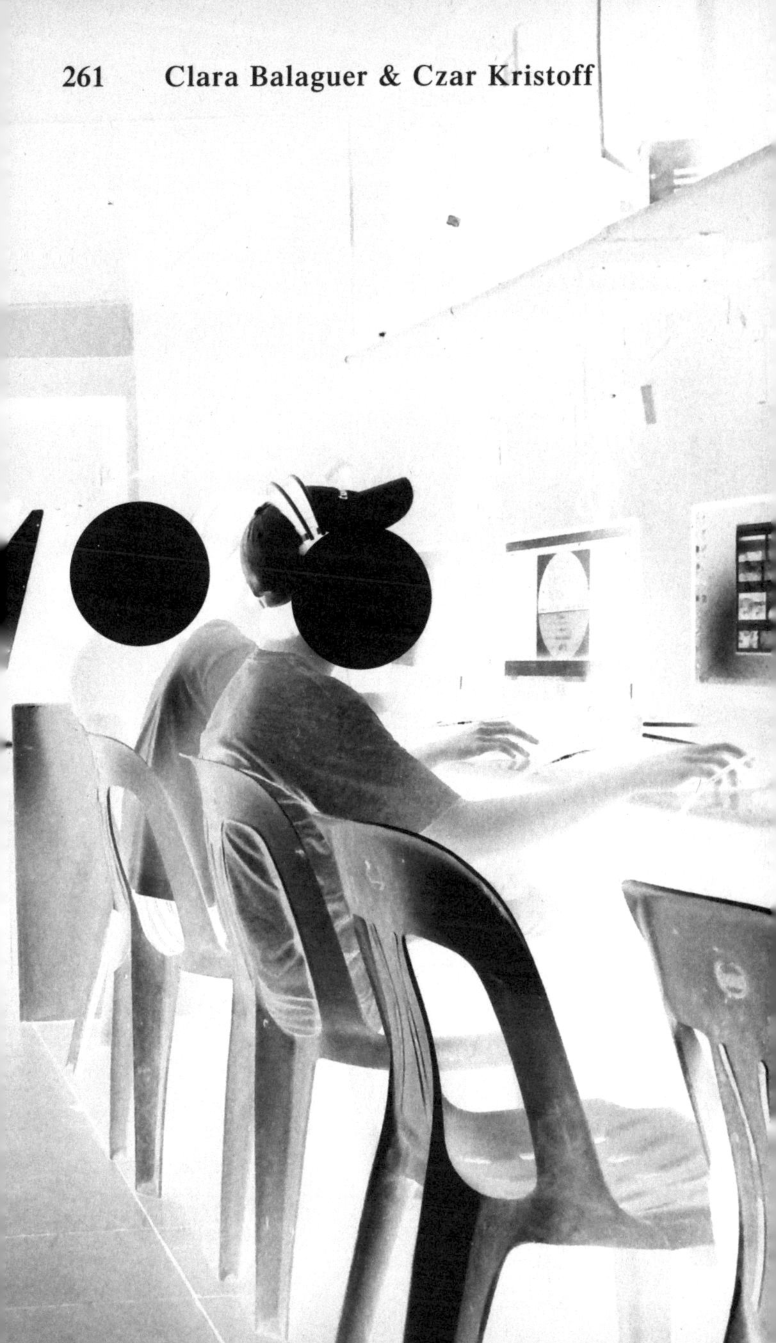

orderly traffic between domain and environment." I have been thinking a lot about this text recently.

The people and organizations I mentioned earlier play a big role in the agency that I have now. They are the portals that provided new possibilities. And I think the formation of URL is a way to extend the goodness of these portals. The act of extending as bootlegging. But I think in reality, there is a lot of work to do. URL is still within the gateways I would say. It operates within privileged domains, those who have access to the internet for example, those who are connected to its network. How about those who are beyond URL's reach? How will the leaking and redistribution reach them? I do admit that URL is imperfect at the moment, but to be sure, the one thing that it will not bootleg is the oppressive structure of Intramuros and its bootlegs.

CB: So what Czar did is make his own art school in reaction to the monolithic art education in the Philippines. We don't have art schools, but we do have certain departments in certain universities, oftentimes turning out artists with a very similar output. So Czar created Temporary URL in defiance of those institutions. And that was also my experience: for so many years doing pedagogy and workshops, and in reality what I was setting up were schools. The workshop is an educational format, it only took me ten years to realize, oh, I'm an educator.

CK: It has been challenging to enter an academy as a teacher. I had to prove that I am worthy and capable, which of course every job application requires. But I guess I was used to conducting workshops without thinking about If what I give is/ I am enough.

But luckily, the school I used to work at was very interested in the pedagogical approach I did for URL and outside of URL. So when I was working on the syllabus for the semester, I was referencing a lot to what URL embodies. I would say that I bootlegged URL for this particular school. :-)

BS: It gets at this idea of infiltration. Maybe the most effective way to change any system is to work from within?

CB: Right, it's all about getting through security.

Title page (p. 240): Logo for The Office of Culture & Design

BLESS Nº 37 New Sheheit

BLESS No 33 Artistcare

BLESS No 28
climate confusion assistance

BLESS Nº 59
Holding on
the Explosion

BLESS swimming together
Nº 61

BLESS (B)

BLESS is the creative polymath lead by partners Desiree Heiss and Ines Kaag. Since 1995, BLESS has succeeded in consistently being inconsistent, seamlessly moving between areas of fashion, home goods, product design, performance, installation, and contemporary art — often thriving in the blurry boundaries of each. The resulting objects are otherworldly, completely familiar yet totally alien, best understood as fully "BLESS." What is surprising is that the motives that shape this utterly unique practice remain quite practical. As Heiss and Kaag explain, their work is strongly tied to ideas of structure, sustainability, reuse, and recontextualization. The Multicollection T-Shirt is a paradigm of this thinking: an official bootleg of an unofficial bootleg, which begins to answer (or ask) what does it mean to bootleg yourself? Interview by Ben Schwartz (BS).

> BS: How do you understand bootlegging today? Do you see a relationship between the idea of bootlegging and your work?

B: Over the past years, our understanding of the word "bootlegging" has changed a lot. Instead of seeing it as a lesser version or reproduction of an object or concept (a copy to be sold at a cheaper price), we have come to view it as a method of research and a means of getting to know an original.

In terms of the reproduction of our own design and ideas, we feel quite inviolable. As a small brand, we consider it an honor if the products we create trigger the desire in others to possess, copy, or reproduce them, as you wouldn't do this with something meaningless. On the contrary, it hurts much more when people who were part of our structure apply laboriously researched contacts and long term relationships to their own or other brands. In such an event, we try to be as easy and Buddhistic as possible. We call our profession "situation design," a sportive and spiritual import/export business.

If bootlegging also means the elegant infiltration of existing systems (consumerism and our society in general) then we would like to reserve a seat in the front row of underground activists. We are constantly working on the sustainability of our structure.

BS: Could you elaborate on how you consider sustainability in your practice?

B: Since 2012, with the creation of BLESS N°46 Contemporary Remediation, we stopped purchasing fabrics at a large scale and began to rely on the leftovers of big fashion houses, such as Hermès and Fendi. This strategy allows us to work with amazing quality, but considerably reduces the number of pieces we can create. Production-wise, it's absolutely inefficient, but it allows us to work with materials we otherwise could not afford. Further, we constantly use and re-use our own design leftovers which is our way to clean our path up and take responsibility for all items that didn't find a satisfied owner. We re-transform them and propose them as unique pieces every season. Examples of such products are:

BLESS N°49 Insert Editions: We cut existing BLESS tops and jackets at the shoulder line and insert a piece of fabric from the current collection to link the pieces. It can then be worn with the additional part around the neck, which makes it look like the piece has an incorporated scarf, or you can let it fall down and it gives a more extended and dramatic silhouette.

BLESS N°67 Overstockjeans: A full pair of BLESS trousers is cut at the back and inserted as a front piece, attached to a jeans backside.

The way we think about sustainability and re-use in design carries over into our business structures. Often people think that designers should always be thinking about the next color of the season, or what crazy shape a product could develop. In reality, we need 98% of our creativity for developing alternative business models, interim solutions to survive with our little structure, and paying our team and rents punctually at the end of the month. Over the years we have developed a stable mix of collaborations, teaching and learning, barter deals, and crossed uses of budgets — the mix of strategies has become a growing experience. Our path allows us to discover how to use and combine interests and inspires us to sometimes interlink different projects: from those that are commercially necessary to those that are more of a hobby.

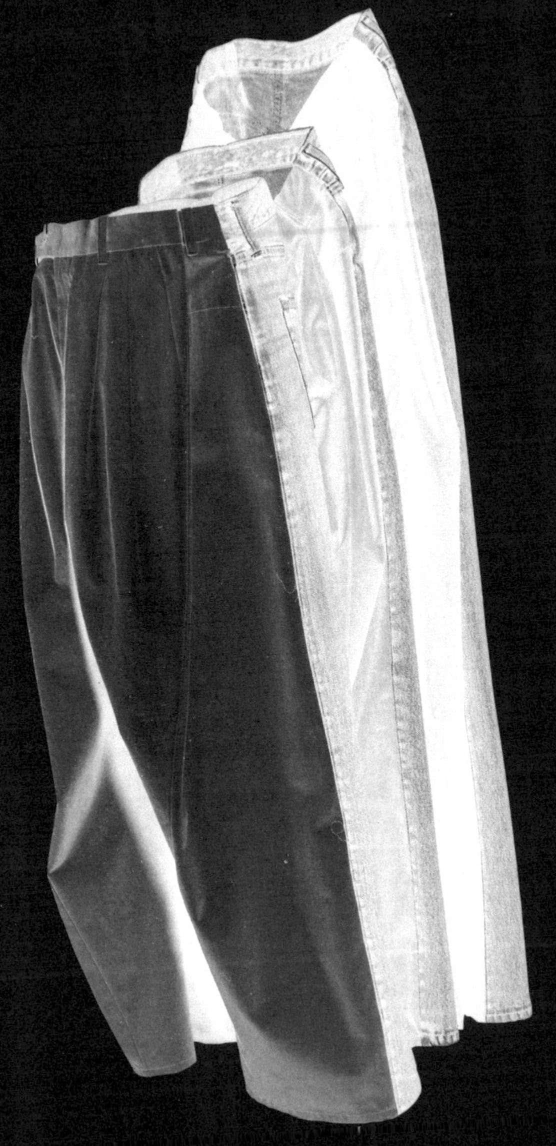

BS: I recently learned the backstory of the Multicollection t-shirt. Could you talk a little more about this piece?

B: Since the beginning, our practice has been mostly interested in re-use and re-assembly: taking existing items and augmenting them, combining them in a different way, bringing them to life in new contexts, reworking the idea of personal style that is always a mix of things, to bring clothing in as lifelong companions.

But we also recently came to copy ourselves with a bootleg BLESS product. One day Wendy from Ooga Booga, a store in LA, sent us a picture showing a young visitor in her shop wearing a T-shirt with a printed BLESS title: BLESS N°28 Climate Confusion Assistance. Wendy asked us if this was a real BLESS product, as she had never seen this before. It in fact wasn't a product from us, but we found it brilliant that someone "sampled" one of our titles in order to communicate it in the form of a product. We honestly felt embarrassed that we didn't do it ourselves in a lifespan of 25 years, especially since "title designing" is one of the dearest hobbies of BLESS!

Even after years of re-consuming our own visual output, it never came to our mind to re-use our own titles. In the middle of this inspirational moment, it felt like a fan product had revealed itself. So the Multicollection T-shirts were born, and we loved the way they developed. We are now in the second season and the T-shirts are having a good spread already.

We are reminded of another example of bootlegging in our work...many years ago, we found a wooden carved Coca-Cola bottle in a market in Zan-

p. 268: BLESS N°67 Situation Designer, Overstockjeans (2019)

zibar. We started to sell the bottle in our BLESS N°08 Found Object collection. This series included found and inexpensive objects that we felt should be aligned to a higher-priced market, as we were in awe of their craftsmanship. Originally we were afraid of getting in trouble with Coca-Cola, but they adored the object and sponsored the catalog and the event. At the time, they understood that the act of carving their banal and cheap product into wood was actually an act of honor. Then, us selling this product through lifestyle boutiques again elevated their image.

> BS: The Coca-Cola bottle seems like an especially intriguing and complex example of bootlegging because of the world of difference between the artisan's reality and the corporate world of Coca Cola. Do you feel the artisan properly benefited from this project? I begin to wonder how bootlegging defies or reinforces disparate power structures and fiscal inequalities?

B: It's a brilliant question and interesting to explore further what happened after this discovery. We later got back in touch with the artisans and re-ordered some bottles as they became quite popular. This then triggered our wish to have other items carved in wood, and we commissioned these Tanzanian woodcarvers to copy classic wristbands and digital watches that we wanted to wear in the form of wooden bangles.

Furthermore, they also carved sleeve parts and jewelry we made out of wood. Apart from the fact

p. 271: BLESS N°67 Situation Designer, Multicollection T-Shirt (2019)

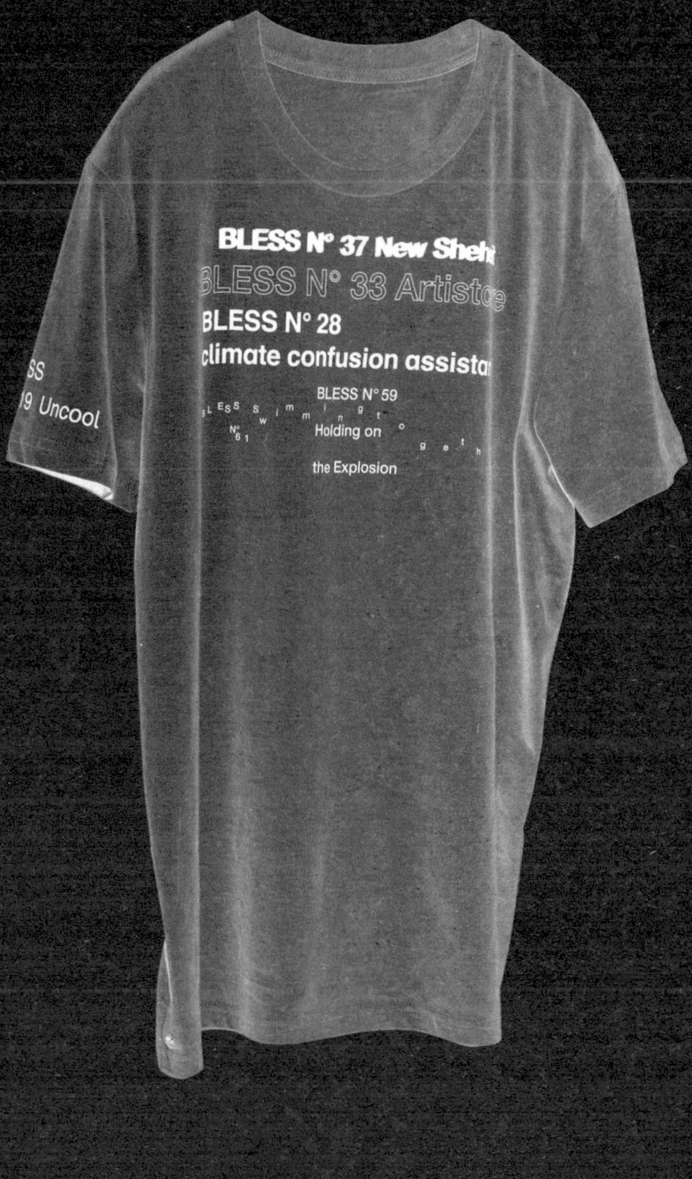

BLESS N° 37 New Shehi
BLESS N° 33 Artistce
BLESS N° 28
climate confusion assistar
SS
19 Uncool
BLESS N° 59
BLESS swimming together
N° 61
Holding on
the Explosion

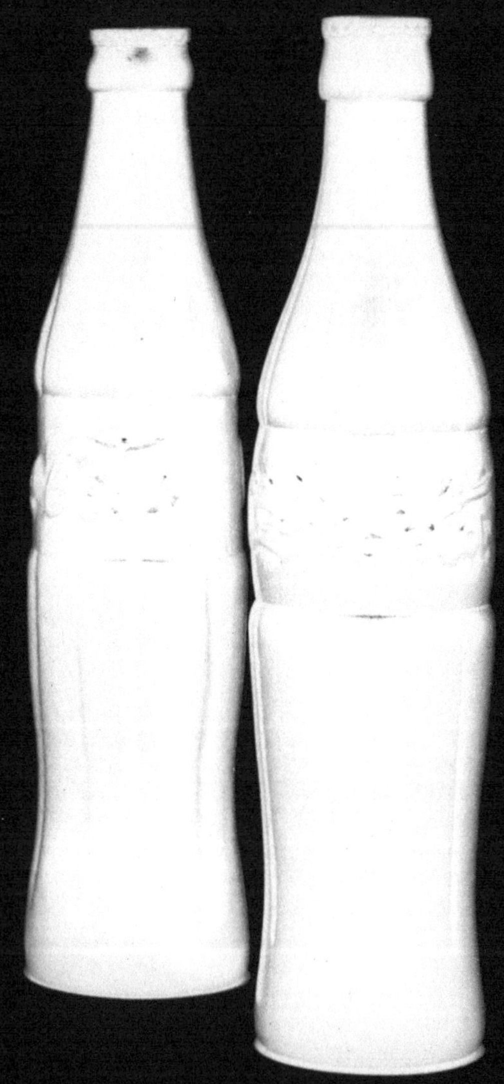

that we commissioned more work from the artisans, it made them aware of unique abilities and inspired them to carve objects other than the traditional statues they would normally sell on the market. We, by the way, also tried to commission traditional German woodcarvers in the Black Forest, and companies that specialized in wooden decorative works in France, but nobody could meet our expectations — the technical skills and knowledge to carve such intricate pieces had become a lost art.

BS: Bootleg fashion seem to be having a particular moment right now. Do you have any thoughts as to why brands have embraced this act and what the implications might be?

B: The bootleg factor is an indicator for objects of desire. No desire for the unreachable, no bootleg. The rarer and more desired the original, the more it gets bootlegged, quantity-wise.

Opposite to this, there are also conceptual and political acts that manifest through projects where partial content was extracted from its original context to create a new original, like a Vetements DHL T-shirt. The almost identical copy (use of the same cheap materials) could on one hand manifest as a message of complicity with low-paid workers. The piece could also be read as irony, spitting on workwear that is now a leisure gown for the rich, a way of devaluing the uniform and the labor behind it.

In this case, it seems as though a circle got closed. In a city like Berlin, it is truly impossible to

p. 272: BLESS N°08 Found Objects, Wooden Coca-Cola Bottle (2004)

distinguish between a well-rested homeless person and a Russian kid dressed in Balenciaga. Let's decide to like this and embrace the vision that the high-fashion-market is ready for occupational retraining.

The popularity of the bootleg as well speaks to the idea of authorship becoming more and more obsolete. Whatever you develop, people will have the right to appropriate and take further, as programmers do when they build based on open source. Everything interrelates and all original creation is influenced/has always been influenced by the pool of inspiration that is provided by its surroundings.

Thus, we as "creators" appreciate seeing the crucial point and goal shifting. Instead of "designers" we would describe what we do as situation design, meaning to be Impulsgeber und Auslöser (stimulator and trigger). The future will hopefully operate more with commonly shared values instead of celebrating single inventors that get pushed in the capitalistic world—concentrating on placing a successful product but forgetting about an all-round responsibility.

BS: Could you elaborate on this idea of "situation design?"

B: The whole process to find that term took us about 20 years. We realized more and more that the main act and special accomplishment of BLESS is not its products but its particularity of a self-defined, made-to-measure profession that is constantly evolving and adapting with the times. It is kind of category-free and could possibly act in whatever field of interest we define.

Since it is driven by personal need, without having to depend on any market, we are able to operate on a more intuitive level. We create whenever we feel the need for something, be it a product or a situation, that we can't find elsewhere. Often it is a situation that we find ourselves in when clients, people, and institutions would invite us to participate or come up with a project. The "term" was born when we had to define our input in a collaboration with a performance artist. Perhaps we were originally intending to develop costumes and set design, but we found ourselves thinking about the why and what for, and the screenplay and the movements itself, and in the end, it became more a situation that was shared with an audience.

BS: What is the future of bootlegs?

B: We imagine bootlegging as a trigger of participatory design: not wanting to purchase a bootlegged product, but creating a copy yourself. In this way you "honor" the existing design; you put in your own effort to personalize it. The time investment and joy of applying personal creative skills might lead that creation to a higher price level than the original (industrial manufactured) version.

Title page (p. 264): Graphic from the BLESS N°67 Situation Designer, Multicollection T-Shirt (2019)

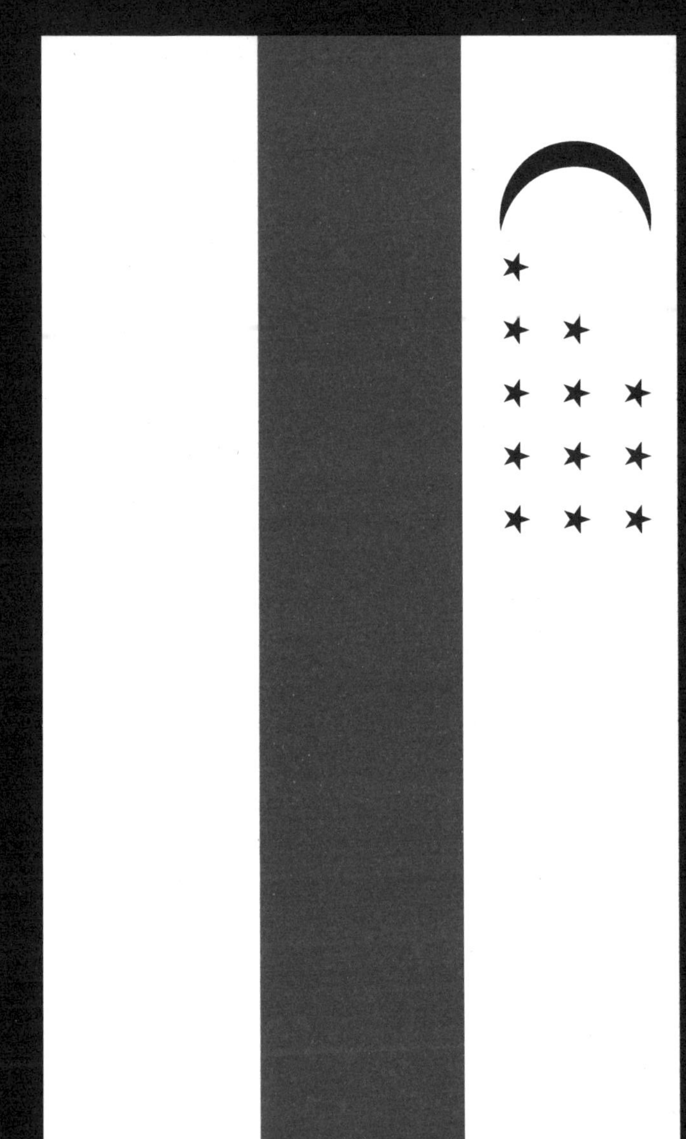

Hassan Kurbanbaev (HK)

Hassan Kurbanbaev is a Tashkent, Uzbekistan-based photographer. Throughout his practice, he explores both the complex history and evolving present of his country through vast landscapes, intimate portraits, and poetic still lifes. In one particular body of work, *Logomania: Owning The World at Half Price*, 2019–2020, Kurbanbaev documents bootleg fashion in Uzbekistan via raw in situ video and high-gloss studio photography. The series of photographs calls into question what happens when logos move across cultures, the creative potential of Chanel head scarves, and what it means for Uzbekistan to be labeled a "bootleg country." Interview by Ben Schwartz (BS).

> BS: In a statement for the 2020 exhibition 'The Real Thing', you wrote, "In a way, Uzbekistan is a bootleg country." Could you elaborate on that? How might the history of Uzbekistan relate to the bootleg obsession that you are documenting today?

HK: It was a figurative expression. I spoke about this in the context of borrowing signs from Western culture since Uzbekistan gained independence after the fall of the USSR. People were so happy about this freedom—from a protracted, wild shortage of goods, we jumped into the hands of the mass market, which began to overwhelm the country, and this was a joy for that time. Just imagine that in the 1990s, a plastic bag with a picture or some kind of logo was something valuable to people, it was stored and even washed. And therefore, for that time, any Western symbol, like Adidas or McDonald's, printed on something—mainly on clothes—was perceived as something important, something that could make you happier. The West opened before us in all its attractive splendor. Of course, huge quantities of poor-quality goods and bootlegs poured into the country, and this could no longer be stopped. A fake West came to us, made somewhere in China, Turkey, and Eastern Europe. Along with the goods came television, which also began to form new values and the desire for wealth, or at least for prosperity. It was a new consumer experience that was firmly embedded in our lives. A lot of time has passed since then, but this mania has remained as before. It seems to me that it only grows over the years; we see the West everywhere (and more recently, the rich Middle East) and we want to immortalize our current architecture, the decoration of our homes, and the clothes that can imitate that luxury and wealth.

BS: In the West, logos like Gucci or Apple symbolize a certain class or sign of quality. What additional meaning do these symbols take on in the context of Uzbekistan?

p. 279: Hassan Kurbanbaev, Image from the series *Logomania: Owning The World at Half Price*, 2019–2020 (2020)

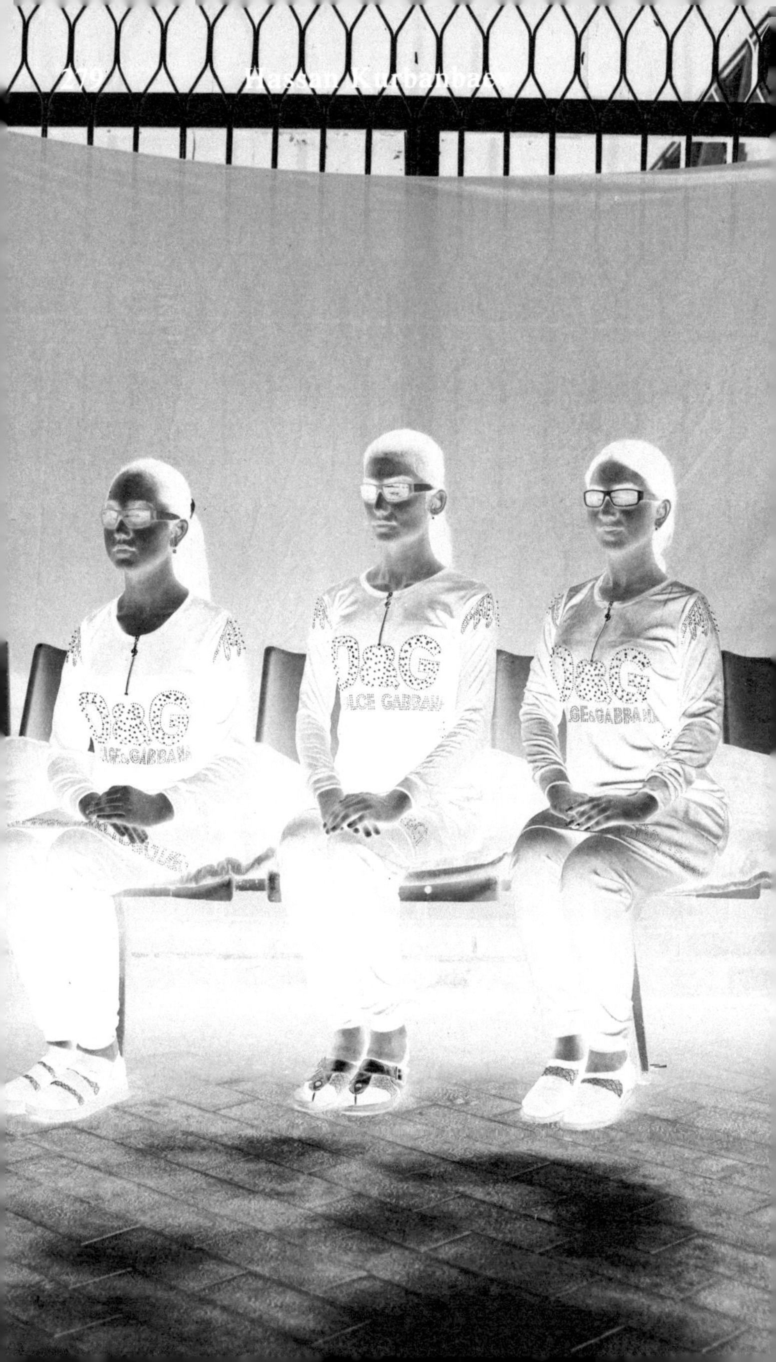
D&G
D&G
D&G

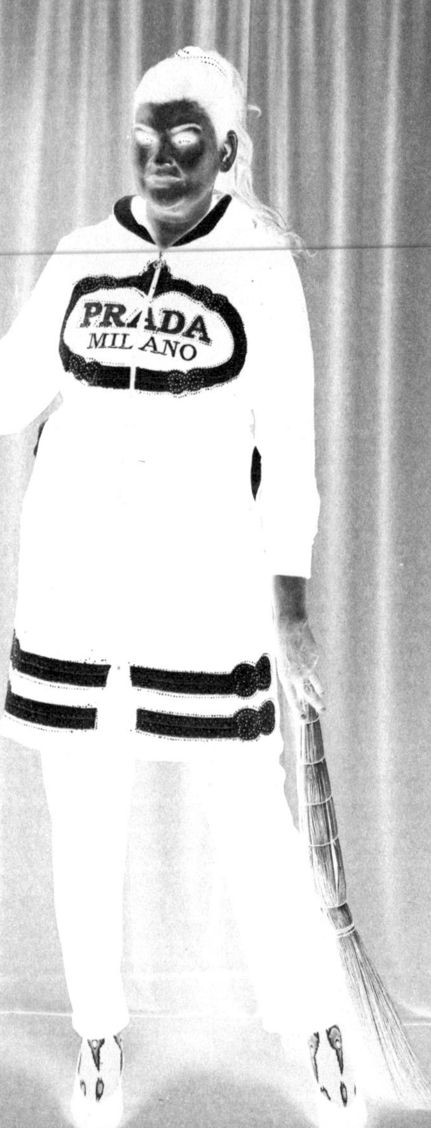
PRADA
MILANO

HK: This is a good question, and one I think about myself. Of course, they have the same meanings, but are perceived differently. Because they are replicated on anything, including store signs or bed linen, for example, the logos themselves are depreciated and become something of a household name. The specific logo does not matter anymore, its presence is more important. This, as I said in the project statement, is the "naive method of appropriation."

BS: Are you critical of this brand obsession and the impact it might have on developing Uzbekistan's own unique cultural identity? Or do you embrace this obsession as symbolic of our globalized capitalistic culture?

HK: In this obsession, I see a kind of crisis in our current culture. It is difficult for me to understand what played the first role here: demand—that is, the need of a local person to be covered with Western logotype—or supply—when manufacturers located somewhere in China or Turkey formed an opinion that having a fashion brand logotype is something that will enrich your clothes, and yourself. I tend towards the latter. This is a billion-dollar consumer goods business, which, together with globalization and approximately the same worldwide ideas about luxury, moves around the planet and has destructive properties for different emerging cultures.

BS: I wonder if you see any creative potential in this obsession with bootlegs. Could

p. 280: Hassan Kurbanbaev, Image from the series *Logomania: Owning The World at Half Price*, 2019–2020 (2020)

they be objects of inspiration? Could they evolve into a unique visual style of their own as they interact, blend, and integrate with more traditional elements of Uzbekistan culture?

HK: I would not make this photo series if it was only about bootlegs. It is not interesting to me. Once walking through the local bazaars, when I saw a thousand golden logotypes on long Muslim robes, I said, "wow, this can be a story." Therefore, as a photographer, it is interesting for me to observe this interaction. This is unique and authentic. Take, for example, women's headscarves, which most often have Chanel logos, or local grandmother's Muslim velour suits with a Gucci logotype on it. This combination of fashion, religion, West and East, and the economy has a strong visual narrative and is a good field for creativity.

BS: Could you talk about the images themselves? The photographs are stunning, sumptuous, and glamorous. They are often shot in-studio, beautifully styled, and carefully composed. For you, what do these formal qualities communicate as opposed to, for example, more in-situ street photographs where bootlegs naturally occur?

HK: As soon as the idea for this series was born, I decided that I wanted to present it as something like family archives or vintage photography postcards. I wanted to elevate the costumes in the same way seeing something in the context of a museum immediately signifies values. In addition, there is a social or cultural subtext in the photographs. Take, for example, a woman in a dressing gown with an embroidery of the Prada Milano crest: she is holding a rose, but also in her hand is her usual broom with which she sweeps the yard. Much is taken from my real-life observations.

> BS: Do you see potential in your photographs as they circulate, to insert Uzbekistan culture into a broader global narrative?

HK: Absolutely. Unfortunately, Uzbekistan is still a country that does not have a clear reference for the Western audience; it is generally very difficult for them to understand what Uzbekistan is. Therefore, I am looking for ideas that can reflect the modern life of my country. And if in the gallery my photos can work in, say, the context of a certain topic or research, then on Instagram this is my personal opportunity to reach a large audience; talk about my country through personal experience; enter into a dialogue with different opinions, positive and negative; and communicate with people who have never been to my country, as well as with Uzbek diasporas living in Europe or the USA.

> BS: On your website you mention the slogan of Uzbekistan, "A country with a great past and a great future." As the bootleg phenomenon seems so rooted in our present, I wonder what you think it might communicate about Uzbekistan culture today?

HK: It should be noted that the bootleg appeared in Uzbekistan before the original. It came first. Hence,

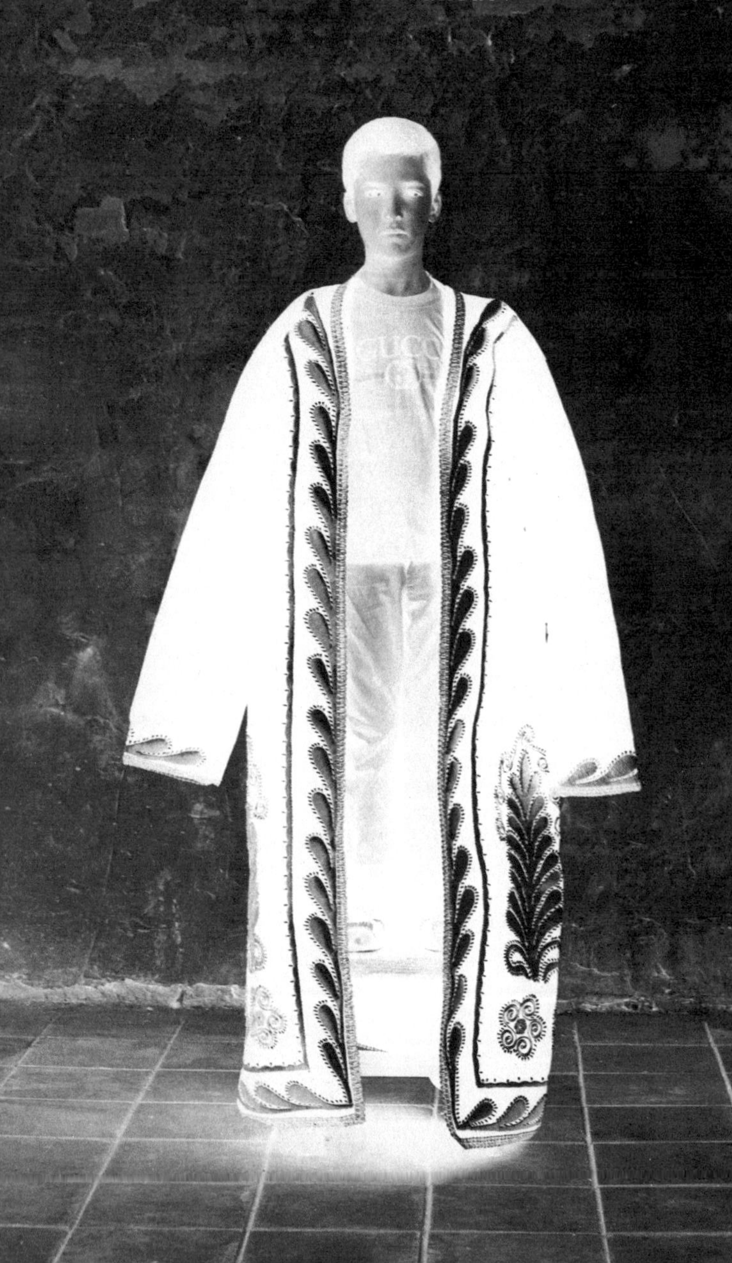

it initially had superiority in our so-called present. There is a feeling that this was reflected in the country itself, in its image. In our life, there is a lot of parody and absurdity, imitation. We strive very much for a beautiful future, while not developing our own modern culture.

p. 284: Hassan Kurbanbaev, Image from the series *Logomania: Owning The World at Half Price*, 2019–2020 (2020)
Title page (p. 276): Flag of Uzbekistan

adidas

SHIRT (S)

SHIRT is a rapper and conceptual artist based in Queens. His unique and prolific practice finds commonality in hip-hop and contemporary art through ideas of sampling and appropriation. The two seemingly disparate disciplines become intertwined in SHIRT's universe, mixing in additional elements of sculpture, performance, and fashion. But to the artist, these distinctions are irrelevant, all of them are really just containers for his ideas. In one work, SHIRT created a fake version of *The New York Times* for an album release; in another he broke the internet with a shirt sporting both Nike and Adidas logos. In a personal favorite, he restaged the iconic 1983 *Blizaard Ball Sale* where he sold snowballs on the street in New York to create a shared experience with the artist David Hammons. As SHIRT concludes in the interview, bootlegging is very much about "extending"—it's the natural evolution of an idea when it enters the world. Interview by Ben Schwartz (BS)

BS: What is your relationship to bootlegging, even outside of your art practice? Growing up, did you have any interaction with bootlegs or any formative experiences with them? Do you think about bootlegging when making work?

S: I probably first heard the word in the context of buying mixtapes and CDs from DJs. I grew up listening to hip-hop music very closely, so sampling is part of the language you learn there. Is sampling bootlegging? Is taking a part of something to conceptually or actually use it for a new thing, bootlegging it? I don't know, maybe not. Are we not speaking here to the very nature of what we do as human beings and how we live? To take, absorb, and evolve? Everything is remixed. Maybe we get a thing right and hold on to it for a long while, but even then there has to be people somewhere fucking with it, trying things, pushing the limits of a thing, expanding a thing. Is expounding on a thing bootlegging it? Bastardizing it? Honoring it? I like the idea of walking near someone having a conversation, thinking you heard them say one thing, then riffing on what you think you heard. It will always be something new but derivative. All the while, other people in your vicinity are doing exactly the same thing. We learn from and bootleg each other, right? Is learning bootlegging? We learn how to live and how to die from each other. I watch you, I try that thing I like, now I'm doing it and someone's watching me. I don't think about this concept of bootlegging when making work. I'm thinking about the work.

BS: Could you talk more about the relationship between bootlegging and hip-hop? Is there a difference between bootlegging and sampling, and is it even important to make that distinction?

S: Yeah, like I was saying, maybe there isn't a real difference. But it'll depend on the context, too. In actual definitions there's a distinction, sure. Typically "bootlegging" is referring to making a new thing 1:1 to the original thing, right? Or it's even often considered a lesser quality version of the original thing. Then also bootlegging as a term has ties to being deceitful and trying to create a deceiving "fake" or counterfeit. Sampling is often referring to taking a small piece of something and using that to make something new. So sampling two seconds of an old hit record to use for a loop through a new song. Or sampling as in trying a piece of something. They're different concepts, yeah. In general, to be honest, I don't like the term and its connotation. I have problems with what gets referred to as a bootleg and what never does. Jimmy Fallon or some other massive pop force will outright steal little Black girl dances on TikTok that go viral all the time but the skits are never referred to as bootlegs. Corporations will always attempt to copy what goes viral, record labels will try to apply the same formula over and over again, any company doing anything will attempt to duplicate what works. Sometimes we fail and it's noticeable. Often the copy is so perfect it works and goes unnoticed. I say "we" because it strikes me as human nature. We're all just trying to bootleg our best days.

> BS: Bootlegging finds its origins in smuggling. Today I think about bootlegging as a way to smuggle ideas back and forth between realms of "high" and "low" culture (as much as I hate those terms). I love the way your work seamlessly moves between hip-hop, historically viewed as pop culture,

and contemporary art, traditionally understood as "high culture." Can you talk about how you work with, and often upend these archaic distinctions? How does this relate to ideas of rebellion or infiltration?

S: We have to stop referring to it as high/low. Bootlegging as a way to smuggle ideas back and forth—period. I willfully ignore these lines and distinctions now. I don't acknowledge them. I am constantly being reminded that they are there in the minds of pretty much every person in the world, but I personally have done a good job operating like the lines do not exist at all. I just make. The idea, and thinking about the idea, dictates the medium the thing ends up in.

Something I've been thinking recently is that maybe there is no bad art but only sentiments expressed in a wrong medium. Like not enough thought was put into what medium would be best, or an idea was forced through a medium by either the artist or a third party. When you think about most instances of what we may consider "bad art," usually the feeling and desire in making the thing is coming from a very genuine place in a person—like the old adage says, "No one has ever written, painted, sculpted, modeled, built, or invented except literally to get out of hell." I do believe that to a large degree. But I don't think about "infiltration" all that much. It's a cool word and idea maybe. But for instance, I find myself in crazy rooms sometimes and might marvel at how I ended up there, marvel at this connection or that. But I don't feel this infiltration thing. I'm supposed to be in that room.

The path I'm on will lead me through all sorts of rooms. If I was an international spy or something, we could talk about the infiltration thing, but I'm not. "Rebellion" is there, but it's more acutely a rebellion against letting a bullshit, racist, inequitable, deeply harsh world dictate how I'm going to personally move through it and approach people and things. I rebel against anyone attempting to dim my flame. I burn hotter in the face of that.

> BS: You're often making art about, or in reference to, other artists, which to me is an expression of fandom. Bootlegging as a fan becomes an act of love. Do you consider yourself a fan? In what ways does this fandom motivate or inspire you? Alternatively, do you use bootlegging as a form of critique?

S: To be honest, I rarely make art "about other artists." I actually can't think of a work I've made specifically about another artist. What happens is I will often come across a work by another artist that I feel is really just perfectly said or done. And then sometimes the idea for me is to do it exactly like they did. My ongoing Neon Book Paintings Series comes to mind, where I read a book for the first time and highlight sentences with a neon marker that stand out to me—and then that is the work itself. Part of that is a feeling like I don't have to or want to add one other thing there. This sentence or idea is worded just right and it's exactly what I myself want to communicate, so I highlight, and in that way I've used it.

It more than often has nothing to do with whoever I saw do it first. Just like I want it not to matter that the next kid might have seen me do it first. Maybe it should be about what the work is saying and only that. For me, it's all in service of whatever larg-

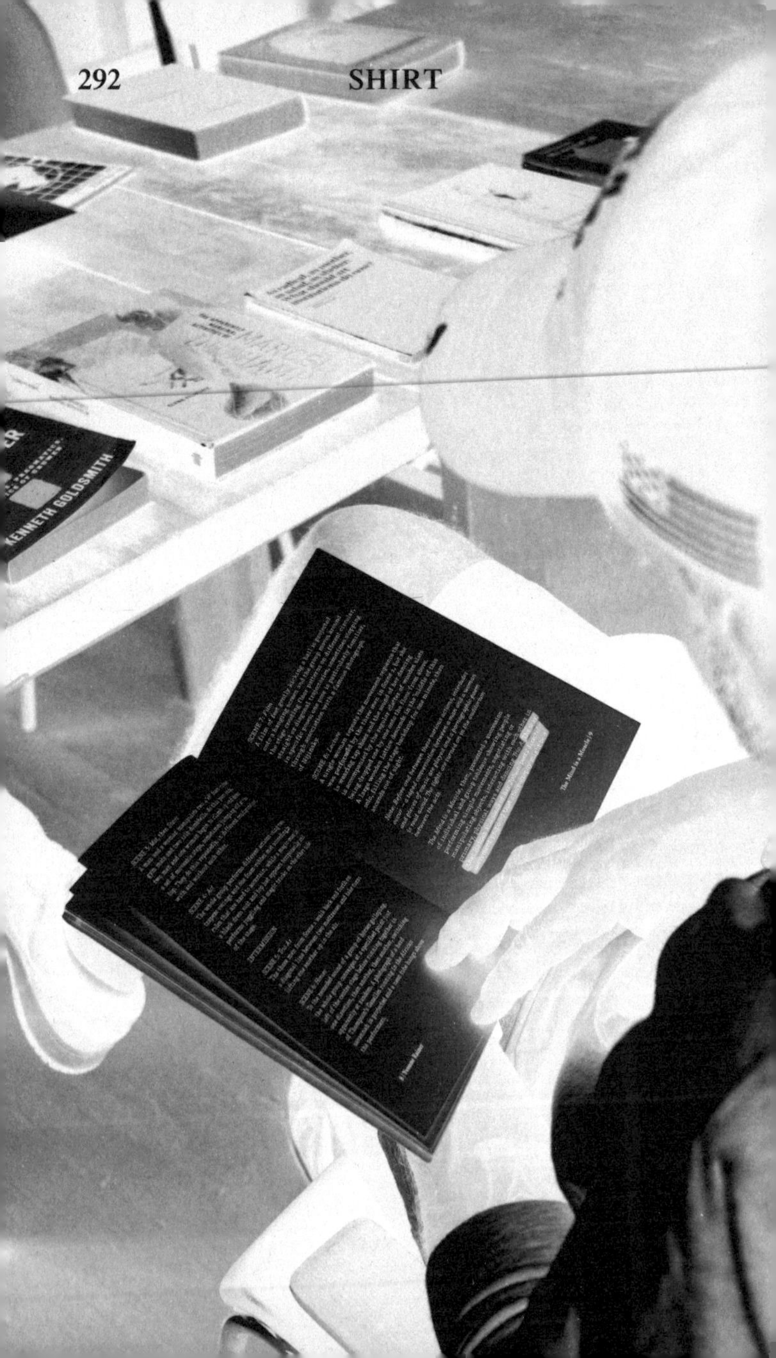
KENNETH GOLDSMITH

er idea I've come to in my practice. So I think the concept of "fan" here is weird. Art and thinking critically has saved my life and in many ways has changed how I approach nearly everything. Is sharing stuff I find inspiring inherently an act of love? Yeah maybe. I know, there's always gonna be people who see stuff you post for the first time and it becomes this universe opening thing. I'm aware of that. Is positively wanting to expand someone's world an act of love? Probably yeah. Of course, I really am a fan of people. I'm a fan of works and ideas and where being open can lead. I'm motivated to learn and to teach. That's what it is to be alive for me. Constant learning and teaching. Whatever you learn should be taught. Could someone use a mode of "bootlegging" as a way to express ideas of critique too? Sure.

> BS: I want to talk about your performance reenactments… Hammons's *Bliz-aard Ball Sale*, your performance of *The Fine Art of Rap* (I know this is a little different than a direct reenactment, but I was really moved by the video) or recreating the sidewalk writing image from the NYPL Image Collection to name a few. I understand this as an embodied form of bootlegging—a copy that involves becoming the original. When you do these performances, how does your relationship with the original change?

S: Yeah it's totally an embodying thing. For me, doing something physically exactly the same as someone else did it is kind of this beautiful collapsing of time and

p. 292: SHIRT, *Neon Book Paintings* (ongoing)

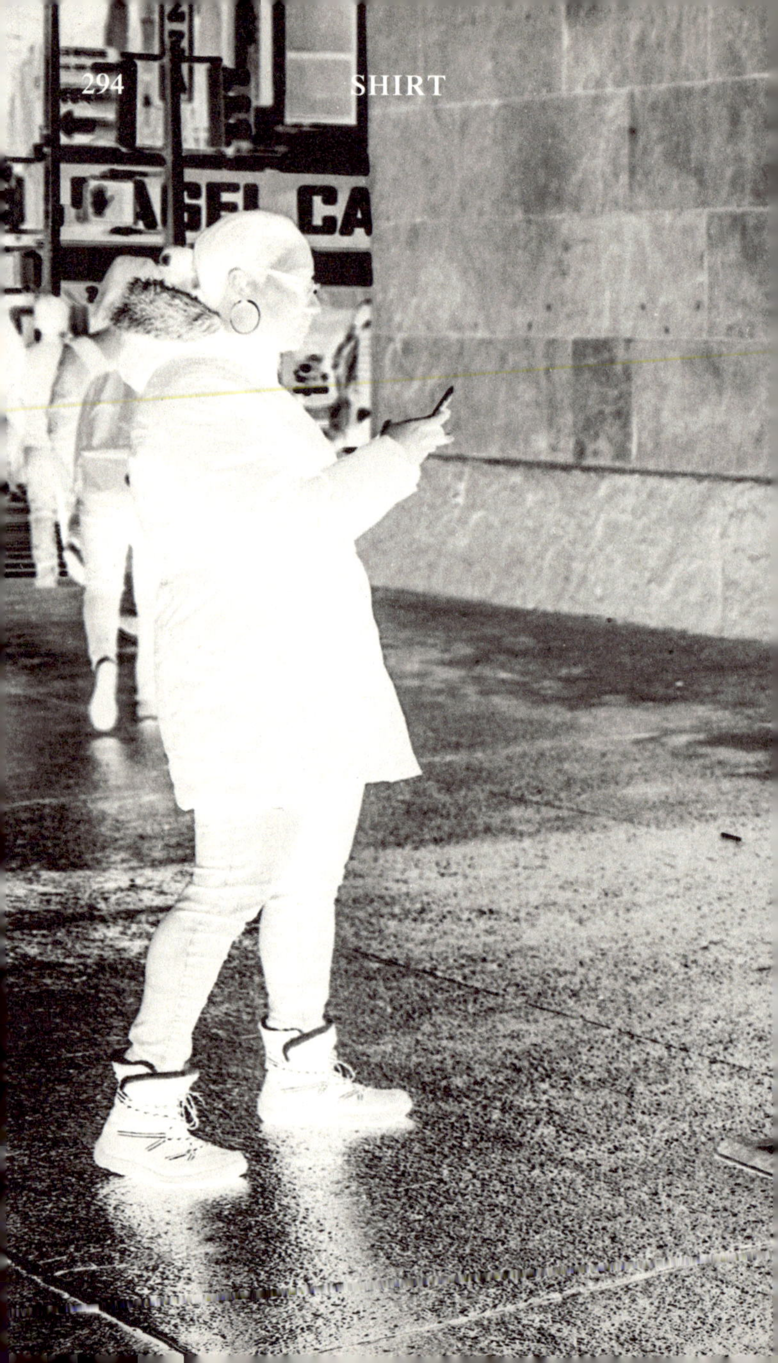

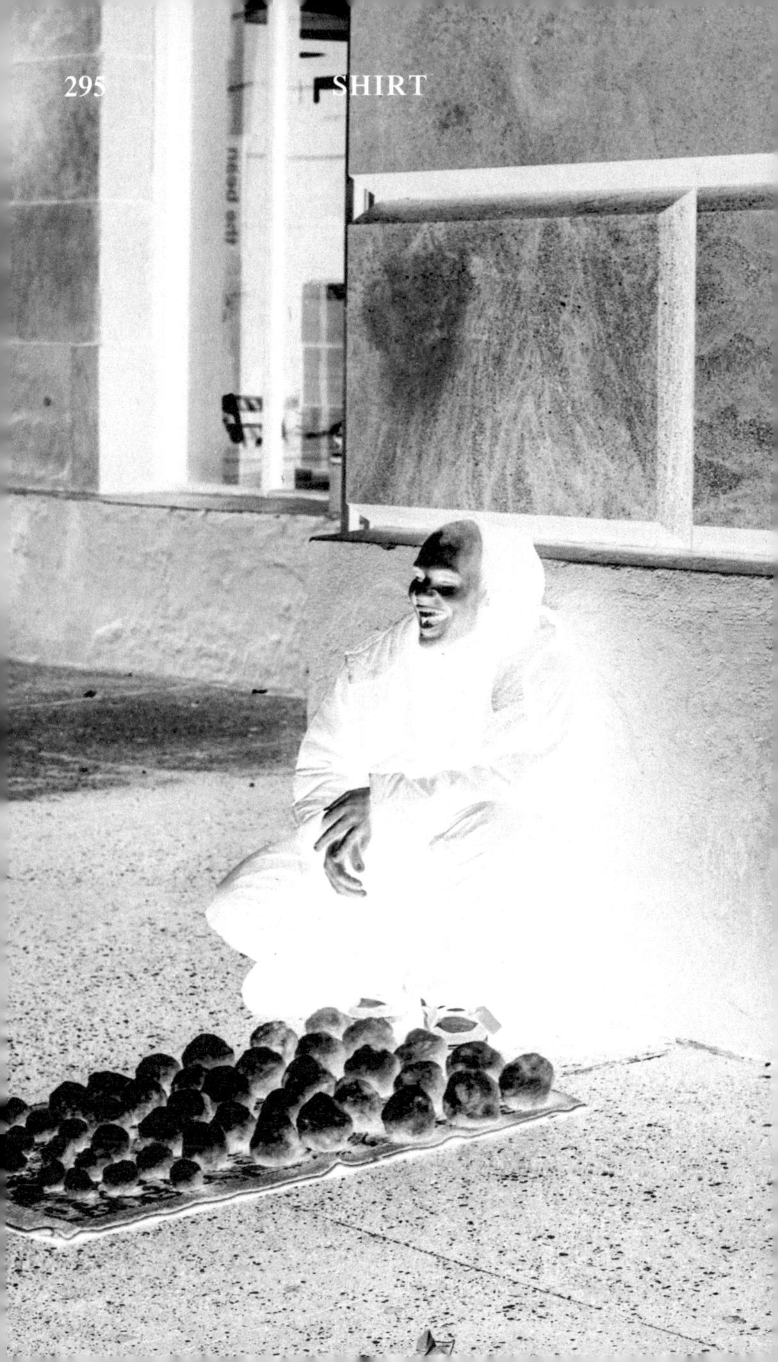

space, a gesture I've come to really like. Maybe it grew out of skating when I was young, trying to emulate tricks I saw and new moves. But yeah, where does it come from? It's a way of being close to a particular person, work, or action, right? And yeah again, you hope that the way the original thing moved you or helped you, in some way in turn does that for someone else. By redoing it you're expanding its reach.

I'm not sure how my relationship to the original thing changes. Does it give me this new insight? Maybe. I remember going to the Matisse Cut-Out show at MoMa in 2014 and wanting to make those Blue Nude shapes out of paper. Then when I did and was making them, I felt the scissors slicing through the paper and there was something there. Matisse himself felt that sensation. Our arms had to bend and contort the same way to get those angles. That's something. Same for the Hammons work. Maybe seeing the gorgeous Dawoud Bey photo you think a guy is just standing out there selling snowballs. But then you do it: you prepare the snowballs, choose the rug, you go out and stand there and people walk by and interact with you. Me and Hammons share that now. It may have been a different day or whatever, some 30+ years apart, but it's a New York City street and people are walking by and you feel this magical connection.

But also this "becoming the original" thing you said. Is that not what we're all doing? We start out as bootlegs or samples of our parents and then living is the process of becoming, right? What happens when you do what heroes do? Do you not become a hero in the process? Do you not become someone else's hero? I look up to people and have always

pp. 294–295: SHIRT, *Snowball Sale (1983)* (2018)

thought, well, to have certain qualities I admire in others, you emulate them. The thing about emulating is it's only emulating conceptually before you do it. Once you do it, maybe it's not emulating anymore. You're just doing it now. I've been trying to be like and emulate and bootleg and learn from smart, caring, thoughtful, fly, ill people for a long time.

> BS: You remade a Virgil Abloh shirt titled *You Can Copy Someone To A T And It Will Never Be The Same*. To you, what is the value of a copy?

S: Yeah, I kept seeing Virgil wearing it and couldn't find any info on it anywhere. I would make up fantastical ideas of where he came to get or make it, what the graphic specifically referenced and his interpretation of it all. It made me think. But I think it's important here to distinguish that before I thought about this as a copy, I thought about it as: it is this black tee with a large white ship graphic on the front, et cetera. We don't experience things as a "copy" even if we know they are. We first and foremost experience them as they are. And that maybe is an inherent value in what a copy is. It is itself a new experience that stands alone and never has to refer to the original. I think I've tapped into some truth there, I've never put it into language until just now. Maybe all we're seeing is "copies" everywhere we look. Only we experience these things as their own original thing. So we have to remember that! Copying as worldmaking. And connecting that to the same positive feeling you get from executing an idea or a dream you want to make reality. I thought that tee should exist. I had

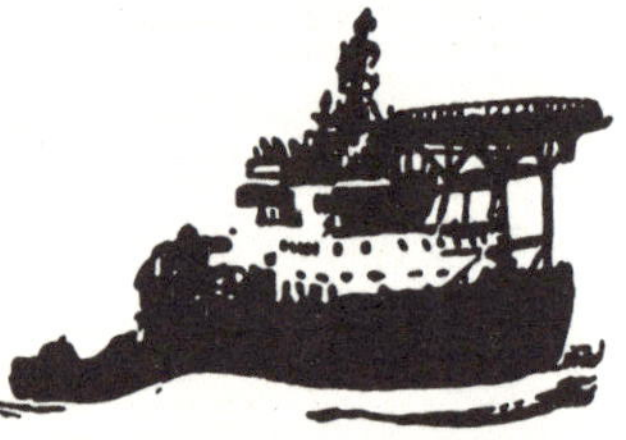
YOU ACTUALLY
FELL IN LOVE
WITH AN IMAGE

to prepare a high quality file from jpegs I found online, then invest a bit of money to make and produce the tees. It's always inspiring as hell to go through that process and end up on the other side with a thing you made. It's gratifying as shit every time, as anyone that does it will attest. Then this person—Virgil in this case, a hero of heroes—dies young. So I never get to give him one, we never get to talk about why it struck me as important, how he came to have it et cetera.

> BS: I want to expand on that project a bit, specifically the way you sent around files allowing people to remake the shirts themselves. I'm really interested in the way you approach distribution, often offering links to tracks, or files on your Instagram. In what ways does bootlegging create or reinforce community? How has that worked in your own practice?

S: Anything you put up public on a social media site should attract people that like the same thing. Does liking some of the same things make us a community? I don't know. I do think it's inevitable that humans clique up. I don't think bootlegging is intrinsically linked to how maybe you're defining community. Or maybe it is and I just don't know the inner workings of some bootlegging community. I really like this idea that maybe we don't experience the concept of a bootleg at all. Maybe a good bootleg means the concept of a bootleg immediately fades and you're really just left

p. 298: SHIRT, *You Can Copy Someone To A T (It Will Never Be The Same)* (2021) with the thing. Maybe the same thing the original produced. So yeah, a few hundred of us experience a thing on socials as we encounter it and we might clique up around it. Community comes into play with being exposed to others' opinions for a prolonged time. I also don't know how I feel about the word community anymore either. I feel very close to certain people for sure, and in conversation with them whether physically and actually or not. You meet people from around the world and it's instant love. So what are the lines of this community if not jagged and raw and glitchy and shifting. I like thinking that people in my IG comments or interacting with my stuff at the same time, downloading from links I make available etc, are finding each other too. I really hope that's actually happening.

> BS: Could you talk about the way you use logos in your work? What meaning do these signs hold for you? I'm thinking specifically of your Adidas × Nike mashups and Nike × Timberland mashups.

S: I don't have a particular way I use logos in my work. In fact, I feel a bit of indifference when it comes to logos. I flirted with having various logos when I was younger, but as my work and career developed I've purposely not established a logo for my own brands. I mean, I have what an invoice looks like from me. I have fonts I like, I guess. But there isn't that one symbol, or rather there's a bunch. When it comes to putting a Nike check on a Timberland boot, for me it's about gesture. The physical gesture of taking a silver Krink and doing specifically this dripping check. The colors are too good together, the materials, that iridescent paint on the suede. The gesture isn't to stand there and write small words on the boot and sentences—that's maybe a different idea for another time. This was about that physical check gesture. It was almost just a bonus that the check mark is a logo for a really popular company, and one that for me there's some history with. So there was all this other meaning able to be layered on to what was initially a really just gestural, and pure motion and desire for the boots customized in this way. I have to say there was also some success I was feeling because growing up, the yellow Timberland was so iconic I used to think all collaborations done with it were corny. As a designer and creative, it becomes a real goal to make a thing like that work. The yellow construction boot is just about untouchable to me, but something about that silver dripping Nike check on the side of it made me feel like I achieved something. (I have one other really good idea.) People reducing all of that to their simple idea of a "bootleg" is so old and played out to me. It's a 6 inch premium Timberland boot with this added paint element from an artist. "Bootleg" damn near has nothing to do with it. I'll say that I do think there's a lot of power in people appropriating corporate logos and imagery and anything else to create commentary, capital, et cetera. There should be absolutely nothing off limits for people to use. The rich already operate like this. Especially if we're talking "legal" limits and bullshit like copyright.

BS: On a related note, what is your relationship to ownership and originality?

S: My relationship to the terms is that they are clearly very real concepts for a lot of people and I believe come from a very human place. I can imagine a lot of people throughout history dying over feeling like someone copied them or took their idea. I can also easily imagine many of the brilliant ideas we live by now and attribute to certain individuals may as well be bootlegged, remixed, stolen, and otherwise interpreted from someone we'll never know the name of. I think it's caused a lot of strife between people and continues to today. I personally think it's all nonsense. I mean, play by the rules too, right? You can't just come take my car. That's my car, right? I'm wearing a jacket, you couldn't just come take my jacket off me. I mean, you could. That's the thing, too. We can say something is ours all we want, but is it?

As far as originality goes, I think we are all co-conspirators of each other. If we're talking as me and you are, then this is our era together. Everyone posting on their Instagram and Twitter their ideas and who they are. I don't know what originality is supposed to mean. I'm original in the sense that my DNA is mine, sure. I'm me, there literally isn't a clone of me. I don't care about originality, like—how could I lose when I'm already chose? I am original no matter what or who I copy or what I do. No one on earth could copy like me, and I can't copy like anyone else. What I'm saying is, in a deep sense, we all are already copying each other. That's how we know to wear pants and take the train and stand there and drive in the lines. I think a cooler game to play is who can find and follow and copy the best people and ideas. Like where's an idea from hundred years ago—or yesterday—that interests me to extend it and keep it going? Who's a person I can find that I feel just fucking gets it, that I can watch as much as they allow and my time here allows. What can come through them? Who are the best people and ideas on their radar? And then of course, your own metric for "best" comes into play. Best for me in this sense is just a loose best and brightest/seems like a good person/ stylish/aware of what's going on/ loving.

> BS: I think the recent work you are doing with pearls is really beautiful. I see it as enshrining something that is overlooked. I think of bootlegging as a form of preservation especially in underrepresented communities. Does this idea resonates with you?

S: I think if we look at what Dapper Dan was doing and all the racism and barriers of entry he was met with and so many others are met with—it becomes more than about preservation. It becomes about doing what you gotta and using what you got. Dap and none of us can compete with these brands spending hundreds of millions, and billions now, to market and sell to our people or anyone who wants that logo on their chest. So what if we just take that logo and do what we want with it? Imagine that. They spend billions to make their symbol so cool that my people work and give all their money to advertise it on their chest, and I can't use it too? All a company logo is to me is another symbol made for me to exploit. We can all exploit. And Dap made original things everyday! No one did it like Dapper Dan. Other people did it like them even when they thought they were doing it like him—see how that works?

Do we understand how aggressive it is to be some Forbes 500 company and buy billboards in neighborhoods and around cities with your logo printed on it? All just to sell to the inhabitants of that

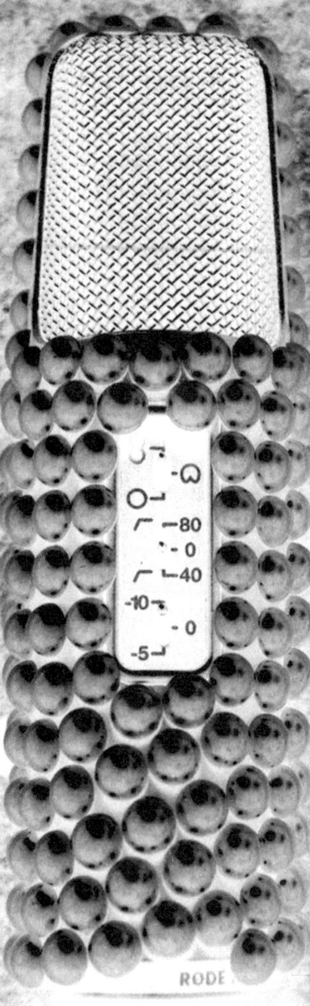
-80
-0
-40
-10
-0
-5
RODE

city and community? It's insane and we've normalized it. And we know the word "bootlegging" but we don't know the word—I don't have the word. What's a word for companies and brands that advertise their products and ideas in neighborhoods that the company's executives and employees don't live in?

How about all a "real" product should mean is made by a person. All "authentic" should be referring to is the type of experience you're going to get. You're not going to get your forty bucks stolen—you're going to buy and receive a T-shirt, it's gonna be a size large, it's gonna be a black tee, et cetera. My Nike Adidas tees aren't bootlegs of anything. That was my whole point, I had never seen the logos just together on a tee like that. I saw people doing things like different words in the same font and shit like that, but never just the logos unaltered next to each other. This is me after I grew up hearing my whole life that it's this taboo thing to wear the two companies at the same time. Like they have some power over me. So I'm a person examining all of our learned bullshit, and I'm going to let that sit with me and not react? No. So in this case I made a tee about it.

"Bootlegging" is just extending. It's exactly what would happen when an idea becomes public or hits the mainstream. If it's a decent idea it can and most often will be adopted, copied and multiplied, and become the invisible normal. It can and does disappear into our psyche. Are the ripples in a body of water bootlegs of previous ripples? Sometimes I make beats repeating sounds I make accidentally.

p. 304: SHIRT, *I Turned Myself Into Myself* (2022), album cover
Title page (p. 286): Nike and Adidas logo referencing a T-shirt made by SHIRT featuring both logos

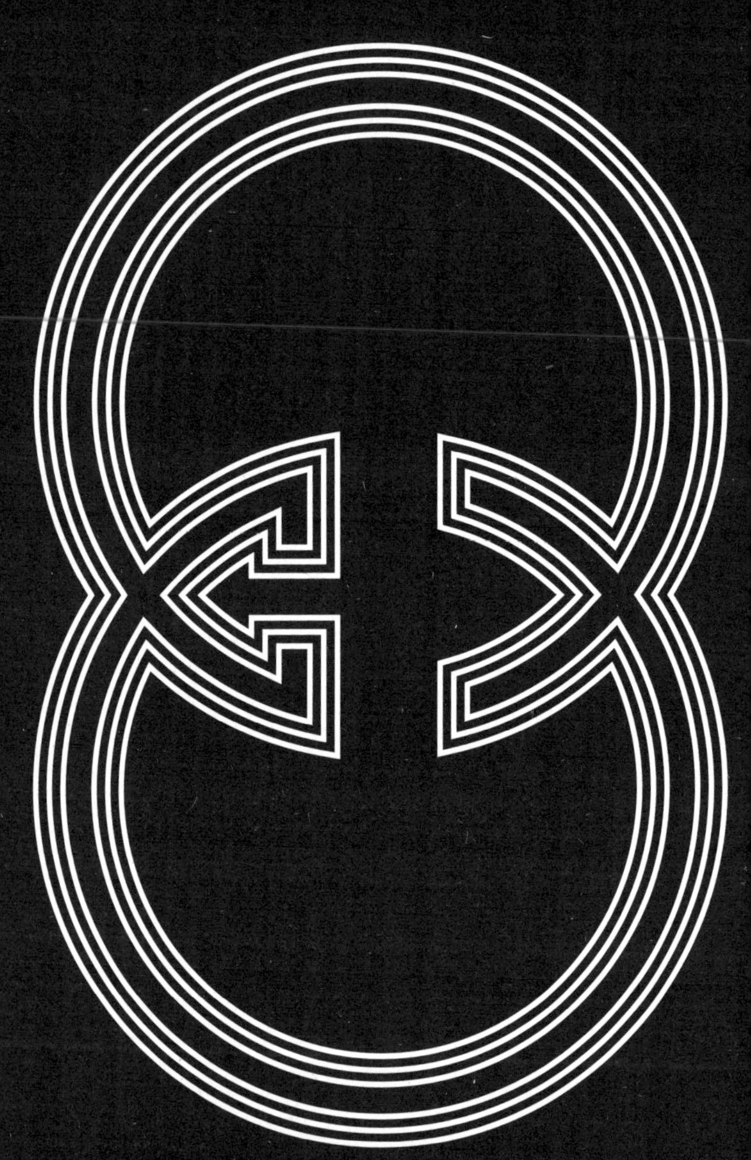

Akinola Davies Jr. (ADJ)

Akinola Davies Jr. is a UK-based filmmaker with a unique ability to portray socio-political issues through a lush, dream-like lens. His work with artists like Blood Orange and brands like Gucci and Kenzo merge the vibrancy of his Nigerian roots with the grit of his hometown of London. His 2018 work *Boot/leg* portrays individuals and groups in bootleg fashion: purses, jewelry, and hijabs patterned with logos from high end luxury brands. Through these intimate portraits, Davies Jr. explores the often unspoken relationships between brand, garment, culture, and status. Interview by Ben Schwartz and Jasio Stefanski (BS/JS), 2020

> BS/JS: We arrived at your practice through your project *Boot/leg*. Could you begin by giving us more context about that piece?

ADJ: *Boot/leg* was my first solo show in Basel, Switzerland at One Point One, a gallery that primarily represents and works with minority artists. I saw the show as an opportunity to situate the culture I saw around me within the context of fashion. The piece was a nine-minute film centered on individuals wearing bootlegged clothing, all framed within the tropes of the fashion industry: muzak, a high-gloss aesthetic, sumptuous color, slick production et cetera. I was interested in featuring a more grassroots-level of fashion through people that high-end industry doesn't usually cater to. These groups of people, however, are very interested in fashion, in these brands and products, and oftentimes insert themselves into the narrative by creating and wearing bootlegs.

> BS/JS: So with the piece, you were not only thinking about the actual objects, but also the systems and contexts that surround these bootleg items?

ADJ: Exactly. I was interested in the cyclical way that fashion finds and exploits trends. These trends often come from the street, are picked up by high-end fashion houses, and then sold at exorbitant prices. Because of their inaccessibility, the street then makes bootlegs of these items, demonstrating demand, and giving more value to the original.

But what's unfortunate is how the fashion industry refuses to have a real dialogue with the communities from which they steal. As a result these communities are creating things for no one but themselves, which inevitably makes these items much more interesting.

> BS/JS: We'd love for you to expand on that relationship—how does bootlegging create, preserve, and even empower disenfranchised communities?

ADJ: Clothes are very coded and are often used as identity signifiers of a particular group. In *Boot//leg*, for example, special attention is placed on the hijab. Clothes of course are also symbols of status and hierarchy within a community; what you wear dictates your position and how others perceive you. In that way, clothes, and bootlegs, become important in creating communities.

But bootlegging itself is its own community or ecosystem: designers, manufacturers, vendors, and consumers. So really you have communities at play, based around commerce, around design, around style, around association. It's so layered on so many levels.

> BS/JS: I wonder how the relationship between these various levels and tiers that you talk about affects what might be considered bootlegging and what might be considered appropriation?

ADJ: Dapper Dan is a great example of this. He garnered attention for his bootlegs of Louis Vuitton, Gucci, Prada, et cetera, but was never welcome in that sphere. Then, of course, years later Gucci bootlegged one of Dapper Dan's designs and sort of claimed Dapper Dan as one of their own. So in that situation it becomes a case of appropriation, versus Dan who was making bootlegs.

I think control and power greatly affect the appropriation vs. bootlegging conversation. And the wonderful aspect of bootlegging is how it really democratizes the narrative of fashion. The people making these items are doing so with very limited resources and perhaps a limited education, and in a way bootlegging becomes a means of education. And now

pp. 310–311: Akinola Davies, Still from *Boot/Leg* (2018)

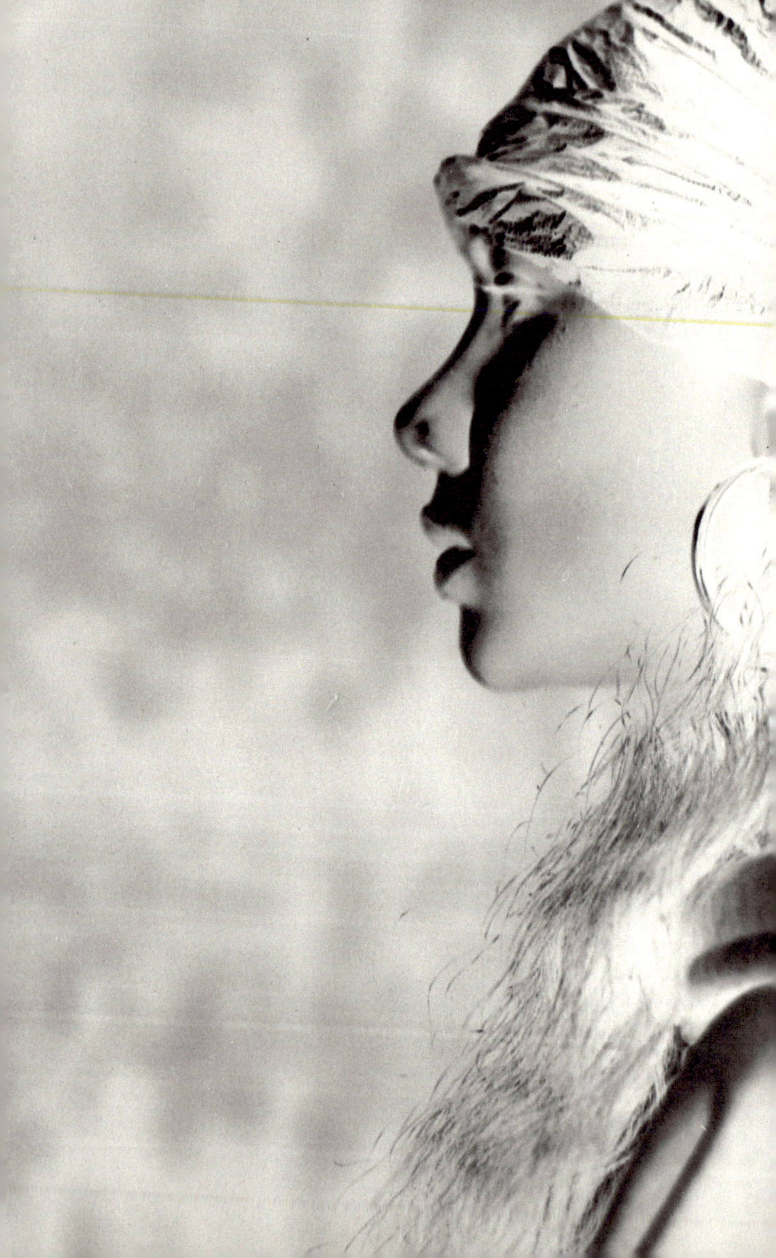

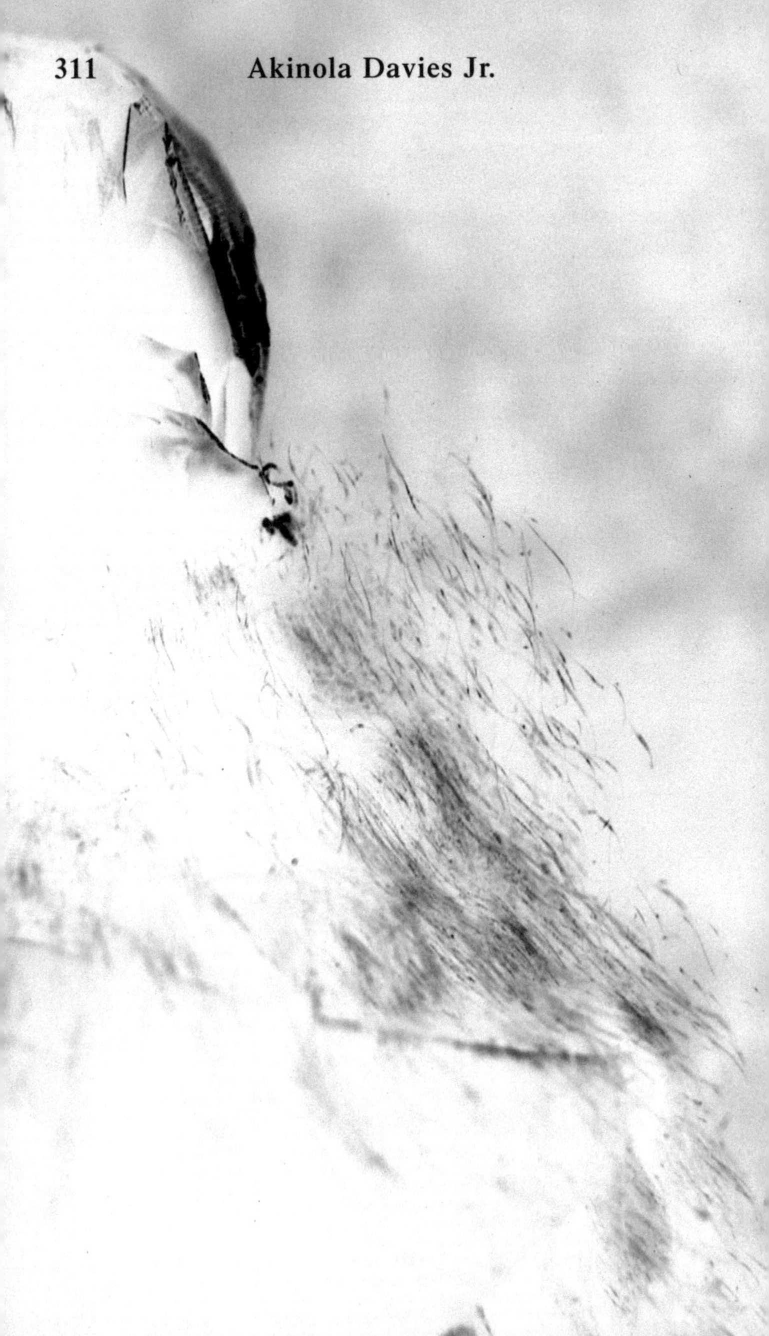

you have companies understanding bootlegging as a complete art form in and of itself. Gucci, for example, released an official version of a bootleg shirt. I just think bootleggers are ingenious, I am eager to see how they will continue to evolve and become more clever in the manner in which they create and distribute.

> BS/JS: As we talk about issues of cultural appropriation, and varying power dynamics, do you see bootlegging as a strategy for minority communities to subvert oppressive power structures?

ADJ: I think ultimately with bootlegging that minority communities have the ability to centralize themselves in how they choose to tell their stories. Beyond bootleg clothing, I am interested in how these communities might bootleg oppressive systems, and how that can be an act of empowerment. For example, growing up in Nigeria I was always really fascinated and impressed by these kids who would learn to use computers and send emails across the world to get money from people. All of this was based on their understanding of how to infiltrate and subvert various systems. It has a very bootleg mindset—it's ingenious—I think that sort of initiative should be celebrated.

> BS/JS: As brands become more aware of these communities, possibly from the result of bootlegging, do you see a way for these structures and communities to work together in an equitable way?

ADJ: Unequivocally there is a way to do it, but I think when you're dealing with big brands, you start engaging more in conversations about profit. For capitalism to work, some people have to be exploited, and so I'm not sure how interested these brands are in having these types of conversations.

Brands need to be more ethically minded in the way they engage with communities. And actually, I think the reason why a lot of communities end up bootlegging is because there isn't that representation within the hierarchy of those systems. I think ultimately that's the starting point. It's about inclusion in the earlier stages of production and planning to affect how and what things are made to account for a broader range of people. And I think if brands really want to engage then there needs to be more structured systems in regards to how to engage, which once again boils down to funding, access, education, et cetera.

BS/JS: So in many ways, bootlegging becomes this vehicle for access…

ADJ: Right. For communities who are left out of the more mainstream narrative, they are forced to adjust and find ways to insert themselves into that narrative. It can be through fashion, it can be through the internet, and I think that has been instrumental in this democratization process.

A friend of mine used to do this project called Photocopy Club because he was fully aware that he could never open up his own gallery. He would write to artists and he would get them to send him a print, and then he would photocopy loads, and he would do a show where people would just buy art straight off the walls. I thought this was a nice example of

pp. 314–315: Akinola Davies, Still from *Boot/Leg* (2018)

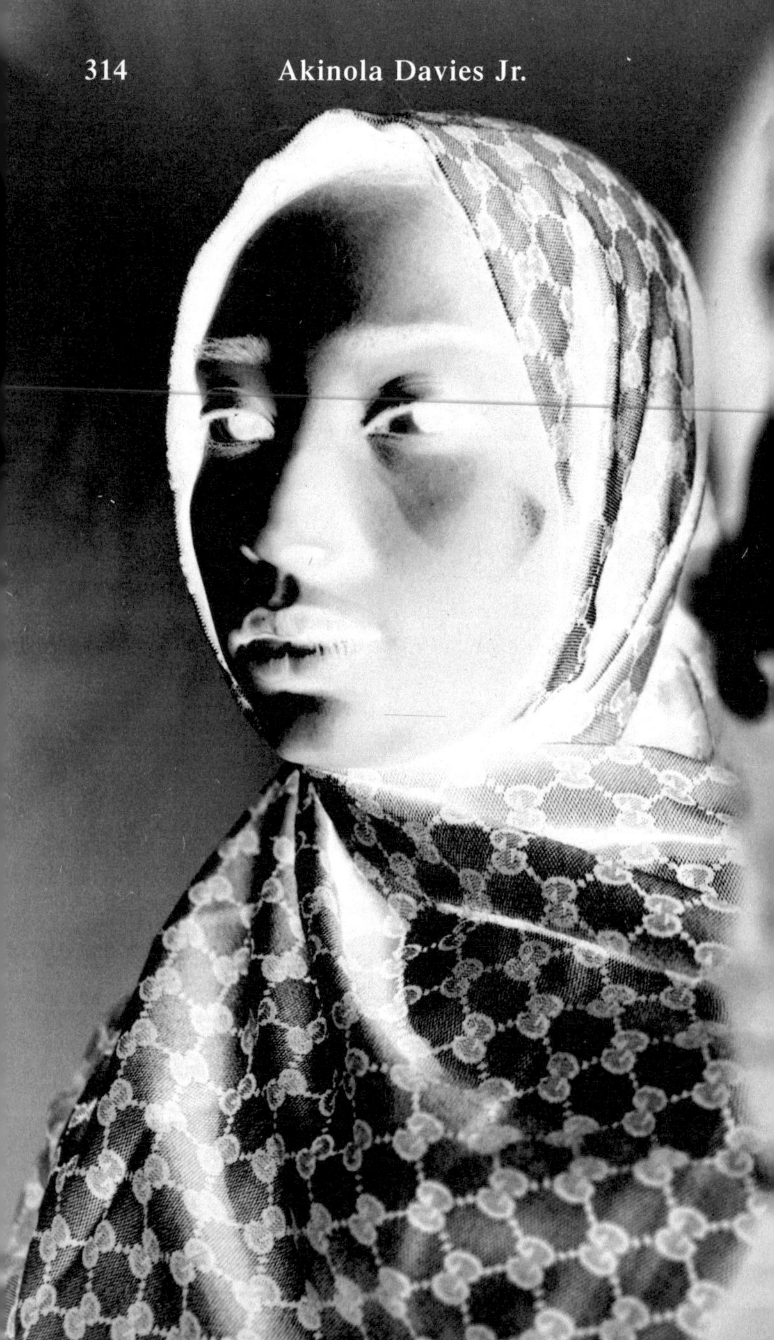

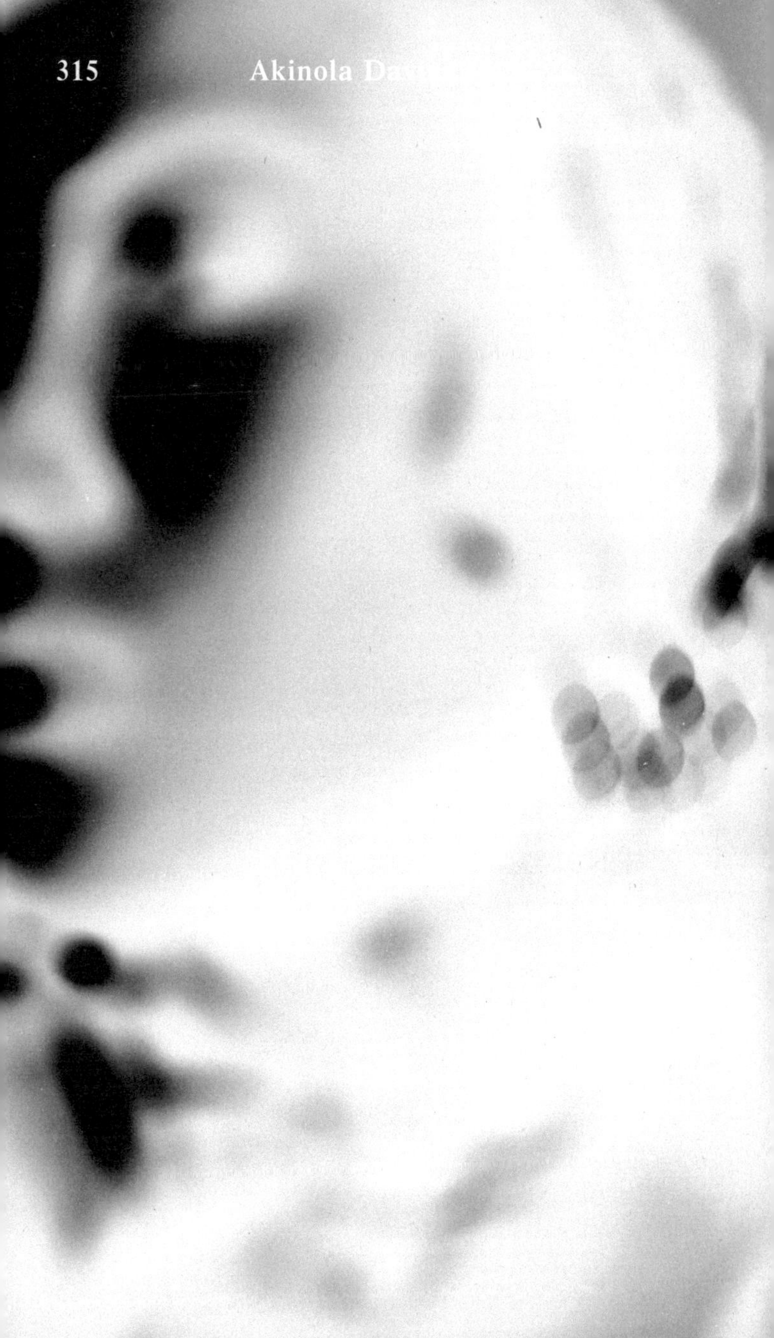

bootlegging as access—access to an artistic space, access to a community, access to a product.

BS/JS: Throughout your work, it seems like you're interested in celebrating points of intersection, especially between things that wouldn't normally interact.

ADJ: I'm really interested in how different generations or cultures speak to each other, especially with the internet and the way things seem to more fluidly mix. I'm interested in finding and surfacing things that unite various communities. In my work I try to play with context, hoping that people can see themselves in areas they may have never expected. I made a film called *Zaza* in Northern Nigeria based around this 500-year-old equestrian festival. A friend from Palestine was surprised about the symmetry of the film and its relationship to Afghani, or Palestinian, or different areas of Muslim culture. People might never see those relationships unless they watch the film. There's so much code that people wouldn't understand.

Most of what I'm really interested in is how to create more dialogue and how to bring different groups of people together to understand—whether it's generationally, whether it's culturally, whether it's racially—what unites us.

BS/JS: Do you see bootlegging as a viable form of activism?

ADJ: Yes, I think the next iteration of bootlegging is very much centered on activism. On one hand, I think bootlegging has always been a form of protest, but I think more recently you've seen an iteration that is much more overt. There is a group of guys called Hype-Peace who basically bootlegged the Palace Skateboarding logo, donating all proceeds to various Middle Eastern causes. Or someone like Jonny Banger, who initially bootlegged a lot of Polo and Ralph Lauren , and in his more recent work, has been attacking the British government during the pandemic.

> BS/JS: Today, bootlegging feels increasingly at risk for becoming a passing design trend. At its core, what power or effect can the act have in this present moment?

ADJ: I think what happens is that the design community is very consumed with trends without much understanding of their greater connection to the outside world. Trends are so quickly consumed and disposed of without allowing any room to evolve. I see at the core of this bootlegging trend a sense of ingenuity and a sense of industry from people working with limited resources. It's almost an evolutionary process, if you can figure out how to make something from nothing, you will last. In places like Africa they are forced to be creative with what they have, and that to me is the core of innovation.

Title page (p. 306): Outlined version of the Gucci monogram

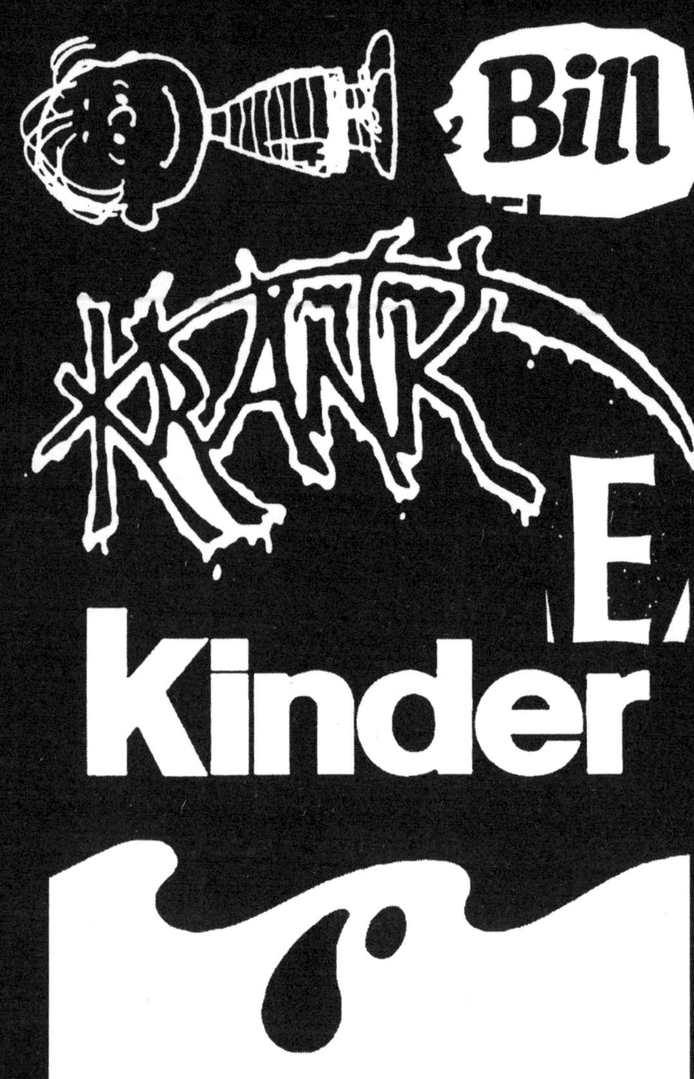

Bill
KRANK
E
Kinder

Urs Lehni (UL) & Olivier Lebrun (OL)

Urs Lehni is a Zurich-based graphic designer and the founder of Rollo Press. Olivier Lebrun is a Paris-based graphic designer. The two have become close collaborators after working together on Lebrun's bootlegged *A Pocket Companion to Books from The Simpsons* which became an instant hit in the art book world as well as with fans of the TV show. They later collaborated on a "monograph" for the French graphic designer Bernard Chadebec, composed of 1:1 prints of his poster works. Both Lehni and Lebrun share a background in skateboard culture which has since permeated into ideologies around publishing, access, and community. Both seem to view their ideas as more urgent than precious, taking on a zine-like approach to publishing and distribution centered on working with and releasing projects for a loyal fanbase and community of friends. Interview by Ben Schwartz (BS).

> BS: Both Urs and Olivier, to begin with, I'm curious about your general understanding of or relationship to bootlegging.

OL: For me, it begins with my background in skateboarding and in music. It's maybe a habit that we acquired through being a part of these cultural practices. I don't think it was ever on purpose, maybe just a natural way for us to affirm our references.

UL: Definitely. Growing up with skateboarding has provided us with a loose understanding of authorship. I think in this culture people generally have been quite generous with sharing content. I think we were just infused with that kind of attitude during our adolescence and it provided us with a pretty blurry idea of authorship, what's up for grabs, what's sacred, where you're not allowed to go or what you're not allowed to touch. I don't have a clear distinction between bootlegging, appropriation, and pirating. There is also open source, which is something that I find really interesting in graphic design, which is almost non-existent. I think with any project, you can either start from scratch or you can see what's already there, and for me, the latter is the thing that interests me. I would like my work to feel like it's embedded in a culture or a history and not so much something I did from scratch. I'm interested in things that look like they are found rather than made.

> BS: Bootlegging is of course tied to this idea of smuggling. If we think about smuggling in graphic design, we can think about moving between different cultural spheres: high and low culture, the "vernacular" and the "arts." This seems to be a common interest for the two of you, looking at "low culture," and through the design/publishing process, bringing it into the realm of "high culture." Why does this interest you, or what effect do you think this has?

OL: I think Urs and I are generally interested in things outside of design. We have this whole chat of images that aren't necessarily design-related. I'm really interested in this idea where people aren't totally aware that what they are doing is design; the results are much more interesting. I am not opposed to contemporary graphic designers who are trying to push the practice forward, but I've always viewed graphic design as my work and not my lifestyle. I've had people advise me to let go of my background in skate culture or be critical of it, and for that reason I'm not so interested in being a part of a certain design community. I'm not trying to match skills with the top graphic designers, I'm interested in using design to work with all of these other things I enjoy.

UL: I think Olivier and I both have one foot in the scene and the other one outside of it. We are skeptical of a too canonical way of making design—I find these ideas very troublesome and also very boring. In Switzerland, we have a lot of tradition, and theres still so many schools that rely on a set of principles that were established in the 1940s and 1950s. I'm always shocked, and to a certain extent also disgusted, that this is still attractive, without looking at the ideological package that these aesthetics come with.

I think a lot of my practice is opposing this and trying to find positions that are outside of it. This ideology might not really be at the forefront of the practice and it's not supplemented by critical readings or texts, it's more through action. It's by publishing small stimulators that are outside of a certain

pp. 322–325: Bernard Chadebec, *Intrus Sympathiques* (2016)

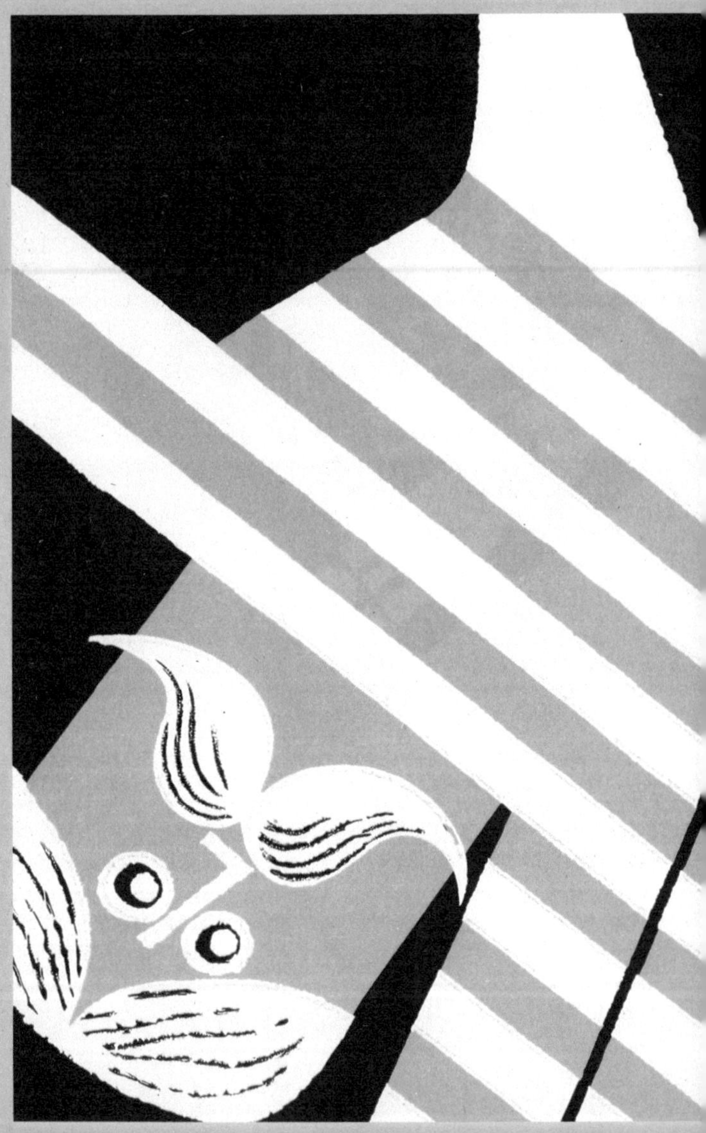

loquée...
RITE : 30, RUE OLIVIER NOYER, 75680 PARIS CEDEX 14. N° 044 D CODE COMMANDE N° 4785
252
15

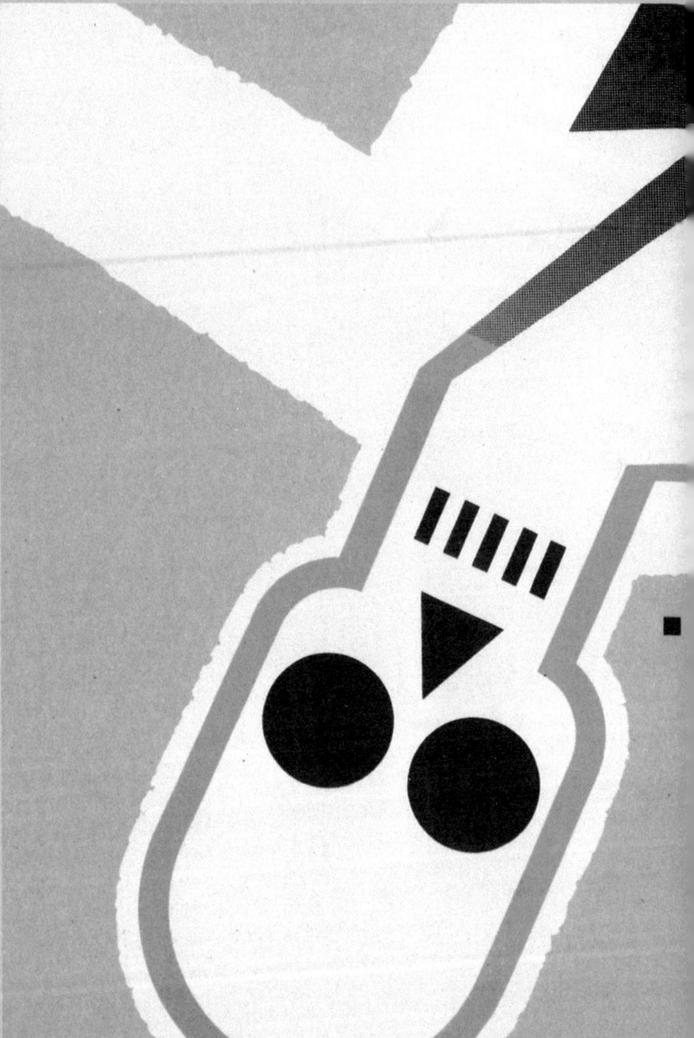

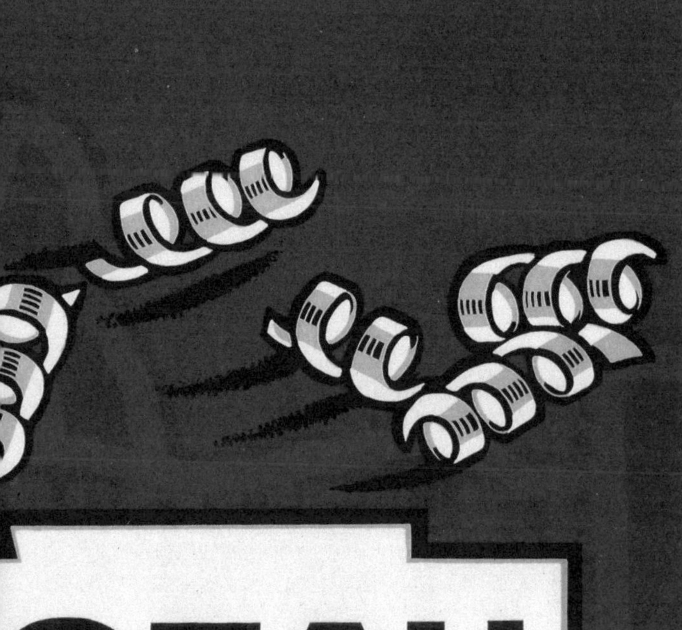
CEAU
main
230
91

canon. I think the [Bernard] Chadebec book is a good example of this because it's just a guy who worked for the industry in a way; he's the French poster designer who has probably reached the highest print runs with his work, but nobody in the design scene ever talked about him because his stuff was just hanging in factories. We were curious as to why nobody has written about him or shown his work.

BS: On a related note, both of you have spoken before of the influence of Hans-Rudolf Lutz. In the States, he's surprisingly and sadly obscure. His work seems to resonate with this interest in "low culture" and the spirit of bootlegging. Can you both talk about his influence on your own practice? and sadly obscure. His work seems to resonate with this interest in "low culture" and the spirit of bootlegging. Can you both talk about his influence on your own practice?

UL: My first contact with his work was because he was a teacher at the school where I was studying. I didn't have him as a teacher because he got sick the year before I went there. When he died he left this huge vacuum; everybody would talk so highly of him. About a year later after his death, the school decided to make an exhibition in his honor, and a teacher gave us the option to help with the show.

Throughout this process, I was able to look at almost everything that he had done in his professional life. Since then, I mean, I'm not a specialist on his work, but I've collected a little bit and I have a lot of contact with Tania Prill, who is his widow and is in charge of his archive.

I think Lutz is also this kind of figure. If you're at the design museum in Zurich and you have a Wolfgang Weingart exhibition, then you should have a Lutz exhibition. I really question why we haven't seen this; we should have a major monograph of his work at this point. He and Weingart are to me the really interesting Swiss postmodernists. One is kind of a technical virtuoso and is exploring in a more formal and aesthetic way. The other has a really broad cultural idea of design, is very active on the political left, is organizing exhibitions with posters from Cuba, and is in a way an outspoken communist and anticapitalist. His broader understanding of design, looking at it as something that is not exclusively done by a field of professionals, I find so contemporary, especially at a moment when we're seeking a more inclusive or participatory field. If you look at his hieroglyphics book, it seems to be in direct opposition to the ideas of Swiss modernist Otl Aicher, where there was a desire to find one way of saying Apple, or toilet. Lutz showed us that there are so many more ways to communicate. I find it fascinating. His way of taking a newspaper and deconstructing it into different parts and finding this immense pleasure in this universe that is so narrow and quotidian—he just goes in there and finds all this amazing stuff.

OL: When I saw the issue of *Typografie Monatsblätter* made by Lutz, I thought it was brilliant, a total skater attitude. With his hieroglyph book, today you could almost see it being some sort of Instagram account and the magic is lost. There is something really nice about the way he collected things from the street over time, or the way he blew up the raster image from the newspaper; he was just so full of surprise. I definitely found him to be an interesting and inspiring figure to look to for inspiration. I'm telling you, Urs and I rarely chat about design, but today we were talking about Virgil Abloh…

UL: Did you interview him by the way?

BS: I've been trying to…

OL: For me, it's very surprising. I didn't see the guy coming, and now he's doing everything from fashion to skateboarding. I recently read a text in *Real Review* that talked about how brands like Fuct and Stussy were built up with bootlegging, and now it's all moving to high fashion and no one can afford it. That part of it, I don't like. I'm beginning to think bootlegging is just becoming a trend and will eventually collapse.

UL: [Abloh] has this 3% rule, where if you do something and it differentiates from the original by 3% you can claim that it's your own. I remember these sorts of disputes in type design, and there I think the number was 5%. I wonder how you can even measure this?

BS: This need to claim ownership feels antithetical to the whole idea of bootlegging…

OL: Both ethically and politically I'm very much against this way of working. We've seen a lot of bootlegs in the fashion world that have co-opted skate culture. It has a lot to do with power and money; I remember a high fashion label that appropriated work from the brand Santa Cruz and would sell the products for such high prices, and these original graphics were made by a small team struggling to stay afloat.

I don't mean to make a political statement about our work, but we really do try to make things affordable, we're not so interested in capitalizing on profits with our work. I think it goes back to the way things freely circulated and were traded in skate communities.

UL: You're right, it's about accessibility. Bootlegging now feels like the opposite of what it was in the past; rather than make something more affordable, it's more expensive. We don't want anyone to think twice about whether or not they can afford our books.

> BS: Bootlegging and community are inherently linked. On one hand, you have communities that make the bootlegs. On the other, you have bootlegs that might create, preserve, or become emblematic of specific communities. Could you each speak to your relationship between publishing and community?

OL: Rollo has an amazing community. I was so happy to have *The Simpsons* book come out on Rollo, it was like the music label I always wanted to be on. I also identified with the other publications and practices that Rollo supported, and they were supportive of the simple idea of having fun making books and having fun reading books. But really Rollo is a community — you have Stefan Marx, Linus Bill. I suppose what made me excited is that these were all people Urs was close with, so it felt like being part of a gang or a team. Having *The Simpsons* book there really allowed me to be welcomed into this community.

I also appreciate how these books end up as a part of a much larger community, on my bookshelf for example. I like how *The Simpsons* book falls in between Dieter Roth and Baldessari or next to a comic book, it just felt like a missing link on my shelf, and I am interested in communicating with people with a similar understanding of this project. It also operates in between the idea of a fan zine and a book. Sometimes we make books that feel like fan zines and other times we make fan zines that feel like books, and I've always been really attracted to this ambiguity. I like that *The Simpsons* book seems to connect a lot of disparate communities—*Simpsons* fans, graphic designers, art book lovers, etc. It felt like a missing link, much in the same way Chadebec was a sort of missing link for Urs and I. I so often see these small communities as being so hermetic, and we are really interested in making connections between these different groups.

UL: I'm really happy that Rollo turned out the way it did. There was no strategy behind it; I just want to make things for my friends. In a weird way, this simple idea feels almost radical, but I don't understand why this should be. I never relied on the sales of those books for my personal life. I would try to keep it as a zero sum game, you know, it makes a bit of money, then you put a little money into it again. And now for the first time, I have a job at this school and I have a bit more financial stability than I used to have before. There's no economical strategy behind it, I don't want to get anywhere with it, it's just the pure pleasure of doing these things together with people I like.

BS: I know Rollo started with a Riso, which perhaps set a precedent for the economic methods of production. Throughout Rollo's catalog, there is an underlying sense of raw, or straight forward, design and production. As the imprint has become established and highly respected, is this aesthetic still the result of economy, or do you think about it as a sort of Rollo "house style?" Do you feel there is a particular "aura" around this type of design? Is there a magic to something that feels found rather than designed?

UL: The best-funded project we ever had was Chadebec, and it turned out a little bit more fancy than other titles. But in general, I guess this is also just linked to my own upbringing coming from the lower spectrum of a Swiss middle class family, and spending my youth skateboarding with a DIY mentality—this is what determines my pricing policy.

I really want things to be affordable and at the same time I'm also really interested in this mass market paperback aesthetic. In that sense, I think we are closely linked to some strands of conceptual art where you use some super mundane objects in order to disseminate your ideas or your content. You don't choose the handmade edition of twelve and charge hundreds of dollars for it. You want the thing to be out there and you want to produce it in the largest possible number. So I think that has informed a lot of design decisions in the end. With limited money, how can we make the most interesting object in the highest possible run.

BS: Speaking of authorship, several of Rollo's titles are reprints of lost, rare, or simply

pp. 332–335: *A Final Companion To Books From The Simpsons* (2018)

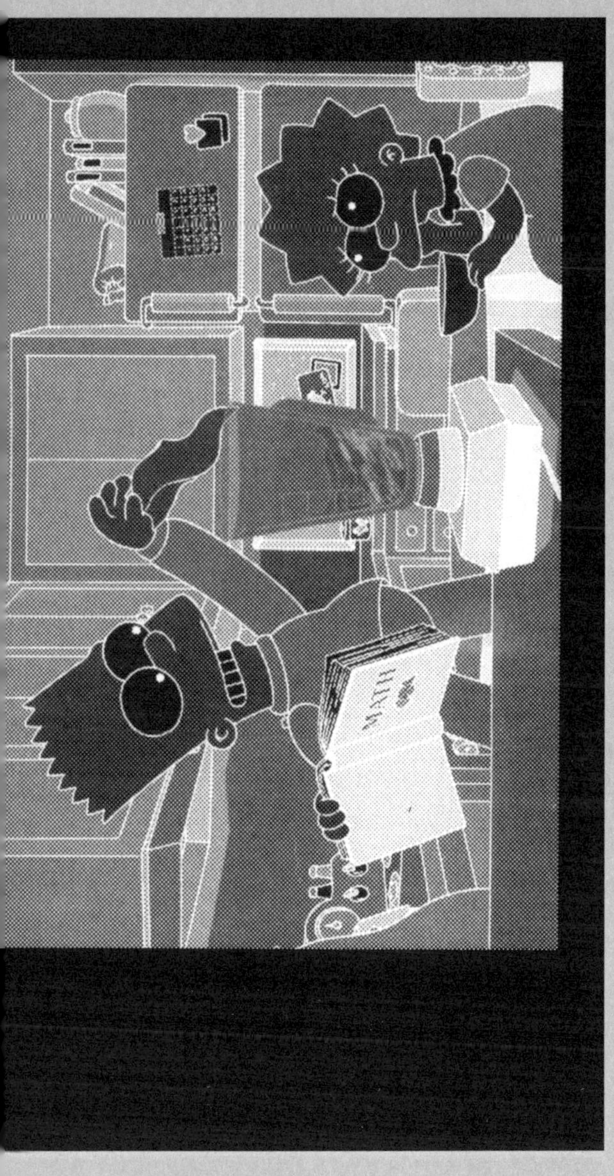

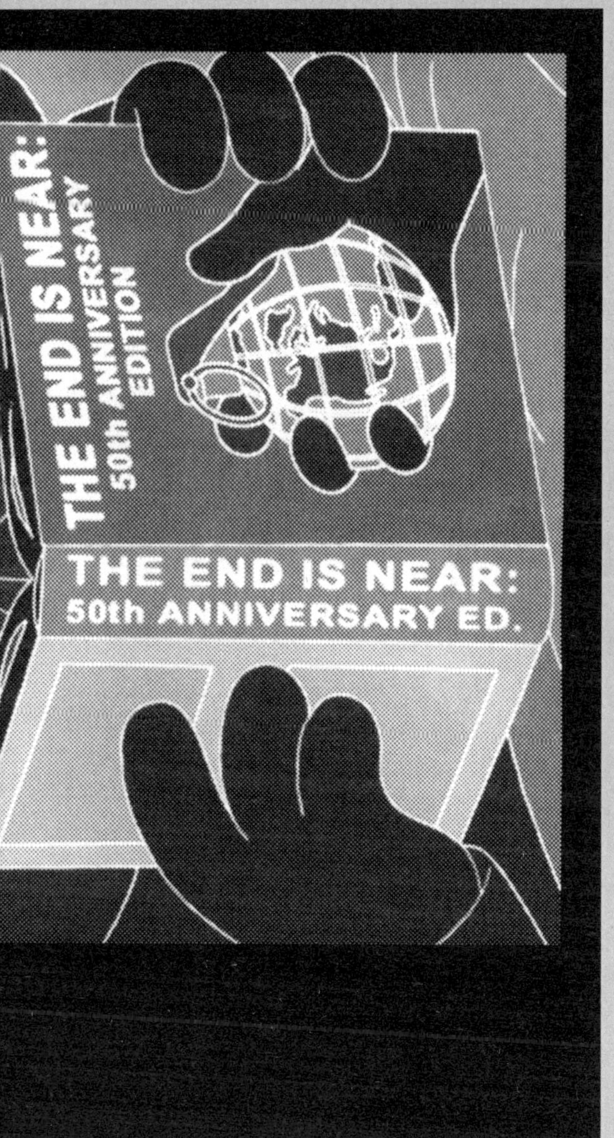
THE END IS NEAR:
50th ANNIVERSARY
EDITION
THE END IS NEAR:
50th ANNIVERSARY ED.

lesser-known historical works (*Xerox Book*, Ken Isaacs, et cetera). Regarding these reprints, have you ever had any issues with copyright? By publishing this sort of work, do you see it as a form of preservation? And lastly, is there an element of authorship in these reprints? I am thinking here of the way Walter Benjamin thinks of a translation: "An act midway between poetry and doctrine." In other words, is your goal to stay as close to the original as possible, or are you interested in some sort of transformation?

UL: We reprinted a Ken Isaacs book that I had ever seen in real life, so I don't know what it would mean to mimic the original as closely as possible. It was more like the idea of reenactment through making something available again that somehow disappeared. There wasn't any big conceptual gesture behind it, it was done in the context of an exhibition and there was a communal printing/binding room where everyone could make their own copy. We had some extra copies left, so I made the book available for trade—you could offer up anything in return for a book. We also reprinted Seth Siegelaub's *Xerox Book*, which was similarly linked to production. Maybe it was more of a stupid joke, but the *Xerox Book* is offset printed and I just figured someone should Xerox it.

OL: Working without so much emphasis on authorship opens up the roles I can play as a designer. I'm always interested in being involved in much more than just putting together the final outcome. And by not being so concerned with authorship, it puts more emphasis on the content. I see so many designers who also work as artists in some way, and there is always this battle of authorship. For me, that's completely the wrong way to think about work. I just want to use design to pay my rent and make sure my family is OK. Again, I look at Chadebec as an example, he was never concerned about being part of graphic design history, it was simply his job that he got paid five days a week to do.

> BS: Urs, you've mentioned the idea of open source as it's related to design. It's something that I feel is also related to bootlegging. Could you expand on this a bit?

UL: It's something that has been in the back of my head for a while, and it is something that was put in my head from the days of *Dot Dot Dot*. I think designers like Will Holder and Stuart Bailey, and later with David Reinfurt, they work a lot with templates such as the one they made for *Metropolis M* and later reused for other magazines. One problem I have with graphic design is that you always need to start from scratch, you know, you're almost like an artist who has to start with a blank canvas and come up with a brilliant idea. There's a history of like 500 years of books, and most are between A5 and A4, and have page numbers, and a container for the body text, et cetera. The principle and the problems have been almost identical over hundreds of years, so why don't we just make use of that knowledge and resources? A lot of it has to do with software; I'm 100% sure there will be a time when this monopoly is cracked open and we will be more willing to share our designs. Another problem that I have is with type design, which

PROVAL
ING

is really playing into that field as well, because there is the possibility to use open-source licenses and then distribute typefaces in this way. So there you have this kind of software infrastructure, but nobody thinks to use it because you are doing something you can actually make millions from. Graphic design is interesting to me because it's always full of these worthwhile dilemmas. Nothing is clear, it's always blurry; there is always something to figure out.

> BS: I like the idea that a bootleg is more truthful in understanding a subject than any sort of original. That, by looking through the eyes of an admirer, we can know a subject on a more personal level. I'm curious if you feel the same way with publishing? Additionally, does your DIY method of production provide an additional lens through which you can understand a subject on a more intimate level?

OL: A bootleg often operates as an homage to the original. It's also a way of speaking to your audience, for example, when we used the Nirvana logo on the Yellow Pages shirt, we entered into a dialogue; we are winking at the community. With the recent Linus Bill book or with *The Simpsons* book, the design of each is meant to reframe the content in an unexpected way. *The Simpsons* book is modeled after an encyclopedia, so there is a slightly more dry or academic framing than you might expect. This is what I like most when Urs is designing something, there is al-

p. 341: Spines from various editions of *A Pocket Companion to Books from The Simpsons* (2012–2018)

LISA I PICK UP BOOKS LIKE YOU PICK UP BEERS.
HOMER THEN YOU HAVE A SERIOUS READING PROBLEM!

MARGE WELL, LET'S CHECK OUT THAT DISCOUNT BOOK WAREHOUSE.
HOMER BUT WE ALREADY OWN A BOOK!

Marge We're taking Maggie to the bookstore, so she can learn the way kids did between 1910 and 2002.

Marge Now, if you ladies recall what this place is supposed to be for!?
Lady Mm… Mm… Smokin' weed?
Marge Reading!

9 783906 213248

Marge DVDs, plush toys, crullers… I don't see many books.
Homer Yeah, the only actual books are coffee table books:
Barn Doors of Topeka,
Dogs Eating Ice Cream,
Jigsaw Puzzles with One Piece Missing,
Man-Killing Snakes of the Amazon…
Clerk Sir! Never say "Amazon" in a bookstore.

ways this idea of displacement which creates these unexpected encounters

UL: I'm not 100% sure that if I buy a bootleg book I get a better understanding of an original. Sam de Groot, for example, compiled and illegally published J.D. Salinger texts as a critical gesture and I'm not totally sure I felt any differently about Salinger. What I can say, though, is as a bootlegger, or somebody who finds a lot of joy and pleasure in re-enacting material from the past, I think it does help me to understand it in closer way. At the moment, I'm working on the reprint of *Today's Hieroglyphics* by Lutz and I have to kind of reverse engineer the project, and it allows me to look at the book from a totally different perspective. Not necessarily what's printed on the page, but the organization and the logic. A lot of it he did manually and with photo composition and cutting and gluing, and so when I do it in InDesign there are different tools being used to rebuild the spread.

That's something I really enjoy, to kind of stick your brain into somebody else's brain and figure out how he or she did something. There is a real learning process that is happening there, and it's how I learned about so much. There is a sort of embodied element to it, you have to actually go through the process, and I think when you do that there is a lot to be gained. Maybe in a future curriculum in an art school there should be a class… "okay Monday morning, time to get to bootlegging 101…"

BS: We've been speaking a lot here about bootleg objects, but I'm also interested in how bootlegging might transcend objects.

How can we think of bootlegging as a mindset or methodology? Do either of you have thoughts on how the act might evolve in this way in the future?

OL: I think it's a fantastic way to show your sources and recirculate information again. There is also power in its ability to provide accessibility. I really can't say much about the future, but my optimism points towards bootlegging as a way to continuously recirculate resources, even if these sorts of activities are transferred to a medium like Instagram. Right now, the hype around bootlegging feels like a trend, and one that will pass. But I think it will continue to exist in smaller communities and help resurface stories that might have otherwise been lost, and interrupt these very linear histories that we gravitate to.

UL: Yeah, I think of bootlegging like a virus that mutates, but I think it has to emancipate itself from what it was before. There is this organic quality to the gesture that somehow always manages to slip away and go under the radar.

Title page (p. 318): Cover of *Kranke Kinder* by Linus Bill published by Yellow Pages (2021) run by Urs Lehni and Olivier Lebrun

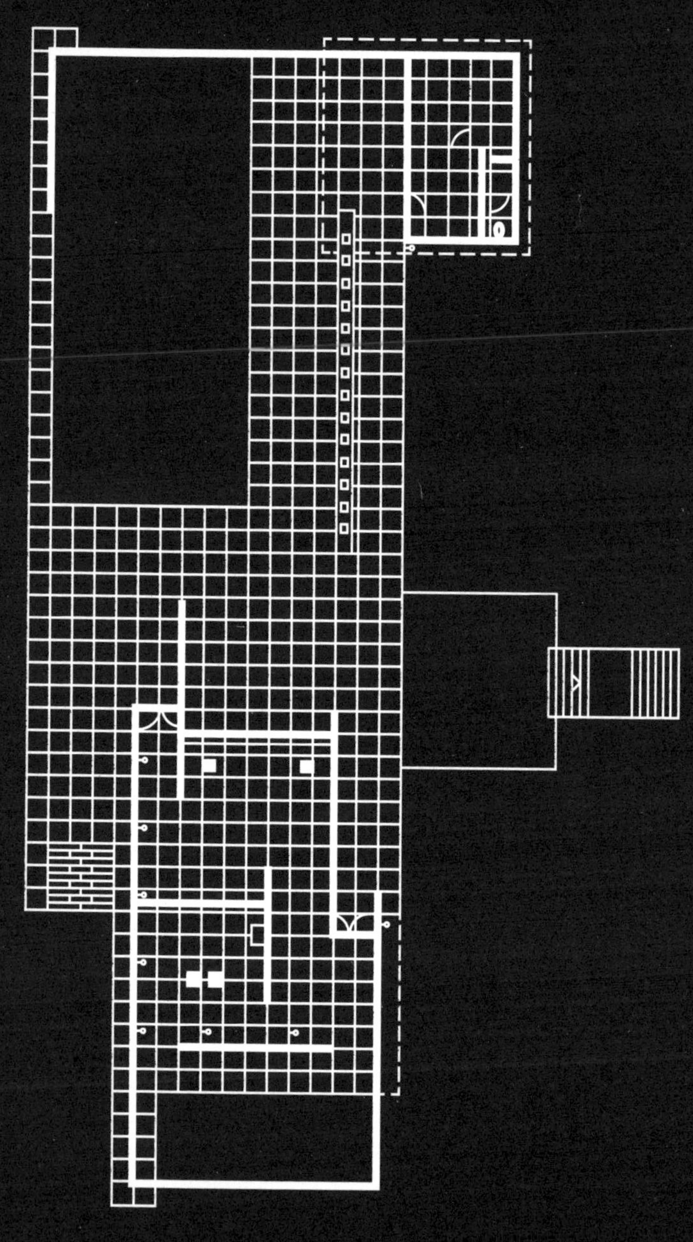

Oana Stănescu (OS)

Oana Stănescu is a New York–based architect and educator. In 2021, Stanescu, along with the German architecture practice Something Fantastic, organized a lecture and workshop at Syracuse University School of Architecture titled 'Covers, Covers, Covers', which investigated the idea of a cover version across a broad spectrum of media. Looking at examples from Cat Power to Alvar Aalto, Mies van der Rohe to Martin Margiela, the speakers presented various case studies that expanded the traditional notion of a cover far beyond its musical origins. The lecture, in addition to Stănescu's architectural collaborations with Virgil Abloh, made me curious about how she saw bootlegging play out in the field of architecture. Our conversation, however, found Stănescu at a unique crossroads in her career after recently dissolving her previous studio FAMILY, and at the cusp of starting her own office. Rather than discuss bootleg buildings, we spoke about the liberating potential of a "bootleg practice"—subverting the rules and expectations of a studio that so often go unconsidered. Interview by Ben Schwartz (BS).

BS: I really enjoyed your recent lecture at Syracuse on cover versions. What inspired this lecture and workshop?

OS: I've had this idea of working with covers for a while now and my goal has been to make a multidisciplinary exhibition which deals with this notion of a "cover" in different aspects of music and architecture, art and writing. There's no creative field that doesn't have some kind of parallel or its own version of a cover. There is even a legal aspect to it, which is of interest to me, and that's where things tend to break down. It all feels really relevant now given this kind of cultural moment we are in. So this idea of a multidisciplinary exhibition has been on my mind for a long time, but until we get there we have this workshop that myself along with Something Fantastic have developed. It felt important because people tend to feel very fragile about covers and the theory and baggage they seem to involve. But really our idea for the workshop involves ideas as banal as saying you can learn a practice by covering it—which is widely accepted when it comes to learning an instrument by playing songs by other artists. In architecture, this is less accepted as a way of learning. Yet when I look back at my time in architecture school, one of the most valuable exercises we did was to rebuild or redraw a Tadao Ando house from scratch. In doing so, you get to know it in an intimate and unique way that you wouldn't get just from looking at plans.

In all the studios I've worked in, and the places I've taught, this notion of the cover is rarely discussed. And I think in architecture, there's still this myth of the genius architect and originality. There's an obsession with looking for the new thing, and I was interested in the simplicity and really the validity of the cover as a creative process. I might be wrong, but it feels more acceptable in Europe than in the U.S. There seems to be less of an obsession with trying to reinvent and a more open mindset with drawing upon certain ideas or objects. In the U.S., there seems to be more of a focus on: what's the brand? What's original? Which doesn't always lead to great things. Introducing the idea of the cover is a way of trying to loosen up the creative conversation and combat the polarization of things like Instagram and a lack of actual conversation. The reality of media, and the ingestion of information, all operate on the same spectrum as the individual genius. We love building them up, and we love tearing them down.

In my most idealistic, wildest dreams, this push for the cover would really just evolve into a new cultural way of thinking. It would reset our expectations. Because as a creator, the moment you let ego and authorship go, there's an immense freedom to just create. Ideally, we would be able to let go of these expectations of ourselves or others driven by this mythical authorial figure.

> BS: What excites me about covers is their ability to become progressive rather than just mimetic. A cover can be so much more than a copy. In the best covers, authorship becomes totally blurred...

OS: Right, there's an element to all of this that forces us to acknowledge that nothing we do is original, that everything is built on something from the past. What

I find most fascinating about this conversation is that some people identify themselves fully with their work. So the moment you remove some of this myth of originality, it destroys a person's identity. This all ties back to how we define success, because we're still distracted by the things that happen out in the open—social media likes, for example. But the most interesting things don't actually happen at that level. The interesting things are rarely at the surface, but still it's hard not to be distracted by that level of the conversation.

> BS: For you, what makes a powerful cover? What does it take for a cover to transcend its source?

OS: I don't think there's a single way in which that happens, but I think there is a point where a cover can become its own thing. A good cover builds on the original, it doesn't take away from it. It couldn't exist without it, but at the same time, it is its own thing in an unquestionable way. In the lecture, we talked about the Alvar Aalto stool and the Ikea "cover," which would have actually been a dream for Aalto to see because he wanted it to become more commercial. Or the plexi version, which works because the shape of the chair is much truer to that material than to the wood. I remember at one point I was working at SANAA in Japan. One of the partners was working on a house, and at one point it started looking like the Prada Aoyama building by Herzog & de Meuron in Tokyo. I remember at the time everyone on the team was freaking out because there was a similarity in a certain type of geometry.

The only person who didn't care was the partner, Kazuyo Sejima, because for her, it was one step out of a long process. At least in architecture, things can take years to arrive at the final solution. And that always stuck with me, her calmness and coolness in remaining unfazed by all of that.

BS: How did the students react to this workshop? Was there anything in particular they struggled with?

OS: I'm hoping to do this workshop in multiple iterations in different contexts. I think there's so much richness within the conversation, and I want to make sure to have the time and space to explore it. In this case, it was first year students in their second semester, so many of them were somewhat new to architecture. I think it was a great moment to try it out because there was less of a struggle to undo deeply rooted ideologies, and more so just giving them the freedom to run with different ideas. I think there were a lot of questions as to what actually makes a cover, and what are the rules of a cover, and I was really just trying to get them to open up to the idea.

I think what was intriguing for students was that the idea of a cover tied in part to larger cultural conversations. Things in architecture tend to be very insular and removed from what's happening in the world around you, because of the long timelines. So I think the workshop allowed them to draw parallels to things outside of the practice and effected their cultural and conceptual understanding of the world… at least I hope.

pp. 350–353: Stills from 'Covers, Covers, Covers' a lecture for Syracuse University of Architecture School by Oana Stănescu with Something Fantastic (2021)

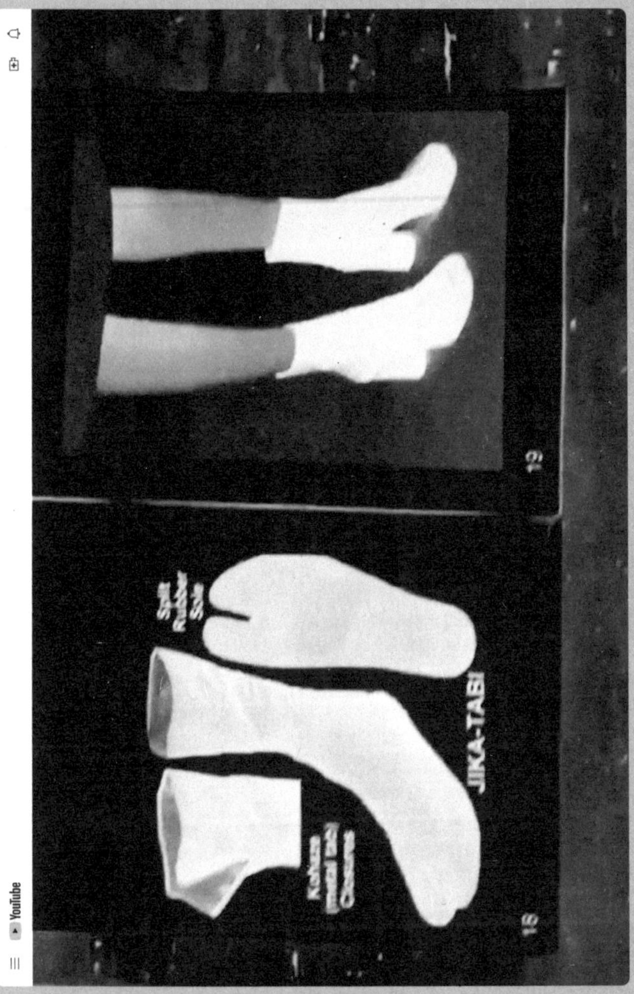
YouTube
JIKA-TABI
15
19

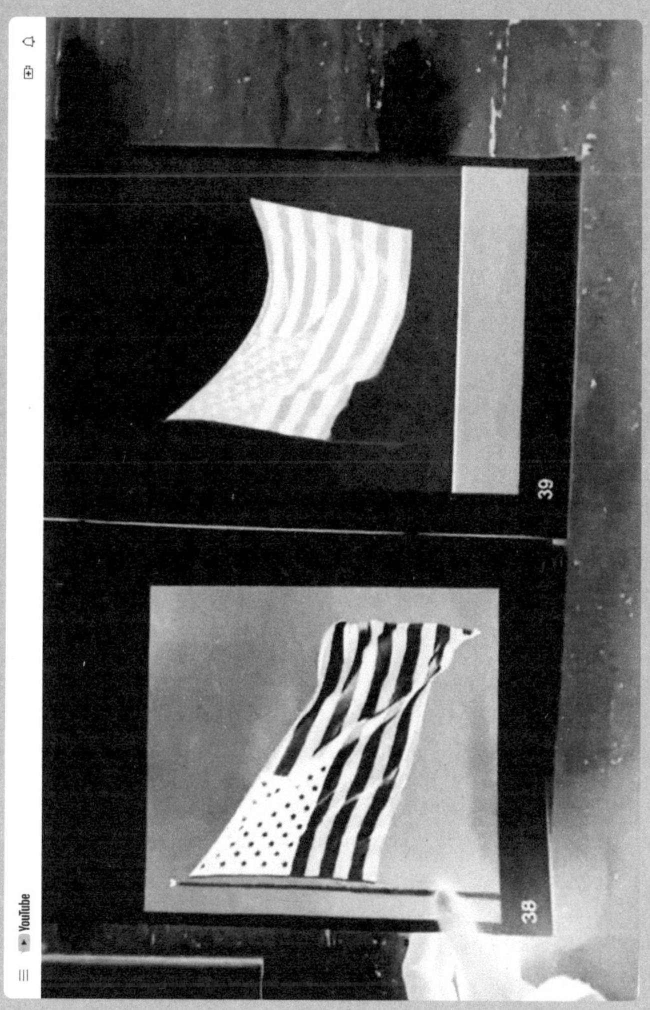
YouTube
39
38

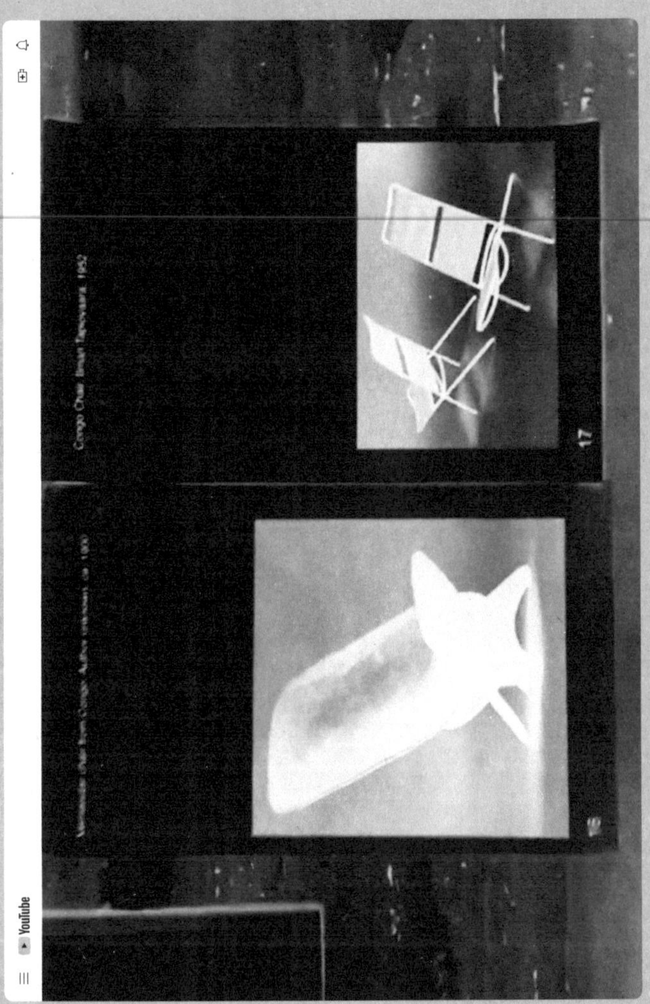
YouTube
Congo Chair
17

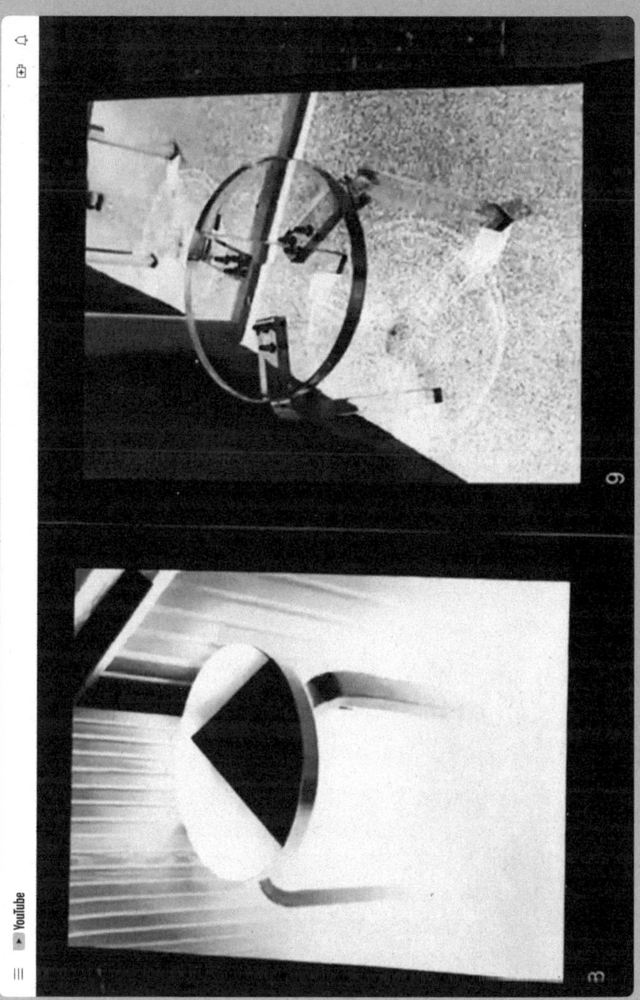
YouTube

BS: And what about in your own practice? Has this focus on covering affected your process at all? Do any projects of yours come to mind where some of this thinking feels particularly important?

OS: Not in a direct way, at least not yet. If anything, it's influenced more so how I am trying to work and run my practice rather than directly affecting the projects I am working on right now. I was in a partnership before and we had worked together for nearly a decade and eventually just wanted different things. It became very clear to me that I wasn't interested in having just another architecture office (nothing against architecture offices). I wasn't quite sure how that would manifest itself, but in the beginning, everyone is telling you what an office is or should be—you need a website, you need to model your practice after this or that architect, et cetera. There is a lot of pressure, and for a long time you just can't answer it.

I very intentionally began to think about how to avoid falling into a trap of just running an office. With architecture, projects get big really quickly and you need staff, you need people to work with. So you end up working with people and of course there still needs to be some structural hierarchy, but I've been trying to work more with a network of collaborators. It's less about being stuck in one partnership, and more about embracing many partnerships on different projects.

Even with the name, it's just my name. Most people that I ended up working with were clients who I had a personal rapport with and to create some sort of brand felt fake in many ways. In that sense, it's my name but I want to be able to put any other name next to it. My goal is to sign the projects with the initials of everyone working on it.

BS: It makes me wonder what a bootleg architectural office looks like. Does something like that resonate with your office at all?

OS: I would use the word hijacking instead. I feel like in any creative project, it's a bit like a game where you set up the rules and parameters that you want to work within. Quite often, we forget to question some of those variables that we set up to begin with. It's the same with practice, you forget to question some of those aspects of your life because you have only so many hours in a day.

To me, the interesting thing with the bootleg is that it has a lot to do with the stupidity of rules and permissions, right? It creates an incentive to find a way around things. It creates access, it fills a particular need. I mean, that was how I discovered music growing up—through bootleg CDs. So, for me, the point of trying to reorient myself in how I do the work came out of the need to reject expectations. Now it seems so banal and obvious, but it took me quite a while to get there. This new formation of a practice came out of a need to find new and different ways of working, because the old ones just weren't fitting.

Title page (p. 344): Diagram of the Barcelona Pavilion by Mies van der Rohe (1928) featured in 'Covers, Covers, Covers' a lecture for Syracuse University of Architecture School by Oana Stănescu with Something Fantastic (2021)

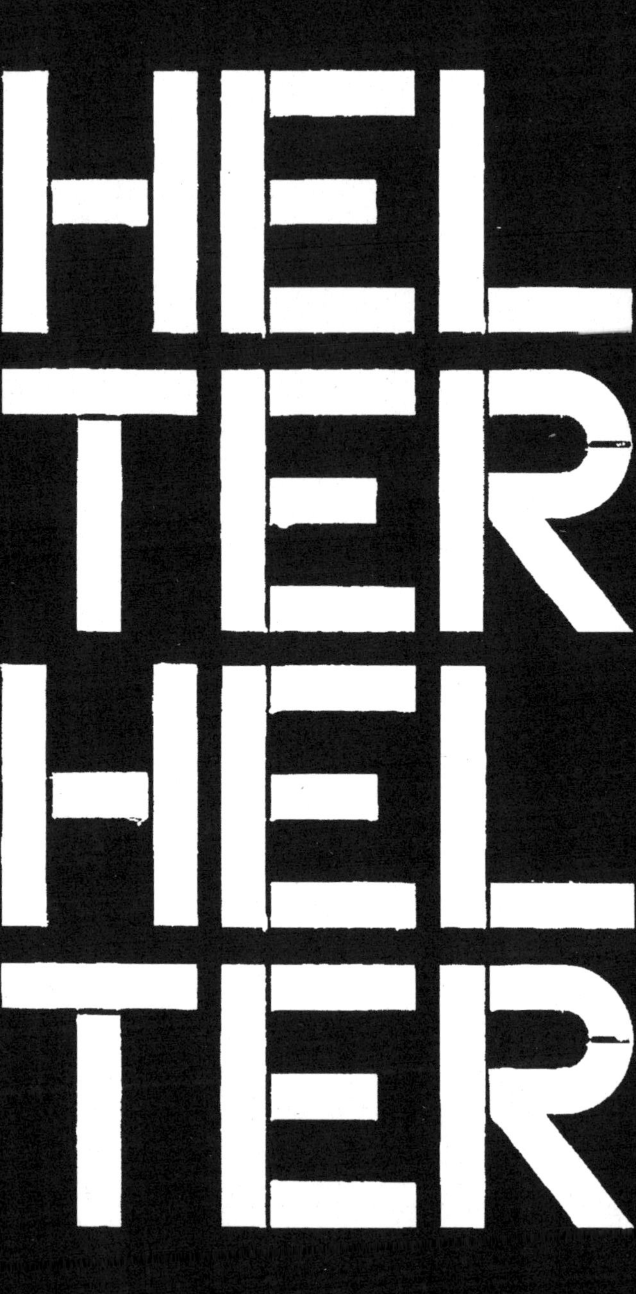
HEL
TER
HEL
TER

Eric Doeringer (ED)

Eric Doeringer is a Los Angeles–based conceptual artist. Doeringer began selling replicas of iconic artworks outside of galleries to the amusement, or more often the annoyance, of those inside. His practice follows closely on the heels of Elaine Sturtevant and Richard Prince as he challenges notions of authorship and originality through his oeuvre of knock-off books, paintings, sculptures, and installations. What becomes particularly interesting is the way Doeringer explores these ideas in the remix-ridden online world, where at times his copies become more "real" than the original. Interview by Ben Schwartz (BS).

> BS: How has your understanding or appreciation of bootlegs evolved over time?

ED: One of the things that first intrigued me about "bootleg" or counterfeit merchandise was that a given item, say a Louis Vuitton handbag, would be reproduced at a variety of price points. At the top end, there's a bag of similar quality to the "real" thing (possibly manufactured at the same factory) but unauthorized. Then there's a range of cheaper knockoffs that look convincing at a distance, but the leather and fasteners are chintzy and the stitching uneven. Finally, there's a copy that isn't trying very hard to look like the original (possibly to avoid legal action)—the LV is replaced by other initials and the bag's design is noticeably different. It was these "bottom tier" copies that captured my attention. At what point did they cease being "copies" and start becoming "originals?" The Monkees weren't The Beatles, but they still had some great songs!

Over time, I've grown more interested in exploring the relationship between the original and the copy. I've learned a lot about copyright law and become more adamant about artists' rights to appropriate, sample, remix, collage, and otherwise repurpose existing works.

> BS: In an interview about bootlegging, I'd like to "bootleg" a question from Robert Rosenblum in a 2003 interview with Mike Bidlo in *Artforum*: "What you do is close to what a lot of artists do: namely, making replicas of, or variations on, well-known works of 20th-century art. You could be grouped together with a predecessor like Elaine Sturtevant, who began doing this work in the 1960s, or with your contemporaries from the 1980s and 1990s like Sherrie Levine or Richard Pettibone. I'm curious to know how you feel about your relationship to these other artists."

ED: I definitely feel a kinship with these artists (I would include a few others like Richard Prince and Jonathan Monk). I think it's interesting that even though we are all doing the "same" thing (i.e, "copying" other artists), we are very different artists with different concerns. We all look back to Warhol and Duchamp, but there's a world of difference between a Pettibone Warhol painting and a Sturtevant Warhol painting (and not just the scale!). We do share some commonalities, like an interest in the ways that repetition changes an image (and the reception of an image) and in challenging traditional notions of authorship and originality.

BS: The art world tends to distinguish itself by labeling mimicry or "bootlegging" as "appropriation." Why do you think this is, and do you personally differentiate between these two ideas?

ED: I would say mimicry is the attempt to copy something perfectly. A mimic is judged on its fidelity to the original. A bootleg is a bad mimic—unauthorized and of lower quality. But, one could view the bootleg as simply "different" from the original, not necessarily "lesser." The slippage between the original and the bootleg provides an opportunity for creative change.

A bootleg is usually "cheap," which could be good or bad depending on your perspective. A bootleg might be available when the original is not—like bootleg liquor during prohibition, a bootleg recording of a live concert, or a bootleg copy of a banned or unreleased book or movie.

The language is complicated. I don't like to use the word "copy" in regards to my work, but it is often

pp. 360–361: Eric Doeringer's bootleg artworks for sale in the streets of New York, (2006)

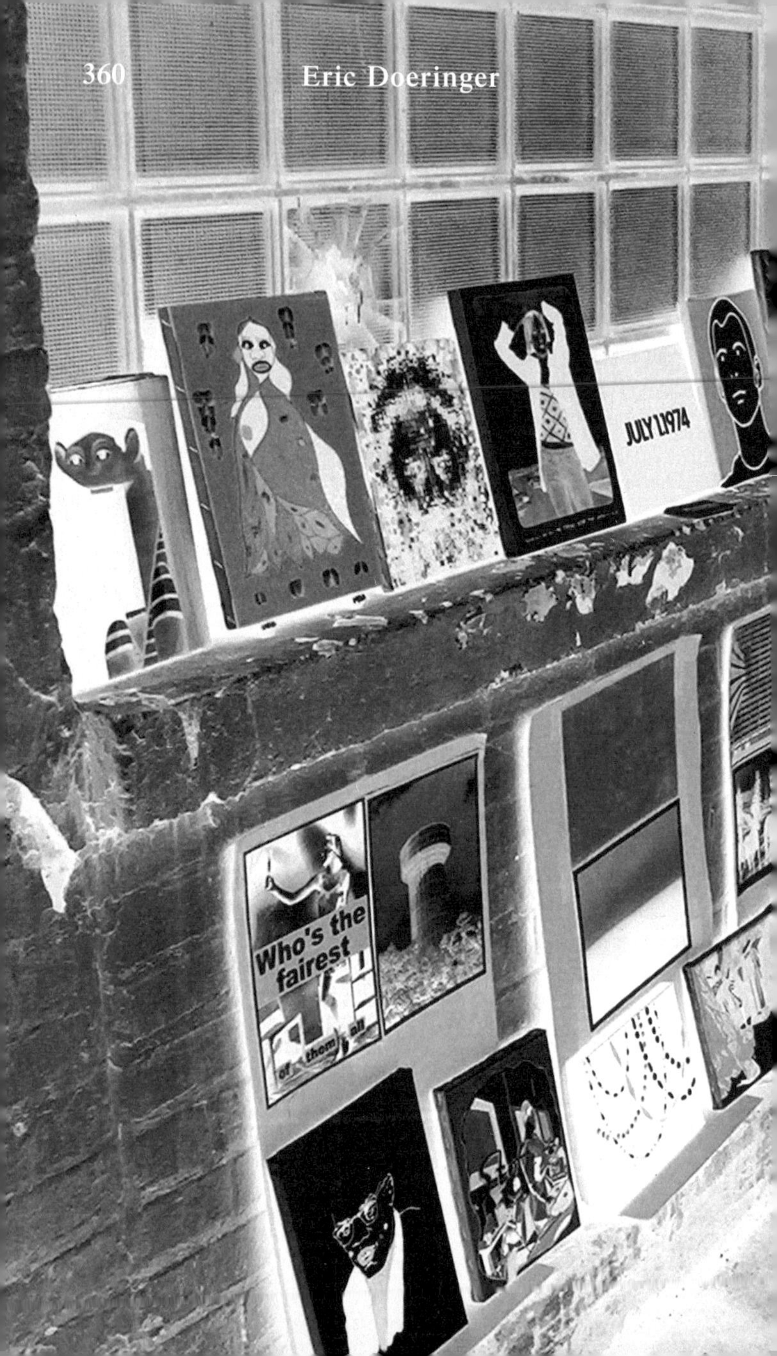
JULY 1 1974
Who's the fairest
of them all

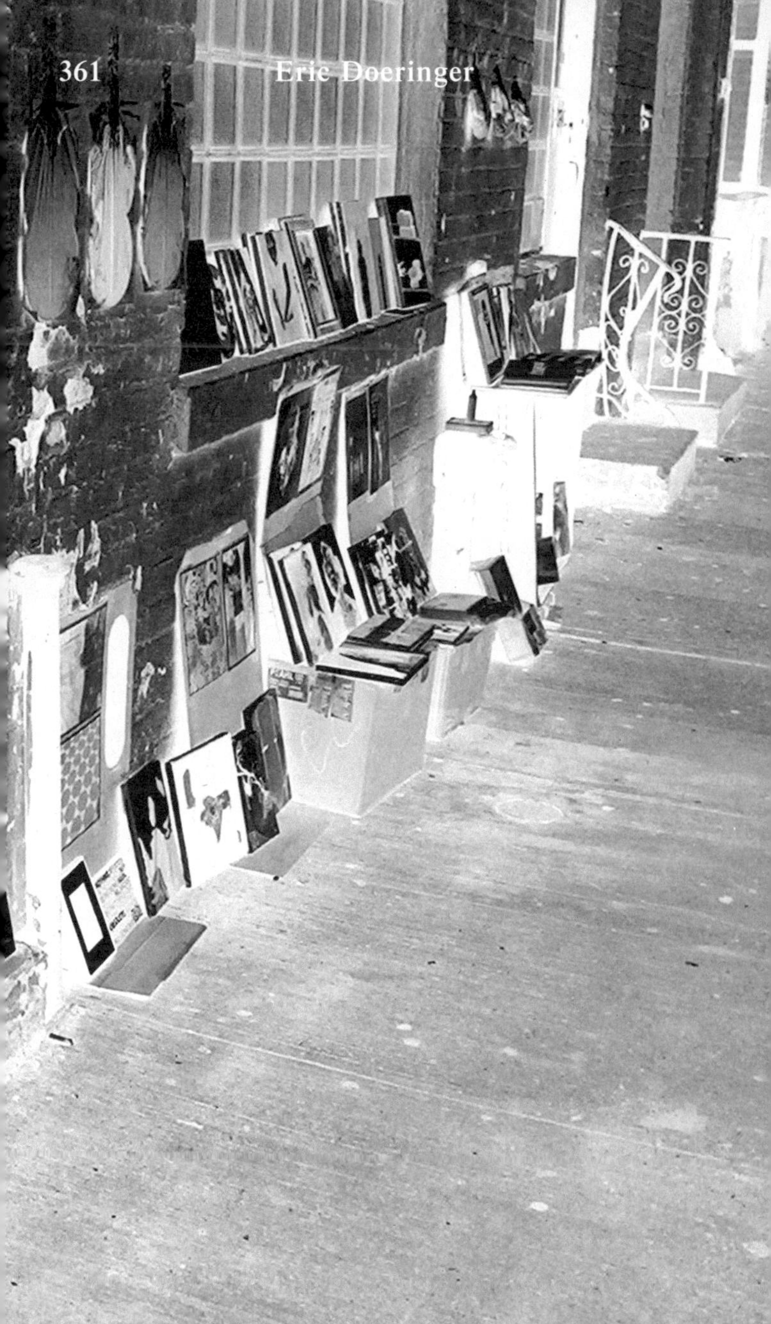

the easiest way to describe what I do. I don't mind the term "appropriation," which I define as repurposing an existing work (image, text, music, et cetera) to express a new idea.

> BS: For Sturtevant, it seems that the question of why she chose to bootleg certain works was often thought of as intuitive. How do you make that decision?

ED: For my Bootleg Series, the choice of artists was determined by their presence in the media and art market. I chose so-called "art stars." I definitely viewed the "curation" of artists, the "installation" of works on the street, and the "performance" of selling the paintings all to be parts of the "artwork."

The artists also had to have a recognizable style—you could say "brand"—that I could imitate relatively quickly and easily. The work had to look good and be "sellable." More Damien Hirst, less Marina Abramović.

When I sold my paintings on the street in Chelsea in the early 2000s, I thought of my selection of artists as a snapshot of the "hot" artists of the time—almost like a yearbook. In some ways, it *was* like bootlegging handbags. I could make a few copies of a few different paintings and see what sold on the street. If one painting proved to be popular, I'd make a bunch more. If another sold slowly, I would "discontinue" it and try something new.

More recently, I've done some thematic exhibitions of Bootleg paintings. I had a show based on works being auctioned at Christie's New York—my exhibition ran concurrently with the sale—and another in Los Angeles featuring works inspired by the

Broad Collection. For these series, I was able to "cherry pick" the works I thought were the strongest—and/or that I felt I could interpret the best—from predetermined collections of "masterpieces."

I also make works that I call "Recreations" which are more similar to the original works in scale, materials, and execution. These pieces are less about the market and more about the concepts explored in the original works. I'm drawn to artists who set up systems to generate their work (On Kawara's Date Paintings), relied on assistants to "make" their artwork (Sol LeWitt's Wall Drawings, Damien Hirst's Spot Paintings), or otherwise strove to remove their "hand" from their artwork (Andy Warhol's silkscreens, Ed Ruscha's photo books).

> BS: Bootlegging can be seen as an act of admiration or, conversely, as a form of subversion. In your practice, does your bootlegging stem from a place of fandom, or does it operate more as a critique?

ED: I definitely conceived the project as a subversion of the art market. Most obviously, I was trying to undercut the market by selling "cheap knockoffs." But, also, unlike traditional art multiples, my Bootlegs are neither signed—my name is rubber-stamped on the back—, numbered, nor issued in a limited quantity. And because the paintings are produced according to demand, I've made many more copies of the popular works, meaning the less "successful" paintings are "rarer" and thus potentially more valuable.

Selling my Bootlegs on the street in Chelsea was also a way to get around the gallery system, which had been daunting to me as a young artist. I liked that vending my paintings on the street—perhaps the least prestigious way for an artist to exhibit their work—was integral to the project. Ironically, many more "important" people from the art world probably saw my paintings on the street than would have seen them inside a little-known "emerging artist" gallery.

I am also a lover—or "fan"—of art. My work involves a lot of research and studying artworks, and I wouldn't make it if I didn't love art and the art world. But I value both a critical eye and a sense of humor. You have to be able to laugh at yourself!

> BS: In 2019, you had a show almost exclusively of Christopher Wool Bootlegs. His work is predominately black and white, generally uses a particular stencil typeface… in a way, his work operates as a brand. A similar idea could be applied to other artists you bootleg, and of course, bootlegging and branding go hand-in-hand. I'm curious about your thoughts around this notion of an artist's practice as a brand? Is that an idea you are exploring in your work?

ED: The idea of artist-as-brand is definitely part of the concept behind my Bootleg series. The works I replicate have to be recognizable—"Oh, that's a Damien Hirst, that's a Warhol, that's a Richard Prince…" I am interested in the ways in which an artwork can function as a status symbol, and in what gives an artwork its value. An authentic Damien Hirst spot painting is worth more than mine, but my spot painting is more valuable than one made by an anonymous artist in China. They're all polka dots painted on white, and Damian didn't paint any of them. Why is Marcel Duchamp's *Fountain*—itself a replica—worth so much more than a similar vintage urinal?

> BS: What is the importance of accuracy in your work? The pieces in your Bootleg series, you mention, are intentionally "bad" recreations of work. Your Art Recreations attempt to be as accurate to the original works as possible. Why is it important to make this distinction?

ED: To me, the word bootleg suggests a "bad" copy. But, something can be "so bad it's good" or "bad" in the sense of "badass." In my artwork, I use the term bootleg to describe a series of works that are produced relatively quickly so that they can be sold inexpensively. They are handmade multiples produced in small batches of the "same" work. They are not signed or numbered and are usually smaller in scale than the original works (I originally sold them on the street so they had to be portable, but the small scale also keeps my production costs low). The Recreations are made with more care. They are usually the same size as the original works and made using the same techniques and materials. But, of course, they are never identical to the original works.

For me, that difference is the interesting part. It could be a vast difference, or what Duchamp called "infrathin." For example, my interpretation of Warhol's *Brillo Box* is a silkscreened plywood box mimicking the current design of a carton of Brillo pads. It looks nothing like Warhol's box (the logo and colors are completely different) but anyone familiar with Warhol will easily see the reference. At the opposite end of the spectrum are my recreations of Sol

LeWitt's Wall Drawings. If a museum were to exhibit an authentic, authorized LeWitt drawing of 10,000 straight 1-inch lines on one wall and my version of the same drawing on the opposite wall, they would be different (every line would be in a different place) but also the same (they would contain 10,000 lines in similar length, density, and area). It would be impossible to discern which was LeWitt's drawing and which was mine. Neither could be judged a "better" drawing. Yet the drawings hold different value (both monetary and historical) and, indeed, are two different artists' attempts to communicate different (if related) ideas.

> BS: I'm curious about your Bootleg books. I've noticed one major difference here is that you replace the artist's name with your own on the actual work. I'm interested in the ideas behind these more apparent alterations and the emphasis on authorship.

ED: I put my name on the cover and/or title page of the books because I am the author, and the original books included the author's name in the same place. I don't see that authorship as being more emphasized than in my other artwork, where my name is listed on a wall label or exhibition checklist, since that is how the original works would be presented. I always sign or otherwise mark my name on the back of works. For me, claiming authorship is the radical step—I would never attempt to pass my works off as works by the original artists.

p. 367: Eric Doeringer, *Gesammelte Werke Band 7 (after Dieter Roth)* (2020)

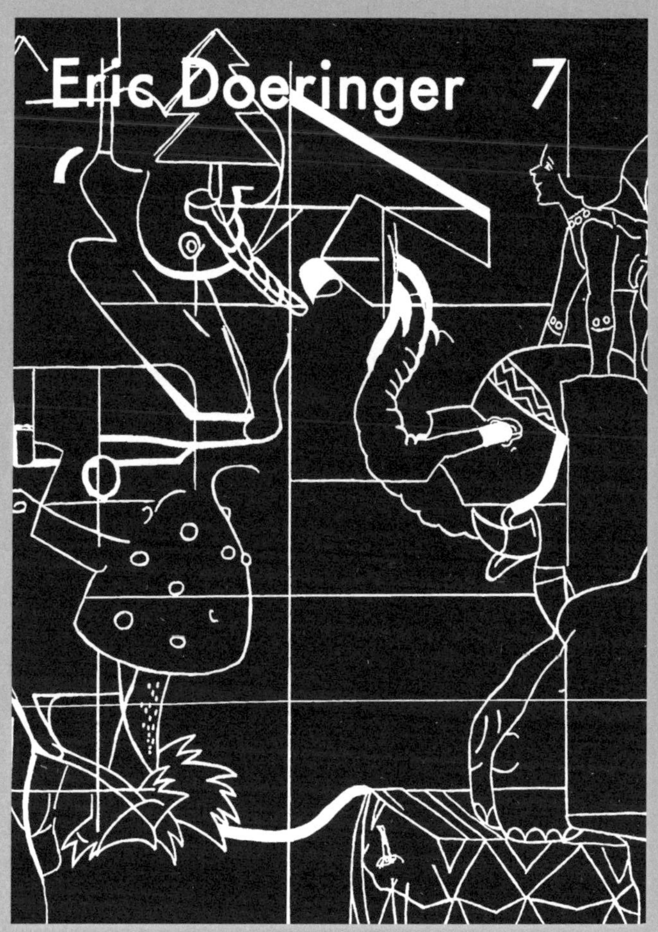
Eric Doeringer 7

> BS: What role does humor or irony play in your work? I'm thinking specifically here about your 2007 setup at the GEISAI Art Fair in Miami, or your experience having your Bootleg stand removed by police after a call from a gallerist in New York.

ED: Humor is very important. How can you participate in the art world and not want to laugh at it? When I sold my Bootleg paintings at the GEISAI Art Fair—which was held during Art Basel Miami Beach—I consciously tried to create an atmosphere that was closer to a 99-cent store than a high end art fair booth. The paintings were hung wall to wall with very little breathing room, I hung "used car lot" flags overhead, and I posted signs touting my low prices.

I think that when the art dealer called the cops on me, it was more about him than me. I hadn't "copied" any artists he represented, he just didn't like having vendors on the sidewalk. Most of the other dealers on the block were supportive, but it only takes one complaint. An artist actually threatened to sue me over an exhibition titled, 'FUCK EM IF THEY CAN'T TAKE A JOKE!'

I have received a number of "cease and desist" letters over the years from artists or their lawyers or galleries. This has actually become a real problem. I haven't ever been sued (I generally agree to cease and desist), but I have been asked to destroy (or, more commonly, forbidden to reproduce/exhibit/sell) some works. I have also lost exhibition and publication opportunities due to fears of legal action. I believe I should be able to make a painting of another artist's painting the same way I might make a painting of some flowers. But, I can't afford a legal fight against a millionaire…

> BS: What potency do you think bootlegging still has today, in the context of the internet and social media, where things are constantly reused, remixed, and reposted?

ED: I love how the internet and social media recontextualize images and create new "realities." I frequently come across images of my Bootleg paintings posted online as examples of the original artists' work. Once they are reproduced as jpegs, it's much harder to tell the difference between my little Bootleg paintings and the "real" ones.

I made a Bootleg "Julian Opie" painting, which is a self-portrait I drew in the style of Julian Opie. Some years later, I discovered a Russian website (selling reproductions of paintings printed on canvas) that was offering knockoffs of my painting as "Eric Doeringer by Julian Opie." Of course I had to buy one!

In fact, the rise of the internet and digital technology has turned pretty much everyone into a bootlegger. Who hasn't streamed a bit of unlicensed video from YouTube or uploaded a copyrighted image to Instagram? Once an image or other file is posted online, the author may legally retain copyright, but for all intents and purposes the work enters the public domain.

Title page (p. 356): Excerpt from Christopher Wool's *Untitled (P80) Helter Helter* (1988)

Online®

CERAMICS

Online Ceramics, Elijah Funk (EF) & Alix Ross (AR)

Online Ceramics have built a bootleg T-shirt empire upon a love and fascination with the Grateful Dead. Branching out from Deadhead designs, the brand has since collaborated with A24 and the Fela Kuti estate to make merch that feels at once contemporary and archival. In their complex designs, the duo scatter in obscure symbols and messages that speak to only the most niche of fan communities. Their efforts are not meant as gate-keeping, but rather as a means to celebrate fandom, community, and obsession. Interview by Ben Schwartz (BS).

> BS: Your practice feels very much related to bootleg culture—DIY T-shirts, proximity to music, a certain lo-fi aesthetic—yet your designs for the most part are entirely original. Is an Online Ceramics shirt a bootleg?

EF: In some ways I don't consider what we do as bootlegging. I think initially some of it was rooted in borrowing graphics from the Grateful Dead and similar concepts. Before Online Ceramics, I was making more straightforward bootlegs. I feel like we've just expanded upon bootlegging into something more similar to fan art. To me, a more traditional bootleg is more like taking an obscure record cover and printing it on a shirt, or like the vendors outside the Los Angeles Forum who are selling shirts on the street, which is something more functional than creative. Really it just feels like an effect of capitalism.

AR: Not to say that bootlegging can't be creative, but for sure, I agree with where Elijah is on that. When I think of bootlegging, I think of some of Elijah's work outside of Online Ceramics. Using extremely rare images or symbols that exist on T-shirts, yet as a way of tapping into a niche community. And that niche element is really important—that moment when one person sees it and immediately identifies with it is powerful.

EF: Right, like on this last T-shirt drop we did, I made a shirt that said Channel 23, which is the Grateful Dead's Sirius XM radio station. It isn't a bootleg, but it is referring to something in the canon. It's like the brand Boot Boyz Biz, even though their brand is explicitly about bootlegging, I see it as something a bit more dynamic because of the design decisions they are making.

> BS: So for you, a bootleg involves a certain amount of copying and pasting. It's more about shifting context while keeping the content or design the same?

pp. 373–374: Online Ceramics shirt modeled by Clue
Photo: Justin Cole Smith

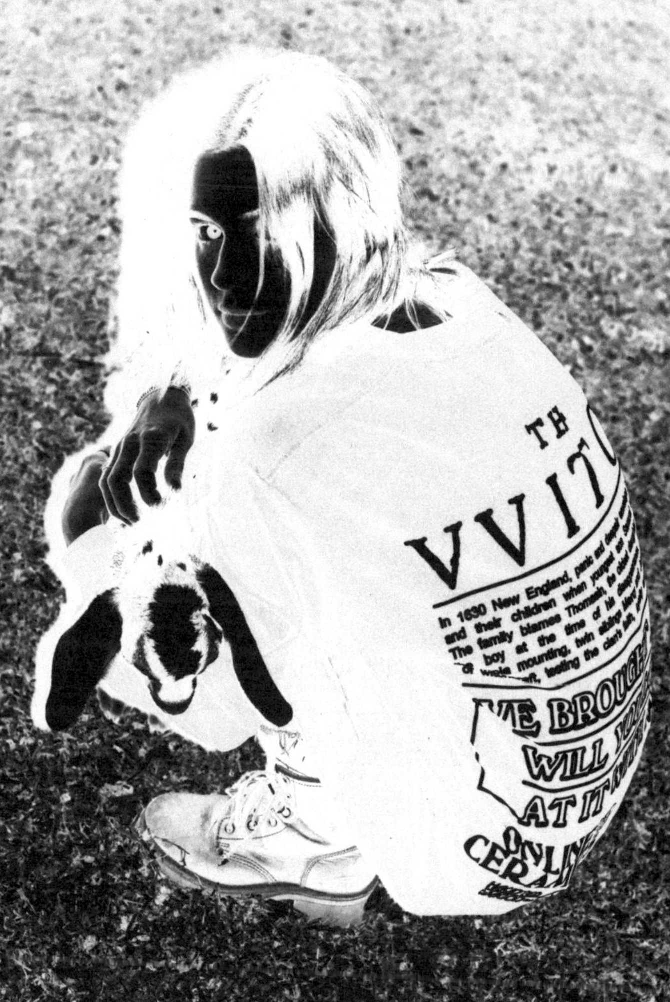
In 1630 New England, panic and
and their children when
The family blames Thomasin, the
boy at the time of his
mounting, twin siblings
tasting the clan's
WILL
AT IT

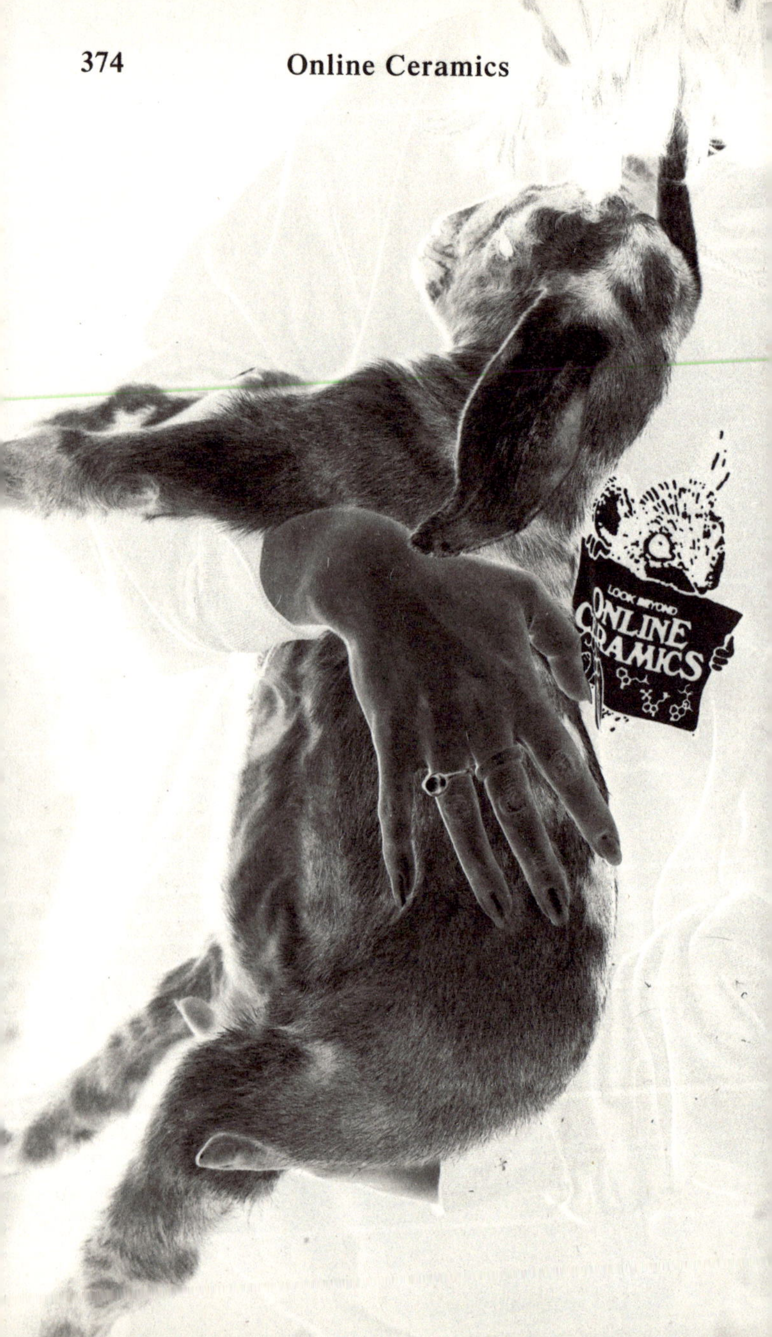
LOOK BEYOND
ONLINE

AR: Visually, I think the emphasis is more on collaging or repurposing. There is also the aspect of the vendors outside venues who don't care about communicating anything visually, and it revolves more around making money.

EF: On that note, this really funny thing happened last year at the L.A. Dead shows, where those guys bootlegged our designs and mixed it with the official artwork from the tour, because they just assumed that it *was* the official work. It was such a cool moment to me where everything had come full circle.

> BS: I'm also interested, and perhaps skeptical, when these lines become blurred between official and bootleg. I'm thinking here of these sanctioned bootlegs by companies like Off-White, Vetements, or Balenciaga.

AR: In my mind, for it to be a proper bootleg, it has to be unsanctioned.

EF: I think part of the reason we took off so early is because we were skirting so many copyright rules. It allowed us to appeal to people outside of the Grateful Dead world because it wasn't just a Grateful Dead T-shirt. Even within the Dead world, it was referencing things that were deep parts of the culture in general. The shirts became markers of knowledge that gravitated towards something like a method of research.

> BS: The Dead community feels like a central tenant to Online Ceramics. Could you talk more about this relationship between niche communities and bootlegging?

AR: For me it becomes a way to contribute something back to the community, which seems to be the goal of everyone on Shakedown Street [makeshift markets outside of Grateful Dead concerts] in some way. Obviously, there's money involved with all of this but we are trying to genuinely give something back.

EF: And really, we initially started all of this as a bartering token to be accepted into the Grateful Dead community. When guys like us roll up to a dead show—like, I don't have long hair, we're young, everything felt really foreign. We were unsure of how we would be able to communicate in this world, and these shirts became our means of communication. We have seen it sort of explode, such as big brands now making Dead shirts, all of which we don't really care for. We began to question if we should stop, but in talking to the community, they really pushed us to keep going. I see it as providing a service to people, to bring them happiness and things that they enjoy. So it's a way of marketing or transmitting joy.

> BS: How important is authorship to you? I ask this knowing that your style has been ripped off by both fans and brands. Does it bother you, or do you see it as a part of this current environment where the boundaries of ownership have become obscured?

EF: When I see younger kids doing it, it really means a lot to me because it means that they're informed, in the same way that we were, by art. I see them as learning in the same way that we did. What I don't like is when I see people finding a way to capitalize on people's sincere feelings, and I think that's where I draw the line. There have been certain people that I've seen ripping us off and I have approached them. I just find it to be a weird way to operate in the world. But with that being said, we wouldn't exist without making Grateful Dead shirts to begin with. So in what sense are we benefiting from people being generous to us?

> BS: Right, but I've always seen bootlegging as a bottom up tactic, one where someone with less power is taking from someone with more.

EF: Anytime there's a new wave of music or something, then someone from the top comes down and squelches the thing, you know, they kill the party as they try to insert themselves into youth culture. But if we can inspire people to make artwork, then that's great. There's certainly a significant amount of younger kids making T-shirts in an alternative style that was not really prevalent when we started. I think that's really cool.

AR: Now that we have some distance from the project—it's been five years since we started—I do see it as reaffirming when people are imitating us. I really do think we turned on a light in a room that people really didn't know was there. It feels like something to continue to build on.

> BS: In what ways do you think of the T-shirt as a medium? Some of your T-shirts, with repeating motifs, can at times feel like a sequel or a second volume. Can a T-shirt be a book, a performance, a film?

EF: T-shirts were the only way people would pay attention to what we were doing. I think that is something that excites people, the fact that we have done sequels of shirts and we have expanded upon our own ideas in our world.

AR: I see wearing a T-shirt as essentially performative; a graphic T-shirt is, no matter what, making a statement. It's a political act. We're interested in creating shirts with messages that people would want to transmit.

> BS: That feels important. There really feels like a genuine connection between the two of you and the Online Ceramics ethos. I say this at a time where new age spirituality has become a bit of a trend and in many cases can feel shallow or reduced to a certain aesthetic. As two people who believe in the messaging of your shirts, does it bother you if people wear them without connecting to what they are saying?

AR: I feel like when people buy a shirt from us, they are genuinely drawn to the message.

EF: I think in some ways we use our platform to be educators. We just did the Fela Kuti shirts, in the same way we wanted to make Dead shirts. We want to turn people on to things that we feel are really important. And now that we have that community, it's so exciting to be able to spread these things that

p. 379: Online Ceramics shirt modeled by Coco
Photo: Justin Cole Smith

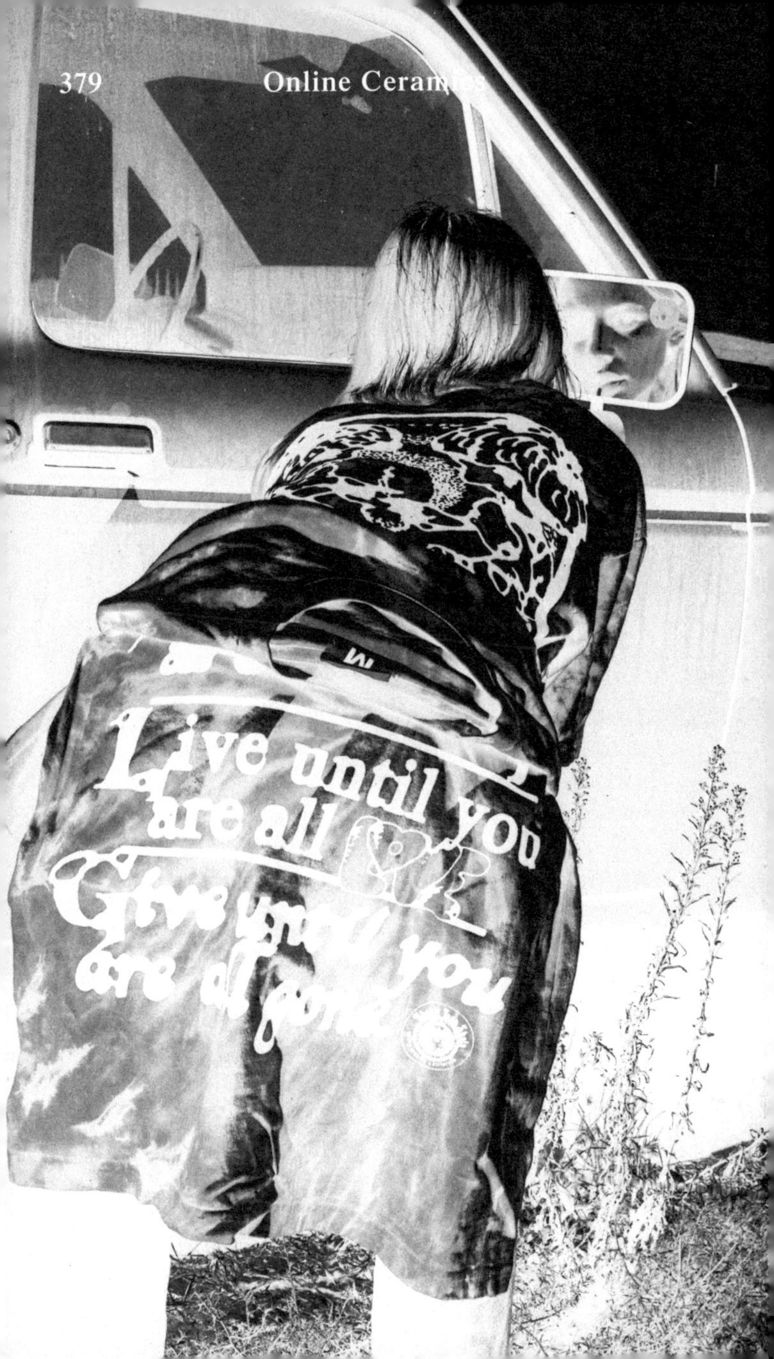
Live until you
are all
Give
you

we find interesting or comforting or affirmative. So I think it's awesome that even if someone doesn't understand the message, it's innately going to seep into their existence. If you live with something long enough, it becomes part of you.

BS: What role does this element of love or fandom play in Online Ceramics and bootlegging on a more general level?

EF: I think the reason Grateful Dead ephemera is so good, and the reason punk visual culture is so good, and the reason psychedelic posters were so good is that they were born from love and passion. Maybe that's why bootlegs, or the "unofficial" merch, is more exciting, because for the people that make it, their goal is to become a part of the community. That amount of passion driven into art is really hard to come by any other way. When you're inspired by something and you love it so much, you've got to channel that into the work you are making.

AR: I think it has something to do with mythology. Before getting into the music of the Grateful Dead, I was so interested in the idea of this band touring around and spreading LSD all over the world. These crazy stories of their manager making the LSD, and the acid tests, I found so compelling, and that really drew me in. I think bootlegs operate in a similar way, generating and spreading these larger-than-life stories...

EF: I grew up in a house where my stepdad had a room that was dedicated to the Grateful Dead. It had cookie jars and bear statues and throw blankets and every bootleg. It was his stash, and I didn't enjoy it at the time, but looking back it deeply resonated with me. I remember looking through those books when I was seven or eight, and even though I was listening to Black Flag, the Dead artwork lured me in. The roses and the skeletons, I just found it all to be really cryptic and fascinating and it made me want to decipher it.

AR: The artwork around the Dead is unparalleled: from *Steal Your Face* to the Grateful Dead bears, and each has its own really amazing history. From the beginning, I always found the visual language around the band to be just as powerful as the music itself.

> BS: So much of the current bootleg trend is steeped in irony. How does humor or irony play into your work?

AR: There's a little bit of irony, but for the most part, we try to be pretty sincere. Humor is a huge part of what we do. But, as you mentioned earlier, we do really care about what we're saying and we think about it deeply. Since the beginning, we are pulling from influences that are rooted in some kind of positive idea. And sometimes we do get dark, like the satanic shirts, and that's where irony comes in for us.

EF: Amidst all of this, we are still trying to entertain ourselves and each other. We could capitalize on this movement and just make shirts that would sell. But the reason it reads so well is, Alix and I have been friends for twelve years now and people that work with us have been our friends for twelve years, and we all have a very similar sense of humor. We know that what clicks with us generally will work beyond our scope—and if it doesn't, at least we'll find it funny.

BS: I do feel there is a certain bootleg aesthetic that Online Ceramics tapped into early on. It feels like an important aspect of this is a desire to communicate a sense of history. That this object or graphic has undergone certain processes which communicate the effect of time. Why do you think our culture feels drawn to visuals that feel so removed from the present moment?

EF: We say the word "classic" a lot, and I think one of my main functions as a designer is to make work that's never dated. As in, it can't really be placed in a specific moment in history. I've gathered a lot of that concept from the Grateful Dead, because their lyrics never really point to a specific moment in history. I read this interview about one of their songs that said "styrofoam" in it and someone got really mad because that's such a marker of time. And I think we, for the most part, try and create in a similar way. Today everyone is making shirts with graphics all over them, sleeve graphics are very 2020, and once we realized that, we stopped doing them.

BS: Given the proliferation of bootleg T-shirts in almost every area of culture, do you see the act as a trend with an expiration date, or a creative gesture that will evolve and prevail?

EF: I think it depends on what sphere you're looking at. Bootlegging is so vast. So you have something like a Redbubble or Zazzle bootleg, which feels truly embedded in capitalism. But then you have people like Total Luxury Spa, and what they are doing has a true integrity and beauty to it. I got back to why I started making bootleg Scandinavian hardcore shirts as a way to spread the message of this thing I was really excited about. So I think the relevancy and power of bootlegging just kind of depends on each particular person's approach.

AR: I also think the ease of reproduction is really empowering. Any kid can save up like a hundred bucks and get all the stuff they need to do screen printing. This current generation is so creative, and bootlegging just feels like a powerful outlet for that creativity.

EF: Bootlegging feels like a natural expression of fandom, even before you might recognize what you're doing as bootlegging.

AR: I think bootlegging will always be alive and well.

Title page (p. 370): America Online logo flip taken from an Online Ceramics T-Shirt

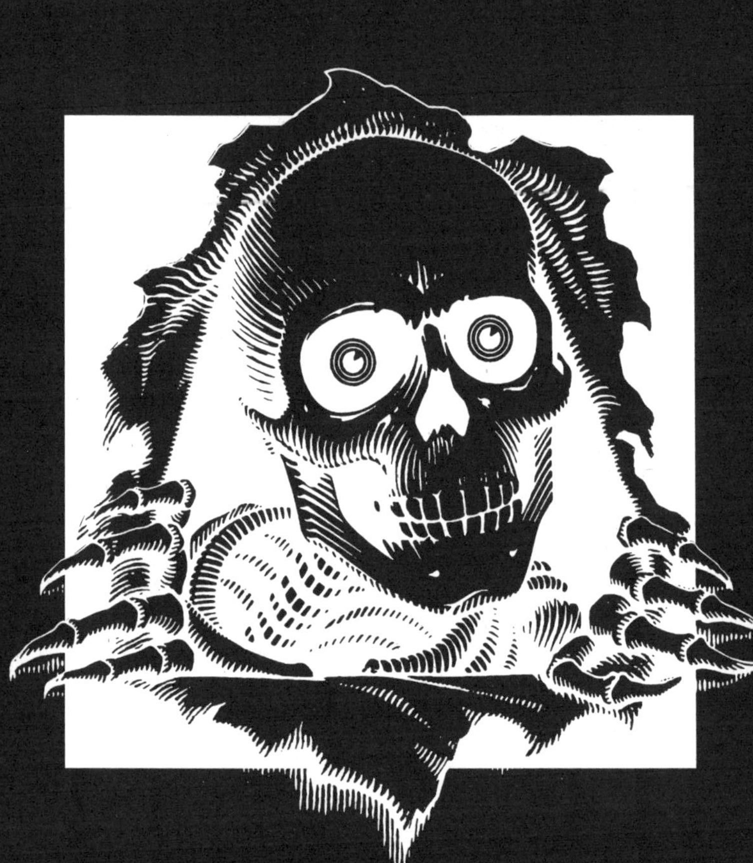

Mark Owens (MO)

Mark Owens is a Philadelphia-based graphic designer, writer, and educator. As a part of his design practice, Owens often writes about the intersection of design, music, and material culture in publications like *PIN-UP*, *IDEA*, *GRAPHIC*, and *Dot Dot Dot*. While his writing touches on subjects from Brutalism to Times New Roman, his specific relationship to punk and hardcore subcultures has given him a unique perspective on the recent bootleg phenomenon. In his teaching, Owens conducts a workshop on hauntology, the concept of elements from a non-existent past reappearing in the present like a ghost. While there is often an archival element to bootlegging, under the guise of hauntology, they have a far greater potential to fill an invented gap between history and fantasy. Interview by Ben Schwartz (BS).

> BS: As someone with such a deep interest in obscure music subcultures, I'd love to hear what bootlegs mean to you. In these communities, what value do bootlegs hold?

MO: For me, the most generative way to distinguish bootlegging from practices like knockoffs or pirating is to emphasize the connection to music, fandom, and modes of circulation. In this respect, bootlegs as we know them are an invention of the late 1960s and describe "unauthorized" recordings such as audience tapes, demos, and studio outtakes that are circulated on vinyl by fans without the permission of the artist or major label. The presumption is that the true fan already has all of the "legitimate" releases by a given artist, and the bootleg is filling a gap that the music industry is either unwilling or unable to fill. The bootleg thus has both an archival value and also provides insight into the artist's creative process that an "official" release that is sanitized and over-dubbed might not. By pressing vinyl records of these recordings and inserting them into the marketplace, bootleggers were also occupying systems of production and distribution. This combination of archival value, fandom, and (mis)use of systems of circulation also opens up an enormous space for creativity in the form of label names, cover artwork, material choices (like colored vinyl), and the sourcing, sequencing, and editing of bootleg material—this is where things like mash-ups find a close proximity to bootlegs.

It is this creative dimension that the current crop of bootleg projects inherit from the earlier bootleg era and transport into the internet-savvy present—whether in music or some other medium. As designers, we are very often working as our own editors, archivists, and researchers, so I think for my own practice this creative potential within the bootleg impulse is one that can help inform design decisions and suggest new possibilities—even if they might be "irresponsible" or "vulgar" ones.

BS: Are there any projects of yours that come to mind where bootlegging played a significant role?

MO: A few years ago my partner, Alex Klein, and I were invited to contribute to a group exhibition at LAXART in Los Angeles loosely organized around the idea of the bootleg. We had always wanted to make a piece of furniture and were fans of the *Ulm Stool*, which was originally created by Max Bill in 1954 for the Ulm School and is still sold by Vitra as an icon of modernist design— a simple form that can double as a portable stool or a bookshelf. At the time, we had also managed to track down some deadstock Memphis Bacterio pattern laminate from a vendor in Studio City, and we wondered what it would be like to cover the outside of Max Bill's Ulm Stool with this pattern designed by Ettore Sottsass, the quintessential postmodern designer, who we were also huge fans of. So, we made one, imagining this bootleg stool as a kind of "lost" collaboration between the two designers. Ironically, the laminate gave the stool, which is normally raw wood, both an added decorative element and an improved functionality.

In terms of client work, a similar idea informed a pair of catalogs I created in collaboration with the artist and curator Justin Beal along with designer Nilas Andersen. These catalogs document two group shows, "Soft Matter" and "Touchpiece," which included design objects and artworks that, very generally, explore connections between materials and the body. Many of the works feature flexible "skins" of various kinds, and we wanted to find a way to get that idea into the book. Justin had suggested revisiting a catalog designed by Andrea Branzi's studio in 1986, *Domestic Animals*. The book is long out of print and somewhat marginal to Branzi's output as an industrial designer, but we tracked it down and attempted to "pour" our contents into its format. Of course, in the process all kinds of unexpected things happened, and we ended up making design decisions that we never would have on our own. The paperback is also a format that is scaled to the size of the human hand and is part of a whole economy of circulation, so we ended up with two books that function as additions to an imagined series and enter into dialogue with their predecessors. The artist Martin Kippenberger did something similar with his *Peter* catalogs (1987), whose format was based on a Sonnabend Piero Manzoni catalog (1973), and his example was also very much on our minds.

> BS: In your writing and teaching practice you've examined the idea of hauntology, which feels related to bootlegging in their mutual desire to exhume the past. Do you consider bootlegging a hauntological act?

MO: Jacques Derrida coined the term hauntology in a very specific context, and his basic insight is that media "spectralizes." When you mediate something, when you put an image of yourself on television or in a broadcast, you're spectralizing—there's a "there" and also a "not there." For me, that's the main thrust of the Derrida quote and is something I was thinking a lot about with my Paul McCartney text ('R.I.P.: Notes on the Paul McCartney Shadow Canon') in *Dot Dot Dot*. There is Hauntology as a style catego-

p. 389: Mark Owens, Alex Klein, Bootleg Ulm stool (2011)

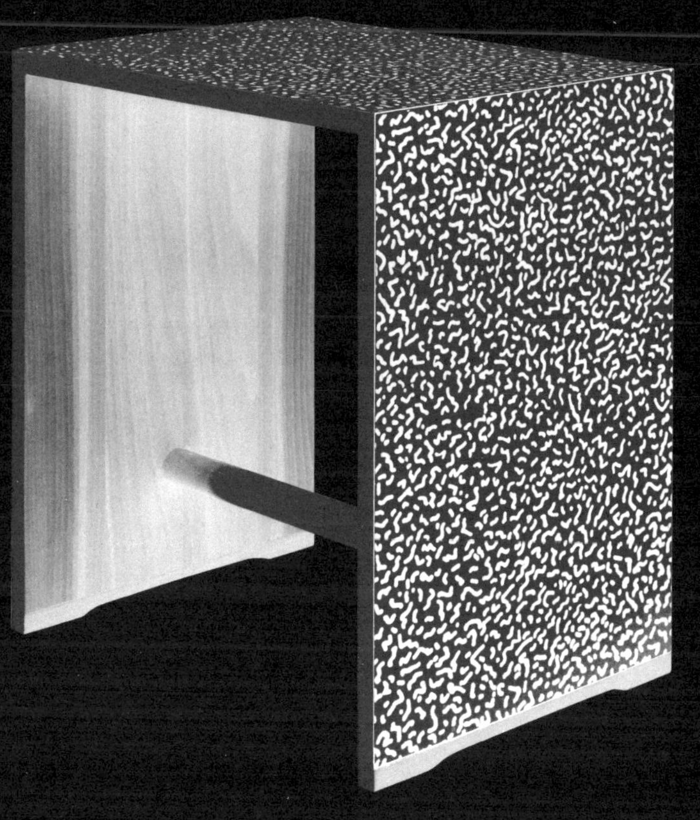

ry, which is related to this idea of plunderphonics and involves taking the textures of the past and creating a past that never really existed. There's a fiction-making element, it's conjuring a shared set of ideas about a time period and creating a new version of that period in the present. There's something creative about it which is related to bootlegging.

> BS: I wonder how this creative element might relate to the bootleg's archival potential? Is there some value in presenting a history that might deviate from the more commonly accepted narrative?

MO: When I think about a project like Boot Boyz Biz, it's less hauntological and more of an archival project. It's taking things that really did exist and mashing together the graphic forms. Perhaps they begin to relate to hauntology in the way they can occupy a sort of imaginative space that at times can be more interesting than a simple recount of historical details.

I think the archival dimension and a sense of desire or fandom is an important part of bootlegging. Studio outtakes, audience tapes, and demos are all the products of a kind of audio archaeology. They take research and digging, and often bootleggers will put these elements together to tell a story, to fill in a gap in the "official" record, or to create an imagined artifact. I think this aspect distinguishes bootlegs from straightforward ripoffs, clones, or copies.

Growing up listening to punk bands at a time when many of the original groups had long since broken up, I encountered the records themselves as historical artifacts and studied the minutiae of type, layout, photography, lyrics, and liner notes with the kind of attention that designers are very familiar with. Bootlegs open up and mine this imaginative space as well.

I agree with the fact that a bootleg might allow us to understand something better than an original. People who can say "I was there" are generally not the best people to understand what's actually going on with some perspective. When you are witnessing something as it's happening, you can't have a clear and informed vantage point until time has passed. A good example of this is minimal wave, which wasn't a genre in 1980. No one was making "minimal wave music." There were people in the States and in Belgium and scattered over Europe that were all making this particular style of music and tape trading, but they were just doing it and not thinking about what it was. The idea of minimal wave is a later formulation of trying to make sense of what was happening at that particular time. There's the continuum of history that's flowing by and things are happening and someone in the present takes that moment, names it, and finds new extensions.

> BS: To me, at least in design, it feels like the bootleg trend has reached a sort of culmination. At one point during this research I was fairly convinced that it would be impossible for bootlegging to move forward in any sort of meaningful way. Is bootlegging dead?

MO: What's happening with bootlegging feels very similar to the vaporwave phenomenon in the sense that it's a genre of music that people have been saying

p. 392: Andrea Branzi, *Animaux Domestiques* (1988)
p. 393: Justin Beal, *Soft Matter* (2014)

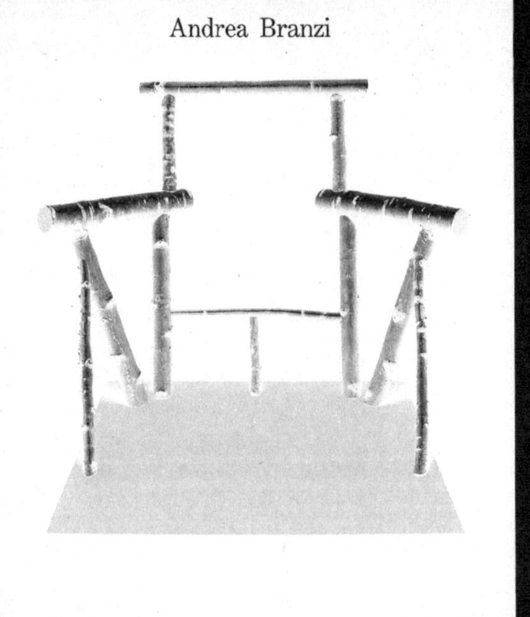
ANIMAUX DOMESTIQUES
Andrea Branzi
PHILIPPE SERS EDITEUR / VILO

SOFT MATTER

Curated by Justin Beal

WALLSPACE

is exhausted since it began in 2012. Every year people claim it is played out and every year someone finds something new and interesting in the genre. It's an interesting phenomenon where it's constantly renewing itself in ways that still feel fresh. People are able to curate a suite of things that they're so deep in and constantly pull out something new. I think that's true of any historical investigation, people right now are looking at the 1920s or 1930s or Ben Franklin's archive and still finding something new and a new way to relate it to the present. I'm reminded of a term from Walter Benjamin, "Jetztzeit" which involves pulling something from the past into the present as a way of understanding its radical potential, and to me that speaks to the power of bootlegs.

I recently saw an Instagram account that only makes Steely Dan bootlegs. I would listen to Steely Dan in college, and it's always been sort of uncool, but then these bootlegs frame them in a super creative and funny way that is exciting to me. So I do agree there's a certain bootleg phenomenon happening now, but what makes it exciting is the content and the cleverness. It's this idea we all inherited from postmodernism, that the pushing together of various reference points makes something entirely different. But what makes it different from postmodernism, which is sort of cynical and ironic and heartless, is this idea of fandom. Bootlegs come from economic opportunism on the one hand, and on the other just this love of a fan, which I think is special.

I absolutely believe in a future for bootlegs. At their best, bootlegs and musical forms like plunderphonics and mash-ups create entirely new forms out of pre-existing material. For me, these internet subgenres tap into larger questions of collective memory, affect, and the material remainder that exceeds the parameters of a given historical moment or even a given material artifact.

Title page (p. 384): Powell Peralta logo taken from Mark Owens' Hauntology class syllabus

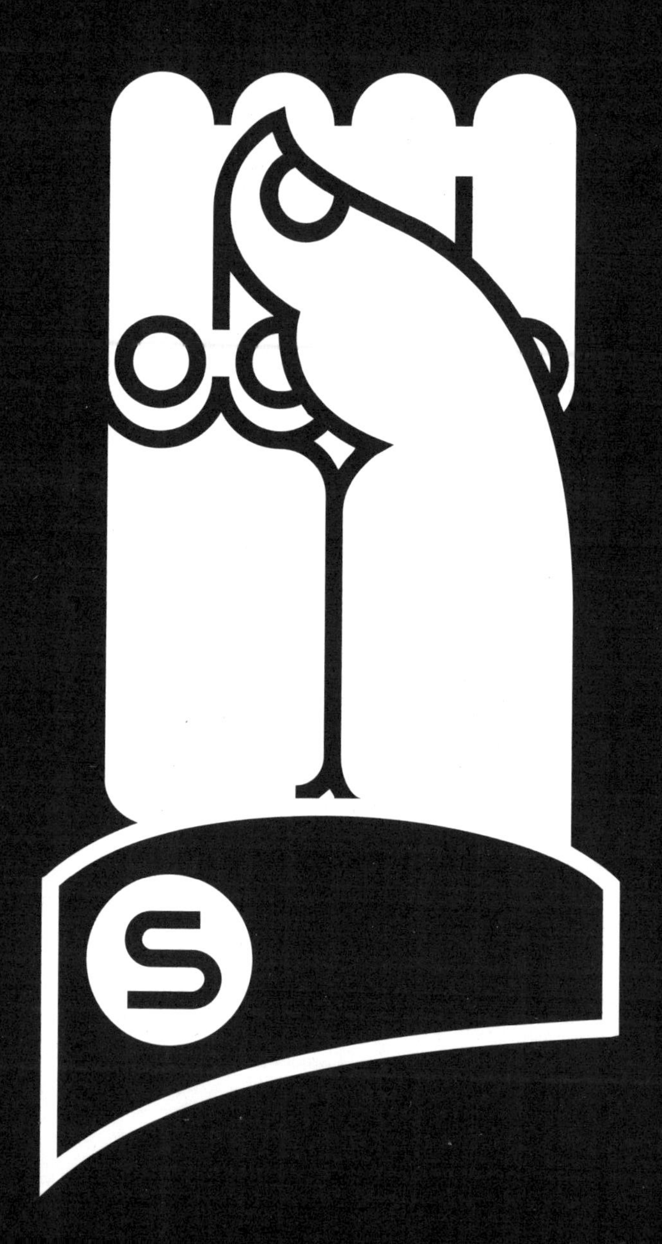
S

Nat Pyper (NP)

Nat Pyper is an artist and designer that seamlessly moves between graphic work, textiles, writing, and performance, using each media as a form of investigation into the alphabet. In their project, *A Queer Year of Love Letters*, Pyper unearths typefaces from seminal moments in queer history and recreates them as a usable font disseminated for free. Their body of work reframes fonts as a means to archive and disseminate essential voices from queer history. The collection of typefaces demonstrates how a bootleg ideology might infiltrate practices such as type design, smuggling histories, and ideologies into new and unexpected territories. Interview by Ben Schwartz (BS).

> BS: So often, the motivation behind a bootleg is love. It's this idea of love that makes me think of your *Queer Year of Love Letters* project. If there is a font revival project that could be considered a bootleg, it's this one. How did love or homage affect the way you dealt with or treated this material?

NP: There are certain literal aspects where the title is a play on words: fonts as "love letters," but also the actual alphabets as "love" "letters." Digging deeper, I see the project as a way to establish a lineage or an inheritance outside of the patriarchal relations of passing down. I was interested in ways to establish a bond with people outside of space and time. The reason I wanted to turn these letters into a font and not something static like a poster or an essay is to highlight the work that these queers were doing, and at the same time put that work to new use. It's a way of establishing that this work is not yet done, it continues, and these fonts are maybe a poetic way of repurposing these forms. It's important that it gets used freely, and in that way the ideas behind them continue to evolve and change.

> BS: For me, these fonts exemplify this idea of a bootleg as a form of alternate archiving. It's a form of preservation, but one that is much more active and participatory, and far less precious than a traditional archive. It allows for a certain amount of power, but also a risk in losing control of the material or ideas.

NP: When I started the project, it was a way to pair my interests in type design with this particular history that I was beginning to create my own relationship to. I put these fonts out there because I wanted people to use them and I didn't necessarily consider the full spectrum of how that might happen or what it might mean. I realized part of letting go is related to the radical nature of this history. So many of the people that I'm highlighting with these fonts were anti-fascist, they were against a certain tyranny of culture and were interested in hijacking that culture through their own work. I totally understand that people are going to put these fonts to all kinds of uses, but I'm more interested in the ideas that propagate, regardless of where or how the font gets used. In fact, the font-object (font file) itself literally always retains this historical information. The OTF contains details about this radical history associated with the typeface, so as it moves it gets deposited in various places often unbeknownst to the user. I really like the idea that even if the history isn't reproduced in the use of the font, it forever remains true to its original intent.

> BS: I love that. It's a way of smuggling and disseminating history which feels very much aligned with the origins of bootlegging. You mentioned how these fonts came out of a particular research, and I'm curious about this idea of bootlegging as a form of research. How might a bootleg allow us to achieve a certain proximity or intimacy with a subject? How has your relationship or understanding of this history changed through the process of recreating these letters?

NP: In the case of the G.B. Jones font, I was able to gain a certain amount of proximity in that I was actually able to speak with her. She's a filmmaker in Toronto, and I shared with her the idea of the font and my interest in it being a more recent history. With this typeface, the particular history it represents deals with people who are still alive, and it's something I'm constantly thinking about, how to achieve certain proximity to history, especially to a past that is not yet that far gone. One that is in many ways still developing. And I should say that I don't see these fonts as a proxy for the voice of these people; I'm not trying to speak on their behalf. I'm more interested in working with these forms and putting them to new use.

I also want to be sensitive to the fact that this history can't be reproduced. Especially the queer punk work, is really resistant to definition, legibility, and categorization. That's why queer punks adopted queer as a label, because it resisted any easy definition. They rejected terms like gay and lesbian, and embraced terms like "fags" and "dykes" and "queers." They were interested in reclaiming these labels, and not as apt descriptors, but rather more like cover for the activities that they wanted to participate in. So when working with these histories, that's the trick that I'm trying to understand—how do you relate or point to a history that resists historicism?

> BS: I've come to understand bootlegging as a valuable tool to preserve and pass on overlooked and underrepresented histories. Do you think bootlegging could be used as a tool for activism and resistance in these communities?

NP: I think you could talk about what queer punk scenesters were doing as a form of bootlegging, but I think importantly, even if you *do* describe what they're doing as bootlegging, the end result I wouldn't describe as such. The breakdown happens because the work is recontextualized, recombined, and changed in such a significant way that it protects them from copyright infringement. The work is altered enough

p. 401: Nat Pyper, G.B. Jones (2018)

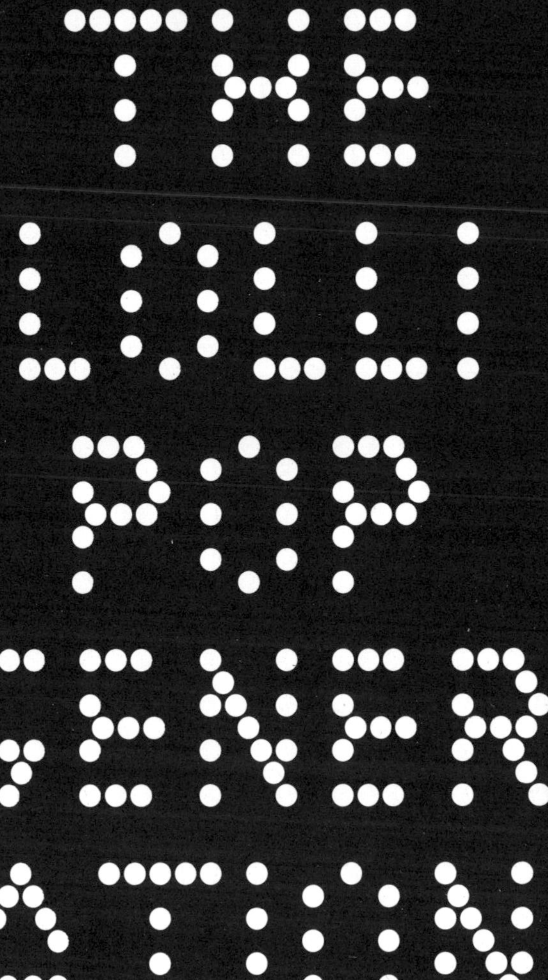
THE
LOLLI
POP
GENER
ATION

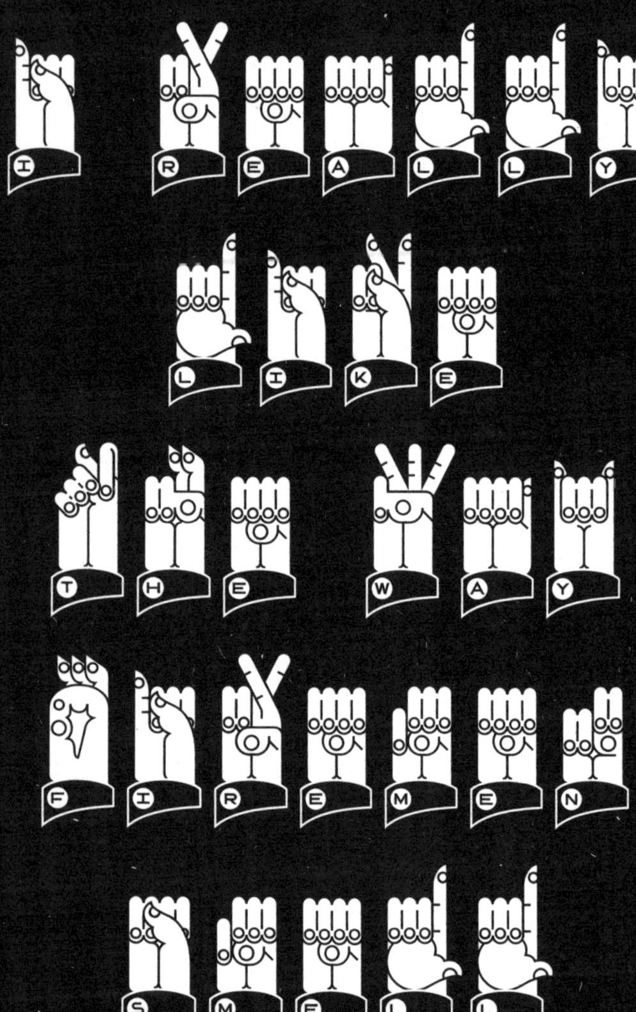
I R E A L L Y
L I K E
T H E W A Y
F I R E M E N
S M E L L

that it's not trying to be the original work, it's using the original to do something new. These punks were adamantly into copyleft regulation so I don't think they would've seen it as a bootleg, they were more interested in the free exchange of ideas.

So if you define bootleg as I originally thought—something reproduced against the law—then I think a lot of these queer anarchists wanted the law abolished in the first place. So a bootleg couldn't exist because the ideas are just so rapidly circulating among themselves. I'm interested in a world where a bootleg can't exist or it goes by another name because there is no law to protect the original thing in the first place.

> BS: But you mentioned earlier how these punks reappropriated the language of oppression as a way of reclaiming it and using it against the original purpose—a form of détournement like the logo flips of the early aughts. If you think of a bootleg in this way, then perhaps it does seem like it could possibly become a resistance tactic?

NP: Yeah there was something kind of meta happening with queer punk zines in the mid- to late-1980s and early 1990s, in that punk zines had already existed for the better part of a decade. Of course, different zines had existed before then too, and specifically, the format of cut and paste as a methodology had existed for a long time. I think where queer zines diverge in an interesting way is that there's this meta level of, they were cutting and pasting from this punk

p. 402: Nat Pyper, Martin Wong (2018)

culture that existed. So all of these values of capitalism and of the state were in fact reproducing themselves without them realizing it. And so, you know, these queer punks were going one step further.

They are using cut and paste as a method for cultural critique, but are also critiquing their punk predecessors, the ones who had passed down this method. And then of course in general with punk there's a lot of interesting staking out and a lot of infighting. And so with the queer zines, there's such a complex ecosystem happening where they're also critiquing each other and using each other's words against them.

I agree with the simple idea that they were repurposing the culture that was around them in order to critique it and gain power and have a voice. A lot of these people were isolated; some of my favorite scenes are from Milwaukee, not just because I lived there, but also because it's such a good example of this isolated queer who has no one around them. There's this really great story in one Milwaukee zine, with this punk who goes to a punk bar and sees this other punk that has a bandana in his pocket. And he thinks, "Oh my God, it's another fag punk, I didn't know these people existed here." He starts talking with them and by the end he realizes that it's just a straight punk that reappropriated gay culture for a look. He really realizes how alone he is, and he's saying all this in a diatribe in his zine that's then going out into the world, and he's connecting with other queer zinesters, going to zine conventions in Toronto, Chicago, New York, et cetera. Ultimately, it's a method for critique, but also to bridge the divides that had existed before then.

p. 405: Nat Pyper, Robert Ford (2018)

SHE

KNOWS

WHO

SHE IS

BS: I am reminded here of your piece on stunt doubling, where you are tasking punks to go further. I feel the same way about bootlegging...

NP: Yeah, the reason I used that analogy was because I was trying to find something that could speak to their embodied experience and this action that is commonly understood as risk-taking. I think that those are important elements of what it means to engage in that kind of activity. There needs to be real risk involved because the payoff is that much more incredible. In the case of queer punks, it's liberation, the possibility of pushing against the culture until it explodes into something more.

BS: I know community is a central tenet of your practice. I see it to be an important element of bootlegging as well. Looking at *Queer Year of Love Letters*, can you talk about what effect these fonts have on creating or preserving communities?

NP: I think that is the root of all of my work—an interest in publishing and in literacy, and how with these acts we can transgress the divides between us. This idea of community becomes really interesting when it's people that are actively interested in this transgression, while also recognizing and valuing these separations. With the fonts, for example, I'm resharing these into the world because I want to find community around these ideas and these histories in the same way that queer punks were publishing and bridging the divides of space and time that were between them. I'm really interested in this idea of establishing community across space and time—people who no longer exist, people who are yet to exist, and with the fonts the potential of supporting writing and ideas that don't yet exist.

Title page (p. 396): "S" from Nat Pyper's Martin Wong font (2018) from *Queer Year of Love Letters*

Hassan Rahim (HR)

Hassan Rahim is a graphic designer from Los Angeles, currently based in New York. His work with clients ranging from Nike to Nine Inch Nails feels both thrilling and rigorous, full of texture and detail that place them from either an underground past or far off acid-laced future. For Rahim, texture tells so much of the story, giving a design its history, whether real or fabricated. For example, in 2018 Rahim collaborated with the Crenshaw streetwear brand Total Luxury Spa for a Sun Ra bootleg from an imagined concert at the LA Coliseum. The shirt exploded online, the idea of the fictional concert connecting followers of the band and streetwear hypebeasts alike. It's a powerful example of how a bootleg might surpass its role as a simple garment and become a bridge between histories, cultures, and communities. Interview by Ben Schwartz (BS).

BS: To begin, I want to pull a quote from a previous interview of yours where you mention two signatures of your work are "inversion" and "subversion." I think you could make the argument that these ideas are very much at the core of bootlegging.

Could you speak about your relationship to bootlegging and the influence it has had on your practice?

HR: I think about bootlegging and sampling in relation to each other, similar but different. A bootleg is something that's attempting to emulate or riff off of an original idea, and then market itself as a version of that idea to a customer who may or may not be able to tell the difference. An early example of that from my youth was going to a sports game and seeing people sell T-shirts in the parking lot for cheaper than the official merch store. I would ask my dad about them and he told me they were bootlegs and we shouldn't buy them, but to me they looked so much more interesting.

Sampling, to me, involves a certain degree of authorship. In the process of copying you create something new from preexisting material. I think about the first hip-hop record which was just looping a funk song, but at a certain point, that loop becomes its own thing. This gray area between the thing that's being sampled and this new creation is the place that I like to explore in my work.

BS: That's interesting because in a lot of ways I see your work as a designer similar to a music producer or maybe a DJ. The way you pull together pre-existing elements, manipulate them, combine them, until you create something that feels fully your own.

HR: It's funny, so much of how I got into design is a result of bootlegging—or pirating software. I downloaded music production software and I downloaded Photoshop, and I happened to be better at design. My approach is a result of the way I needed to teach myself how to design. Growing up I was living in a group home, my parents couldn't provide for me, I just needed to stay out of trouble. I think from that situation there is a certain amount of resourcefulness and resilience that develops. Going back to the idea of the DJ looping the record, it was a degree of necessity, using what you had at your disposal. And that's how I got started—always sampling, making use of what was around.

BS: I've been thinking a lot about bootlegging as a form of learning. In Shanzhai culture, if you create a believable copy you become as respected as the original author.

It reminds of something Kanye said (sorry to mention his name) when he was learning to produce. He just tried to recreate this Dr. Dre song sound for sound, an exact copy. And he really learned the nuances of production from doing this. For me, I didn't go to school, I learned from watching online tutorials where you would be given a project file that you had to recreate. They are teaching you how to use the tools, but then you have to develop the way you think, your approach with the tools. Someone can teach you how to use a hammer, then you can decide to hit a nail or bash in a window. I think the issue with that approach comes when people don't develop their own way of thinking… they can't break out of copying.

BS: I want to ask you about your Sun Ra bootleg. Throughout this research, I've been really interested in the idea that a bootleg can allow us to get closer to a subject than the source. Perhaps it has something to do with perspective, or seeing something through the eyes of someone who loved that thing. Or maybe it's about the process of making. Did making your Sun Ra T-shirt bring you closer to that moment in time and to the work of Sun Ra?

HR: Totally, a lot opened up for us with that shirt. Initially, I didn't think anyone would see it, I thought it was gonna be just for the heads. The idea of our shirt was to make an imaginary concert tee as if they were going to perform at the LA Coliseum. We made two colorways for Total Luxury Spa and it sold out immediately. This all felt a little before the new wave of bootleg band T-shirts on the internet. We ended up doing a second print run and realized that this money had to go to the band, and we were able to make a generous donation and it really opened up this dialog with the members of the group. I think that's an important consideration with bootlegging, whether you're affecting someone's bottom line or taking money away from people that really need it. The shirt eventually allowed us to do some merch for the band in conjunction with a livestreamed concert during the pandemic, with all proceeds going to Sun Ra Arkestra and World Stage. It was this really beautiful collaboration that all started with a bootleg shirt.

BS: Throughout your practice, and in this particular example, runs this throughline of

p. 413: Hassan Rahim, Total Luxury Spa, Sun Ra T-Shirt (2018)

SUN RA
SAT. & SU.
SEPT. 9 & 10
ONLY!
L.A.

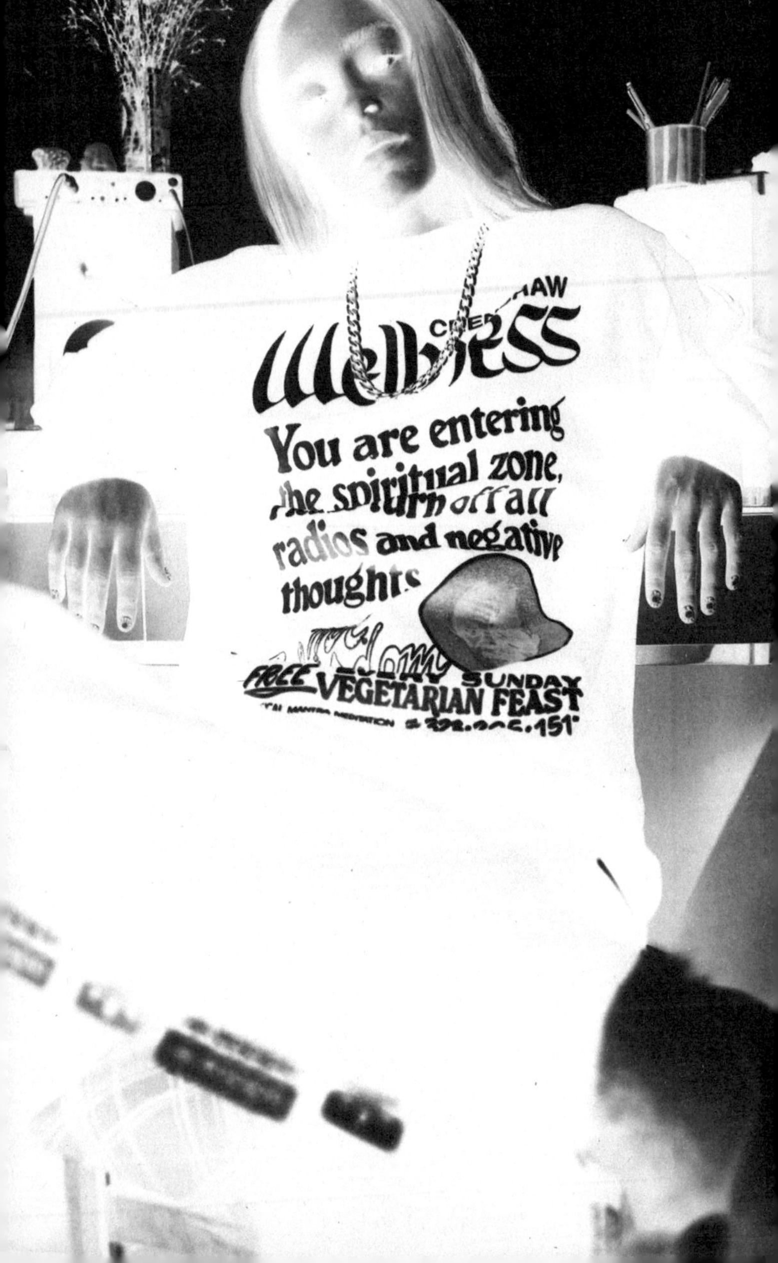

You are entering
the spiritual zone,
turn off all
radios and negative
thoughts
FREE
SUNDAY
VEGETARIAN FEAST

fandom. I'm wondering if you can speak to how that drives what you make.

HR: There's a lot of ego in this industry and people are too cool to be obsessed with something. It just comes off as so ingenuine. I love the idea of being a fan. And it's a whole other level of fandom to then want to make something to honor this thing, like we did with the Sun Ra Arkestra. You have to really care about something to push it to that degree of homage. Think about the time when fanzines were being produced and bands had mailing lists—what an amazing culture. It was like the epitome of fandom and even bootlegging. Look at the Grateful Dead, it's all just bootlegs of bootlegs, I'm not sure if there ever really was an original.

BS: The Grateful Dead makes me think about the relationship between bootlegging and community (fan communities, maker communities, et cetera). The Los Angeles-based clothing store Total Luxury Spa seems to tap into this idea, specifically with the Crenshaw community of LA, in a unique way. From this project, have you learned anything about bootlegging as a means of creating and preserving communities?

HR: I absolutely see bootlegs as markers of communities. I think about skating as a kid, and how particular brands of skate gear really established who you were connected to. And of course that's carried over

p. 414: Hassan Rahim, Total Luxury Spa, Crenshaw Wellness T-Shirt (2017)

into streetwear and trends with graphic T-shirts. So by wearing these, or wearing some obscure bootleg shirt, you immediately find your people. Again, with the Sun Ra shirt, I was fascinated by the people who bought them. Some were fans of the band, others just liked the aesthetic and the shirt became a way for them to learn about the group. I saw a resurgence of interest in Sun Ra after we made that shirt and I realized how much power a simple bootleg shirt could have. It connected old and new fans across all generations without the gatekeeping that can sometimes happen with niche communities. Since that shirt, I've wanted to use bootlegs as a way to open people up to lesser known bands who influenced hip hop—bands like ESG, who are a gateway to a whole genre of music, a community, a certain place and time.

> BS: Given the way you embrace bootlegging, what are your thoughts around ideas of authorship and originality? Especially as someone whose work has been very influential and highly referenced by a younger generation of designers.

HR: I'm less concerned with originality, I think what needs to change is this desire to call people out. At this point, I'm tired of the drama and tea of things like Diet Prada. I'm more interested in putting my references on display rather than trying to keep them for myself. That way the people who are really interested will dig deeper—who's the designer? What else did they design? Who were they influenced by, what movement were they a part of? You allow people to find their own way into a particular subject matter.

I've really come around to this idea of open source. At first I was very protective, but I think that stemmed from insecurity and ego. I came to realize we all have the same tools, the only thing I can really claim as my own is my process, the way I think about things. I'm less concerned with some sort of aesthetic signature, I'm aiming more for a signature approach which feels very tied to the idea of subversion you mentioned earlier. The filters and effects and textures that I use, which might seem like my style, actually come from a very particular way of approaching material. It's not something you can just apply to every project. Someone once told me that I owned "inversion" and I laughed. How self-centered would that be, to think you invented a negative image? When you get over this idea of originality, you can put that effort into building a community with like-minded interest. Coming from punk and indie cultures, no one was really trying to one up each other, you were just trying to find your people.

BS: How do you feel about graphic design's latest obsession with bootlegging?

HR: What I see as the main difference between bootlegs today and in the past is the availability of resources. Look, for example, at a 1990s rap T-shirt. You often find some odd system font, the colors are slightly off and misregistered, images are clumsily cut-out. That wasn't by design, it was out of necessity. You know, they can only afford a certain amount of colors, so they had to make do, and these limitations created a really interesting effect.

I think a lot of this "bootleg look" today comes down to texture. Texture really tells a story, it talks about where something comes from, it gives something a history. When I use textures, it isn't random, it's still about communicating something. And in order to understand textures you have to understand the techniques and limitations that produce them. I have people reaching out all the time asking for me to give them my textures, thinking they can just apply them to any design. There's even a marketplace where you can buy textures and effects to make things look old or worn… it feels like a new form of skeuomorphism. One time someone asked me for a certain halftone texture and I just DM'd him a link to a specific Xerox Phaser printer. I wasn't trying to be protective, it was just an attempt to encourage research and really promote the techniques that produce these visual results.

I'm reminded of an interview I saw with Timbaland. He had gotten to a point where he had every keyboard, synth, plugin, and rack that you could buy. But to challenge himself to make something different he realized he needed to change his approach. For the Nelly Furtado record he ended up just using trash cans, pots, and pans. They were sounds you couldn't emulate with new technology, he had to go back to the source.

> BS: As we look at contemporary bootlegs, it's interesting to ask why this "textured" look is so alluring. I wonder if it has something to do with nostalgia or the way we equate things from the past with a certain sense of authenticity?

HR: Time is the texture in most scenarios. However, a lot of the newer generation, especially those on Instagram, or post-Tumblr, seem to rely heavily on texture. I think the texture gives otherwise cold vector graphics a sense of character. Perhaps it's a slight rebellion to the digitality of our world. In the 2000s everything was slick, hyper-3D, a vision of the future. Now we seem much more interested in trying to create a sense of the past.

> BS: A lot of what you are saying with these effect marketplaces taps into my concern that today there are designers trying to replicate a "bootleg look" despite having an abundance of resources, techniques, and forms of distribution at their disposal. It reduces bootlegging to an aesthetic.

HR: I'm reminded of a conversation I was having with someone asking if punk was dead, because punk used to be a community, a scene, a way of life. Today, punk has gotten distilled into an aesthetic or a style. I think that it's the same issue, it's the gentrification of an aesthetic. To me, bootlegging isn't dead. I think bootlegging is evolving into more of a way of thinking and at the end of the day, it's always a means of honoring something or showing love. Even today you can tell when these projects are starting from a place of true fandom rather than superficially tapping into a trend. Despite everything, I think that one of the most genuine ways to signal a love of something is to wear it on your back.

Title page (p. 408): Logo from the Crenshaw Wellness T-Shirt (2017) by Hassan Rahim and Total Luxury Spa

References:
Index, Biographies & Acknowledgments

Author:

Ben Schwartz is a graphic designer and editor based in New York. sourcetype.com

Interviewees:

Line Arngaard is a graphic designer based in Amsterdam. linearngaard.com

Clara Balaguer is an artist based in Rotterdam.

BLESS is a fashion house and design studio based in Berlin and Paris consisting of Desiree Heiss and Ines Kaag. bless-service.de

Boot Boyz Biz is a clothing label based in New York, started by Kevin McCaughey. boot-boyz.biz

Akinola Davies Jr. is a director based in London. akinoladaviesjr.com

Eric Doeringer is an artist based in Los Angeles. ericdoeringer.com

Experimental Jetset is a graphic design studio based in Amsterdam consisting of Marieke Stolk, Erwin Brinkers, and Danny van den Dungen.jetset.nl

Elisa van Joolen is an artist and educator based in Amsterdam. elisavanjoolen.com

Czar Kristoff is an artist based in Laguna. czarkristoff.tumblr.com

Hassan Kurbanbaev is a photographer based in Tashkent. cargocollective.com/hassankurbanbaev

Olivier Lebrun is a graphic designer based in Paris. olivierlebrun.fr

Urs Lehni is a graphic designer and publisher based in Zurich. rollo-press.com

Jonathan Monk is an artist based in Berlin.

Jordan Nassar is an artist based in New York. jordannassar.com

Sonia Oet is a ceramist based in Brussels.

Matt Olson is an artist based in Minneapolis. ooiee.me

Online Ceramics is a clothing label based in Los Angeles started by Alix Ross and Elijah Funk. online-ceramics.com

Mark Owens is a graphic designer based in Minneapolis. lifeofthemind.net

Printed Matter is an independent bookstore and publisher based in New York. printedmatter.org

Nat Pyper is an artist based in New York. natpyper.com

Babak Radboy is an artist based in New York.

Hassan Rahim is a graphic designer based in New York. hassanrahim.com / 1201.am

Christopher Schulz is an artist and publisher based in New York. pinupsmag.com

Shanzhai Lyric is an artist collective based in New York consisting of Ming Lin and Alexandra Tartarsky. shanzhailyric.info

SHIRT is an artist based in New York. rapartist.org

Oana Stănescu is an architect based in New York. oanas.net

Collaborators:

Laurenz Brunner is an art director, graphic designer, and type designer based in Zurich. sourcetype.com

Meg Miller is a writer and editor based in Berlin. megmiller.world

Emmet Byrne is a curator, graphic designer, art director, musician, and writer based in Boston.

Marie Hoejlund is a graphic designer based in Copenhagen. mariehoejlund.com

Jasio Stefanski is a graphic designer and developer based in Minneapolis.

Simone Wegman is an Amsterdam-based researcher and writer. She is working as a project editor and researcher at Valiz.

Valiz is an independent international publisher addressing contemporary developments in art, design, and urban affairs. Valiz is headed by Astrid Vorstermans and Pia Pol. valiz.nl

Source Type is an international platform for typographic research and visual literacy. Source Type is headed by Laurenz Brunner with Ben Schwartz. sourcetype.com

The Unlicensed Interviews began in 2018 at the Walker Art Center. This project, which has taken five or so years to realize, could not have been completed without numerous individuals who I would like to recognize here. First and foremost is my wife Coral Saucedo Lomelí. Whether it be moving to the Netherlands during COVID to join me during the Jan van Eyck residency, or debating the merits of originality over morning coffee—her love, positive energy, and creative spirit has, and always will be, a guiding force in all that I pursue. I would also like to sincerely thank my wonderful family who has been an unwavering support system in all my endeavors.

UNLICENSED would not exist without the guidance, intellect, wit, and humor of my mentor Emmet Byrne. I am forever grateful for the ways he challenged and pushed this project into areas that I could never have imagined. Additionally I am extremely grateful for the team of collaborators who helped materialize this publication. My deepest thanks to Laurenz Brunner for believing in me and for welcoming me into the Source Type family. Thanks to Astrid Vorstermans and Simone Wegman at Valiz for their guidance and trust in wanting to make an inverted "shadow book". Thank you to Meg Miller whose poetic sensibilities imbue any text she works on with an element of magic. And lastly my deepest gratitude to all of the brilliant artists and designers who allowed me to interview them. I am humbled by your generosity, and your insights have forever shaped the way I will make work.

I would like to as well thank several other individuals who have contributed to this project in one way or another. In alphabetical order: Bruno Alves de Almeida, Kian Ansari, Aryn Beitz, Simon Browne, Bryan Chu, Jo Frenken, Ryan Gerald Nelson, Rudy Guedj, Geoff Han, Marie Hoejlund, Paul John, Natalie Kelapire, Hicham Khalidi, Aliki van der Kruijs, Ming Lin, Stuart Mouritzen, Austin Redman, Sereina Rothenberger, David Schatz, Ryan J. Simons, Patrick Slack, Jasio Stefanski, Melia Tandiono, Nicholas Weltyk, Johnny Woods, Brian You, and the staff, advisors, and residents at the Jan van Eyck Academie.

UNLICENSED: Bootlegging as Creative Practice

Author, Concept:
Ben Schwartz

Design:
Ben Schwartz

Creative Director
Source Type:
Laurenz Brunner

Copy-editing:
Meg Miller

Typefaces:
Times LT Semibold

Lithography:
Mariska Bijl,
Wilco Art Books

Paper Inside:
Holmen Trnd 70 gr, 2.0

Paper Cover:
Invercote 200 gr

Printing and Binding:
Wilco Art Books, Amersfoort

Project Editor Valiz:
Simone Wegman

Publisher:
Valiz, Amsterdam, 2023
www.valiz.nl
Astrid Vorstermans
& Pia Pol
with Source Type, 2023
www.sourcetype.com
Laurenz Brunner
& Ben Schwartz

This publication has been printed on FSC-certified paper by an FSC-certified printer. The FSC, Forest Stewardship Council, promotes environmentally appropriate, socially beneficial, and economically viable management of the world's forests. fsc.org

Distribution:
NL/LU: Centraal Boekhuis, www.cb.nl
BE: EPO, www.epo.be
Europe (excl. Benelux, GB, IE)/ Asia: Idea Books, www.ideabooks.nl
GB/IE: Central Books, www.centralbooks.com
USA/Canada/Latin America: D.A.P., www.artbook.com
Australia: Perimeter Books, www.perimeterdistribution.com

This publication was made possible through the generous support of:

het Prins Bernhard cultuurfonds

creative industries fund NL

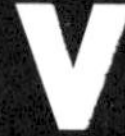

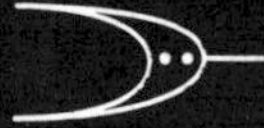

Amsterdam, 2023
ISBN 978-94-93246-29-4
Printed and bound in the EU

Front Cover Images:
Top: The Great Sphinx of Giza located in Giza, Egypt.
Bottom: Replica of the Great Sphynx of Giza at the Luxor Hotel located in Las Vegas, NV.

Back Cover Image:
Cell phone tower camouflaged as a palm tree.